Queer and
Trans Migrations

DISSIDENT FEMINISMS

Elora Halim Chowdhury, Editor

A list of books in the series appears at the end of this book.

Queer and Trans Migrations

Dynamics of Illegalization, Detention, and Deportation

Edited by
EITHNE LUIBHÉID AND
KARMA R. CHÁVEZ

UNIVERSITY OF
ILLINOIS PRESS
Urbana, Chicago, and Springfield

© 2020 by the Board of Trustees
of the University of Illinois
All rights reserved
Manufactured in the United States of America
1 2 3 4 5 C P 5 4 3 2 1
∞ This book is printed on acid-free paper.

Library of Congress Cataloging-in-Publication Data
Names: Luibhéid, Eithne, editor. | Chávez, Karma R., editor.
Title: Queer and trans migrations: dynamics of illegalization, detention,
    deportation / edited by Eithne Luibhéid and Karma R Chávez.
Description: Urbana, Chicago: University of Illinois Press, [2020] |
    Series: Dissident feminisms | Includes bibliographical references and
    index.
Identifiers: LCCN 2020015415 (print) | LCCN 2020015416 (ebook) | ISBN
    9780252043314 (cloth) | ISBN 9780252085239 (paperback) | ISBN
    9780252052194 (ebook)
Subjects: LCSH: Sexual minority immigrants—Social conditions—Case
    studies. | Sexual minority immigrants—Government policy—Case
    studies. | Detention of persons—Social aspects—Case studies. |
    Deportation—Social aspects—Case studies.
Classification: LCC JV6346.5 .Q44 2020 (print) | LCC JV6346.5 (ebook) |
    DDC 306.76086/912—dc23
LC record available at https://lccn.loc.gov/2020015415
LC ebook record available at https://lccn.loc.gov/2020015416

Dedicated with much love to Colm Luibhéid
(January 22, 1936–October 9, 2017)
I hope that now you can fly

Contents

Illustrations and Artist Statements follow page 130

Acknowledgments

Many people have helped to make this book possible. We are, foremost, very grateful to each of the contributors to this volume. In addition, we are appreciative to the help and assistance of the following people: Adela C. Licona, Erica Rand, Julio Salgado, Scott Morgensen, Lisa Kahaleole Hall, Katy Buchanan, Humaira Saeed, and the anonymous reviewers of the manuscript. We are also very thankful to the staff at the University of Illinois Press, especially our acquisitions editor, Dawn Durante, who makes every process transparent and efficient, and the wonderful Jennifer Argo. Thank you to the Department of Mexican American and Latina/o Studies and the College of Liberal Arts at the University of Texas at Austin for financial backing of this project. We are appreciative of UT's Latino Research Institute and Director Deborah Parra-Medina for providing Eithne with a fellowship so that we could be in the same place during the final stages of the book. Finally, we thank our partners, Hai Ren and Annie Hill, for all their support, always.

Queer and
Trans Migrations

Introduction

KARMA R. CHÁVEZ AND EITHNE LUIBHÉID

Globally, nearly 300 million people live either as international migrants[1] or internally displaced people.[2] Over the past several decades, the number of people compelled to leave their homes has continued to grow, and along with such growth, migrant detentions and deportations have skyrocketed in the United States (from where we live and write) and globally. Except for those who can show that they fit into a narrow spectrum of state-designated family ties, skill sets, large bank accounts, or protection needs, possibilities for acquiring legal status have been greatly reduced or entirely cut. Legally present migrants, too, increasingly lose status and become routed into detention and deportation. Legal channels disappear even as countries like the United States remain "reliant on the . . . dispossession and disavowal of Indigenous peoples, global circuits of expropriated labor, economies of racialization, and its expansive network of military bases," which generate continual international migration.[3]

Western media outlets and government officials alike declare that the arrival and presence of large numbers of migrants evidence a "migration crisis." Certainly, in places such as Greece, Turkey, Lebanon, and Uganda, the increase in new arrivals strains social services, placing burdens on health care providers, social workers, low-income neighborhoods and more. Yet, movement and arrivals do not on their own constitute a crisis. Jenna M. Loyd, Matt Mitchelson, and Andrew Burridge offer important reframing of the crisis rhetoric: "Borders and prisons—walls and cages—are global crises."[4] We build on this claim: if there is a migration crisis, it concerns the unaddressed conditions that push many to migrate when they would prefer not to, and the impacts of punitive state, supranational, and populist responses including expanding illegalization, detention, and deportation.

Responses to the mass migration from and within Syria since 2011 as a result of civil war between President Bashar al-Assad and opposition forces are instructive about how states frame and respond to migrants, rather than structural causes of migration as "crises." As people have fled to neighboring states in the Middle East and Turkey and risked sea travel to other parts of Europe, especially Greece, countries have responded in numerous ways, rhetorically and materially. In 2015, German Chancellor Angela Merkel announced the suspension of a 1990 protocol that required asylum seekers to apply for asylum in whichever country they first entered. Merkel proclaimed Germany would allow all Syrian asylum seekers to stay.[5] The proclamation landed Merkel on the cover of *Time* as its person of the year but was almost immediately followed by a series of actions designed to secure Germany's borders, speed up deportations of refused asylum seekers, suspend family reunifications for certain asylum seekers, fight smuggling of migrants, and stop the flow of people into Europe.[6] Although Merkel's government rapidly modified its "openness" through efforts to close people out, Merkel faced significant backlash from members of her own government, ordinary Germans, and members of the far right alike. A handful of violent incidents across Germany perpetrated by Middle Eastern and North African asylum seekers further fueled the backlash. The number of people seeking and receiving asylum in Germany has drastically decreased as deportations have increased.[7]

Germany's attempt to address the volume of refugees directly contrasted with Israel's during the same period. Israeli Interior Minister Silvan Shalom announced, "I continue to fight, with all my effort, against the phenomenon of illegal infiltration, in light of the hundreds of thousands of infiltrators to Europe in these days and hours. I will not relent until we reach a framework that will allow the removal of the infiltrators from Israel."[8] Although viewing essentially all migrants to Israel as economically driven "infiltrators," Prime Minister Benjamin Netanyahu noted that Israel was "not indifferent to the human tragedy" of Syrian and African refugees. He nevertheless explained: "Israel is a small country, a very small country, that lacks demographic and geographic depth; therefore, we must control our borders, against both illegal migrants and terrorism."[9] Notably, official Israeli framing of migration as matters of crime, border security, illegality, and terrorism has long functioned to animate its practices of detention and deportation, including its detention of refugees in a large, open-air detention center called Holot in the Negev desert[10] and its deportation of 40,000 African refugees in late 2017, in part, Netanyahu claimed, so that they could close down Holot.[11] Germany's and Israel's rhetorical proclamations could not seem more different, but the material results were quite similar: an increase in processes of migrant illegalization, detention, and deportation. *These crises* deserve urgent attention.

Around the globe, political leaders and activists respond to the presence of migrants in ways that share logics with places like Germany and Israel, even as each set of responses and the contexts out of which they emerge differ. Criminalizing, detaining and deporting migrants, and closing and militarizing borders, is the norm. Populist and fascist rhetoric decrying insufficiently fortressed borders and migrants as the source of all societal ills augments political practices and policies. U.S. President Donald Trump famously launched his 2016 bid for the presidency by declaring his want for a border wall to keep out Mexican "rapists." His anti-immigrant rhetoric, coupled with his executive orders targeting numerous migrant groups, remains the fuel that energizes his political base. In early 2018, Hungarian Prime Minister Viktor Orbán insisted that his country would not accept refugees because the Hungarian people did not want "Muslim invaders."[12] Orbán has long been considered one of the most vocal proponents of Fortress Europe and has employed numerous measures ranging from razor wire fences to tear gas to keep migrants out of Hungary.[13] Examples of anti-immigrant populist policy, rhetoric, rallies, and campaign platforms can be found everywhere.[14]

In this second decade of the 21st century, the responses to migration and migrants feel fevered, but they have developed over long periods of time and resonate with other historical moments. Throughout history, migrants and "foreigners" have been targets of various kinds: as scapegoats for social and economic ills, problems to be maintained and/or expunged, subversives, threats, criminals, and sources of disease. As Loyd, Mitchelson, and Burridge note, the expansion of global apartheid whereby wealthy countries erect barriers to prevent the movement of people from poorer countries, combined with policing and prison regimes—"when the state is built and society is governed through crime legislation"—must be part of our sense making (p.1). The creation of physical sites like walls and cages in order to protect and generate wealth works in tandem with laws that criminalize more people and practices that terrorize migrants. "Governing immigration through crime," works not just through legal means,[15] but through a barrage of images and ideologies that render migrants as suspicious and threatening, and thus vulnerable.[16]

Vulnerability does not affect all migrants equally since those who are already subalternized due to country of origin, race, class, ability, religion, gender, and sexuality often find themselves facing the most difficult conditions before, during, and after migration. For example, in the process of migration, LGBTQI people, especially those who are trans and gender nonconforming, face exacerbated risks of violence, policing, and containment at the hands of state and non-state entities.[17] In detention, LGBTQI migrants often get placed in solitary confinement, allegedly for their own protection, and are at increased risk of sexual and physical violence at the hands of detention officials and other detainees and a higher risk of illness and medical neglect.[18] LGBTQI claims of persecution have sometimes generated sympathy, political will, and pathways to resettlement.[19] Yet, LGBTQI claims are widely used by states as a means to extend what Jasbir Puar calls homonationalism: the selective incorporation of some LGBTQI people in ways that bolster neoliberal capitalist and militaristic logics and practices, while abandoning the most vulnerable.[20] Thus, purported concern for LGBTQI migrants often does not lead to actual pathways for legal migration.[21]

How nonnormative gender and sexuality impact international migration processes and migrant lives is thus very complicated, and it has been a matter of serious intellectual consideration for roughly only two decades. In a 2004 call for change, Eithne Luibhéid insisted, sexuality "structures every aspect of immigrant experiences. Yet immigration scholarship virtually ignores the connections among heteronormativity, sexuality, and immigration."[22] Since Luibhéid's call for change, an impressive volume of work in Queer and Trans Migration Studies (QTMS) has emerged.[23] It is impossible to capture the entirety of this emergence or the breadth of this field of study, which Luibhéid characterizes as an "unruly body of scholarship" that is continually transforming and revising itself.[24] This volume, which expands QTMS, is situated at the intersections among the growing, interdisciplinary scholarship on migrant criminalization, illegalization, detention, and deportation; prison abolition; and queer, trans, and gendered asylum and refuge. Works in the volume are not intended to be "representative" but, instead, grounded, innovative interventions that invite conversation, collaborations, and action in response to the urgencies of the moment.

As scholarship in this area has grown, activism and art by and about queer and trans migrants has also increased dramatically. In the U.S. context, for example, and following the large immigration justice marches in 2006, queers have taken center stage in leading activist and artistic movements, some of which are documented and reflected in this book. The 2007 Queers for Economic Justice, "Queers and Immigration: A Vision Statement," laid out a map for how truly comprehensive immigration reform would keep the most vulnerable queers at its center. Since then, numerous activist, artist and "artivist" groups, including the Immigrant Youth Justice League, United We Dream, Culture Strike, the Queer Undocumented Immigrant Project, Mariposas Sin Fronteras, Familia, the Queer Detainee Empowerment Project, the Los Angeles Queer Contingent, and others have made important inroads into checking the gender- and heteronormativity of the immigration movement, setting queer and trans migration agendas, challenging the treatment of trans migrants in detention, and more. In the United Kingdom, activists have confronted the "gay imperialism" of white British gay rights leader Peter Tatchell, who regularly denounces Muslims and Islamic cultures for antigay politics while silencing the voices of queer Muslims.[25] Others have developed nonprofit organizations and collectives, such as "LGBTQI+ Refugees Welcome in Greece" and the Canadian "Rainbow Refugee," to support queer and trans refugees. These are just a few examples of queer and trans migration activisms and cultural work. Although some of these efforts undeniably reproduce and uphold neoliberalism by emphasizing identity over economics, reifying narrow views of LGBTQI identity, or positioning certain countries as backward in order to make someone from there a better candidate for inclusion, all of this work has occurred in the midst of—and in response to—skyrocketing migrant detention and deportation.

Queer and Trans Migrations brings together academics, activists, and artists to explore how LGBTQI migrants experience and resist dynamics of illegalization, detention, and deportation. The dynamics also affect citizens with migrant family members and citizens who are regularly racialized as "foreign," as well as communities and families whose lives span national borders. Centering LGBTQI migrants, affected citizens, and cross-border communities and families as interlinked, this book addresses not only how these groups are affected by current enforcement strategies, but also how a queer approach may contribute toward imagining migration controls and national citizenship differently. The volume also models the value of diverse, interdisciplinary methodologies that illuminate and intervene into these dynamics.

Queer and Trans Migrations is envisioned as the companion to an earlier edited collection, *Queer Migrations: Sexuality, U.S. Citizenship, and Border Crossings.*[26] *Queer Migrations* was published at a different global moment and brought interdisciplinary immigration scholarship into productive conversation with sexuality scholarship. Centering queer of color migrants and communities, and questions of citizenship and border crossing, the book considered "how sexual arrangements, ideologies and modes of regulation shape migration to and incorporation into the United States."[27] *Queer and Trans Migrations* extends that exploration by analyzing how illegalization, detention, and deportation thoroughly define migrants' (and citizens') lives at local, national, and transnational scales.

Although we widely circulated the call for contributors, *Queer and Trans Migrations* remains heavy on contributors from and research about the United States. This troubling overrepresentation reflects U.S. power and hegemony in the production and circulation of academic knowledge. The book is not intended to suggest that U.S. experiences are universal or generalizable; thus, contributors also engage processes of illegalization, detention, and deportation in Turkey, Greece, Canada, and Indigenous Nations. At the same time, the United States does offer an important focus when analyzing and challenging migration regimes that operate transnationally as well as nationally. Similar to the ways that what Natalia Molina calls "racial scripts"[28] apply across racialized groups, nation-state migration, detention, deportation, and security regimes draw from and influence one another. Asylum decisions in one country often draw upon rationales used in another. Countries like Israel test technologies of border control, security, and containment that are then used around the world.[29] And in a broad sense capitalism creates the scripts for countries and corporations alike to draw and exploit migrant labor, profiting at every step. Understanding detention, deportation, and illegalization across transnational as well as national contexts helps to identify such scripts and resist them.

As a field-defining book, *Queer Migrations* emphasized the voices of scholars almost entirely. Since its publication, "queer and trans migration" has shifted from a then-surprising linking of immigration and sexuality scholarship, or a matter of concern for binational same-sex couples, to a robust body of scholarship, a naming of the most active voices and organizers within the immigration justice movement, and an immense site of cultural and intellectual creativity. This growth within scholarship, organizing and activism, and art and cultural production has not happened in isolation. In fact, many queer and trans migration scholars researching and teaching at universities are organizers and activists in their communities, and many activists and organizers have produced some of the most profound intellectual insights about the ways racialized gender and sexuality constitute migrant communities and migration policy. Artists have created the visual rhetoric of the movement and a source of inspiration and conversation for scholars, and they are shapers of thought and action in their own right. Artists and activists have also functioned as an important accountability mechanism for scholars, ensuring that scholars don't just take the intellectual labor of others but give credit where it is due. Given the overlaps among these groups and the proliferation of discourse across these groups in the 21st century, in *Queer and Trans Migrations*, we put academic, activist, and artist voices side by side. Whereas the academics all responded to our call for papers, we found activists and artists by reaching out to our extended circles and, in some cases, sending solicitations to people we did not know personally. The activist reflections discuss the authors' experiences and analyses based on their long-standing engagement in struggles at the interface between queer, trans, and migrant issues. Regardless of whether we agree with the analyses, we view the reflections as offering important knowledge and perspectives, which we edited for clarity and consistency. Neither of us has expertise in art so we selected pieces that were thematically relevant, had a powerful message, and that we found visually compelling.

Key Terms and Concepts

In the collection, *queer* is used in a dual sense: as an identity category that either stands on its own or serves as a synonym for LGBTI, and as an analytic rubric. As an identity category, *queer* (like *lesbian, gay, bisexual, transgender, intersex, heterosexual, cisgender, transformista, loca, fa'fafine, bakla*, and many related terms)[30] requires us to navigate complicated political, ethical, and theoretical mandates. There is nothing essential, universal, timeless, or unchanging about the term *queer*; it has emerged through and remains implicated in histories and geographies of power. It involves self-attribution or attribution by others, is tied to and upholds state regimes for making populations legible and governable and offers compromised but important means for making claims. People are never reducible to state and other dominant logics and are never "outside" of these logics, either; people variously navigate state and other institutional demands in relation to identities and legibilities; people claim, inhabit, and give meaning to identity categories in ways that must be respectfully explored; and people transit among identities, too.[31]

Trans people are among those who are included in *queer*, yet Trans Studies scholars suggest that *queer* has often functioned as a synonym for lesbian and gay people and questions of sexual nonconformity, rather than as a category that meaningfully engages trans lives and theories and questions of gender nonconformity.[32] In this collection, the terms *transgender* and *trans* are also used. Enke describes *transgender* as "an identity that some people embrace for themselves" and "an ever expanding social category that incorporates the broadest possible range of gender nonconformity for the purposes of movement building, organizing, and social service recognition."[33]

Trans and *queer*, as analytic rubrics, may not refer to identities or identifications at all. *Queer* as an analytic rubric generally "calls into question the stability of any . . . categories of identity"; critically historicizes the material and ideological work performed by all identity categories; and directs attention to questions of power, intersectionality, normalization, dispossession, and transformation.[34] *Trans* as an analytic rubric is similarly multidimensional. The editors of a special issue of *Women's Studies Quarterly* suggest that *trans-ing* "is a practice that assembles gender into contingent structures of association with other attributes of bodily being, and that allows for their reassembly. Transing can function as a disciplinary tool. . . . It can also function as an escape vector, a line of flight, or pathway toward liberation."[35] *Queer* and *trans* as analytic rubrics highlight the need to analyze how sexual and gender regimes do not affect just nonnormative subjects but everyone (e.g., centering trans women in immigration detention illuminates how oppressive gender norms can be for all detainees, and how achieving gains for trans women benefits all those impacted by immigration regimes). Moreover, since whiteness is constitutive of sexual and gender normativity, an intersectional approach that addresses racialization, colonialism, and capitalism is necessary. Thus, scholarship and activism must critically address how migrant illegalization, detention, and deportation processes work through, remake, and are contested in terms of white-normed sexual and gender standards and ideologies that impact everyone.[36]

This collection also uses the term *migrant*. As in *Queer Migrations*, the term is used here to refer to anyone who has crossed an international border, without making distinctions based on people's state-conferred legal statuses. This is because legal statuses reflect not "types" of migrants but the workings of power and knowledge that seek to differentiate among migrants; delimit rights and protections that they will be granted or denied; and shape forms of surveillance, discipline, normalization, and dispossession to which they are subjected.[37] Thus, our usage of the term participates in the call by militant migration researchers to problematize scholarship that serves the state by reifying and objectifying people on the move by uncritically recirculating the state's categories.[38] As Nigel Harris describes, although elaborate categorical distinctions reflect and further operationalize the state's belief that migrants represent problems to be variously governed or expelled, from the point of view of migrants, states are the problem.[39]

Sometimes the collection uses the terms *asylum seeker* or *refugee*, which are statuses that some migrants seek or acquire through a different process than the state's immigration system. The terms emerged after World War II and commonly refer to people who have crossed an international border and who seek protection under international human rights (rather than national immigration) law.[40] The protection process depends on and reproduces a binary distinction between forced (political) and voluntary (economic) migration, even though no such clear-cut distinction operates in the lives of most migrants.[41] We sometimes use the terms *refugee* and *asylum seeker* to trace and encourage further critical analysis of the so-called protection regime through which some migrants acquire status, but we do not accept the binary distinction between forced and voluntary migration that dispossesses migrants through both nation-state immigration systems and the refugee and asylum systems.

Works in This Volume

Part I, "Contextualizing" begins with Luibhéid's overview of the historical development of heteronormative U.S. immigration controls that position heterogenous people as vulnerable to illegalization, detention, and deportation on multiple grounds. Luibhéid also considers how queer and trans resistance has intervened in these processes. Julio Capó Jr. illustrates and extends the analysis by discussing the experiences of Black Bahamians, particularly women, who migrated or attempted to migrate to Miami during the late 19th and early 20th centuries. Capó shows how the state's multifaceted approach to controlling moving bodies that it deemed undesirable produced complex grammars and praxes of illegality, confinement, and deportability that remain significant today. Showing the importance of these histories in the present, Sasha Wijeyeratne—formerly of the National Queer Asian and Pacific Islander Alliance—discusses strategies for building deeper solidarity between marginalized queer and trans Asian/Pacific Islanders and Black Lives Matter agendas. They also discuss community actions exploring practices of surveillance, profiling, policing, and criminalization that make API communities unsafe and innovative strategies for intervening into these Department of Homeland Security policies and practices.

In Part II, "Negotiating Systems," Suyapa G. Portillo Villeda, who writes in her combined capacity as academic and activist, considers the work she's done as an expert witness in immigration courtrooms for Central American asylum seekers in the United States, particularly for LGBTI people. Portillo argues that U.S. foreign policy has a debilitating impact on Central America, making migration one of the only viable options, and LGBTI people face exceptional dangers within this context. Fadi Saleh explores the predicament of queer Syrian asylum seekers in Turkey who have simultaneously become the recipients of humanitarian attention, but often obtain asylum only if they disavow the civil war that caused them to flee and instead indict Syrian homophobia as the catalyst. Saleh thus parses out the meaning of "well-founded fear of persecution" for Syrians. Elif Sarı also focuses on Turkey, analyzing how LGBTI asylum seekers from Iran negotiate their limbo status between increasingly restrictive policies in places of possible resettlement like the United States and Canada and the present, politically unstable situation in Turkey. Sarı shows how people respond to and survive uncertain lives and futures. Rafael Ramirez Solórzano takes us to Miami, Florida, offering a place-specific understanding of queer undocumented youth organizing efforts. Solórzano explores how the organizers navigate the racial legacies of Jim Crow, the Civil Rights Movement, and the "Cuban Immigrant Power Structure" in order to create possibilities for solidarities and transformation. Ryan Conrad, a longtime HIV/AIDS and queer activist, writes of his experiences migrating to Canada and regularizing his status. Despite his relative privilege as a white man from the United States, Conrad details the difficulties of navigating the Canadian immigration system due to Canada's health-based restrictions, which can have disproportionate impacts on queer people.

Following Part II, we have included a multipage insert with high-quality, color images of seven works by the following artists: Myisha Arellanus, Felipe Baeza, Adela C. Licona and Greg Bal, Molly Fair, Matice Moore, María Inés Taracena, and Rommy Torrico. They represent both emerging and well-known artists who have contributed to mobilizing for justice. Some artists are directly impacted by the dynamics addressed in the book, while others are accomplices to the movement for queer and trans migrant justice. Each work offers important ways for people to engage the themes of this book and the movement.

In Part III, "Resisting/Refusing," Jamila Hammami, founding and longtime executive director of the Queer Detainee Empowerment Project in New York City, discusses the project's work of bridging the prison abolition and immigration justice movements while providing support to queer and trans migrants inside and outside of carceral facilities. Hammami insists that the only way to achieve justice is by bridging these two movements with an emphasis on those who suffer the worst impacts of these brutal systems. Myrto Tsilimpounidi and Anna Carastathis raise compelling questions about how refugees and refugee crises become framed. They center the "Facing Crisis" photography workshop that they conducted with LGBTQI refugees in Athens, Greece, which sought to intervene into the construct of the "deserving refugee" that relies on heteronormalizing displaced people and instead allow for participants' own self-representations. Ultimately, workshop participants created images of places, rather than people, as a way to bring questions of subjectivity to light. AB Brown also discusses the complex positionalities of LGBTQI refugees—in this case from the Democratic Republic of Congo, Uganda, and Malawi—who arrived in the United States via South Africa. Using a performance lens, Brown explores how their informants (or collaborators, as they describe them) seek assimilation into neoliberal capitalist structures of the United States even while critiquing how those structures operate. Brown argues that their collaborators' performances of self may offer new and expansive models of belonging.

Continuing the exploration of resisting and refusing, scholar and activist Jack Cáraves and Bamby Salcedo, president and CEO of the TransLatin@ Coalition, detail the work of the coalition. Salcedo begins with a history of how the organization started with advocating for trans Latina immigrants, but has expanded and modified over time. Cáraves discusses their participatory research with the Coalition that resulted in a community report on trans Latina health, and the two reflect on the power of collaborative scholarship in creating visibility and furthering the well-being and liberation of trans people. Ruben Zecena takes up the question of trans migrant liberation through his analysis of what he calls "shameless interruptions." Focusing on Jennicet Gutiérrez's 2015 interruption of President Obama's Pride celebration and Trans Queer Pueblo's interruption of the 2017 Phoenix Pride parade, Zecena theorizes these interruptions as a queer migration politics that refuses the silencing and shaming of brown bodies and offers coalitional possibilities for survival.

The final part, "Critiquing," begins with Yasmin Nair's retrospective on the status of the immigrant justice movement. A longtime organizer in the Chicago scene, and one of the first to bring queer and immigration issues together beyond concerns about binational same-sex couples, Nair offers a searing commentary on what she perceives as the role of undocuqueer activism in entrenching neoliberal logics within the immigration justice movement by focusing on identity and "feel good" stories. José Guadalupe Herrera Soto, also a longtime Chicago-based organizer with several autonomous collectives, frames and shares two letters he wrote. The first asked people with resources for support in getting his father back from Mexico, where he went to visit his mother before she died. The second is a "thank you" letter to those who supported his efforts. Herrera's complex framing of the letters details both the harsh realities of "family separation" and problems with gestures of solidarity and help. Unlike personal narratives that are crafted to serve neoliberalism,[42] Nair and Herrera critically situate themselves within broad, intersecting dynamics of inequality and the urgencies of challenging these through thoughtful collective action. Karma R. Chávez and Hana Masri explore how liberal activist framing of the United States' "child migration crisis" in summer 2014 provided then–President Obama the language with which to create and promote more draconian immigration policies just months later. Chávez and Masri draw from queer migration scholars and activists to offer resources for movement organizers in developing alternative rhetorical strategies. Part IV concludes with a roundtable discussion among scholar-activists Leece Lee-Oliver, Monisha Das Gupta, Katherine Fobear, and Edward Ou Jin Lee who offer insights on the vexed relationship between queer and trans migration struggles and Indigenous organizing for sovereignty and self-determination.

We hope that this volume shows that any so-called "migration crisis" results from state policies and practices, and those who suffer most are migrants themselves. We also hope this volume provides readers with resources to intervene in the state's work.

Notes

1. Phillip Connor, "International Migration: Key Findings from the U.S., Europe, and the World," Pew Research Center, December 15, 2016, http://www.pewresearch.org/fact-tank/2016/12/15/international-migration-key-findings-from-the-u-s-europe-and-the-world/.

2. "Figures at a Glance," United Nations High Commissioner on Refugees, 2018, http://www.unhcr.org/figures-at-a-glance.html.

3. Alyosha Goldstein, "Introduction: Toward a Genealogy of the US Colonial Present," in Formations of United States Colonialism, ed. Alyosha Goldstein (Durham, N.C.: Duke University Press, 2014), 1–2.

4. Jenna M. Loyd, Matt Mitchelson, and Andrew Burridge, "Introduction: Borders, Prisons, and Abolitionist Visions," in Beyond Walls and Cages: Prisons, Borders, and Global Crisis, eds. Jenna M. Loyd, Matt Mitchelson, and Andrew Burridge (Athens: University of Georgia Press, 2012), 1.

5. Allan Hall and John Lichfield, "Germany Opens Its Gates," Independent, August 24, 2015, https://www.independent.co.uk/news/world/europe/germany-opens-its-gates-berlin-says-all-syrian-asylum-seekers-are-welcome-to-remain-as-britain-is-10470062.html.

6. Wesley Dockery, "Two Years since Germany Opened Its Borders to Refugees: A Chronology," *Deutsche Welle*, September 4, 2017, https://www.dw.com/en/two-years-since-germany-opened-its-borders-to-refugees-a-chronology/a-40327634.

7. Judith Vonberg, "Why Angela Merkel is No Longer the 'Refugee Chancellor,'" *CNN*, July 6, 2018, https://www.cnn.com/2018/07/06/europe/angela-merkel-migration-germany-intl/index.html.

8. Ben Sales, "As Europe Takes in Migrants, Israel Tries to Keep Them Out," *Times of Israel*, September 9, 2015, https://www.timesofisrael.com/as-europe-takes-in-migrants-israel-tries-to-keep-them-out/.

9. "Netanyahu: Israel 'Too Small' to Absorb Syrian Refugees," *Jewish Telegraphic Agency*, September 6, 2015, https://www.jta.org/2015/09/06/news-opinion/israel-middle-east/israel-too-small-to-absorb-syrian-refugees-netanyahu-says.

10. Robert Tait, "'We Are Prisoners Here,' say Migrants at Israel's Desert Detention Camp," *The Telegraph*, April 4, 2014, https://www.telegraph.co.uk/news/worldnews/middleeast/israel/10743910/We-are-prisoners-here-say-migrants-at-Israels-desert-detention-camp.html.

11. "Israel to Deport 40,000 African Refugees without Their Consent," *Deutsche Welle*, November 19, 2017, https://www.dw.com/en/israel-to-deport-40000-african-refugees-without-their-consent/a-41443084.

12. Emily Schultheis, "Viktor Orbán: Hungary Doesn't Want 'Muslim Invaders,'" *Politico*, January 1, 2018, https://www.politico.eu/article/viktor-orban-hungary-doesnt-want-muslim-invaders/.

13. Nick Robins-Early, "How Hungary's Viktor Orbán Became the Villain of Europe's Refugee Crisis," *The Huffington Post*, September 23, 2015, https://www.huffingtonpost.com/entry/viktor-orban-hungary-refugee-crisis_us_5601b038e4b0fde8b0d021e3.

14. For example, Adam Nosslter, "Marine Le Pen Leads Far-Right Fight to Make France 'More French,'" *New York Times*, April 20, 2017, https://www.nytimes.com/2017/04/20/world/europe/france-election-marine-le-pen.html; "Migrant Crisis: Finland's Case against Immigration," *BBC News*, September 9, 2015, https://www.bbc.com/news/world-europe-34185297; Robyn Dixon, "In South Africa, A Protest against Foreigners Turns Violent," *Los Angeles Times*, February 24, 2017, http://www.latimes.com/world/africa/la-fg-south-africa-foreigners-20170224-story.html; Chris Irvine, "South Korea Fearful Yemeni Asylum Seekers Will Exploit Visa Loophole," *Fox News*, June 27, 2018, http://www.foxnews.com/world/2018/06/27/south-korea-fearful-yemeni-asylum-seekers-will-exploit-visa-loophole.html; John Otis, "Inside Colombia and Venezuela's Border and Refugee Crisis," *Time*, September 8, 2015, http://time.com/4025305/colombia-venezuela-borders/.

15. Jonathan Xavier Inda and Julie A. Dowling, "Introduction: Governing Migrant Illegality," in *Governing Immigration through Crime: A Reader*, ed. Jonathan Xavier Inda and Julie A. Dowling (Stanford: Stanford University Press, 2013).

16. Leo Chavez, *The Latino Threat Narrative: Constructing Immigrants, Citizens and the Nation* (Stanford: Stanford University Press, 2008).

17. Martha Balaguera, "Trans-Migrations: Agency and Confinement at the Limits of Sovereignty," *Signs: Journal of Women in Culture & Society* 43, no. 3 (2018): 641–664; Vek Lewis, "Forging 'Moral Geographies': Law, Sexual Minorities and Internal Tensions in

Northern Mexico Border Towns," in *Transgender Migrations: The Bodies, Borders, and Politics of Transition*, ed. Trystan Cotten (New York: Routledge, 2012), 32–56.

18. Shana Tabak and Rachel Levitan, "LGBTI Migrants in Immigration Detention: A Global Perspective," *Harvard Journal of Law and Gender* 37, no. 1 (2014): 1–44.

19. For example, UNHCR, *Guidelines on International Protection No. 9*, October 23, 2012, http://www.refworld.org/docid/50348afc2.html; Farida Deif, "Canada Levels the Playing Field for LGBTI Refugees," *Human Rights Watch*, May 5, 2017, https://www.hrw.org/news/2017/05/05/canada-levels-playing-field-lgbti-refugees.

20. Jasbir K. Puar, *Terrorist Assemblages: Homonationalism in Queer Times* (Durham, N.C.: Duke University Press, 2007).

21. Sima Shakshari, "The Queer Time of Death: Temporality, Geopolitics, and Refugee Rights," *Sexualities* 17, no. 8 (2014): 998–1015.

22. Eithne Luibhéid, "Heteronormativity and Immigration Scholarship: A Call for Change," *GLQ* 10, no. 2 (2004): 227.

23. Below is an incomplete list of English-language, authored (not edited) books in QTMS: Aren Z. Aizura, *Mobile Subjects: Transnational Imaginaries of Gender Reassignment* (Durham, N.C.: Duke University Press, 2018); Hila Amit, *A Queer Way Out: The Politics of Queer Emigration from Israel* (Albany: State University of New York Press, 2018); Toby Beauchamp, *Going Stealth: Transgender Politics and US Surveillance Practices* (Durham, N.C.: Duke University Press, 2019); Bobby Benedicto, *Under Bright Lights: Gay Manila and the Global Scene* (Minneapolis: University of Minnesota Press, 2014); B Camminga, *Transgender Refugees and the Imagined South Africa* (New York: Palgrave Macmillan, 2019); Margot Canaday, *The Straight State: Sexuality and Citizenship in Twentieth-Century America* (Princeton, N.J.: Princeton University Press, 2009); Lionel Cantú Jr., *The Sexuality of Migration: Border Crossings and Mexican Immigrant Men*, ed. Nancy A. Naples and Salvador Vidal-Ortiz (New York: New York University Press, 2009); Julio Capó Jr., *Welcome to Fairyland: Queer Miami before 1940* (Chapel Hill: University of North Carolina Press, 2017); Héctor Carrillo, *Pathways of Desire: The Sexual Migration of Mexican Gay Men* (Chicago: University of Chicago Press, 2018); Karma R. Chávez, *Queer Migration Politics: Activist Rhetoric and Coalitional Possibilities* (Urbana: University of Illinois Press, 2013); Monisha Das Gupta, *Unruly Immigrants: Rights, Activism, and Transnational South Asian Politics in the United States* (Durham, N.C.: Duke University Press, 2006); Carlos Ulises Decena, *Tacit Subjects: Belonging and Same-Sex Desire among Dominican Immigrant Men* (Durham, N.C.: Duke University Press, 2011); Oliva Espín, *Latina Realities: Essays on Healing, Migration, and Sexuality* (Boulder, Colo.: Westview Press, 1997); Kale Bantigue Fajardo, *Filipino Crosscurrents: Oceanographies of Seafaring, Masculinities and Globalization* (Minneapolis: University of Minnesota Press, 2011); Calogero Giametta, *The Sexual Politics of Asylum: Sexual Orientation and Gender Identity in the UK Asylum System* (London: Routledge, 2017); Gayatri Gopinath, *Impossible Desires: Queer Diasporas and South Asian Public Cultures* (Durham, N.C.: Duke University Press, 2005); Jin Haritaworn, *Queer Lovers and Hateful Others: Regenerating Violent Times and Places* (London: Pluto Press, 2015); Adi Kuntsman, *Figurations of Violence and Belonging: Queerness, Migranthood and Nationalism in Cyberspace and Beyond* (Oxford: Peter Lang, 2009); Lawrence

La Fountain-Stokes, *Queer Ricans: Cultures and Sexualities in the Diaspora* (Minneapolis: University of Minnesota Press, 2009); Eithne Luibhéid, *Entry Denied: Controlling Sexuality at the Border* (Minneapolis: University of Minnesota Press, 2002); *Pregnant on Arrival: Making the Illegal Immigrant* (Minneapolis: University of Minnesota Press, 2013); Martin F. Manalansan IV, *Global Divas: Filipino Gay Men in the Diaspora* (Durham, N.C.: Duke University Press, 2003); David A. B. Murray, *Real Queer? Sexual Orientation and Gender Identity Refugees in the Canadian Refugee Apparatus* (Lanham, Md.: Rowman and Littlefield, 2015); Susana Peña, *¡Oye Loca! From the Mariel Boatlift to Gay Cuban Miami* (Minneapolis: University of Minnesota Press, 2013); Wim Peumans, *Queer Muslims in Europe: Sexuality, Religion and Migration in Belgium* (New York: I.B. Tauris, 2017); Thibaut Raboin, *Discourses on LGBT Asylum in the UK: Constructing a Queer Haven* (Manchester: Manchester University Press, 2017); Nayan Shah, *Contagious Divides: Epidemics and Race in San Francisco's Chinatown* (Berkeley: University of California Press, 2001); *Stranger Intimacy: Contesting Race, Sexuality and the Law in the North American West* (Berkeley: University of California Press, 2012); Fatima El-Tayeb, *European Others: Queering Ethnicity in Postnational Europe* (Minneapolis: University of Minnesota Press, 2011); Julieta Vartabedian, *Brazilian 'Travesti' Migrations: Genders, Sexualities, and Embodiment Experiences* (New York: Palgrave Macmillan, 2018); Gloria Wekker, *The Politics of Passion: Women's Sexual Culture in the Afro-Surinamese Diaspora* (New York: Columbia University Press, 2006); Chiou-Ling Yeh, *Making an American Festival: Chinese New Year in San Francisco's Chinatown* (Berkeley: University of California Press, 2008).

24. Eithne Luibhéid, "Queer/Migration: An Unruly Body of Scholarship," *GLQ* 14, nos.2–3 (2008): 169–190.

25. Jin Haritaworn, Tamsila Tauqir, and Esra Erdem, "Gay Imperialism: Gender and Sexuality Discourse in the 'War on Terror,'" in *Out of Place: Interrogating Silences in Queerness/Raciality*, eds. Adi Kuntsman and Esperanza Miyake (York, U.K.: Raw Nerve Books, 2008).

26. Eithne Luibhéid and Lionel Cantú Jr., eds. *Queer Migrations: Sexuality, U.S. Citizenship, and Border Crossings* (Minneapolis: University of Minnesota Press, 2005).

27. Eithne Luibhéid, "Introduction: Queer Migration and Citizenship," in *Queer Migrations*, ix.

28. Natalia Molina, *How Race Is Made in America: Immigration, Citizenship, and the Historical Power of Racial Scripts* (Berkeley: University of California Press, 2014).

29. Jeff Halper, *War against the People: Israel, The Palestinians and Global Pacification* (London: Pluto Press, 2015).

30. These terms may be related, but they should not be treated merely as synonyms; each has its own history and trajectory that is not necessarily commensurate with any other.

31. Luibhéid, "Queer/Migration."

32. Heather Love, "Queer," *Transgender Studies Quarterly* 1, nos. 1–2 (2014): 172–175. Love writes, "transgender functions as an umbrella term, able to conjure up a spectrum that can include transsexuals, cross-dressers, and butches and femmes" (173)—though Love also notes that "it also signals a resistance to the taxonomic framework implied by the model of the spectrum (even as it 'overcomes' it)" (173).

33. A. Finn Enke, "Notes on Terms and Concepts," in *Transfeminist Perspectives in and Beyond Gender Studies*, ed. A. Finn Enke (Philadelphia: Temple University Press, 2012), 18–19.

34. Siobhan Somerville, "Queer," in *Keywords for American Cultural Studies*, 2nd ed., eds. Bruce Burgett and Glenn Hendler (New York: New York University Press, 2014), 203; see also Cathy J. Cohen, "Punks, Bulldaggers, and Welfare Queens: The Real Radical Potential of Queer Politics?" *GLQ* 3, no. 4 (1997): 437–465.

35. Susan Stryker, Paisley Currah, and Lisa Jean Moore, "Introduction: Trans-, Trans, or Transgender?" *Women's Studies Quarterly* 36, no. 3/4 (2008): 13. They ask us to further explore the intellectual labor that "critical deployment of 'trans-' operations and movements" can accomplish (13).

36. Illustrating this, Marcia Ochoa describes that the femininities of transgender women in Venezuela are not exceptional; on the contrary, they emerge from the dynamics that produce normative femininities and indeed, beauty queens. Marcia Ochoa, *Queen for a Day: Transformistas, Beauty Queens, and the Performance of Femininity in Venezuela* (Durham, N.C.: Duke University Press, 2014). In regard to queer as an analytic rubric for thinking about migration, see Nicholas De Genova, "The Queer Politics of Migration: Reflections on Illegality and Incorrigibility," *Studies in Social Justice* 4, no. 2 (2010): 101–126.

37. Luibhéid, "Introduction," xi.

38. See Glenda Garelli, Martina Tazzioli, Sandro Mezzadra, Bernd Kasparek and Irene Peano, "Militant Investigation" in. "New Keywords: Migration and Borders," ed. Nicholas De Genova, Sandro Mezzadra and John Pickles, *Cultural Studies* 29, no. 1 (2015): 63–64.

39. States are the problem in multiple senses including in terms of how states' (in)actions may impel migration in the first place, and how state immigration regimes classify, contain, and often punish migrants. See also: Alyshia Gálvez, "Migration," in *Keywords for American Cultural Studies*; Sandro Mezzadra, Brett Nielson, Stephan Scheel and Federico Rahola, "Migration/Migration Studies" in "New Keywords," 61–63.

40. See Liisa Malkki, "Refugees and Exile: From 'Refugee Studies' to the National Order of Things," *Annual Review of Anthropology* 24 (1995): 495–523.

41. Stephan Scheel, Glenda Garelli, and Martina Tazzioli, "Politics of Protection" in "New Keywords," 72.

42. Sujatha Fernandes, *Curated Stories: The Uses and Misuses of Storytelling* (Oxford: Oxford University Press, 2017).

PART I

Contextualizing

1

"Treated neither with Respect nor with Dignity"

Contextualizing Queer and Trans Migrant "Illegalization," Detention, and Deportation

EITHNE LUIBHÉID

On April 10, 2014, current and formerly undocumented migrants released recommendations urging President Obama to stop deportations and undo the laws and practices that pipelined as many as 400,000 migrants a year into deportation. This self-described Blue Ribbon Commission, which included LGBTQ-identified members, had come together in response to President Obama's call to make deportation "more humane" (*sic*) through a consultative process that included few affected migrants.

A blue ribbon commission is typically comprised of "exceptional people [who are] appointed to investigate, study or analyze a given question."[1] Although members have no direct authority, their participation signals that they are deemed to be among the "best and the brightest," and that their recommendations may "be used by those with decision-making power to act."[2] The move by undocumented and formerly undocumented migrants to constitute themselves as a Blue Ribbon Commission brilliantly appropriated standard government strategies for addressing important issues. Although immigration law, backed by state violence, constructs undocumented people as neither present nor having political voice, the Blue Ribbon Commission insisted that members' voices should be heard and recognized as expert, and their recommendations to dismantle the deportation pipeline should be taken seriously.

The release of the Commission's recommendations reflects struggles and concerns that motivate this collection: questions of migrant "illegalization," detention, and deportation; the role of self-identified LGBTQ migrants working independently and in coalition with allies, using queer and trans frameworks, in the struggles; and the importance of radical interventions into the current system that funnels people into undocumented status, detention, and deportation in record-breaking, catastrophic numbers.[3] This chapter provides history and context for understanding how these struggles affect some one million self-identified LGBTQ migrants in the United States.[4] Many U.S. dynamics link with struggles in other nation-states and regions, but it is beyond the scope of this chapter to adequately address those.

This chapter first provides historical context for understanding the development of U.S. immigration controls that seek to reproduce a heteronormative nation and citizenry. The next sections historicize how these controls generate migrants deemed to be "illegal" and subject to detention and deportation. The final section describes how these developments reproduce inequalities among the citizenry while also subordinating migrants; yet, activisms and cultural works by queer and trans migrants and allies have sought to transform these dynamics and create a more just, sustainable world.

Nation-State Immigration Controls

U.S. national level immigration controls began taking shape in the late nineteenth century. The controls operate at the interface between, and shiftingly reproduce, the "transnational" and the "national." They reproduce the transnational as a site of inequality by treating immigration as primarily generated by individual decision-making, rather than by transnational dynamics and inequalities in which the United States plays a significant role. Immigration controls reproduce the nation and citizenship as sites of inequality, too, by legally admitting migrants who serve white, patriarchal, heterosexual, middle-class norms, while criminalizing, "illegalizing," and making disposable other migrants. Queer theorists have glossed these intersecting logics as constituting "heteronormativity," which is the framework that guides this chapter.

A heteronormativity framework underlines the fact that there is a distinction between heterosexuality understood as "object choice" and heteronormativity understood as entailing sexual and gender norms that are inextricable from racial, economic, and colonial logics that structure property relations, resource distribution, public/private distinctions, and the differential valuation of people.[5] A heteronormativity framework highlights that all societies are structured according to sexual/gender norms that change across time and place, yet generally normalize sexual reproduction channeled into patriarchal forms that uphold dominant racial/ethnic, economic, and settler/colonial interests. That norm produces a range of sexual and gender subalterns including those who, in contemporary terms, self-identify or are identified by others as LGBTQ—as well as poor and racialized women who bear children, interracial couples, sex workers, genderqueer people, and others.

Immigration controls have served as key technologies for producing a heteronormative U.S. nation and citizenry—and as a locus for challenging these norms. Beginning in the 1880s, nation-state federal-level immigration policies and practices became key instruments for producing and policing changing forms of nationalist heteronormativity.[6] Immigration controls took shape in the context of "westward expansion"; ongoing dispossession of Native communities including through the Dawes Act of 1887; efforts to recruit recently freed Black people into state-sanctioned forms of marriage and subordinated labor that upheld white sexual, gender, and property relationships and logics; and a growing overseas empire.[7] Early-twentieth-century immigration policies and practices steadily codified dual tracks: one for admission and settlement by primarily migrants from Northern and Western Europe, structured around a heteronuclear family with a male breadwinner;[8] and another track that built on the history of exclusion of Chinese and other Asian migrants while making migrants from Mexico, Central and South America, and the Caribbean primarily temporary, exploitable labor that could be summoned when needed and then dismissed. Immigration law also codified growing bans on migrants deemed to threaten these arrangements, including sex workers; those deemed immoral; men who had sexual, erotic, and romantic relationships with other men; women who had sexual, erotic, and romantic relationships with other women; and anarchists, labor organizers, and political dissidents, among others.[9] Nayan Shah argues that by policing migrants, the norm of settlement within conjugal, patriarchal, white, propertied marriage became the only legitimate form of political subjectivity in the United States and Canada by the mid–twentieth century.[10]

The 1965 Hart Cellar Immigration and Nationality Act (1965 INA), which forms the basis for current immigration law, is generally lauded for ending explicitly ethnic and racial discrimination in U.S. immigration law. Yet, historians have shown that the act was deliberately calculated to enable continued racial and ethnic discrimination by elevating nuclear family and sibling ties as the primary grounds for legal admission.[11] The Act's model of family remained grounded in patriarchal marriage comprised by a breadwinning husband, a childbearing wife consigned to the domestic realm, and children. Lest there be any confusion, a ban on migration by "sexual deviates" was codified. Skilled labor remained a basis for legal admission, too, but on a much smaller scale.

By the 1970s, neoliberalism was becoming an ascendant framework that thoroughly depended on, yet denied the relevance of, institutionalized racism, (hetero)sexism, capitalist exploitation, and empire. Tanya Golash-Boza explains that neoliberalism involves:

(1) an ideology that the state's primary role is to protect property rights, free markets, and free trade; (2) a mode of governance based on a logic of competitiveness, individuality, and entrepreneurship; and (3) a policy package designed to slim down social welfare and integrate countries into the global economy.[12]

From within this framework, the United States further globalized goods, services, finances, cultural products, and more. It also entered into new rounds of military conflict designed to shore up capitalism. These initiatives interfaced with many long-standing capitalist and colonialist engagements between the United States and other countries, and also created new entanglements. These processes deepened the material, institutional, and ideological ties that comprise the "bridges for migration" to the United States.[13] At the same time, the impacts of neoliberalism in other countries, including structural adjustment programs, mobilized increasing numbers of people to migrate internationally. Migrants included Indigenous people throughout the Americas.[14] Yet, even as the United States fueled neoliberal globalization processes that significantly contributed to migration, it simultaneously enacted new barriers against people who sought to enter, or remain, legally. These contradictions vastly expanded the numbers of people who would become designated as undocumented and deportable migrants.[15]

In 1980, the United States codified a distinct institutional and legal process for responding to migrants seeking protection from persecution. Historically, the international refugee system was structured around the experiences of normatively gendered males facing persecution for political activism in the public sphere. In 1965, the United States further defined refugees as those fleeing communism and the Middle East. However, the United States Refugee Act of 1980 incorporated the international definition of a refugee: someone who has crossed an international border and has experienced, or fears experiencing in the future, persecution on account of their race, religion, nationality, political opinion, or membership in a particular social group.[16] The Refugee Act of 1980 also set up processes for selecting and administering the resettlement of people who entered the United States through the refugee system.

Unlike migrants admitted through the 1965 INA, those admitted through the Refugee Act received government assistance (which has steadily declined). Nonetheless, "economic self-sufficiency was the cornerstone of the Refugee Act of 1980," and resources were administered in a manner that was intended to inculcate neoliberal logics among the migrants.[17] The state's processes for selecting and resettling racializes and (hetero)genders them in ways that condition their possibilities within labor markets, the welfare state, and citizenship norms.[18]

In the early 1990s, after tireless efforts by feminist, queer, and other activists and scholars, U.S. law began to recognize that sexuality or gender could comprise a basis for social group identity or a tool of persecution on which refugee or asylum claims could be made. Yet, this insight became incorporated into refugee/asylum law and policy in a way that largely reflected the neoliberal multicultural politics of recognition, which essentialized sexuality and gender as individual attributes of marginalized people rather than as broad social axes of power and struggle that are relevant to everyone. This approach created numerous barriers for migrants who sought asylum on the basis of sexual or gender identity or persecution. For example, successful claims hinge on credibility, which is often evaluated according to deeply ethnocentric and essentialist norms or stereotypes about LGBTQ people or cisgender heterosexual women's lives, which are unable to account for intersecting vulnerabilities that include but extend beyond sexuality and gender. The process often reproduces colonialist logics of "third world difference," "backwardness," and LGBTQ people and women who are "victimized" by "their culture" and need rescue, while letting Global Northern nation-states off the hook for their role in generating migration and in the systemic violence that migrants endure while seeking status and afterward.[19] The relatively small numbers whose applications result in legal status endure homophobia, transphobia, misogyny, racism, and exploitation throughout the process and after settlement, too. Effectively, as Sima Shakhsari describes, seeking state recognition as an asylum seeker or refugee requires making oneself legible within specific legal and social norms of sexuality and gender that have been set by powerful others, and that reproduce colonial, racial, and class logics. As a result, many migrants become systemically and violently "stripped of rights" through a process that claims to uphold their rights.[20]

In 1996, the Defense of Marriage Act (DOMA) codified marriage as involving one man and one woman; thus, marriage could not provide a basis for legal immigration by same-sex couples, and couples that included trans partners often faced complex difficulties in legally immigrating.[21] Also in 1996, in line with neoliberalizing logics and technologies of privatization and personal responsibility, anyone sponsoring a spouse or other family members for migration became required to meet minimum income/asset requirements and sign legally binding affidavits of support. Authorized immigrants were also barred from numerous forms of public assistance for at least five years.[22] Chandan Reddy describes that for decades, family-sponsored migration has provided the largest pool of legally admitted "unskilled workers," whose labor remains in high demand. Yet, by admitting them through "family reunification," their migration gets coded as being "produced by the petitioning activity of resident immigrants living in the United States," to which the benevolent state responds. Moreover, their social needs become the privatized responsibility of the petitioning sponsor.[23] An array of temporary rather than permanent immigration visas for additional low-wage workers, and the labor of international students, supplements the system.[24]

As part of the production of "responsibilized" migrant families who served state austerity agendas, migrants' childbearing and children became further problematized. Exclusionists and white nationalists circulated incendiary claims that migrant women were "targeting" the United States to give birth to children who, as U.S. citizens, would supposedly reap enormous benefits and sponsor their undocumented parent(s) for legal status. The claims are manifestly inaccurate.[25] Nonetheless, the claims legitimized policies and practices that materially disenfranchised the women and their children, including in terms of access to health care, food, shelter, and educational opportunities.[26] Research has not addressed how LGBTQ migrant parents, and children with LGBTQ migrant parents, were affected, but the impacts of these anti-immigrant policies and discourses were surely compounded by the ways that same-sex and trans families remain vilified, criminalized, and made invisible, and parent/child ties within these families are rendered unstable or illegible by both domestic and immigration law.[27]

Congress and numerous state governments repeatedly introduced bills seeking to repeal birthright citizenship for children who were born in the United States to migrant parents. Dorothy Roberts highlights the links between these anti-immigrant discourses and policies, and discourses and policies that criminalize, pathologize, and seek to prevent childbearing and parenting in communities of color and Native communities. As Roberts describes, anti-immigrant policies went hand in hand with welfare "reforms" in the 1990s that targeted U.S. citizen women who were poor, of color, and/or Native through "family caps," encouragement to use the long-lasting but risky contraceptive Norplant, and other measures.[28] Roberts concludes that such efforts "send a powerful message about who is [and is not] worthy to add their children to the future community of citizens."[29]

These struggles over children implicated not just local and national, but also transnational, hierarchies. As Tamar Wilson explains, U.S. immigration policies historically ensured that the costs of socially reproducing families were borne by Latin American, Caribbean, and Asian nation-states from which migrants came. But when more women became international migrants, stayed abroad longer, and birthed children, these circumstances resituated social reproduction costs.[30] Exclusionist rhetoric and policies, operating in tandem with racist welfare and criminal (in)justice and deportation policies that reassert the norm of the United States as a nation grounded in white, middle class domesticity and reproduction, sought to refuse and "offshore" these costs.

In June 2013, the Supreme Court struck down section 3 of DOMA that defined marriage as a relationship between one man and one woman. On July 1, 2013, Secretary of Homeland Security Janet Napolitano issued a statement saying, "effective immediately, I have directed U.S. Citizenship and Immigration Services (USCIS) to review immigration visa petitions filed on behalf of a same-sex spouse in the same manner as those filed on behalf of an opposite-sex spouse."[31] The statement was accompanied by a list of "Frequently Asked Questions" with answers about how the process would work. This change opened the door to legal migration for some same-sex couples. Yet, as Priya Kandaswamy describes, the struggle for recognition of same-sex marriage was waged without challenging or transforming the ways that marriage preserves white privilege, patriarchy, and the restricted transfer of wealth.[32] Not surprisingly, in order to receive legal status based on marriage, same-sex and trans couples, like normative male/female couples, had to meet income requirements; prove the bona fides of their marriages; demonstrate lack of criminalization; and conform to norms of privacy, domesticity, and consumption. This reformist change incorporated relatively privileged same-sex and trans couples within the existing system and logics of structured inequalities.

These developments make clear that heteronormativity always involves questions about how sexualities and genders comprise axes for governance, discipline, resistance, dispossession, and displacement that thoroughly articulate the long history of settler colonialism, empire, white supremacy, and capitalism through which the United States is constituted. Dynamics of migrant illegalization, detention, and deportation, which are the focus of this collection, stem from these histories.

"Illegalization"

In the United States today, it is commonly believed that "illegal" or undocumented status reflects the inherent, undesirable character of individual migrants who have "broken the law." That individualizing and depoliticizing approach ignores the dynamics that drive global migration in the first place and the United States' role in those dynamics. It also ignores how U.S. immigration policies reinforce multiple inequalities at global, national, and local scales—thus ensuring that migration will continue—and how U.S. immigration regimes configure who may, or may not, acquire or keep legal status and on what terms. Plainly stated, undocumented status reflects not a "type" of person but rather, a person who has been *made* undocumented through relations of power, knowledge, and struggle.

The very possibility that someone might become designated as undocumented is relatively recent. Moreover, scholars have shown that the line between documented and undocumented status is never stable, but rather, migrants transition among statuses depending on the changing rules for admission, residence, and work.[33] The meanings and experiences of being designated as undocumented also greatly vary.[34] Scholars have analyzed how dynamics of settler colonialism, capitalism, racism, and empire significantly shape who is likely to become routed into undocumented status; recent works, to which this collection contributes, further explore how sexual and gender hierarchies articulate these histories.[35]

The immigration system's rules concerning eligibility for admission, described earlier, thoroughly configure people's possibilities for acquiring legal status or not. Migrants are also made undocumented through the refugee and asylum system. The fact that there are two different systems for migrant admission reflects the distinction between forced (political) and voluntary (economic) migrants, even though force and economics are not easily separable in most migrants' lives.[36] Insisting on the distinction, however, allows the United States to invalidate claims by poor and working-class migrants seeking protection by asserting that they are "really" economic migrants trying to "take advantage" of the refugee/asylum system. Media frequently echo that assertion, which has legitimized expanding measures to prevent migrants from ever arriving to apply for asylum. The measures include turning migrants' boats around at sea, housing them on islands and deconstitutionalized zones to ensure they cannot apply for asylum, using bribes or threats to persuade other countries through which they pass to contain or stop them, and outrightly refusing to allow them to apply for asylum when they arrive at U.S. border checkpoints. The distinction between forced and voluntary migration also enables the United States to deny asylum claims by migrants who cannot conform to narrow, Eurocentric norms of gay, lesbian, or transgender identities and identifications; women who cannot fit the narrative of the United States "saving brown women from brown men" (though only when women are sufficiently middle class and there's no prospect of more than a handful of applicants); those seeking protection on the grounds of persecution and violence in which the United States is directly implicated; and others. Assertions that migrants fail to meet the dizzying maze of technical, bureaucratic, or evidentiary standards that are required to "prove" their need for protection further enable denial of claims in these situations. Once their protection claims and appeals are denied, migrants no longer have a basis for continued presence or claims on the state, and they become recast as unauthorized and deportable, including to circumstances that may result in death.[37] Even while the refugee and asylum system remains a major engine for producing migrants who are undocumented, detainable, and deportable, the existence of that system "obscures the political context that produces displaced people in the first place" and the role of the United States and other nations in that context.[38] It also further legitimizes harsh immigration controls. These U.S. approaches are widely echoed around the world.

When migrants become unable to acquire or retain legal status because of these processes, this does not mean that they are deported.[39] On the contrary, they often become differentially included in the United States in a manner that makes them highly vulnerable and exploitable.[40] Differential inclusion "describes how inclusion in a sphere, society, or realm can involve various degrees of subordination, rule, discrimination, racism, disenfranchisement, exploitation and segmentation."[41]

The experiences of LGBTQ holders of DACA status offer one illustration of how migrants may transition among documented and undocumented statuses and the forms that differential inclusion may take. President Obama created DACA, or Deferred Action for Childhood Arrivals, in 2012, after Congress repeatedly failed to pass legislation that would have provided a pathway to legal status for millions of young people who had been brought as undocumented children to the United States. They faced blocked opportunities at every turn and the constant possibility of detention and deportation. The DACA program allowed undocumented migrants who had entered the United States before the age of 16 and met other requirements to get temporary work authorization and protection from deportation for a two-year period.[42] Yet, DACA-holders were not considered to be "legally present" even though they were physically, socially, economically, and in every other way present. Moreover, DACA offered no path to more secure status and had to be regularly renewed, which meant it could be denied. Some 800,000 migrants, including an estimated 36,000 who identified as LGBTQ, received DACA status.[43]

The DACA program reflected a neoliberal dream (or nightmare) in terms of allowing for the extraction of value while providing no social benefits. Yet, the sheer fact of not being deportable, combined with having work authorization, made a demonstrable difference in the lives of DACA recipients and their families/social networks. A Williams Institute study found that LGBTQ DACA holders reported an average increase of 45 percent in hourly wages and expanded access to jobs with benefits, and 92 percent reported pursuing educational opportunities that would have otherwise been unavailable.[44]

Under the Obama administration, DACA holders seeking to renew their status were sometimes denied, including for petty infractions, which illustrates the tenuousness of that status. In Fiscal Year 2017, under the Trump administration, 840 DACA holders' statuses were revoked.[45] In September 2017, the Trump administration stopped accepting any new applications for DACA status, and effective March 5, 2018, DACA status began to expire for all holders—without any prospect for renewal. The Migration Policy Institute estimated that as a result, 915 DACA holders would lose status every day.[46] Several courts enjoined the Trump administration from dismantling the program. In June 2019, the Supreme Court agreed to review whether the Trump administration could end the program; as of this writing, that decision is pending.

The experiences of LGBTQ DACA recipients illustrate some of the complexities involved in getting, keeping, or losing legal status: the extraordinary variety of statuses available and the (im)possibilities and constraints associated with each one; how legal statuses intersect with other axes of privilege or vulnerability; and how migrants may transit among statuses, which impacts not just themselves but also those around them.[47]

All of this connects with risks and experiences of detention and deportation.

Detention and Deportation

In the 1980s and '90s, the United States significantly expanded militarization of the U.S./Mexico border and immigration enforcement both inward and outward from the territorial boundaries of the United States. Militarizing the border involved a steady buildup of surveillance and military equipment; material and virtual walling; a massive escalation in numbers of agents patrolling the border, who were also more visible in everyday and neighborhood settings; the rise of armed vigilante groups; tech and private prison companies flocking to the border to seek profit; and a consistent lack of accountability for abuses and shooting deaths.[48]

Militarization and expanded immigration enforcement are grounded in and shore up settler colonial logics, especially for peoples like the Tohono O'odham, whose nation spans the U.S.-Mexico border. U.S. border enforcement has deepened the experience of violent occupation. Border Patrol agents routinely engage in "coercive, abusive and threatening behavior" toward citizens going about their everyday business, treating them as suspected unauthorized migrants on their own land.[49] Border Patrol presence has resulted in walling, checkpoints, helicopters overhead, drones, and more; this has harmed the earth and plants, disrupted traditional ways of life, and reflects ongoing abrogation of the nation's sovereignty.[50] Other Native nations have been similarly affected.

When militarization of the southern border failed to prevent migration (and instead produced many more dead, deeper smuggling networks, and longer migrant stays in the United States), detention started to become the major strategy for responding to undocumented migration. Detention had already been significantly developed as a response to Haitian and Cuban asylum seekers arriving by boat in the 1980s.[51] In 1996, new laws drastically ramped up the processes whereby migrants became criminalized (dubbed "crimmigration" by Juliet Strumpf), which greatly expanded illegalization, detention and deportation logics, processes, and institutions.[52] The laws mandated the deportation of all noncitizens, authorized or not, who were convicted of an "aggravated felony." The laws redefined what counted as an aggravated felony so that even minor violations like shoplifting or nonpayment of taxes were potentially included. The laws applied retroactively, such that noncitizen legal residents who had minor brushes with the law long in the past suddenly found themselves deportable. Crimmigration also involved the enhancement or literal creation of criminal sanctions for immigration-related acts, for example, reentering the United States after being deported for unauthorized presence. Further driving crimmigration and deportation were the ways that local and state law enforcement became increasingly linked into supporting federal immigration authorities. The convergence between crime control, immigration control, and deportation has tightened the popular and political equation of undocumented status with inherent criminality. The events of September 11, 2001, also deepened the equally unjustified association of undocumented migration with terrorism.

The United States now has the largest immigrant detention system in the world.[53] Detainees include long-term U.S. residents, both documented and not, and recent border crossers, including those planning to apply for asylum. They are held in a sprawling network of county jails, Department of Homeland Security (DHS)–run facilities, and private facilities that are paid a daily rate for each detainee.

Sexual and gender logics, in their intersections with economic dispossession, racialization, settler colonialism, and empire, shape who is targeted for detention and eventual deportation. Golash-Boza has shown that working-class men from Latin America and the Caribbean are overwhelmingly targeted.[54] Monisha Das Gupta suggests that they are targeted "*precisely because* they do not and cannot structurally live up to the . . . gender and sexual arrangements" prescribed by settler white heteronormativity.[55] LGBTQ migrants, especially when they are trans women, of color, from Latin America or the Caribbean, and/or poor, are also highly vulnerable to becoming detained. Vulnerabilities include being targets of violence in the countries from which they came, while crossing through transit countries, and upon arrival in the United States; heightened likelihood of interaction with police because of the discriminatory enforcement of laws and with criminal gangs who know they are largely unprotected; and being pushed into homelessness, survival sex work, and the underground economy. HIV-positive migrants are also vulnerable, especially in jurisdictions that criminalize otherwise legal conduct or increase penalties for illicit conduct based on HIV-positive status.[56] Detained HIV-positive people generally experience significant difficulties accessing vital medicines and health care.

Immigration and Customs Enforcement (ICE) may release migrants who are not subject to mandatory detention, present no flight risk, and do not threaten public safety. ICE uses an automated Risk Classification Assessment tool to evaluate whether to detain or release migrants. Sharita Gruberg found that in 2015, even when ICE's own risk assessment tool recommended release, ICE did not release LGBTQ migrants in 88 percent of those instances.[57] For those few who were offered release, ICE required the payment of extremely high bonds that most could not afford, so they remained detained anyway.

While in detention, conditions are organized around and perpetuate sexualized, gendered, racialized, and economic abuse. In a 2011 groundbreaking challenge, Heartland Alliance's National Immigrant Justice Center filed complaints documenting allegations of abuse on behalf of 13 detained LGBTQ migrants with the Office of Civil Rights and Civil Liberties and the Office of the Inspector General. The complaints described sexual assault, denial of adequate medical care and mental health treatment, arbitrary long-term solitary confinement, frequent discrimination and abuse by officers and facility staff, and ineffective complaints and appeals processes.[58] "[O]ther complaints have documented LGBT detainees being called names such as 'faggot' by guards and being told to 'walk like a man, not a gay man' and 'act male.'"[59] Trans women are very frequently detained in all-male facilities.

Sexual abuse is particularly rampant and unchecked in immigrant detention facilities. ICE insists that it has a zero tolerance policy toward sexual abuse in detention facilities.[60] Fliers in detention facilities urge detainees to "break the silence" about sexual assault, and detainees are provided with information about how to file complaints.[61] Nonetheless, Human Rights Watch, the ACLU, MALDEF, and others have consistently documented systemic, unchecked sexual abuse within immigrant detention facilities. A 2018 report by *The Intercept* affirms that "sexual abuse and harassment in immigration detention facilities are not only widespread but systemic, and enabled by an agency that regularly fails to hold itself accountable."[62] The author concludes that the data "paint a damning portrait and suggest institutional complicity to sexual abuse on a mass scale."[63] Institutionalized complicity and lack of accountability are also shown by the fact that ICE has asked the National Archives to erase records of abuse and deaths in detention.[64] Transgender women are particularly at risk of sexual abuse in detention; it's estimated that they represent 1 in 500 of all detained migrants, but according to a 2013 report, 1 in 5 substantiated cases of sexual abuse in immigrant detention facilities.[65] Trans migrants are also routinely subjected to gendered harassment and denial of hormones and appropriate medical care.

Sexual abuse and coercion may result in pregnancy, or migrants may already be pregnant when detained. Under the Obama administration, pregnant women were regarded as a vulnerable population and generally not detained except under extraordinary circumstances. In December 2017, the Trump administration rescinded that policy. Some detained women have miscarried due to lack of proper medical care, staff indifference, generally abusive conditions, and the stress of their situation.[66] For detained women and girls who may not want to carry a pregnancy to term, including when the pregnancy stemmed from sexual violence, abortion access is extremely difficult. The case of detained migrant 17-year-old Jane Doe, whose struggle for an abortion reached the Supreme Court in 2018, demonstrates the difficulties.[67]

Vulnerability to sexual abuse and coercion combines with high rates of physical and psychological threats, abuse, and coercion. Detainees also report consistent difficulties accessing adequate food, basic hygiene, and health care. Lawsuits charge that detained migrants comprise a captive workforce that is frequently compelled to work for $1 a day. Not surprisingly, but tragically, migrants have died in detention under conditions that have yet to be remedied. Recent deaths include Roxsana Hernández, a 33-year-old transgender woman from Honduras, who died on May 25, 2018. A statement by Pueblo Sin Fronteras, Al Otro Lado, and Diversided Sin Fronteras expressed deep grief that Roxsana had died after traveling "over 2,000 miles through Mexican territory on foot, by train, by bus because her last aspiration and hope was to save her own life."[68] Yet, in the United States, she encountered entrenched indifference to the circumstances that motivated her migration, brutal conditions including detention in an "ice box" that caused severe deterioration to her health, and loss of hope. "Treated neither with respect nor with dignity," these cumulative conditions led to her death.[69]

While not every facility is the same, the system as a whole fosters "a culture of cruelty."[70] Cruelty including neglect, abuse, and death persists because facilities lack oversight or accountability. A patchwork of different detention standards applies (though mainly in the breach); the complaints process is utterly inadequate; ICE has been aware for years of that conditions in many detention facilities are abysmal, but their response is characterized by "systemic indifference." Facilities with a record of inhumane and degrading treatment of people, and unexplained deaths, continue to receive contracts to detain migrants.[71] The Trump administration has been rolling back the meager protections that are supposed to be in place—while vastly expanding the numbers detained. It has also promoted brazen indifference to human rights violations, systemic abuse, and death.

Rachel Lewis argues that illegalization and detention frequently produces lesbian-identified women as deportable subjects.[72] Martha Balaguera describes that Central American trans women on the run from violence and persecution, whose bodies "fill detention facilities, shelters, and the migrant trails across Mexico," experience "confinement in motion" that includes, but extends far beyond, the violence inflicted by the U.S. state.[73] Shannon Speed suggests that Indigenous women fleeing violence, including lesbian, trans, and cisgender women, find that their rights are "functionally eliminated" at every step of their journey, and the process of seeking protection through asylum further *contributes* to that elimination.[74]

These practices and logics draw from and further contribute to the vast expansion of the prison industrial complex that targets poor, racialized, and queered U.S. citizen communities. They also contribute to restructuring states and other institutions of governance around social abandonment, imprisonment, and impunity.[75] Finally, the practices and logics articulate with the global detention regime in which the United States is a major participant.[76]

Because of these practices, the numbers who are deported have reached horrifying levels. Golash-Boza describes that "the current numbers of deportations are unprecedented in the history of the USA"; between 1998 and 2012 alone, there were over 4.1 million deportations.[77] Despite DHS's claims that it targets dangerous criminals for detention and deportation, most deportees have no criminal record or records related to traffic offenses, low-level drug offenses, or reentry after a previous deportation; deportees are also frequently people who sought humanitarian protection but were denied.[78]

Although state research and policy often individualize and normalize deportation, Khosravi and others highlight that it is a deeply brutal process, and moreover, as suggested by Lewis, Balaguera, Speed, and many more, individual experiences of brutality through detention and deportation connect to systemic inequalities and structural violence—which do not end when migrants are dropped off or dumped outside of U.S. territorial borders.[79] Instead, people may enter cycles of incarceration-deportation-abuse-return-incarceration and so on that contribute to stripping them of rights at every step. In some cases, migrants including LGBTQ people and other vulnerable groups are deported directly to death.[80] In other cases, they experience slow and systemic death.

Citizenship, Citizen/Migrant Hierarchies, and Struggles for Transformation

U.S. citizenship stems from and reproduces settler colonialist, racializing, heterogendering and anti-poor logics.[81] Immigration controls including illegalization, detention, and deportation support this form of U.S. citizenship. At the same time, these controls are transforming the meaning of citizenship. Transformations are evidenced by the experiences of literally millions of citizens and legal permanent residents whose family members and friends have been tracked into illegalization, detention, and deportation. A growing scholarship documents the multiple harmful and destructive impacts on families and communities who live under these conditions. Their experiences reflect and reproduce hierarchies among the U.S. citizenry, while also reshaping how nation-based citizenship functions transnationally.[82] For example, migrants' deportation affects citizenries in the countries to which they are forcibly sent, as well as U.S. citizens who are left behind; U.S. citizen family members sometimes leave with deported migrants; and many migrants conceive themselves as de facto U.S. Americans even after being deported.

Publicizing the pain and disenfranchisement of citizens who are impacted by immigration enforcement practices, including through deportation of their family members, has offered an important means for challenging current immigration controls. Yet this strategy remains fraught with risk because only *some* citizens' pain and disenfranchisement appear capable of generating change. For example, appeals to stop the deportation of family members have most often gained traction when the families involved are normatively gendered, have some degree of racial privilege or economic means, have not been criminalized, or can otherwise appeal to mainstream values like military service. Other citizens' pain and disenfranchisement seemingly do not count and instead, reiterate or deepen their devaluation.[83] These disparities underscore how immigration struggles often reflect, and further shore up, inequalities among citizens, as well as among migrants.[84]

Promising approaches for grasping and reworking the co-implication of citizen and migrant statuses stem from treating citizenship as "not just a status that precedes immigration enforcement but also one that is, in a functional sense, produced by such enforcement."[85] For example, citizens and migrants have worked together to challenge racist immigration enforcement practices that "overlap and intersect with historical and contemporary geographies of racist state violence and mass incarceration" that target citizens.[86] Engin Isin characterizes these kinds of challenges as "acts of citizenship . . . through which citizens, strangers, outsiders and aliens emerge not as subjects already defined, but as ways of being with others."[87]

The United States has a long history of migrant justice struggles that link with citizens' issues. Since 2006, there has been a resurgence of these struggles. The resurgence has spanned the political spectrum from those seeking liberal reforms around legalization while accepting militarization of borders, to revolutionary approaches demanding open borders, the abolition of ICE, and more.[88] Mainstream LGBT organizations began to incorporate immigration issues into their platforms with a particular focus on lobbying for recognition of same-sex and trans couples' relationships as a basis for legal immigration. This focus generated significant criticism because it affirmed normalizing visions of which families, relationships, and individuals "deserve" protection and incorporation, thereby serving rather than challenging immigration enforcement practices that routinely illegalize, detain, and deport queer and trans migrants who are racialized, criminalized, and economically dispossessed.[89] More radical queer migrant justice platforms (for example, by the now-defunct Queers for Economic Justice and the Audre Lorde Project) also emerged and continue to inspire.

Queer and trans migrants, who are positioned at the intersections of multiple identities, hierarchies, and movements that often overlook them or seek advancement at their expense, emerged as leaders and made significant interventions into the framing of demands and the tactics used. Their interventions often entailed seizing or creating "coalitional moments." Karma R. Chávez explains that coalitional moments arise when political issues overlap in ways "that create space to reenvision and potentially reconstruct rhetorical imaginaries" and open up possibilities for "radical social and political change."[90] Coalitional moments have been evidenced by the work of young queer and trans migrants who "put a vibrant face (or faces) to a nationwide movement that is intent on highlighting the simultaneity of LGBT and migrant struggles."[91] Some migrants borrowed from the LGBT movement's tactic of "coming out of the closet," proclaiming themselves "undocumented and unafraid" while pushing to end deportation and open up legalization.[92] "Undocuqueer" also emerged as a critical framework through which queer and trans migrant subjectivities, collectivities, coalitions, and political projects caught fire, sparking pride, resistance, and new forms of organizing. Julio Salgado's "I am Undocuqueer" series, comprised of vivid portraits and short narratives, significantly fueled these efforts.[93]

LGBTQ migrant detention particularly sparked coalitional moments while highlighting differences. After complaints were filed against the Department of Homeland Security (DHS) in 2011, DHS created a special detention unit for transgender and gay migrants (the LGBT "pod"); yet reports of the abuse of LGBT detainees continued, leading to nationwide protests and Congressional concern. In 2015, undocumented trans migrant Jennicet Gutiérrez interrupted President Obama at a White House event to protest the abuse of detained trans immigrants and demand the release of all LGBTQ detainees. In 2016, undocumented trans and queer migrants who advocated confrontational, transformational, and nonassimilative approaches to social justice struggles bravely went on a public hunger strike to protest the LGBT detention pod and all immigrant detentions. Queer and trans migrants also mobilized around the arrival of caravans of gay and trans Central American migrants seeking asylum in the United States in 2017 and 2018 and numerous other struggles.

Artistic and cultural works (including the works in this volume) have been indispensable for queer and trans migrant organizing. Social media have also been indispensable. Migrants have deftly navigated social media's implication in dominant economic, cultural, and social regimes, opening up space for new subjectivities, imaginaries, activisms, and communities. And even while ICE increasingly depends on information technology to surveil, incarcerate, and deport, queer and trans migrants and allies have used information technologies to contest deportations and enable border crossings, and for other purposes (see Herrera in this volume).[94]

Struggles against migrant illegalization, detention, and deportation have deeply tangled roots that connect multiple forms of violence and freedom dreams. Understanding these historical entanglements offers resources, roadmaps, and inspiration for the difficult present.

Notes

1. Wikipedia, "Blue Ribbon Panel," https://en.wikipedia.org/wiki/Blue-ribbon_panel.

2. Ibid.

3. The term *illegal* has been widely criticized on multiple grounds including because it contributes to normalizing the criminalization and dehumanization of migrants. Race Forward (formerly the Applied Research Center) launched a "Drop the I-Word" campaign in 2010 (https://www.raceforward.org/practice/tools/drop-i-word). In this chapter, I retain the term *illegal* in order to critically historicize, problematize, and denaturalize it but place quotation marks around it to signal that it is highly problematic.

4. This estimate uses 2011 data; a more updated estimate is not available. See Gary J. Gates, "LGBT Adult Immigrants in the United States," The Williams Institute, March 2013, https://williamsinstitute.law.ucla.edu/wp-content/uploads/LGBTImmigrants-Gates -Mar-2013.pdf.

5. Mark Rifkin, *When Did Indians Become Straight? Kinship, The History of Sexuality, and Native Sovereignty* (Oxford: Oxford University Press, 2011), 32–33.

6. Eithne Luibhéid, *Entry Denied: Controlling Sexuality at the Border* (Minneapolis: University of Minnesota Press, 2002); Margot Canaday, *The Straight State: Sexuality and Citizenship in Twentieth-Century America* (Princeton, N.J.: Princeton University Press, 2011).

7. Lindsey Schneider, "(Re)producing the Nation: Treaty Rights, Gay Marriage, and the Settler State," in *Critical Ethnic Studies: A Reader*, ed. Nadia Elia et al. (Durham, N.C.: Duke University Press, 2016), 92–105.

8. Ibid., 93.

9. As state immigration controls delimit who may become a legal migrant in relation to nationalist heteronormativity, this co-constitutes boundaries of who *cannot* legalize or may lose legal status.

10. Nayan Shah, *Stranger Intimacy: Contesting Race, Sexuality and the Law in North America* (Berkeley: University of California Press, 2011), 262.

11. David Reimers, *Still the Golden Door* (New York: Columbia University Press, 1992).

12. Tanya Golash-Boza, *Deported: Immigrant Policing, Disposable Labor, and Global Capitalism* (New York: New York University Press, 2015), 11. See also David Harvey, *A Brief History of Neoliberalism* (Oxford: Oxford University Press, 2007).

13. Saskia Sassen, "Why Migration?" *NACLA Report on the Americas* xxvi, no. 1 (July 1992): 14–19.

14. See the special issue of *Latino Studies* 15 (2017) on "Critical Latinx Indigeneities," edited by Maylei Blackwell, Floridalma Boj Lopez, and Luis Urrieta Jr.

15. Migration from Mexico was especially affected. See Douglas Massey, Jorge Durand, and Nolan J. Malone, *Beyond Smoke and Mirrors: Mexican Immigration in an Era of Economic Integration* (New York: Russell Sage Foundation, 2002).

16. See United Nations Human Rights, Office of the High Commissioner, "Convention Relating to the Status of Refugees," https://www.ohchr.org/en/professionalinterest/pages/ statusofrefugees.aspx.

17. Aihwa Ong, *Buddha Is Hiding: Refugees, Citizenship, the New America* (Berkeley: University of California Press, 2003), 85; Odessa Gonzalez Benson, "Refugee Resettlement

in an Era of Neoliberalism: A Policy Discourse Analysis of the Refugee Act of 1980," *Social Service Review* 90, no. 3 (2016): 515.

18. Ong, *Buddha is Hiding*.

19. E.g., *Sexualities* 17, no. 8 (December 2014), special issue on "Queer Migration, Asylum, and Displacement," ed. Rachel Lewis and Nancy Naples; Calogero Giametta, *The Sexual Politics of Asylum: Sexual Orientation and Gender Identity* (New York: Routledge, 2017); David Murray, *Real Queer? Sexual Orientation and Gender Identity in the Canadian Refugee Apparatus* (Lanham, Md.: Rowman and Littlefield, 2015).

20. Sima Shakhsari, "The Queer Time of Death: Temporality, Geopolitics, and Refugee Rights," *Sexualities* 17, no. 8 (2014): 1007.

21. The Immigration Marriage Fraud Amendments of 1986 further strengthened the state's ability to confine and govern migrants from within normative marriage.

22. Those who are not legally present were already barred from everything but emergency care, even though many pay into federal benefit programs through taxes.

23. Chandan Reddy, "Asian Diasporas, Neoliberalism and Family," *Social Text* 23, nos. 2–3 (Fall-Winter 2005): 109.

24. Ibid.

25. E.g., Robin Templeton, "Baby-Baiting," *The Nation* (August 16–23, 2010), https://www.thenation.com/article/baby-baiting/.

26. E.g., Hirokazu Yoshikawa, *Immigrants Raising Citizens: Undocumented Parents and Their Children* (New York: Russell Sage Foundation, 2012).

27. See Gates's estimate of numbers of children being raised in same-sex couples where one or both partners are foreign-born in Gates, "LGBT Adult Immigrants."

28. Dorothy E. Roberts, "Who May Give Birth to Citizens? Reproduction, Eugenics and Immigration," in *Immigrants Out!* ed. Juan Perea (New York: New York University Press, 1997), 214.

29. Ibid., 205.

30. Tamar Diana Wilson, "Strapping the Mexican Woman Immigrant: The Convergence of Reproduction and Production," *Anthropology Quarterly* 79, no. 2 (Spring 2006): 295–302.

31. "Same-Sex Marriages," US Citizenship and Immigration Services, last modified, July 1, 2013, https://www.uscis.gov/family/same-sex-marriages.

32. Priya Kandaswamy, "State Austerity and the Racial Politics of Same-Sex Marriage," *Sexualities* 11, no. 6 (2008): 706–725.

33. E.g., Mae Ngai, *Impossible Subjects: Illegal Aliens and the Making of Modern America* (Princeton, N.J.: Princeton University Press, 2005); Joseph Nevins, *Operation Gatekeeper: The Rise of the 'Illegal Alien' and the Remaking of the U.S.-Mexico Boundary* (New York: Routledge, 2001); Jonathan Inda, *Targeting Immigrants: Government, Technology, and Ethics* (Malden, Mass.: Wiley-Blackwell, 2005). Inda explores how knowledge production literally "makes up" the undocumented as a new political subject and does so in a manner that suggests ways for governing (against) them.

34. Cecilia Menjívar and Daniel Kanstroom, eds. *Constructing Immigrant 'Illegality': Critiques, Experiences, and Responses* (Cambridge: Cambridge University Press, 2013).

35. E.g., Eithne Luibhéid, *Pregnant on Arrival: Making the 'Illegal' Immigrant* (Minneapolis: University of Minnesota Press, 2013).

36. Stephan Scheel, Glenda Garelli and Martina Tazzioli, "Politics of Protection," in Nicholas De Genova, Sandro Mezzadra, and John Pickles, eds. "New Keywords: Migration and Borders," *Cultural Studies* 29, no. 1 (2015): 71–72.

37. See the scholarship on queer necropolitics, e.g., Jin Haritaworn, Adi Kuntsman, and Silvia Posocco, eds. *Queer Necropolitics* (New York: Routledge, 2014).

38. Scheel, Garelli and Tazzioli, "Politics of Protection," 71.

39. Nicholas De Genova, "Migrant 'Illegality' and Deportability in Everyday Life," *Annual Review of Anthropology* 31 (2002): 419–447.

40. As De Genova describes, "it is deportability, and not deportation per se, that has historically rendered undocumented migrant labor as a distinctly disposable commodity" (438). See also Nicholas De Genova and Natalie Peutz, eds., *The Deportation Regime: Sovereignty, Space, and the Freedom of Movement* (Durham, N.C.: Duke University Press, 2010).

41. Sandro Mezzadra, Brett Nielson, Lisa Reidner, Stephan Scheel, Glenda Garelli, Martina Taziolli, and Federico Rahola, "Differential Inclusion," in De Genova, Mezzadra, and Pickles, "New Keywords," 79.

42. Full listing of requirements in United We Dream, *No More Closets*, January 2016, https://unitedwedream.org/wp-content/uploads/2017/07/Report-No-More-Closets-1.pdf, 8.

43. Kerith Conron and Taylor N. T. Brown, "LGBT Dreamers and Deferred Action for Childhood Arrivals," The Williams Institute, February 2017, https://williamsinstitute.law.ucla.edu/wp-content/uploads/LGBT-DREAMers-and-DACA-February-2017.pdf.

44. Yet, they faced varying barriers; only some states allowed DACA recipients to qualify for lower, in-state tuition or access state-based financial aid.

45. Lori Robertson, "The Facts on DACA," last modified January 18, 2018, *FactCheck.org*, https://www.factcheck.org/2018/01/the-facts-on-daca/.

46. Ibid.

47. The complexities of legal status are further captured by United We Dream's *No More Closets*: "the survey indicates that the LGBTQ immigrant community cannot be split into a binary of documented and undocumented. Indeed . . . many individuals reported confusion about the question or did not know their current immigration status" (8).

48. See Jenna M. Loyd, Matt Mitchelson, and Andrew Burridge, eds. *Beyond Walls and Cages: Prisons, Borders, and Global Crisis* (Athens: University of Georgia Press, 2012); Daniel Martínez, Guillermo Cantor, and Walter Ewing, *No Action Taken: Lack of CPB Accountability in Responding to Complaints of Abuse* (Washington, D.C.: American Immigration Council, May 2014), https://www.americanimmigrationcouncil.org/research/no-action-taken-lack-cbp-accountability-responding-complaints-abuse; Todd Miller, *Border Patrol Nation* (San Francisco: Open Media Series/City Lights Books, 2014).

49. Miller, *Border Patrol Nation*, 145.

50. See "There's No O'Odham Word for Wall," https://www.youtube.com/watch?v=RQu-YEmKCN8.

51. Jenna Loyd and Alison Mountz, *Boats, Borders, and Bases: Race, the Cold War, and the Rise of Migration Detention in the United States* (Berkeley: University of California Press, 2018).

52. Key laws include the Illegal Immigration Reform and Immigrant Responsibility Act, and the Anti-Terrorism and Effective Death Penalty Act. Juliet Stumpf, "The Crimmigration Crisis: Immigrants, Crime, and Sovereign Power," *American University Law Review* 56, no. 2 (December 2006): 367–419.

53. Numbers of migrants detained each year significantly exceed numbers of prisoners detained in federal prison each year.

54. Golash-Boza, *Deported*, 8.

55. Monisha Das Gupta, "Don't Deport Our Daddies: Gendering State Deportation Practices and Immigrant Organizing," *Gender and Society* 28, no. 1 (February 2014): 85.

56. The Williams Institute, "For immigrants, HIV criminalization can mean incarceration and deportation," October 4, 2016, https://williamsinstitute.law.ucla.edu/press/for-immigrants-hiv-criminalization-can-mean-incarceration-and-deportation-2/.

57. Sharita Gruberg, "ICE Officers Overwhelmingly Use Their Discretion to Detain LGBT Immigrants," Center for American Progress, October 26, 2016. https://cdn.americanprogress.org/content/uploads/2016/10/26065442/ICEandLGBTdetentionPDF.pdf/.

58. "Mass Civil Rights Complaint Details Systemic Abuse of Sexual Minorities in U.S. Immigration Detention," Press Release, National Immigrant Justice Center, April 13, 2011, https://www.immigrantjustice.org/press_releases/mass-civil-rights-complaint-details-systemic-abuse-sexual-minorities-us-immigration-d, 3.

59. Gruberg, "Dignity Denied: LGBT Immigrants in U.S. Immigration Detention," Washington, D.C.: Center for American Progress, November 25, 2013, https://www.americanprogress.org/issues/immigration/reports/2013/11/25/79987/dignity-denied-lgbt-immigrants-in-u-s-immigration-detention/, 4.

60. In 2003, Congress passed the Prison Rape Elimination Act (PREA); eight years later, the Department of Justice drafted PREA standards to apply to detention facilities. Immigrant detention facilities were not included since they fell under DHS. In 2014, DHS issued its own PREA policy; by 2016, it covered 64 percent of immigrant detention facilities—in theory, but not in practice.

61. Alice Speri, "Detained, Then Violated," *The Intercept*, April 11, 2018, https://theintercept.com/2018/04/11/immigration-detention-sexual-abuse-ice-dhs/.

62. Ibid.

63. Ibid.

64. See John Washington, "ICE Wants to Destroy Its In-Custody Records of Death, Sexual Assault, and Other Detainee Files," *The Nation*, September 13, 2017, https://www.thenation.com/article/ice-wants-to-destroy-its-records-of-in-custody-deaths-sexual-assault-and-other-detainee-files/. The ACLU has petitioned to prevent the erasure.

65. The Government Accountability Office, "Immigration Detention: Additional Actions Could Strengthen DHS Efforts to Address Sexual Abuse," November 2016, last modified December 2016, https://www.gao.gov/assets/660/659145.pdf.

66. E.g., see Human Rights Watch, *Systemic Indifference: Dangerous and Substandard Medical Care in US Immigration Detention*, May 2017, https://www.hrw.org/sites/default/files/report_pdf/usimmigration0517_web_0.pdf.

67. E.g., Vivian Yee, "After Court Ruling, Detained Teenage Immigrants are Allowed to Obtain Abortions," *The New York Times*, December 20, 2017.

68. May 29, 2018, "Statement by Pueblo Sin Fronteras, Al Otro Lado and Diversidad Sin Fronteras on The Institutional Murder of Roxana Hernandez," https://www.facebook.com/diversidadsinfronteraz/posts/378858885957426%20accessed%20July%2030.

69. Ibid.

70. No More Deaths/No Más Muertes, *A Culture of Cruelty*, 2011, http://forms.nomoredeaths.org/wp-content/uploads/2014/10/CultureOfCruelty-full.compressed.pdf.

71. American Civil Liberties Union, Detention Watch Network, and Heartland Alliance's National Immigrant Justice Center, *Fatal Neglect: How ICE Ignores Deaths in Detention*, 2016, https://www.aclu.org/sites/default/files/field_document/fatal_neglect_acludwnnijc.pdf. Similarly, the Federal government found "problems that undermine the protection of detainees' rights, their humane treatment, and the provision of a safe and healthy environment" (2017). See Office of the Inspector General, "Concerns about ICE Detainee Treatment and Care at Detention Facilities," December 11, 2017, https://www.oig.dhs.gov/sites/default/files/assets/2017–12/OIG-18-32-Dec17.pdf.

72. See Lewis in this volume, and Rachel Lewis, "Deportable Subjects: Lesbians and Political Asylum," *Feminist Formations* 25, no. 2 (2013): 174–194.

73. Martha Balaguera, "Trans-migrations: Agency and Confinement at the Limits of Sovereignty," *Signs: Journal of Women in Culture and Society* 43, no. 3 (Spring 2018): 641.

74. Shannon Speed, "States of Violence. Indigenous Women Migrants in an Era of Neoliberal Multicriminalism," *Critique of Anthropology* 36, no. 3 (June 2016): 282.

75. E.g., Deirdre Conlon and Nancy Hiemstra, eds., *Intimate Economies of Immigrant Detention* (New York: Routledge, 2017); Martha Escobar, *Captivity Beyond Prisons* (Austin: University of Texas Press, 2016).

76. David M. Hernández, "Surrogates and Subcontractors: Flexibility and Obscurity in U.S. Immigrant Detention," in *Critical Ethnic Studies: A Reader*, ed. Nadia Elia, et. al (Durham, N.C.: Duke University Press, 2016), 303–325.

77. Tanya Golash-Boza, "Targeting Latino Men: Mass Deportation from the USA, 1998–2012," *Racial and Ethnic Studies* 38, no. 8 (2015): 1221.

78. E.g., Sarah Stillman, "When Deportation Is a Death Sentence," *The New Yorker*, January 15, 2018, https://www.newyorker.com/magazine/2018/01/15/when-deportation-is-a-death-sentence.

79. Shahram Khosravi, ed., *After Deportation: Ethnographic Perspectives* (New York: Palgrave Macmillan, 2018).

80. E.g., Stillman, "When Deportation Is a Death Sentence."

81. On citizenship in global northern states as an inherited status that stems from and perpetuates global apartheid, see Nandita Sharma, *Home Economics: Nationalism and*

the Making of 'Migrant Workers' in Canada (Toronto: University of Toronto Press, 2006); Aylet Shachar, *The Birthright Lottery: Citizenship and Global Inequality* (Cambridge, Mass.: Harvard University Press, 2009).

82. E.g., Deborah Boehm, *Intimate Migrations* (New York: New York University Press, 2012); Joanna Dreby, *Everyday Illegal: When Policies Undermine Immigrant Families* (Berkeley: University of California Press, 2015).

83. See scholarship on racialization and affect, e.g., Paula Ioanide, *The Emotional Politics of Racism: How Feelings Trump Facts in an Era of Colorblindness* (Stanford: Stanford University Press, 2015).

84. Furthermore, using citizens' pain and disenfranchisement to argue for changing migration enforcement risks turning migrants into the silenced ground from which citizens make their claims—which also serves dominant nation-making processes.

85. Rachel Rosenbloom, "The Citizenship Line: Rethinking Immigration Exceptionalism," *Boston College Law Review* 54, no. 5 (2013): 1965.

86. Geoffrey Alan Boyce, "Appearing 'Out of Place': Automobility and the Everyday Policing of Threat and Suspicion in the US/Canada Frontier," *Political Geography* 64 (2018): 10.

87. Engin F. Isin, "Claiming European Citizenship," in *Enacting European Citizenship*, eds. Engin F. Isin and Michael Saward (Cambridge, U.K.: Cambridge University Press, 2013), 41. Here, I am not advocating for investment in nation-state citizenship. Rather, I am suggesting that to dismantle migrant illegalization, detention, and deportation, we cannot bypass but must instead continue grappling with investments in nation-based citizenship. At the same time, we could, as Schmidt Camacho suggests, create another category of membership that acknowledges the rights of those who are not citizens and honors bonds of community beyond national borders (Alicia Schmidt Camacho, "Hailing the Twelve Million," *Social Text* 105, 28, no. 4 [Winter 2010]: 19).

88. Thank you, Karma, for this framing.

89. Couples must conform to standards of domesticity, privatization, and consumption, while also meeting income thresholds, and not being excludable on grounds of crime, suspicion of terrorism, or anything else.

90. Karma R. Chávez, *Queer Migration Politics: Activist Rhetoric and Coalitional Possibilities* (Urbana: University of Illinois Press, 2013), 8, 146.

91. Melissa Autumn White, "Documenting the Undocumented: Toward a Queer Politics of No Borders," *Sexualities* 17, no. 8 (2014): 986.

92. See Chávez, chapter 3, *Queer Migration Politics* for a thorough analysis of the possibilities and limits of appropriating "coming out" for purposes of challenging migrant criminalization, illegalization, detention, and deportation.

93. The Undocumented Queer Youth Collective and United We Dream's Queer Undocumented Immigrant Project (QUIP) were also key.

94. E.g., Minyoung Park, "5 Must-Have Apps for Undocumented Immigrants," March 17, 2017, https://money.cnn.com/2017/03/30/technology/immigrant-apps/index.html.

2

"Prevent Miami from Becoming a Refugium Peccatorum"

Policing Black Bahamian Women and Making the Straight, White State, 1890–1940

JULIO CAPÓ JR.

Writing in Nassau's *Tribune* in 1911, a Bahamian man described an immigrant officer based in the then-nascent city of Miami as "vigilant as the fabled Cerberus," a reference to the mythological hellhound guarding the underworld.[1] In conjuring the well-known image of the multiheaded hound as a means of describing the city's immigrant officer, the man conceded several connections no doubt intelligible to his contemporaries: the need to protect borders, the violence inherent in such security mechanisms, and the undesirability of particular bodies. While Cerberus was tasked with keeping dead subjects from leaving the underworld, Miami's immigration officer was responsible for regulating Bahamians and others who sought some form of relief, opportunity, and reconciliation through their mobility.

Take the case of an unmarried Black Bahamian woman whose name is not known to us who tried to enter Miami during this period. A man who awaited her arrival rushed to the schooner she sailed in with a marriage license in hand. He hoped this would change her status to that of a respectable married woman who would thereby become eligible to disembark and settle in Miami, even if just temporarily. It didn't work. The "obdurate" officer did not allow a brief ceremony to take place on the vessel nor could the "distressed young woman" step foot on Miami soil. Immigration officers ordered the vessel's captain to take the woman—who, at that point, was in "tears and sobs"—back to the Bahamas.[2]

While exclusion at the border for single or unaccompanied Black Bahamian women was fairly commonplace, most Bahamian male laborers—including some who had been arrested in Miami on felony charges for committing homosexual acts—had a different experience. Immediately after residents voted to incorporate the city of Miami in 1896, white settler-capitalists from the U.S. North, Midwest, and South began populating the frontier-land and looked to seasonal male migrants from the then-British colony of the Bahamas to build southern Florida's infrastructure and economy. In large part because city powerbrokers and employers relied heavily on the cheap and experienced labor Black Bahamian men offered, Miami's borders proved mostly permeable for them before the early 1920s.[3]

This work offers a transnational analysis of Bahamians, with a particular emphasis on the experiences of women, who entered or tried to enter Miami during the early twentieth century. It highlights the gendered migration patterns that found Bahamian men living in "bachelor" societies in Miami's urban frontier and created female-dominated, homosocial spaces on the archipelago. During the early 1900s, women and men who engaged in—or, largely as a product of their race and class, were believed to likely engage in—transgressive sexual acts were more likely to be excluded at the border as liable to become a "public charge" to the state. As the case of Black Bahamian men suggests, however, racialized and gendered labor practices often valorized certain bodies that then more readily circumvented such exclusion. Through these imperatives, Black Bahamian women at the Caribbean-U.S. borders subverted the state's norms of whiteness, binary gender, reproductive heterosexuality, and labor productivity that shaped its assessment of a migrant or immigrant's desirability. While we have come to understand the exclusion of "the homosexual" at the borders—that is, through official U.S. immigration policy in effect from 1952 to 1990—this history urges us to think more broadly about sexuality-based regimes of exclusion that were intrinsically informed by racialized, gendered, and economic imperatives.

The case of Bahamians in Miami elucidates the critical nature of racialized narratives in promoting the formation of what Margot Canaday calls the "straight state," bringing us closer, through a queer transcolonial and transnational analysis, to M. Jacqui Alexander's appeal that we view formations of citizenship through the naturalization of both heterosexuality and whiteness. Centering Bahamians highlights that the state was crafted not just as straight, but also as white, and that hegemonies of straightness and whiteness are co-constituted. In privileging white, hetero-patriarchal norms, the U.S. state created apparatuses to exclude so-called undesirable bodies that transgressed these norms. The Bahamians' experiences in Miami yield significant insight on how the formation of the "straight state" worked in concert with capitalist imperatives facilitated through the productivity and selectivity of a racialized "free labor" system. The legacies of slavery and colonialism in the West Indies constructed the corporeal logics in which, as Alexander argues, "Black bodies, the economic pivot of slave-plantation economy, were sexualized" and, she later adds, "essentially subordinated."[4]

Black border crossers navigated distinct colonial practices in both the Bahamas and the United States that valorized the labor potential of their bodies; the state created apparatuses as a means to gauge its ability to regulate and encourage particular types of labor. So, while Black Bahamian migrants, especially men, were highly encouraged to enter Miami *because* of their desirable labor, Black Bahamian women were more likely to be excluded at the borders on account of predisposed beliefs that they had no or limited labor potential—or, at least, no respectable labor potential that the state understood as valuable. John D'Emilio has traced the centrality of capitalism—in particular, the tenets of the "free labor" system and the radical transformation of the nuclear family—to the formation of distinct sexual identities.[5] Indeed, just as the U.S. state exploited Black Bahamian bodies seeking to enter Miami through the structures of racial capitalism, the migrants' household economies and traditional family models gradually broke down on both sides of the Florida Straits. This, along with greater economic independence that migration at least temporarily offered them, helped disassociate sexual acts from their previous defining core, procreation, and increasingly helped the state and state actors produce a more coherent understanding of bodies in relation to constructs of an inherent sexuality. In particular, the formulation of normative, white heterosexuality became the lynchpin against which a matrix of transgressive sexual expressions—both real or imagined—were measured.

This work also traces how vigilance, regulation, and violence far extended the borders; law enforcement and other state actors heavily policed and surveilled those who managed to pass Cerberus-like inspectors. This surveillance found release in a violent form of state welfare that paralleled and buttressed some of the greatest anxieties at the borders; their confinement at hospitals, asylums, and holding cells created a state logic in which restrictive immigration measures successfully predicted that Black women from the Bahamas would become a public charge. That is, the state's heightened criminalization, policing, and detainment of Black Bahamian women in Miami literally made them public charges and seemed to validate the restrictive immigration policy. Altogether, this queer analysis of Bahamian migration to Miami, which centers on various racialized and class-based formations of gender and sexual transgression across colonial settings, highlights how the state's multiheaded approach of controlling moving bodies it deemed undesirable—not unlike what "the fabled Cerberus" was thought to have achieved—produced grammars and praxes of illegality, confinement, and deportability.

*   *   *

Miami's early entrepreneurs exercised imperialist power to capitalize on tourism, travel, and labor to and from the Bahamas. Venture capitalist Henry Flagler built a lucrative empire throughout Florida that went farther south than Miami, as he understood the area's proximity to the Caribbean would be one of its greatest selling points.[6] Once his enterprise brought railroads that blazed through Miami, Flagler made sure travelers could board a steamship from Miami to the Bahamian capital of Nassau. He struck a deal with the Bahamian government that provided him with an annual subsidy for his business. In return, he provided the Bahamas and Miami regular mail and freight service through his steamships.[7] Parts of the Bahamas depended on Florida to import resources to meet a growing tourism market.[8] Miami and the Bahamas, along with their economies, were indelibly linked. This too was a direct product of the Bahamas' colonial status, because the archipelago remained a British backwater to the metropole. So, while U.S. capitalists saw potential in the Bahamians' experienced labor, Bahamians increasingly looked to the United States to counteract colonial neglect and inaction, particularly the deterioration by the early twentieth century of the colony's key exports: pineapples and sisal.[9]

Although some Bahamians boarded these steamships for leisure travel, they more frequently used them to find work; their labor proved instrumental in the expansion of southern Florida's agribusiness. For Bahamians in the late nineteenth and early twentieth centuries, traveling to and from Miami proved no more difficult than crossing from one island to another in the archipelago. Like the thousands of Europeans and Asians who entered Ellis and Angel Islands before restrictive immigration laws curbed their passage, economic opportunity largely attracted Bahamians to Miami. Bahamians had long frequented the Florida Keys as fishers, spongers, and turtlers. Bahamians specifically looked to Miami, however, after the city's incorporation in 1896. British West Indians were particularly mobile during this period largely due to the construction of the Panama Canal and other U.S. operations throughout the Americas that provided steady work.[10] Unlike the majority of their British-subject brethren, Bahamians primarily found work in Florida. Those from the northern islands, such as Abaco, Bimini, Cat Island, and Harbour Island, especially traveled to Miami.[11] Roughly one-fifth of the entire Bahamian population went to Florida between 1900 and 1920.[12] There, they often earned significantly higher wages while also cordoning off West Indian competition. Some Bahamians told stories of Miami as the "young Magic City where money could be 'shaken from trees.'"[13]

Bahamian migration patterns to Miami largely included women, men, and children until about 1905, when the port became easier for travelers to access and when the city's labor needs and a strengthened immigration control system came to privilege male migrants.[14] Miami agribusiness particularly desired Black Bahamian men's labor, as well as their seasonal presence in the city. Their desirability as laborers helped secure their place in the new city, albeit under the rubric of Jim Crow segregation, discrimination, and violence. Bahamian men

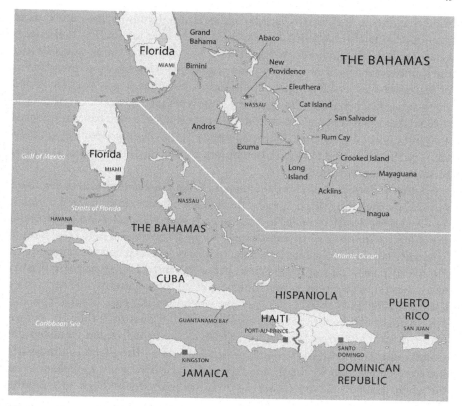

Photo 2.1. Greater Antilles and the Bahamas in the Caribbean in relation to southern Florida. Map by Eamonn Edge.

increasingly entered Miami as seasonal or temporary migrant workers, without women, children, or family members, for a few months at a time.

We should not interpret the capitalist-motivated impetus for welcoming Black Bahamian men to Miami as a sign that they were free from the state's surveillance, subjugation, and criminalization independent of their bodies' gender designation and presumed suitability for particular labor. Bahamian emigration to Florida drained the archipelago of so many young men and their manual labor that by 1921, the male-to-female ratio of those aged twenty-five to thirty-four in the Bahamas reached 1.3:2. That is, among this age group, the female population in the Bahamas was nearly double that of the men.[15] While most of these Bahamian men seemed to have had little trouble passing through the Cerberus-like immigration inspectors in Miami, state actors like law enforcement, judges, and politicians heavily surveilled and policed them once they entered Miami. Arrest records show that during the first two decades of the twentieth century, law enforcement disproportionately charged Bahamian men in the area for sodomy and crimes against nature, among other charges. While the evidence certainly suggests that the homosocial spaces created by their migration—wherein large populations of Bahamian men resided together in Miami, for instance—may have facilitated same-sex sexual behaviors, the archives also reveal that the state discriminatorily policed them as Black migrants whom they believed had a penchant for undesirable and immoral behaviors. Their desirability at the borders, premised on their labor potential, proved to be at once tenuous, constrained, and subject to greater scrutiny upon admission.[16]

Southern Florida's drain on Bahamian male labor created several anxieties on the islands, including discussions of the so-called destruction of the Bahamian family and the dearth of male laborers. In early 1913, Nassau's *Tribune* presented "a matter that for some time past has given us great concern." It noted that despite aggressive labor recruitment in the Bahamas, workers gravitated toward southern Florida and caused "a scarcity of labour in these islands." Higher wages in Florida and a depressed economy in the Bahamas fueled these patterns. "It seems to us useless to offer men 2s.[shillings] per day when they can take a night's run and find themselves where they can earn 6s. per day." It posed: "If they go, can we blame them?"[17] By 1920, for example, the Bahamian government lamented the scarcity of men in Watling's Island, or San Salvador: "The island is almost denuded of young men. . . . I regret to report that . . . there is not a single man on the whole island. . . . If something out of the ordinary doesn't turn up soon, the district will be manless, because the married as well as the single are going."[18]

This gender-imbalanced migration placed new burdens on women on the islands that helped challenge traditional gender norms; it is important to emphasize that while these migration patterns created homosocial male spaces in Miami, they similarly created female-dominant spaces throughout the Bahamian islands. A Bahamian colonial official recalled an instance in the Watlings Island district when the community mourned the death of one of their residents. Because the settlement was "denuded of men," "women had to be the pall-bearers," a role generally associated with masculinity.[19] Another Bahamian expressed concern about how "women have to do all the farm work to maintain themselves and their children, for in the majority of cases in which the men have emigrated, the remittances to their families do not compensate for moral and financial losses."[20]

Evidence suggests transnational anxieties about other "moral . . . losses" in the Bahamas that resulted from these predominantly male migration patterns, such as the breakdown of traditional family models and multiple forms of women's sexual transgression. Most Bahamian women remained on the islands with any children a couple may have had. Colonial sources suggested that the men's prolonged and disruptive absence from the islands seems to have caused several women to turn to others for intimacy. Based on Miami's criminal records for this period, this was not unlike what some Bahamian men did in Miami with other men and new women.[21] In some instances, both parents migrated to Miami, abandoning their children altogether.[22] The men who made the trip to Florida, Bahamian colonial officials claimed, "leave their families to punish." "The wife or mother endures these hardships for a time," but later decides to go to Miami as well, "leaving . . . little children in care of her old parents who are not able to look after themselves." This practice found "scores of children . . . strolling over the District, with no proper care or correction." Local governments worried this would breed "thieves and vagabonds."[23] In Miami and the Bahamas, officials expressed concern that these circumstances might create a new generation of idle laborers and vagrants—a recipe, they also suggested, for undesirable behaviors.

As a result of these shifts, Bahamian women entered new industries, including the service industry and sex work. Women from Rum Cay started using unsold sisal to make hats, for instance.[24] Others attempted to sell sharkskin as a substitute for cowskin leather.[25] While evidence does not specifically reveal that married or partnered women turned to prostitution during these times, colonial sources certainly indicate increased anxieties over the pervasiveness of brothels and sex work during this period. Whether these women were single or married, by 1917 the Bahamian colonial government proposed an Act to curb sex work, particularly in the capital, from which most schooners headed to Florida departed.[26] These "moral . . . losses," colonial officers worried, had also led to an increase in venereal disease. While sex work in the Bahamas no doubt contributed to this, colonial sources saw the greatest increase in infection among "seamen returning from their voyages abroad." The breakdown of morals and the family, they believed, was widespread and occurring in both the British colony and Florida.[27]

These social circumstances particularly affected women attempting to make their way into the United States; their gender, race, ethnicity, and socioeconomic status challenged state-crafted ideals of womanliness and they were categorized as prone to become dependents of the state and its resources. One expansive charge more discretely regulated gender and sexual transgression: the "likely to become a public charge" provision. Despite clear articulation of such a policy in U.S. immigration laws from 1882 and 1891, as Hidetaka Hirota reminds us, the clause originated from earlier state passenger laws that sought to exclude Irish "paupers" and others whom officials broadly construed as undesirable through their discretionary powers. The roots of a "finality clause" that granted inspection officers with largely unchecked exclusionary powers could be found in the immigration policies legislated in Massachusetts and New York.[28] By the turn of the century, when the process of resolutely charging the federal government with immigration control had been consolidated, the construction of undesirable immigrants would more willfully turn to southern and eastern Europeans and, while the nativist fervor targeting the Irish would increasingly diminish, anti-Asian sentiment persisted. Although the clause banning those likely to become a public charge was technically gender-neutral, as Donna Gabaccia and others have argued, it proved particularly effective in excluding single or unaccompanied women because they were already, as women, viewed as inherently dependent on men or a patriarchal system to survive.[29] Furthermore, as Emily Skidmore has observed, we must not overlook the "power of whiteness in rendering queer [and trans] individuals as potential citizens." That is, their relative privilege often stood in stark contrast to those read outside the rubric of whiteness and therefore less likely to be perceived as a threat to the nation.[30]

These forms of exclusion, surveillance, and regulation were further strengthened by racialized mythologies of laziness, hypersexuality, and promiscuity. Rather than view Bahamian women as productive laborers, as the state had tentatively done with Bahamian men, Miami nativists maintained they would burden the city's resources. "[T]hese negro women are not 'farm labor,' nor do they often know how to do any kind of work in a way that is worthy of wages. They are illiterate and frequently so mentally unsound as to be incapable of learning to work in even a passably acceptable way," noted a local newspaper. "They and their children become dependents." Living in Miami, with greater access to income, the newspaper continued, would inevitably lead to a lack of productivity and the so-called immoral vices nativists long associated with Black, immigrant, and working-class communities. In this way, "their idleness contribut[ed], of course, to all sorts of baneful things that are already a grave problem, if the white citizens of Dade county were wise enough to know it." Exclusions at the border were necessary, they believed, because "every boat from the Bahamas brings in undesirables that are bound to become charges and a public nuisance."[31]

These nativist beliefs and gendered economic imperatives contributed to the belief among U.S. immigration officials in Miami that unmarried Bahamian women might be prostitutes or other undesirable entrants likely to burden the state's coffers. In order to reach Miami, Bahamians boarded small schooners "so crowded with people that there was barely standing room on their decks."[32] Many complained that vessels were "over-crowded" and equipped with "absolutely no comforts, not even a latrine."[33] Some Bahamian officials suggested how the travel was particularly troublesome for women. They could not imagine how anyone would "take passage on such boats unless compelled to by necessity."[34] They believed any woman who made the voyage to Miami under such precarious conditions did so in desperation—which rendered her vulnerable to immoral influences—and would otherwise be read as suspect for undergoing a passage unbecoming of a decent woman.

Once Bahamians arrived at Miami's port, they were met by U.S. immigration officials, which included a physician and quarantine officer. These authorities boarded the vessel and conducted medical inspections on incoming migrants, weeding out those deemed undesirable. According to one Miami source, 10 percent of the Bahamian migrants had been "sent back for one reason and another, in failing to meet the requirements of the immigration laws." Those "who appeared to be in such a condition as to perhaps become a public charge" and "persons of questionable character" were "immediately returned from whence they came."[35] The inspectors at the port of entry were charged with identifying and reporting "all insane persons, idiots, persons suffering from a loathsome or a dangerous contagious disease, and all persons whose mental or physical condition will affect their ability to earn a living."[36] In 1914, Miami's immigration inspector told reporters that his official statistics showed that the "percentage of deportation from the port of Miami, based on the number of immigrants" was "higher than at Ellis Island" in New York.[37]

Upon arrival, the quarantine officer conducted "a veritable quiz" on the Bahamians wishing to enter the United States that served as a means of excluding undesirables, particularly women suspected of being prostitutes and others they deemed likely to become a public charge. The questions asked of these women, one Bahamian believed, proved "too personal and embarrassing." He maintained that there was "evidently a desire to prevent Miami from becoming a sort of *refugium peccatorum*," or a refuge for sinners.[38] In addition to these interrogations, it seems likely that, as Eithne Luibhéid has posited with the surveillance of Chinese women at U.S. borders, immigration officers also policed Bahamian women by making individual assessments of their bodies and clothing, which were thought to offer "possible clues about 'inner character,'" or sexual propriety.[39] One Bahamian observer believed the quarantine officers' "praiseworthy . . . effort[s]" had "sternly closed the doors to questionable characters that have not come to seek a living by *bona fide* means," at least in part a reference to Miami's sexual economy.[40]

At the Caribbean-Miami border, a single, Black Bahamian woman seeking admission became cause for alarm, her gender comportment and sexuality immediately suspect. "It is useless for any unmarried woman of the working class to seek admission," noted one man, "unless she have there some married female relative, known to be living a respectable life, to come forward and stand sponsor for her."[41] Both the medical and immigration officers in Miami had a great deal of power and discretion when making these decisions. After all, racialized interpretations of their sexualities stripped these women of their respectability by design.

Meanwhile, the gender imbalance created by immigration screenings greatly contributed to cultural perceptions that Bahamian men on the islands remained attached and under the watchful eyes of women and traditional families while those who ventured to Miami attained greater access to sexual experiences outside the traditional family unit, including extramarital and sometimes commercialized cross-sex and same-sex intimacies. In 1909, a colonial official from the Andros district maintained that several of the returning migrants from Florida were inclined to "what is called a sporting life," suggesting they had grown accustomed to idleness and vice in Miami. It was also, of course, difficult to ignore that the Bahamians in Miami had more income available to them. Instead of working again in Bahamian fields or finding work at sea, those who had traveled to Miami "more fully develop[ed] what in their natures appeals to the lower creation," believed one Bahamian official.[42]

In stark contrast to the majority of the available employment in Miami, several plantation jobs on the islands catered to entire Bahamian families. A 1913 ad in Nassau's *Tribune* promised "employment for every and any one and all the time on our sisal plantations down west." The company offered "small cottages for men and their families" on the plantation.[43] Men who took jobs like this in the Bahamas did not have to separate from their families. Most seasonal jobs in Miami, however, attracted young men who sent much of their cash wages back to the Bahamas. These remittances helped sustain some families and communities back on the islands and became a critical component of the Bahamian economy. Some women, of course, found their own sources of income, at times by migrating.[44]

By the late 1910s, women, children, and families increasingly also went to Miami. In 1920, one Bahamian in Cat Island wrote to the *Nassau Guardian* lamenting how the "steady stream [of migration to Florida] has already accounted for nearly four-fifths of our strongest men." By that point, the writer maintained, when the men returned to the island it was "merely to take their families back with them."[45] This shift was also, in part, a product of a U.S. immigration policy that favored white, hetero-patriarchal family reunification. More than before, many families attempted to make their stays permanent lest the law change and keep them from entering again.[46] Some worked alongside other working-class Bahamians and U.S. African Americans as maids, hotel porters, bellmen, cooks, waiters, dishwashers, servants, and domestics.[47] Even then, many of the Bahamians who managed to settle in Miami often did not feel safe there; some sought to return to the Bahamas. One British traveler overheard a Black Bahamian woman who worked as a maid in one of the city's tourist accommodations discuss fears of being deported while in Miami and how "she considered Nassau infinitely superior to Florida."[48]

For many of the Bahamians who entered Miami, permanent settlement in Miami or the United States was often not the desired outcome. Bahamians experienced a radically different set of racial codes from which they had grown accustomed to in the West Indies. The bifurcated Black-white backdrop of the U.S. South marked them as racial inferiors in Miami and manifested in local law enforcement's hyper-policing of them. One U.S. observer noted in 1922 how "under the British colonial policy the natives are placed on an equal footing with the white, which is quite a contrast to one having lived in the [U.S.] South."[49] One Bahamian noted that while in the Bahamas "colored men were addressed as gentlemen," they became "niggers" in Miami.[50]

The Bahamians' circumstances changed yet again by the early 1920s when new immigration restrictions curtailed Miami's regular flow of West Indian laborers and, at times, led to the repatriation of some already in the city.[51] The 1917 Immigration Act included a prohibitive measure that determined an immigrant's eligibility to enter the United States based on their ability to read. This measure greatly concerned some pro-emigration colonial officials in the Bahamas, as they had come to rely on the regular flow of remittances to sustain the islands' unstable economies.[52] By 1920, Miami's immigration inspector noted he would enforce "the literacy test which is destroying hope in the hearts of many who would embark for this port."[53] Two years later, a Bahamian colonial official observed how only the "young men who possessed the means and were able to pass the literacy test emigrated to Florida."[54] It appeared "most of the labouring class . . . able to read and write" went "regularly to Florida," while the rest stayed behind.[55]

Other U.S. immigration policies squeezed Miami's regular flow of migrants from the Bahamas. In 1921, U.S. Congress introduced a quota system based on perceived assimilability. It limited the "number of aliens of any nationality who may be admitted" to 3 percent of the number of foreign-born people from that country, as listed in the 1910 census. Exceptions were generally made for those in the Western Hemisphere. As such, those from the British Caribbean were exempt from the new restrictions and instead subject to the "remote control" system, or a case-by-case evaluation conducted by U.S. consuls.[56] Working on the foundation of the 1921 Emergency Quota Act, U.S. Congress passed the Johnson-Reed Act in 1924. It included the National Origins Act, which further restricted immigration from Asia and southern and eastern Europe. While the Western Hemisphere was generally exempt again, migrants under British colonial rule were included in a 2 percent "cap" based on the percentage of immigrants living in the United States—now determined by the 1890 census—from the metropole. As a dependent colony, the Bahamas was neither given a separate quota nor exempt; rather, it was included in the numerical restrictions afforded to Great Britain. Despite that, this "nominally race-neutral" policy all but sealed the fate for Bahamians and other West Indians under colonial rule who then faced de facto exclusion in a system that privileged white immigrants from the metropole.[57] Altogether, these policies effectively doomed the legal flow of Bahamians to Miami.

For many of the Bahamian women who successfully passed the "fabled Cerberus" at the border, interethnic marriages and the sharing of intimate spaces with others represented another way they became transgressive in the eyes of Miami's residents and law enforcement. Some Bahamian women became lodgers in others' homes. Unaccompanied women and those who traveled with their children without an adult man often leased boarding spaces with other families, many of whom were U.S. African American. In these intimate spaces, Bahamian women often met other lodgers, women and men alike. While tensions existed between Bahamians and U.S. African Americans, as they often competed for work and were pitted against each other by white nativists in Miami, they often intermarried and united in the face of tightening racial codes that targeted them collectively as Blacks. As Melanie Shell-Weiss has shown, Bahamian women were much more likely to marry U.S. African American men than Bahamian men were to find U.S. African American wives.[58] One possible explanation may be that Bahamian women found comfort in their new and perhaps liberating circumstances in Miami—especially those who had access to greater income than what was available in the economically depressed islands. Other Bahamian women never married at all, of course, and just like many had done back in the islands, they lived independent of a man's control in southern Florida. Altogether, these realities informed a state gaze on their bodies once in the United States. Police and other state actors targeted Black Bahamian women for a variety of offenses, including vagrancy, disorderly conduct, and fornication.

Indeed, while deportations occurred and many Bahamian women were excluded at Miami's borders, the white urban authority also surveilled, sequestered, and incarcerated them as "undesirable" Black immigrant women upon entering the city; thus, the state's earlier suspicion that these women would become a public charge proved to be a self-fulfilling prophecy. By 1935, the chairman of the Dade County Commission wrote the Florida governor about the area's "situation" concerning "insane persons," which proved "very expensive." The Commission asked the Florida State Hospital, located in Chattahoochee in northern Florida, to "relieve" the city of "insane persons as rapidly as they are thrown upon us." In some instances, these "insane persons" were held "in private institutions" at the county's expense. Much more frequently, lack of funds and resources led to the inmates being kept "in the County Jail."[59]

Commitment and medical records reveal that several of these "insane persons" were deemed such because of their transience, unemployment, drunkenness, and racial, gender, and sexual difference. By the turn of the century, the Florida State Hospital had earned a reputation "as a dumping ground for unwanted people regardless of their actual mental state."[60] In fact, while the Florida State Hospital largely served as a mental institute and the Florida Farm Colony operated as a facility for epileptic and feeble-minded youths, their services were often blurred. Feeble-minded Black patients, in particular, often found themselves in the Florida State Hospital since the Florida Farm Colony followed strict Jim Crow laws prohibiting the admission of "colored patients."[61] Also, by 1931, state law eased the commitment process and patient transfers from the Florida Farm Colony, the state's only public institution for the "feeble-minded" during this period.[62]

While many patients at the Florida State Hospital were quite ill—both mentally and physically—records reveal how some patients were committed for senility, alcoholism, anemia, epilepsy, homosexuality, and gender-transgressive behavior. In Miami, one of the more common paths to commitment was being arrested and having police vouch before a county judge that the subject in question was indigent, incapable of self-support, and likely to become a public charge or burden of the state.[63] The parallels to the policing and exclusion of Black Bahamian women at the Caribbean-U.S. border are indeed striking. With broad local laws on the books that criminalized so-called vagrants, particularly in the midst of economic depression, the Florida State Hospital became a vicious and violent form of state welfare.

As several historians have observed, this institutionalization was part of a larger project to regulate populations and curb the reproduction of the "unfit," defined as such through racial, ethnic, class, and sexual lines. In 1913, a prominent Florida white women's organization pleaded, "In order to decrease the number of feeble-minded, insane and blind, defectives of these classes must be prevented from reproducing their kind."[64] These eugenicist policies particularly targeted the state's "unfit" women. As feeble-mindedness and degeneracy was linked to "moral delinquency," Florida officials expressed the desire to enforce sterilization on such women. This reflected a larger eugenics movement that took off during the Progressive period throughout the country wherein "the growing use of state power" was put into effect "to intercede in previously private affairs for an assumed public benefit."[65] So-called delinquent young women and girls in Florida, defined as such largely through their race, ethnicity, and class, were recommended for sterilization because they were known "habitual sex delinquent[s]" or thought to live lives of "immorality and prostitution."[66] Unlike other states, however, Florida failed to pass a sterilization law, so institutional administrators settled on these women's segregated status and containment in the name of advancing civilization.[67]

This high inmate representation of Blacks, both native- and foreign-born, suggests the heightened policing of these communities in places like Miami as well as the violent substitute for social welfare in the form of racially segregated containment that parallels border containment and exclusion in the service of a straight, white state. In Miami, committed patients were often single or unattached, or their families were similarly destitute and incapable of assisting them. Much like Miami's arrest records for sodomy and crime against nature charges, it seems Black Bahamians were disproportionately committed. A 20-year-old Bahamian maid named Vienna Joseph spent several months at the Florida State Hospital in 1929, even though she was "not acutely ill." Officials discharged her once she received antisyphilitic treatment.[68] Once committed, medical examinations of Black women appear to have been particularly invasive and reports reveal physicians operated under racialized assumptions about the patients' sexual proclivities. Some doctors believed female genitals "offered clues for detecting a woman's proclivity toward lesbianism, masturbation, frigidity, and promiscuity."[69] Florida physicians observed how one Miami Black woman's vagina "readily admit[ted] two extending fingers." While such pelvic exams were customary, the ad hoc description—which insinuated she was a "loose" woman—stood in stark contrast to the commentary traditionally made of committed married white women: "marital."[70] Many Black women resisted these invasive examinations and the findings they purported to yield. Tislane Russell, a Bahamian woman living in Miami who also proved "uncooperative" in permitting the exam, told examiners she had "never been seen by any man but her husband."[71] While much of the exam may have been procedure—including recording the size of the cervix and whether there was any tenderness—this supplemental commentary suggests physicians were informed by preconceived notions about Black and immigrant women, particularly that they were hypersexual, nonmonogamous, and sexually suspect.

* * *

In the early decades of the twentieth century, the state created or strengthened systems and instruments of power to surveil, regulate, and exclude those whose gender and sexual nonconformity positioned them outside an increasingly choate construct of the heterosexual and whose ethno-racial categorizations helped fuel nativist mythologies that, in turn, cemented beliefs of their undesirability, criminality, and likelihood to burden the state. As Canaday has argued, U.S. immigration law in the early twentieth century "lumped together aliens who exhibited gender inversion, had anatomical defects, or engaged in sodomy as degenerates." The latter, in particular, "was a racial and economic construct that explained 'the immorality of the poor.'" After all, "perversion" was associated "with 'primitive' races and lower classes, and poor immigrants and nonwhites were believed to be especially inclined."[72]

The straight, white state was built through a matrix of racialized, sexualized, gendered, and economic imperatives that must be understood in concert with one another. Ironically, in promoting the desirability of admitting seasonal, Bahamian male laborers in Miami while excluding many Bahamian women, U.S. immigration policy helped facilitate erotic same-sex and other transgressive expressions and desires in the nascent city and, at the very least, challenged traditional gender norms on parts of the archipelago. Immigration policy was but one manifestation of this. For Black immigrant women who managed to pass the "Cerberus" waiting for them at the border, the state exercised its power to police, confine, and purge undesirable bodies when it ultimately saw to it that Bahamian women became public charges once in the United States. In this way, the state appeared justified in maintaining its imperative of crafting perceived racialized and sexualized hierarchies of desirability for citizenship—based solely on its ability to surveil and exert power over these Black women's bodies.

The state strengthened and created new instruments of powers to render illegal, detain, and deport bodies it deemed undesirable and perverse during this period that remain legible to us today. Residual and new machinations of those powers are manifest in modern-day immigration policies that have redoubled efforts to fortify borders and enable a punitive and carceral system to detract the mobility of people deemed undesirable, albeit under new vocabularies and logics.[73] They have found new life amid the neoliberal backdrop that promotes open borders for trade and business but, alas, not for the people left to suffer from liberal markets, or the many other forms of state-led violence that have prompted them to flee in the first place.

Notes

Portions of this chapter previously appeared in Julio Capó Jr., *Welcome to Fairyland: Queer Miami before 1940* (Chapel Hill: University of North Carolina Press, 2017). Used by permission of the University of North Carolina Press, www.uncpress.org.

The author is forever grateful to the volume editors, Eithne P. Luibhéid and Karma R. Chávez, Ana Raquel Minian, and the late Horacio N. Roque Ramírez, for their thoughtful feedback on this or other iterations of this work and for inspiring the questions it seeks to answer in the first place. Any possible errors in the text, however, are entirely my own.

1. "Florida, Impressions of a Visitor," *The Tribune (Nassau)*, December 2, 1911.

2. Ibid.

3. For more on oceanic borderlands as potentially fluid and contested spaces that can subvert statist powers and reach, see Kale Bantigue Fajardo, *Filipino Crosscurrents: Oceanographies of Seafaring, Masculinities, and Globalization* (Minneapolis: University of Minnesota Press, 2011); Omise'eke Natasha Tinsley, *Thiefing Sugar: Eroticism between Women in Caribbean Literature* (Durham, N.C.: Duke University Press, 2010); Jenna M. Loyd and Alison Mountz, *Boats, Borders, and Bases: Race, the Cold War, and the Rise of Migration Detention in the United States* (Berkeley: University of California Press, 2018).

4. For more on the "straight state," see Margot Canaday, *The Straight State: Sexuality and Citizenship in Twentieth-Century America* (Princeton, N.J.: Princeton University Press,

2009); M. Jacqui Alexander, "Not Just (Any) Body Can Be a Citizen: The Politics of Law, Sexuality and Postcoloniality in Trinidad and Tobago and the Bahamas," *Feminist Review*, no. 48 (Autumn 1994): 12.

5. John D'Emilio, "Capitalism and Gay Identity," in *Powers of Desire: The Politics of Sexuality*, ed. Ann Barr Snitow, Christine Stansell, and Sharon Thompson (New York: Monthly Review Press, 1983), 100–113.

6. Samuel E. Moffett, "Henry Morrison Flagler," *Cosmopolitan*, August 1902, 418.

7. Nathan D. Shappee, "Flagler's Undertaking in Miami in 1897," *Tequesta* 1, no. 19 (1959): 9–12.

8. "An Isolated Plant at Nassau, Bahama Islands," *Electrical World and Engineer* 37, no. 22 (June 1, 1901): 914.

9. Howard Johnson, "Bahamian Labor Migration to Florida in the Late Nineteenth and Early Twentieth Centuries," *International Migration Review* 22, no. 1 (Spring 1988): 84–103; Raymond A. Mohl, "Black Immigrants: Bahamians in Early Twentieth-Century Miami," *Florida Historical Quarterly* 65, no. 3 (January 1987): 271–297; Melanie Shell-Weiss, "Coming North to the South: Migration, Labor and City-Building in Twentieth-Century Miami," *Florida Historical Quarterly* 84, no. 1 (Summer 2005): 79–99.

10. Lara Putnam, *Radical Moves: Caribbean Migrants and the Politics of Race in the Jazz Age* (Chapel Hill: University of North Carolina Press, 2013).

11. Mohl, "Black Immigrants," 280.

12. Ibid., 273–75.

13. Ira De Augustine Reid, *The Negro Immigrant: His Background, Characteristics, and Social Adjustment, 1899–1937* (New York: Columbia University Press, 1939), 184.

14. Melanie Shell-Weiss, *Coming to Miami: A Social History* (Gainesville: University Press of Florida, 2009), 47–48; Arthur Chapman, "'Watch the Port of Miami,'" *Tequesta* 53 (1993): 12.

15. Bahamas Department of Statistics, *Demographic Aspects of the Bahamian Population, 1901–1974* (Nassau: Bahamas Department of Statistics, 1976), 12.

16. Capó Jr., *Welcome to Fairyland*, Chap. 2.

17. "The Exodus to Florida," *The Tribune (Nassau)*, January 11, 1913, 2.

18. Johnson, "Bahamian Labor Migration to Florida," 94.

19. Report on Watlings Island, in Appendix to *Votes of the Honourable Legislative Council of the Bahama Islands* (hereafter AV), March 23, 1922–May 23, 1922, 166, National Archives of the Bahamas, Nassau, New Providence (hereafter NATB).

20. "Letter to the Editor: Out Island Development," *Nassau Guardian*, January 28, 1920, 2.

21. General Index to Criminal Cases—Defendants Dade County, Florida, Prior 1929, A-F, G-M, and N-Z, Miami-Dade Clerk of the Court Archives, Miami, Florida.

22. Johnson, "Bahamian Labor Migration to Florida," 102.

23. Report on Andros (Mangrove Cay), AV, March 23, 1922–May 23, 1922, 63–64, NATB.

24. Report on Rum Cay, AV, February 3, 1920–August 26, 1920, 180, NATB.

25. AV, March 23, 1922–May 23, 1922, 30–31, NATB.

26. An Act for the Regulation of Places Ordinarily Used for Public Dancing or Music or Other Public Entertainment of the Like Kind, October 4, 1919, 23/284/510, Colonial Office Records (hereafter COR), NATB.

27. Health Report on Harbour Island, AV, March 23, 1922–May 23, 1922, 120, NATB.

28. Hidetaka Hirota, *Expelling the Poor: Atlantic Seaboard States and the 19th-Century Origins of American Immigration Policy* (New York: Oxford University Press, 2017).

29. Donna Gabaccia, *From the Other Side: Women, Gender, and Immigrant Life in the U.S., 1820–1990* (Bloomington: Indiana University Press, 1994), 37.

30. Emily Skidmore, *True Sex: The Lives of Trans Men at the Turn of the Twentieth Century* (New York: New York University Press, 2017), 80.

31. "As to That 'Farm Labor' Business," *Miami Metropolis*, June 27, 1919, 8.

32. Qtd. in Mohl, "Black Immigrants," 284.

33. Report on Exuma, AV, March 23, 1922–May 23, 1922, 94, NATB.

34. Report on Eleuthera (Rock Sound and Tarmpum Bay), AV, February 3, 1920–August 26, 1920, 143, NATB.

35. Oscar Conklin, "More than Thousand Bahama Islanders Reach Miami during Year," *Miami Metropolis*, June 12, 1909, 1.

36. Treasury Department, Bureau of Public Health and Marine-Hospital Service, *Book of Instructions for the Medical Inspection of Immigrants* (Washington, D.C.: Government Printing Office, 1903), 14. Also see Alan M. Kraut, *Silent Travelers: Germs, Genes, and the Immigrant Menace* (Baltimore: Johns Hopkins University Press, 1995); Nayan Shah, *Contagious Divides: Epidemics and Race in San Francisco's Chinatown* (Berkeley: University of California Press, 2001).

37. "Under Present Immigration Laws, Hard to Keep Negroes from Landing," *Miami Daily Metropolis*, November 17, 1914, 1.

38. "Florida, Impressions of a Visitor."

39. Eithne Luibhéid, *Entry Denied: Controlling Sexuality at the Border* (Minneapolis: University of Minnesota Press, 2002), 50.

40. "Florida, Impressions of a Visitor."

41. Ibid.

42. Report on Andros (Nicoll's Town), AV, March 9, 1909–August 23, 1909, 68, NATB.

43. *The Tribune (Nassau)*, January 7, 1913.

44. Johnson, "Bahamian Labor Migration to Florida," 100–101.

45. "Letter to the Editor: Emigration," *Nassau Guardian*, April 28, 1920, 2.

46. Michael Craton and Gail Saunders, *Islanders in the Stream: A History of the Bahamian People, Volume 2: From the Ending of Slavery to the Twenty-First Century* (Athens: University of Georgia Press, 1998), 219; Shell-Weiss, "Coming North to the South," 83–84.

47. Shell-Weiss, *Coming to Miami*, 48; Mohl, "Black Immigrants," 284.

48. Alan Parsons, *A Winter in Paradise* (London: A. M. Philpot Ltd., 1926), 83–84.

49. Gordon E. Mayer, "A Cruise to Nassau from Miami," *The Rudder*, February 1922, 18.

50. Reid, *The Negro Immigrant*, 184, 189.

51. Jerome L. McElory and Klaus de Albuquerque, "Migration Transition in Small Northern and Eastern Caribbean States," *International Migration Review* 22, no. 3 (Autumn 1988): 32.

52. Alien Immigration to U.S., February, 1919, COR 23/284, NATB.

53. "Movement of Vessels," *Miami Metropolis*, May 1, 1920, 14.

54. Report on Long Island, AV, March 23, 1922–May 23, 1922, 141, NATB.

55. Report on Exuma, AV, March 23, 1922–May 23, 1922, 96, NATB.

56. Putnam, *Radical Moves*, 85–86.

57. *Ibid.*, 82–122.

58. Shell-Weiss, "Coming North to the South," 87–91.

59. Cecil A. Turner to Governor David Sholtz, July 11, 1935, File 6, Box 28, Governor David Sholtz Correspondence, no. S 278, State Archives of Florida (hereafter SAF), Tallahassee, Florida; *Miami Retreat Foundation v. Ervin* 66 So. 2d 748 (Fla. 1952).

60. Dave Nelson, "'More of a Prison than an Asylum': Florida Hospital for the Indigent Insane during the Progressive Era," *Southern Studies: An Interdisciplinary Journal of the South* 14, no. 2 (Fall/Winter 2009): 75.

61. Steven Noll, *Feeble-Minded in Our Midst: Institutions for the Mentally Retarded in the South, 1900–1940* (Chapel Hill: University of North Carolina Press, 1995), 93–95, 123.

62. Steven Noll, "Care and Control of the Feeble-Minded: Florida Farm Colony, 1920–1945," *Florida Historical Quarterly* 69, no. 1 (July 1990): 71–72.

63. See "Elizabeth Collins," File 1, Box 123, Florida State Hospital Medical Records, no. S1063 (hereafter FSHMR), SAF; "A. B. Anderson," Box 2, Florida State Hospital Commitment Records, no. S1062, SAF.

64. Qtd. in Edward J. Larson, *Sex, Race, and Science: Eugenics in the Deep South* (Baltimore: Johns Hopkins University Press, 1995), 74.

65. Noll, *Feeble-Minded in Our Midst*, 65.

66. Ibid., 74–75.

67. Ibid., 74–78; Wendy Kline, *Building a Better Race: Gender, Sexuality, and Eugenics from the Turn of the Century to the Baby Boom* (Berkeley: University of California Press, 2005), Ch. 2.

68. "Vienna Joseph," File 4, Box 8, FSHMR, SAF.

69. Qtd. in Kline, *Building a Better Race*, 54–55.

70. Archibald MacLaren, "Clinical Lecture," *Northwestern Lancet* 20 (1900): 1–3.

71. "Tislane Russell," File 34, Box 123, FSHMR, SAF.

72. Canaday, *The Straight State*, 22, 29.

73. For example, the U.S. Supreme Court ruled in 2020 that President Donald J. Trump's administration can further expand the "public charge" policy to potentially deny permanent residency to those who use a number of government social services. See https://www.nytimes.com/2020/01/27/us/supreme-court-trump-green-cards.html.

3

From Potlucks to Protests

*Reflections from Organizing Queer
and Trans API Communities*

SASHA WIJEYERATNE

When I first came on staff at the National Queer Asian Pacific Islander Alliance (NQAPIA), I had been organizing in Queer and Trans Asian Pacific Islander (QTAPI) communities for five years. I had been part of organizations built around developing shared community and support, organizing around LGBTQ immigrants' rights and reform, creating our own mental health services, and more. I was drawn to the potential to organize our communities around the issues that impact our lives, to stake our place in the movement through our bodies and our work, and not just to create alternatives but also to change the systems that hurt us.

I joined NQAPIA soon after Mike Brown's murder catapulted the Black Lives Matter movement into international prominence. All around the country, API (Asian Pacific Islander) or Asians for Black Lives collectives were forming, doing the critical work of organizing Asian and API people to put our bodies on the line for Black liberation. Asian and API people offered to follow and support Black leadership in a multitude of ways, from fundraising to forming hard and soft blockades with their bodies.

I was involved in these spaces in multiple cities, across the East and West Coasts and the Midwest. I found political home in these spaces, and yet—as a queer, gender nonconforming, South Asian person, there was often something that felt missing from the dominant analyses and praxis. These spaces often replicated a "white allyship" model of organizing, where white people are urged to use their privilege without actually engaging their own lives, self-interest, or needs. Calls for allyship from white communities often ask people to become "race traitors," to prioritize broad values of social justice and liberation over their day-to-day material privilege.

As queer and trans Asian and API organizers, our communities experience more racial privilege than Black, Indigenous, and Latinx communities; yet we still experience oppression and material costs from racism and queerphobia. How would our strategies shift and our power grow if we engaged people through both the material conditions of their lives and a desire for solidarity?[1] When we say "when Black people get free, everybody gets free,"[2] what did that mean for API people? This analysis isn't new—grassroots Asian organizations like Freedom Inc.,[3] PrYSM,[4] DRUM,[5] CAAAV,[6] and more have been putting forth this analysis for years.

We grounded our queer and trans API organizing in this analysis. How could we organize the margins of our communities—trans people and femmes, gender nonconforming people, Muslim queers, darker-skinned APIs, working-class queers, and more—around our own material needs, as a way to organize more deeply in solidarity with the Movement for Black Lives?[7] How would this transform our existing QTAPI community organizing, which is often centered around potlucks and community building? Within the context of the movement moment we were in and using tools that we suspected would resonate with our base, we embarked on a series of experiments to build QTAPI political power.

We began by making visible the costs of racism and queerphobia within our own communities. We created a media piece called "#QAPIsforBlackLives"[8] with organizers who were South Asian, Southeast Asian, trans and trans femme, working-class, and organizing in solidarity with the Movement for Black Lives. They shared stories about their experiences with police violence—watching family members violated by police in their own homes, experiencing harassment for being gender nonconforming, being blamed for a friend's murder by the police, feeling guttural fear in the blare of sirens. These organizers described how their experiences of police violence and power crafted their understandings and practices of organizing. Instead of understanding themselves as "Asian race traitors," they organized from a place of shared investment and a deep personal and community commitment to undoing the systems that hurt Black people the most and that have ripple effects across our queer and trans API communities.

We wanted to create even more space in NQAPIA for those at the margins of our communities to share their stories. Our next experiment was a deeper dive into political education with our base. We held a week of action called "Redefine Security," based on questioning ideas of "safety" that leave our communities feeling profiled and unsafe. Seven QTAPI people shared their own stories of being shamed and harassed by Transportation Security Authority (TSA), targeted through police informants, pulled over while driving, and targeted while doing sex work.[9] These stories, along with the #QAPIsforBlackLives video, opened up unexpected space for people across our communities to share their stories. Suddenly, stories were emerging from people I had known for years, breaking the silence that tells us that these experiences are normal, that this profiling is for our own safety. Through tears, rage, and fear, QTAPI people shared stories of getting targeted and assaulted by TSA, harassed by police in the street and in their homes, and carrying the constant anxiety that "safety" would actually mean violence.

As we listened to these stories, a few themes emerged. From our Muslim and trans base, we heard endless stories about profiling at the airport. For trans folks, the new full body scanners led to physical violation by TSA agents unable to read our bodies in the binary of their machines and protocols. For Muslim folks, and those perceived to be Muslim, being pulled aside for "random questioning" and invasive searches hadn't felt random for years. And of course, for those living at the intersections of these identities, the harassment and violations intensified. This mirrored the surveillance of Black travelers, and especially the marking of Black women's hair as inherently dangerous.[10] When TSA agents couldn't "read" our bodies with their eyes and machines, they resorted to touch, making invasive body checks, hair checks, and more our new normal.[11] Though there are privileges—especially around class, documentation, and ability—in accessing airports, we decided to organize against TSA as a starting point. This issue was deeply and widely felt across the margins of our communities and brought us into the fight against profiling, policing, and surveillance.

These stories, unearthed through political education, made it clear that community building and potlucks weren't enough. We needed power and strategy. Up to this point, most of the organizations in NQAPIA primarily organized through shared social and community space. This work is deeply political—in a world where our communities throw us out, abuse us, and even kill us, surviving and creating our own beloved spaces is a political act. And yet, it's not enough. As we build community through potlucks, social gatherings, and community space, we also need to build political power to challenge the forces we're up against.

Our next experiment was to build enough political power to shift the practices of policing and surveillance that target our communities. A few of our queer and trans Muslim and South Asian members suggested using 9/11 as a launching and mobilizing event in 2016. Islamophobia didn't start on 9/11, but the aftermath of the Twin Towers falling marked an increase in Islamophobia, similar to what we are living through under Trump's Muslim bans. On 9/11 the collective remembering of the United States vilifies a "Muslim enemy," and racist, violent patriotism runs rampant. For many of our community members, this is a day when people choose not to leave their homes if they can, where we make phone calls to our loved ones to make sure that everyone made it home in the evening.

Responding to our base's experiences of Islamophobia, transphobia, and racism, we developed a campaign targeted at one of the root causes of this profiling, policing, and surveillance: the Department of Homeland Security (DHS). DHS houses the TSA and was formed as a national security response after 9/11. Specifically, our target was DHS Secretary Jeh Johnson. We were excited for the possibility to change a system that seemed invincible yet was only thirteen years old, and to build campaign alliances with other Black, people of color, and queer trans people of color movements and organizations from a place of solidarity and shared struggle.

After building through storytelling and political education and deciding to embark on an experiment to build political power, we took it to the streets. We organized a guerilla street theater action called #15YearsLater, on the 15th anniversary of 9/11. We went to gentrifying areas of D.C. and erected pop-up "checkpoints," replicating the violation, fear, and indignity of "random" profiling in our communities for white people in these historically Black and Latinx neighborhoods. As people stepped through our checkpoint, we asked them the questions that we were used to being asked, such as: "Where are you from? Oh, I've heard that D.C. has become a hotbed of terrorist activity lately"; "Who are you going to meet? Where? Why?"; "That name sounds Christian. Are you Christian? Well then, we'll need to hold you for investigation." White participants had varying reactions, from disbelief to understanding, from rage to curiosity.

There were multiple goals for this action. We created controversy around our DHS target, getting Johnson's name into D.C. and national media.[12] We collected postcards aimed at Johnson and DHS, with the goal of pressuring them into abolitionist reforms.[13] Perhaps most importantly, we continued building the capacities of our base to have these conversations. We spent four hours the day before training people across our communities—trans and queer Muslims, QTAPI people, cis straight Asian folks, non-API people of color—to break down complicated policies into everyday language, centering the impact that these policies have on our people. We built political power by leaning into the strengths of our queer and trans community's ways of organizing and creating a sense of family and safety on a day when most of us would rather hide.

The pressure worked. We got noticed by DHS through pressuring them from the outside and used that leverage to build avenues on the inside. We were invited to submit a model policy that could shift their practices of profiling by taking away some of DHS's power. We had a long road ahead to really make those shifts, but we opened a door that we never imagined possible and were ready to keep building power.

The 2016 election marked the end of our campaign. We made a strategic decision not to fight even for abolitionist reforms under Trump and the shifting terrain of DHS leadership. Any victories we sought were too likely to be turned against us and used to recriminalize our communities. Despite the abrupt ending, we claimed this work and campaign as a victory—for NQAPIA and QTAPI organizing.

There were certainly limitations and failures in our work—that's why these were experiments! To name a few: tackling the entire Department of Homeland Security led to powerful base building on our end but was a national target too large for our current capacity, base, and power. As we worked to organize from the margins of our communities, we were still working on building base, particularly within working-class communities. Though there are certainly working-class members of our base, the majority of the people we organized were middle to upper-middle class. We continued to struggle with how to fight for the issues impacting our people and show up through a solidarity lens, without falling back on "white allyship" models.

And even with those limitations, there are a few lessons that I am proud to draw from our work and that I hope can be useful for other QTAPI organizers. Again, to name a few: we deepened our solidarity work in a queer and trans API context to work from a place of shared material needs and targets, not just a place of using our privilege. We brought the margins of our communities to the center of our work through base-building, leadership development, and shared power, which had ripple effects across NQAPIA and QTAPI communities. We harnessed the strengths of our community's ways of building, through potlucks and storytelling, and used these tools to build toward political power.

I am proud of the ways that NQAPIA and QTAPI people and organizations across the country have organized and built people power from potlucks to protests. I am excited for our people to harness the brilliance from our lessons, celebrate and learn from our failures, and continue to transform our organizational and political homes, our movements, and our worlds.

Notes

1. I have written about this previously through a lens of "selfish solidarity": Sasha Wijeyeratne, "Towards a 'Selfish Solidarity': Building Deep Investment in the Movement for Black Lives," *To Speak a Song*, February 29, 2016, https://tospeakasong.com/2016/02/29/towards-a-selfish-solidarity-building-deep-investment-in-the-movement-for-black-lives/.

2. Alicia Garza, "A Herstory of the #BlackLivesMatter Movement," *The Feminist Wire*, October 7, 2014, http://www.thefeministwire.com/2014/10/blacklivesmatter-2/.

3. Freedom Inc: http://freedom-inc.org/.

4. Providence Youth Student Movement: http://www.prysm.us/.

5. Desis Rising Up and Moving: http://www.drumnyc.org/.

6. CAAAV: Organizing Asian Communities: http://caaav.org/.

7. "Platform," The Movement for Black Lives, no date, https://policy.m4bl.org/platform/.

8. National Queer Asian Pacific Islander Alliance, "#QAPIsforBlackLives," YouTube video, April 8, 2016, https://www.youtube.com/watch?v=Gorrtv1bw7o.

9. #RedefineSecurity Story Bank, last modified September 23, 2017, http://www.nqapia.org/wpp/category/redefinesecurity/redefinesecurity-stories/.

10. See Brenda Medina and Thomas Frank, "TSA Agents Say They're Not Discriminating against Black Women, But Their Body Scanners Might Be," *ProPublica*, April 17, 2019, https://www.propublica.org/article/tsa-not-discriminating-against-black-women -but-their-body-scanners-might-be.

11. #RedefineSecurity Story Bank, https://www.nqapia.org/wpp/redefinesecurity-sahar -shafqat/.

12. There is more information in our Race Files article, "Jeh Johnson, Can You Hear Us Now?": https://www.racefiles.com/2016/09/16/jeh-johnson-can-you-hear-us-now-15years later-queer-trans-muslims-and-south-asians-demand-an-end-to-racial-and-religious -profiling/.

13. Based on Mariame Kaba's work: http://www.truth-out.org/news/item/22604-prison -reforms-in-vogue-and-other-strange-things.

PART II

Negotiating Systems

4

Central American Migrants

LGBTI Asylum Cases Seeking Justice and Making History

SUYAPA G. PORTILLO VILLEDA

After the 2009 coup d'état in Honduras, violence increased exponentially in the country. By 2011, the United Nations named Honduras one of the worst places in the world for violence and impunity. That year, which recorded the most deaths since the 2009 coup, marked the beginning of a new exodus of migrant youth from Honduras, Guatemala, and El Salvador, escaping violence and state neglect for "a better life." Transgender, gay, and lesbian youth were among the people who fled, along with entire families, women, and children. Since 2014, and the arrival of over 64,000 unaccompanied minors at the U.S.-Mexico border—24 percent from Honduras—the need has grown for scholars to provide declarations and testimony in U.S. immigration courtrooms about country conditions and threats to migrants in order to help prevent deportations of people who would face certain death if returned. This work is especially needed for vulnerable populations, among them transgender women.

Since 2006, I have served as an expert on Honduras, El Salvador, and Guatemala in dozens of immigration court cases seeking to prevent deportation of migrants claiming asylum and other forms of relief. Most of these cases have been successful, and often my expert testimonies on country conditions were significant factors in these rulings. As an academic dedicated to researching and teaching the history of the Central American region and its migrants, I find it gratifying, as well as a duty, to share my knowledge of Central America and migration in these immigration cases. As a result of frequent research trips to the region for oral history gathering and archival research, as well as my personal lived experience as an out queer fem, I can speak to conditions in these countries. In line with my scholarly work, in these immigration cases I provide historical context for the cases, including the political history of the country and information gleaned from reports produced by local organizations, which often are more detailed and accurate than international reports.

My work in this area has elucidated two major factors that stand out as culprits for the suffering of many Central American migrants in the Western Hemisphere. First, U.S. foreign policy, along with its linked immigration policy, has been an irresponsible and destabilizing force in the region, thereby rendering people's livelihoods in Central American countries nearly impossible. Second, lesbian, gay, bisexual, transgender, and queer migrants, whose narratives are often invisible, face exceptionally life-threatening hardships, both in their home countries and in their migration trajectories, and require urgent and appropriately tailored protection.

The Violence and Migration Caused by U.S. Foreign Policy

Since the 1980s Civil and Revolutionary wars in Central America, Guatemala, El Salvador, and Nicaragua have been hit with strife leading to a nearly unparalleled exodus of migrants to the United States, Spain, and Canada. While exact figures for the exodus of Central Americans in the 1970s and '80s are dodgy, given the U.S. covert wars and U.S. complicity in human rights violations, it is estimated that 400,000 Salvadorans, or by some accounts 25 percent of the population, fled the country, while 80,000 people were murdered. In Guatemala, since the coup d'état in 1954, there were 200,000 murders, over 90 percent of them Mayans. In the 1970s and '80s, as many as 1.5 million people fled Guatemala seeking refuge in Mexico and the United States. No clear figures exist for Hondurans until after Hurricane Mitch in 1998, which left 1.5 million people homeless in the region. As Peace Accords were signed in 1992 in El Salvador and 1996 in Guatemala, the entire region was pushed into a neoliberal economic model of modernity; "fast track" ushered in *maquiladora* jobs as "development" alongside privatization of the public sector.

Workers in Central America face flexibilized economies, characterized by informal labor with scant worker protections, antiunion blacklists, and few ways to climb the ladder toward prosperity. Domestic education and health care suffered greatly as these countries attempted to compete in a global market by privatizing public services. This move toward neoliberal development was undertaken without accounting for the past, overlooking U.S. complicity in the murders, brutality, and injustices of the 1980s. Although Honduras did not experience a civil war like the other countries, it served as the U.S. backyard, hosting over seven U.S. military air bases and providing the training ground for *contrarevolucionarios*, paid for by then–President Ronald Reagan. While El Salvador, Guatemala, and Nicaragua grapple with slow and fragmented postwar truth commissions and processes of reconciliation, Honduras's history of this period and its legacy have been opaque domestically and internationally. Also, Honduras saw no democratization in tandem with neoliberalization of its economy—resulting in a multitiered economic system that exploited the very poor, made the rich richer, eroded labor protections, and fostered growing corruption.

This context normalized the neglect of marginalized communities, and we can see a continuity of U.S. complicity. Years of U.S. military intervention and occupation in Honduras and the region, coupled with dominance by Honduras's own military rulers, stalled the development of gender and LGBTI rights. U.S. military presence exacerbated exposure to sexually transmitted infections, including HIV-AIDS. In the 1990s, supported by international funding, organizations emerged to prevent HIV-AIDS through services and education among LGBTI populations. In these spaces, LGBTI leadership began to form; previously, they lived in the shadows, though some participated in leftist organizations mobilizing for democracy and justice in the nation.[1] For the most part, however, the infrastructure for advocacy and human rights claims remained weak, subordinated to a U.S.-propelled neoliberalism.

Fast forward to 2009: an elite group of technocrats destabilized Honduras, with support of then–U.S. President Barack Obama and then–Secretary of State Clinton, by ousting Manuel Zelaya Rosales in the first coup d'état of the 21st century. The repression against the resistance movement fighting the coup cost lives. Many emigrated, fearing for their lives or because the destabilization of the country led to joblessness and hunger. In 2017, government-sponsored election fraud further stifled opposition. The newly created *Libertad y Refundación* party, which united with various other parties as the Alliance against the Dictatorship, won the most votes in the national elections, but their candidate was not declared the winner. The ruling party's electoral college withheld election results for over five days and ultimately declared victory for the neoliberal candidate, after numerous voting and vote-counting irregularities. Hondurans widely believe the ruling Nationalist Party "stole" the presidency with the hearty endorsement of the U.S. State Department under Donald Trump.

Central American nations are characterized as economically and politically "weak," virtually dependent on the U.S. economy and aid and now on immigrant remittances for survival. It is impossible to ignore the reality that U.S. invasion throughout the 20th century, and particularly since the 1980s, has not only generated economic and political dependency, but has also thwarted possibilities for nations like Honduras to be sovereign and democratic and to offer democratic processes and policies for LGBTI individuals and other disenfranchised communities. The United States has historically utilized immigration policies to suit its foreign policy agenda to control and dominate a region, often obfuscating conditions in migrants' home countries while exploiting racialized tropes and anti-immigrant sentiments domestically. This contradiction truncates the possibility of a productive and progressive comprehensive immigration policy reform.

LGBTI Migrant Challenges: The Need for a "Queer" Narrative

Migrating LGBTI people face particular challenges, because the community has long lived at the margins of the official historical record of the United States and their home countries. The lives of undocumented immigrants, many of whom are also LGBTI, often fall out of that record into oblivion—they are not recognizable, even to immigration reform movements in the United States or progressive social movements in their own countries. This absence is a matter of critical importance for scholars, who seek to build and contribute to a Central American historical record that is accurate and inclusive, as well as for immigrants, who are reliant on recognition of their hardships to obtain safety and just relief in immigration proceedings. The work of amplifying and illustrating the queer narratives of LGBTI migrants is both an important scholarly project and a procedural and practical necessity in immigration cases and advocacy.

For LGBTI immigrants' cases, such as those of transgender women seeking asylum, experts can provide insights about the experiences of queer bodies and explain the gendered dynamics in each country. Trans bodies often go through repeated disciplining. They are commonly misunderstood and misgendered in official documents and proceedings. In jails, prisons, and detention centers in the United States and abroad, trans and gender nonconforming people are treated and categorized according to their gender assigned at birth or their legal documentation, as opposed to their gender identity, resulting in harassment and mistreatment. Even attorneys representing trans migrants may misgender their clients. Intake declarations at the border, or psychological evaluations, often also obscure an individual's identity when they and their responses—indeed, their very lives and existences—do not fit easily into perfunctory and legalistic forms. Furthermore, the burden of proof falls on the migrant to generate information about their own victimhood—often at the hands of a state apparatus that recognizes neither their lives nor their abuse.

In gathering information and preparing affidavits for Central American LGBTI cases, I have seen the challenges for LGBTI people in detention and court systems. For instance, Josie is a butch-looking lesbian who was detained and deported twice as she attempted to enter the country without documents. The first time she did not reveal to border patrol agents that she was fleeing gender violence in Honduras. She had been raped multiple times by the police there. In one instance, her girlfriend was gang-raped by multiple policemen and Josie was forced to watch. She lived essentially as a prisoner in her *barrio*, in her house, policed by gang members and national police officers for being a lesbian and having a fem girlfriend. Yet, due to fear, she did not come out to Immigration and Customs Enforcement (ICE) officials; the police in her home country were her torturers, so she reasonably believed that authority figures could hurt her and could not be trusted. She was deported. The second time ICE arrested her, she did come out. Despite having a strong case, she was perceived to be lying when she sought asylum, in part because during her previous deportation she had not said anything. This egregious case lost in court, despite my written and oral testimony. Perhaps the judge felt that she was lying because she had not shared her full story the first time she was arrested, or perhaps the case was not compelling enough for other reasons. She was again deported.

The case of Clementina, who transitioned into a transgender man in the United States, proved more compelling because in Honduras, Clementina had been a public figure and contestant in beauty pageants. Clementina's records were part of public newspaper accounts, and her gender identity transition would have made Clementina very vulnerable in her small town in northern Honduras. The challenge in writing affidavits for cases like Josie's and Clementina's is to share an unknown history and context in a way that is recognizable to the audience of immigration judges and government attorneys who often do not have comprehensive and detailed knowledge of home countries' histories and conditions or migrants' experiences. These accounts become part of the official records of the U.S. immigration court, which comprises history in the making, especially for LGBTI immigrants whose stories are documented for the first and only time. LGBTI testimonies, required in legal filings, are redolent with the deep pain of horrific experiences. They trigger raw responses of human emotion and expose the cruelty of the human condition. Often, I know the individuals only through legal documents and on occasion speak directly to them at the attorneys' discretion. But their stories, told through legal declaration and interpreted by an attorney or office staff, leave silences to explore. As a researcher and oral historian, I wish I could know more, engage more, or follow the story longer.

Reflection on the Challenges of Being an "Expert" and an Academic

Most of my affidavits for Central Americans include a brief history of the civil wars, the coup d'état in Honduras in 2009 for Honduran cases, the history of U.S. foreign policy in the country, which ultimately led to the over-militarization of the region, as well as migration trajectories. Often citing U.S. State Department reports or United Nations documents, one can make the case for a human rights disaster in the region. At the same time, I incorporate underutilized sources: oral histories; participant observations; and reports produced by human rights groups, feminist groups, and LGBTI organizations of the home country. A triangulation of reports from the State Department and international and local organizations provides a balanced view of the situation and reorients a narrative about the community and the reasons why people flee. At the same time, this approach helps marginalized communities tell their story, a contribution that almost always feels rewarding.

I have also come to appreciate a few important challenges inherent in this work: (1) the uneasy balance of providing comprehensive history and context with practicing strategic essentialism[2] concerning an individual or a country; (2) the weighted prioritization or creation of the official record; and (3) the need to queer the system at multiple levels.

Drafting affidavits and declarations can be a minefield of contradictions for scholars, attorneys, and migrants alike. On the one hand, the duty of the expert to the court and to the asylum seeker is to provide a true account of the dangers the migrant would face if returned to the country of origin. I utilize data from my own primary research in addition to published reports that detail violence or threats to substantiate my testimony to the court. It is an important story to tell; yet in that process I also recognize the impact of submitting a document to the court, and therefore the historical record, that constructs a particular narrative about the country in question and the communities involved. Often it is not our intention to cement a particular narrative or a monolithic essentialized view, but inevitably, when focusing on one particular issue, this can happen. It is never my intention to comment on Honduran (or any country's) culture or suggest that gender violence is part of an unchangeable culture, but an attorney may present it in that way, or the state's and the judge's questions may take the narrative in this direction. The affidavit can become a one-dimensional document that points to one "truth" according to the situation of that person in relation to the home country. Nonetheless, I have come to appreciate this work as an opportunity to document a country's problems for a historical record, to share the stories of LGBTI community members that may otherwise be omitted from the historical record of either country, and to raise alarm about human rights violations. Sometimes I can accept that I am producing a document that aches of strategic essentialism but was necessary to save a life.

Historians often rely on legal archives for their specificity and detail, and their ability to reveal gender dynamics and marginal social actors that official record obfuscates. Legal archives, however, are tricky and are often accepted by the courts as the only objective truth, yet, like all sources they can be read in multiple ways. Time and format are significant challenges to this work. Once a case is done, it is done. The legal format does not allow for time and space for the migrants to share a full context or a more extensive history of their lives. We really only learn about only one period in time and one context. In an LGBTI case it may be necessary to emphasize strategically one aspect of individuals' identities: their LGBTI identity as the primary source of all their victimization living under homophobic and transphobic conditions that threaten their life. This approach undermines any attempt at providing an intersectional understanding of their identity or the violence they experienced.

This process can also alter our notions of justice, as well as our archives of history itself. The legacy of U.S. foreign policy in Central America has generated multigenerational violence—sometimes burying the potential for true human rights redemption. Asylum may be achieved one individual at a time, but the history, scars, and suffering of U.S. foreign policy are not fully addressed through these cases. The record entered through experts and their attorneys illuminates just a little bit of the systemic and structural violence and may equally elide some of these enduring legacies. But this often-imperfect process can change the life of an LGBTI migrant. For many immigrants, achieving asylum is a new and life-saving start.

Notes

I wrote this piece while a Fulbright Scholar in Honduras (2018).

1. Suyapa Portillo Villeda, "Honduras LGBTI: Landscape Analysis of Political, Economic and Social Conditions," Astraea Lesbian Foundation for Justice, 2015.

2. The notion of strategic essentialism simultaneously recognizes the impossibility of any essentialism and the necessity of essentialism for the sake of strategic action. Gayatri Chakravorty Spivak, "Can the Subaltern Speak?" in *Marxism and the Interpretation of Culture*, ed. Cary Nelson and Lawrence Grossberg (Urbana: University of Illinois Press, 1988), 271–313.

5

Resettlement as Securitization

War, Humanitarianism, and the Production of Syrian LGBT Refugees

FADI SALEH

On November 8, 2016, Jaafar and Hasan,[1] two gay[2] Syrian asylum seekers resid-
ing in Istanbul, both received emails from the International Catholic Migration
Commission (ICMC) in Turkey with letters from the United States Citizenship
and Immigration Services (USCIS) informing them of their ineligibility for refugee resettlement in the United States. These emails arrived a day before Donald
Trump was announced the winner of the presidential elections and a day after
they received word from the United Nations High Commissioner for Refugees
(UNHCR) in Ankara, Turkey, that their files had been withdrawn from the United
States and that Norway was to be their new country of resettlement. The news of
their inadmissibility into the United States did not come as a major surprise—
the two had been waiting to be resettled for almost three years and had almost
lost hope. What was shocking about the rejection letter/email, however, was the
grounds on which they were deemed unresettleable: "a matter of discretion for
security-related reasons."[3]

In 2014, both Jaafar and Hasan applied at UNHCR in Ankara for asylum based
on sexual orientation and were some of the first Syrians to do so. Moreover, they
did not apply alone, but as a trio with a third friend, Wissam, from their hometown of Latakia. Although the three friends applied as a part of the same flight
experience and story, only Wissam tasted the exceptionalism and fast-tracking
promised to refugees seeking asylum based on gender identity and sexual orientation, a discourse that was heavily embraced by, circulated, and perpetuated among
Syrian LGBT refugees in Turkey. He was resettled to Nashville, Tennessee, in a
little over a year. Especially in 2015, with a few precedents of Syrian gay refugees
who were resettled in phenomenally short periods, including Wissam, most of
the gay Syrian refugees I met and spoke with during my field visits to Istanbul

would constantly cite the discourse of a homogenous group called "Syrian LGBT refugees" who were exceptional objects of UNHCR's humanitarian programs and whose asylum procedures, including registration, refugee status determination (RSD) interviews, health and security checks, and interviews with delegations, were supposed to run smoothly and without major hindrances. That said, speculation loomed large as to what could have led to Wissam's quick resettlement while Jaafar and Hasan were stuck in Turkey.

Sometimes the three friends wondered whether it was Wissam's Christianity that expedited his resettlement process, whereas Jaafar's being an Alawite and Hasan's being a Sunni, both predominant Muslim sects in Syria, had negatively affected their cases. At other times, they recalled various encounters with UNHCR's implementing partners, the different interviews, the many questions they were asked, and even the gestures, facial expressions, or affective atmosphere surrounding the settings of and their interactions with the humanitarian-asylum institutions they dealt with throughout the application process. It is important to mention that all of this speculation occurred long before the USCIS ineligibility notice arrived in Jaafar and Hasan's inboxes. Although the email cleared up some of the confusion surrounding their cases' three-year processing time, it could not fully explain why they were rejected. How could two gay refugees be considered a "threat" or "potential terrorists"? they often cynically commented. It was clear that being an LGBT refugee was not reason enough for them to be granted expedited asylum. Given these disappointing encounters with UNHCR and the larger humanitarian-asylum complex, how did Syrian queer populations come to imagine themselves as belonging to a homogenous constituency of Syrian LGBT refugees, and what were the conditions that enabled this imagined constituency? Why were Jaafar and Hasan surprised that a Syrian gay refugee could be rejected due to "security-related reasons," and what logic governs the interrelations between UNHCR's third-country resettlement paradigm, the security apparatuses of resettlement countries, and Syrian LGBT refugees?

To answer these questions, this chapter provides a partial, critical ethnographic account of the relatively recent emergence of the narrative that Syrian LGBT refugees are a homogenous, exceptional group. To achieve this, I focus on what I consider to be the most central and constitutive moment in the construction of this narrative: the encounter between Syrian LGBT refugees and the refugee resettlement program at UNHCR in the context of Turkey. The focus on this encounter proceeds from two observations: first, prior to 2011, Syrian queer persons were at best an obscure and irrelevant population on the global LGBT political scene. Knowledge of their histories, subjectivities, and Syrian queer cultures was, and to a large extent remains, virtually nonexistent. Second, since 2011, due to extensive media representation and circulation concerning the so-called Syrian refugee crisis,[4] the very mention of Syrian LGBT refugees invokes an array of often repetitive histories, narratives, and experiences of exceptional suffering, victim-hood, and vulnerability that have become inevitably linked to and constitutive of this homogenized group-identity. With these two contrasting, yet complemen-tary, observations in mind, this chapter contends that the recent emergence of a normative Syrian gay subject is strongly interlinked with the parallel ascendancy of UNHCR's refugee resettlement program as the humanitarian paradigm par excellence for Syrian queer refugees fleeing to Turkey.

Far from being a neutral humanitarian scheme, resettlement is a complicit, active arbiter in the discursive production of gay subjects that are co-terminus with specific narratives of sexual injury and persecution. Resettlement is a vital component of a global security assemblage invested in "the policing of populations and borders,"[5] as well as "rendering governable and 'managing' populations in Turkey."[6] However, in centralizing my examination of resettlement through UN-HCR, I do not intend to focus on the well-documented and already-established critique and exposure of the tacit (re)enforcement and imposition of Western narratives of what counts as intelligible sexual and gender identities, persecu-tion, or injury.[7] Rather, I propose that the resettlement paradigm is complicit and actively invests in the production, disciplining, and modulation of Syrian queer refugees not only as normative LGBT subjects, but, more importantly, as secure (read: nonterrorist), future citizens of the country of resettlement.[8] In other words, this chapter argues that the birth of the Syrian gay subject is (partially) contingent upon the applicant's capacity to produce her/himself not only as a subject that corresponds to dominant, mainstream notions of sexual injury and identity, but as a secure, nonthreatening gay subject. Further, this chapter demonstrates how the emergence of the Syrian gay subject is enabled by the intensification of what Jasbir Puar aptly calls "queer exceptionalism,"[9] whereby Syrian LGBT refugees, by virtue of being LGBT, are posited as exceptionally secure, nonterrorist sub-jects in contradistinction to an imagined population of non-LGBT/heterosexual counterparts. Only by disavowing their national belonging, ethnic and religious backgrounds, potentially problematic political stances, and any other identities or components that might be perceived as security threats—to the United States, in this instance—can the Syrian refugees' gayness emerge as that which renders them exceptionally worthy of protection and being folded into life in their re-settlement country.

Karam, Jaafar, Hasan, Wissam, and Hussam, all gay men in their twenties (at the time of my fieldwork) from Syria's coastal city of Latakia, are at the center of this article. While I followed Karam's story through intensive online contact during his time as an asylum seeker in 2013, my engagement with the stories of the other four was through both online communication and continuous field visits to Istanbul between 2014 and 2015. There, I spent extensive amounts of time and lived with them, conducted open-ended and semi-structured interviews, and followed their everyday lives and interactions with UNHCR and the larger humanitarian-asylum complex. My choice to follow these specific participants was neither arbitrary nor fully intentional, but was primarily a result of: first, having been close friends and a part of the same queer circles in Syria before I arrived in Germany in 2010 (with the exception of Hasan, whom I first met in 2015); and, second, due to my increasing engagements with different LGBT organizations and movements both in the diaspora and within the Middle East and North Africa region.

While the first part of this chapter focuses on Karam's story and the dynamics of his successful resettlement case, the second part shifts its emphasis to instances where the applicants curiously, and in different ways, inhabit the seemingly paradoxical positions of queerness and potential security threat—an intersection deemed impossible by the dominant discourses surrounding Syrian LGBT refugees and the resettlement paradigm.

A Well-Founded Fear of Which Persecution?
The Production of Narratives of Sexual Injury

Directly after the uprisings in 2011, Syrians started to flee to Turkey to escape the intensifying conflicts and seek protection. This prompted the Turkish government to immediately establish what it called a "temporary protection regime" to regulate the influx of Syrian refugees.[10] Until October 2014, when it became a fully-fledged legal regulation governing the status of Syrian refugees,[11] this regime was "based entirely on political and administrative discretion, which led to spontaneous, ad hoc measures and changing practices."[12] Under the temporary protection regime, Syrians occupy a particular position that sets them apart from other nationalities/groups. Although a signatory to the 1951 Geneva Refugee Convention and its 1967 Protocol, Turkey still applies a "geographical limitation" to the Convention.[13] This limitation stipulates that only Europeans can seek asylum and be considered refugees in Turkey, whereas non-Europeans are only allowed to reside in Turkey temporarily while seeking international protection through UNHCR's resettlement program.[14] Syrian nationals or stateless persons originating from Syria are neither of these two categories.[15] With the temporary protection status, they were granted "a right of legal stay as well as some level of access to basic rights and services," which restricted their right to apply for asylum at UNHCR.[16] Notwithstanding this restriction, there was a select number of people whom UNHCR deemed to be highly vulnerable groups among Syrians.[17] Although not explicitly named, Syrian LGBT refugees gradually emerged as a *de facto* vulnerable group under UNHCR's mandate, and they could apply for asylum if they could prove a "well-founded fear of persecution" due to their sexual orientation and/or gender identity.[18] It was at the early stages of the crystallization of these conditions that Karam decided to come to Turkey in 2013 to apply for asylum at UNHCR.

In April 2013, Karam made up his mind to leave Latakia and embark on a long bus journey to the Turkish city of Balikesir. Shortly after his arrival, Karam went to the UNHCR office in Ankara to register; but, to his surprise, he was informed that Syrian nationals were not allowed to apply for international protection at UNHCR, a piece of information that Karam was unaware of at the time. Upon being denied entry to the UNHCR office, Karam was advised to go to UNHCR's implementing partner, the Association for Solidarity with Asylum Seekers and Migrants (ASAM), but also to no avail: the staff at ASAM also told him that they could not help him because they do not register Syrians, regardless of the reasons of flight. After all, it was 2013, and a general sense of confusion regarding the humanitarian governance of Syrian nationals still prevailed. An Iranian friend of Karam's, who had already been resettled to the United States through the UNHCR and was therefore more experienced in matters of third-country resettlement, chided him for failing to emphasize that he was not applying as *just* a Syrian, but as a gay man—that he was fleeing persecution due to homophobia, not war. Upon being denied entry to the UNHCR office in Turkey, Karam contacted their offices in Geneva and New York, explaining his situation, requesting assistance and permission to enter and seek asylum based on sexual orientation. This impromptu advocacy strategy worked, and UNHCR indeed contacted Karam with an interview date. According to Karam, his interviews, with UNHCR and later with the Swedish delegation revolved around two overarching factors: proving that he was actually gay and that he had a well-founded fear of persecution due to his sexual orientation. During the many talks I had with Karam, he never recalled or mentioned that any questions about incidents that did not directly connect to his sexuality were asked. For example, he was not asked about the uprisings, the ongoing conflict in Syria, or any other "identities" he inhabits, all of which might have played a role in his decision to flee the country. Therefore, he stuck to stories of homophobia in the family, at the workplace, in law and society, and in his everyday life in Latakia—a piece of advice that he forwarded to the next group of queer friends planning to flee to Turkey.

Karam was initially denied entry into the UNHCR office for failing to present his claim for asylum as a result of a sexual injury, and not as an effect of war; a condition that, I argue, inadvertently becomes quintessential to the production of a Syrian gay subject untainted by the affective force of war and conflict. With this condition, "war" becomes problematically equated with being Syrian, an equation that requires the active detachment of Karam's sexual subjectivity from this Syr-ianness-as-war identity. Second, through this performative bifurcation, another identity is arbitrarily produced, one that associates Syrianness-as-war with hetero-sexuality.[19] Third, this becomes more complicated when considering the fact that perceiving oneself as a refugee who bears a "right" to seek international protection became an option, also for queer persons, as a result of, and not regardless of, war. In other words, Karam's successful resettlement did not depend solely on his abil-ity to provide a convincing narrative of sexual injury that both derives from his gayness and corresponds to the decision-makers' ideas of what constitutes such an injury. Rather, I contend, his emergence as an intelligible gay subject worthy of resettlement was achieved through the performative splitting of his sexual identity from its being a (partial) effect of war. This process does not demand the deliber-ate construction of an intelligible gay identity; rather, it requires the successful narration of an injury that comes to function as that identity's origin.[20] Wendy Brown's thinking on subject formation and its relation to suffering and injury is quite informative on this point. She offers a viable critique of minorities' preoc-cupation with and overinvestment in seeking "legal redress for injuries related to social subordination,"[21] whereby these injuries are rendered "foundational to identity," "suffering [becomes] lived as identity";[22] and the gay refugee's sexuality as a "politicized identity . . . becomes attached to its own exclusion . . . because it is premised on this exclusion for its very existence as identity."[23] It is this attachment and investment in sustaining, rather than expunging, the injury as the source of one's identity that Brown aptly names "wounded attachments."[24]

While Brown's partial account of identity's self-preservation through attach-ment to injury is very helpful, her analytical framework needs to be expanded if we are to account for the experiences of Syrian gay refugee resettlement. Return-ing to Karam's case and his initial encounter with the homophobia-versus-war binary, one could argue that his emergence as a gay subject not only depends on his attachment to or repetition of sexual injuries and persecution,[25] but also on what one could perhaps mundanely call a "wounded *detachment*," whereby it is incumbent on the gay applicant himself to construct his sexual injury through actively and repetitively detaching all of those elements that might challenge, complicate, or completely discombobulate the hegemonic narratives or under-standings of what counts as constitutive of one's sexual subjectivity. In Brown's critique, injury is, understandably, something perpetrated by "others"; in my reading, I contend that it becomes the subject's responsibility to curate specific narratives of injury, which then come to stand for the injury itself, by detaching oneself from the "home" country understood as "war." Consequently, this de-tachment becomes the condition of possibility for an intelligible gay subject to emerge as proper, exceptional, and, thus, eligible for resettlement.

The news of Karam's speedy resettlement to Sweden (he left Turkey in early January 2014) and the slow but steady dissemination of the knowledge that queers could seek international protection through the UNHCR offices in Turkey has produced a certain sense of queerness as potentially exceptional within the asylum complex and has simultaneously intensified exceptionalism as a property of being queer—two discourses that feed into and constitute one another. Karam's story has thus prompted other queer persons to flee. But unlike Karam, the conditions under which the next queer asylum seekers came to Turkey and applied for asylum at UNHCR radically changed, and not in a good way. The terrorist group Daesh came to power.[26]

By November 2014, the first reports of the brutal execution of allegedly gay men in Daesh-controlled areas had started to emerge and spread.[27] It was at this historical juncture that Syrian LGBT refugees started to gain considerable visibility and discursive weight, most prominently as an exceptionally vulnerable population whose protection required deliberate humanitarian intervention by UNHCR. Narratives of the vulnerability and exceptionalism of Syrian LGBT refugees started to circulate at high velocities. Increasingly, UNHCR's third-country resettlement schema emerged as the humanitarian paradigm par excellence for Syrian LGBT refugees in Turkey, a relationship that was powerfully produced and maintained in journalistic accounts, NGO reports, press releases, and the increasing attention of Western governments to the plight of Syrian LGBT refugees. Between 2014 and 2016, statements proliferated in which characterizations of Syrian LGBT refugees as some of the "most vulnerable groups" were discursively tied to their being a "target of resettlement policies."[28] Even the Obama White House voiced its concerns for the situation of Syrian LGBT refugees and translated these concerns into the need to prioritize Syrian LGBT refugees within the U.S. resettlement program.[29] Articulations of resettlement as "the most appropriate solution"[30] and "the only durable solution to guarantee the safety of LGBTI people" proliferated, and a consequent need to develop better measures to "identify" or "quantify" those vulnerable LGBT populations from Syria emerged.[31] These discourses steadily intensified, reaching the status of mainstream narratives and foundational truths, and even constituting definitive histories of Syrian LGBT refugees. With every new visit to Istanbul from 2014 onward, I noticed a rising tendency among Syrian LGBT refugees, who had applied or intend to apply for asylum through UNHCR, to employ, reproduce, and circulate these discourses as evidence of their exceptionalism in comparison to their non-LGBT counterparts.

This discourse of exceptionalism reached an unprecedented apogee when, near the end of 2015, the Canadian government announced that it was not going to resettle single straight men, but only single gay men.[32] This added a new layer of international legitimation to the homophobia-versus-war dichotomy, whereby queerness is co-opted and deployed as *the* optic through which "a very specific production of terrorist bodies against properly" LGBT subjects takes place,[33] on the one hand; and a binary of "migrants are always heterosexual (or on their way to becoming so) and [LGBTs] are citizens (even though second-class ones)" is produced, on the other.[34] These two observations, though not automatically connected, feed into each other in ways that help explain the Canadian resettlement policy and how it actively constructs certain subjects as worthy of being folded into Canadian life, understood as resettlement. Although resettled Syrian refugees, whether LGBT or non-LGBT, are not citizens of Canada, the United States, or other Western resettlement countries, citizenship is the highly affective promise at the heart of resettlement: a promise that Syrian LGBT refugees are expected to tend to and invest in. In the case of Syrian LGBT refugees, their LGBTness signifies the potential for them to "become citizens." However, this potential can be activated only if properly detached from their Syrianness-as-war identity. This "undesirable" property becomes automatically attributed to migrants/refugees who seek asylum through resettlement for reasons other than sexual orientation or gender identity, who are then produced as simultaneously inhabiting a terrorist, "perverse heterosexuality."[35] While I do not wish to question the real, negative effects of this logic on migrants and refugees who are perceived as heterosexual, I argue that the exceptionalism accorded to Syrian LGBT refugees, discursively and politically, begs for some problematization and further probing. In the next section, I focus on ethnographic accounts wherein certain Syrian queer subjects are perceived to have failed to properly detach themselves from Syrianness-as-war, and are thus produced as inhabiting the seemingly paradoxical positions of gay refugees and security threats.

Being Both a Gay Refugee and a Potential Terrorist Is No Anomaly

Hussam arrived in Istanbul in the winter of 2014 and applied for asylum in early 2015. After registering with ASAM, it took quite a few months before UNHCR called to give him an interview date sometime in the winter of 2015. Shortly after his first interview with UNHCR in Ankara, Hussam learned that the United States was to be his resettlement country. Soon enough, Hussam had his most decisive interview to date: that with the delegation of the U.S. Department of Homeland Security (DHS) at the ICMC offices in Istanbul.

On the eve of October 29, 2015, Jaafar, Hasan, and I eagerly waited for Hussam at their shared apartment to hear how his interview had gone. Jaafar and Hasan were also from Latakia and were in fact some of the first people to apply for asylum at UNHCR in May 2014. In fact, all three even lived together for some time in Balikesir before moving to Istanbul by the end of 2014. Given that the United States was also their country of resettlement, they underwent almost the same procedures as Hussam. Not wasting a second after his arrival, Hussam told us that what was most striking about his interview was the limited focus on familiar narratives of persecution due to his sexuality, and a hyper-focus on the stories that involved his military service and his unfortunate encounter with one of Syria's warring factions in 2012.

Engaging with Hussam's reflection on the overall interview, Jaafar and Hasan also vividly recalled the DHS delegation's intensive preoccupation with questions that seemed primarily concerned with establishing whether or not these queer refugees were a security threat. On another occasion, Jaafar told me, reflecting on the types of questions he was asked, that "around two or three questions were related to my story, but the rest were about the oppression of gays in Syria, and the case and stories of Daesh. . . . [I was asked] what do you think of the regime, of its politics. . . . They focused a lot on the issue of military service, but luckily neither of us [Jaafar and Hasan] did it . . . they focused on Daesh and on whether demonstrations took place in our region." Hasan added, "They asked me whether I think that the regime was protecting me from Daesh; I told them both are two sides of the same coin," implying that both are differently oppressive of LGBT people.[36] This answer worried him for months to come. Whereas Jaafar and Hasan exerted an effort to manage a poised attitude and (eventually unsuccessfully) tried to sieve out narratives of Syria and the war, Hussam's framing of his sexual injury and its relation to his sexual identity proved fatal for his resettlement. The most central story in Hussam's narrative was, in fact, neither exceptional in a warzone nor strictly gender- or sexuality-related:[37] he had been kidnapped and beaten by what turned out to be a faction of the Free Syrian Army on the outskirts of Damascus. Nonetheless, this quotidian warzone happening was related as a part of his asylum claim based on sexual orientation during his DHS interview on that day.

Hussam had carried out his military service in Damascus, and during that period, he met his boyfriend, who was from Aleppo. After both were exempted from service, Hussam and his now–ex-boyfriend lost contact. In August 2012, Hussam received a phone call from the mother of an acquaintance who was still serving at the same military base where Hussam served. She told Hussam that she had not heard from her son for days and was wondering whether Hussam knew anything. Hussam, whose concern for this acquaintance coincided with his desire to know how his ex-boyfriend was doing, decided to pay a visit to his old military base in order to retrieve his ex-boyfriend's contact information. Ignorant of the security situation, Hussam took a bus to al-Ghouta on the outskirts of Damascus, where he was subjected to different checkpoints. The first checkpoint was managed by the

Syrian regime forces, and since he is from Latakia, a city associated with the Syrian regime, he had no problem moving forward. The second checkpoint, however, belonged to the Free Syrian Army. Like many others, Hussam was asked to get into a car. After a ten-minute drive, he was led into the basement of a villa, where he found many other people. Hussam knew that, unlike the first check-point, his being from Latakia had become a disadvantage. His affiliation with Latakia raises the suspicion that he might be an Alawite or a Shiite (minority Muslim sects associated with the regime), which is why Hussam's kidnappers persistently inquired about his background. Hussam immediately informed them that he was a Sunni Muslim and gave them the name of the village where his parents originally come from, hoping that they would believe that he was a Sunni.[38] It was Ramadan, the fasting month, and luckily Hussam was fasting, which elicited some sympathy. After eight full days of capture, coupled with beatings, "mild" torture, and intensive investigations into Hussam's background, they eventually believed his claim that he was not a regime spy, and he was released.

Commenting on the interviewers' reactions to his story, Hussam vividly recalls, "They were not convinced about how these factions were killing people, but [I] was taken in by them, and although I am gay, they did not find out 'you were gay,' and I was not killed. . . . I told them that the main reason [why they let me go] was really my religious denomination."[39] Hussam, in his recounting of the horrific story, confirmed that he was asked only once by one of the kidnappers about why "he was soft like that," an incident that Hussam deemed negligible, thus completely dismissing the theory that his kidnapping had anything to do with his "queer" appearance, an ascription ironically assumed more by the interviewers than the kidnappers themselves. Later that evening, when Hussam and I went out alone to Kafeka Café, our queer hangout in the touristic Istiklal Street, he further added, "I felt that the essence of the DHS delegation's questions was not to find out whether I was LGBT, but whether I was with or against terrorism."[40]

In this encounter, Hussam did not recognize the thick line between war-suffering and suffering due to a well-founded fear of persecution that is strictly anchored in one's sexual identity. In Hussam's narrative, his sexual identity is strongly tied to its becoming a subject *after* 2011—that is, because of the war, and not before it. Hussam clearly did not see a contradiction between his narrative at the interviews and his self-identification as gay, wherein many injuries that were constitutive of his sexual subjectivity were perceived by the interviewers as both a performative failure and a subject of excessive interrogation. The walls separating war and sexuality collapse in Hussam's account, rendering his self-articulation unintelligibly queer—but not legibly gay—for the decision-makers.

Lastly, it is important to note that religious denomination (and not simply religion) is one of the most structuring axes of identity in the Syrian context, and it invariably affects and produces our senses of our sexual and gendered identifications, relations, and self-understanding. However, in Jaafar and Hasan's interviews, their religious backgrounds became a site of intensive investigation and probing not as constituents of their sexual subjectivities but as antithetical to the decision-makers' notions of what counts as a proper gay refugee subject and hence as sites of potential threat. Thus, both were still the target of affective disciplinary measures, whereby the decision-makers continued to look for nonlinguistic cues in their religious backgrounds or the way they answered the questions to decide on whether they were secure enough and thus worthy of resettlement. In Hussam's surprise at the interviewers' suspicion that he was released from captivity despite "being gay," and in Jaafar and Hasan's continuous avoidance of including other vectors of identification into the narration of their sexual identities and, still failing, intersectionality becomes literally inaccessible to Syrian gay subjects, who must produce themselves in the single-identity sameness of an imaginary, global LGBT subject, while detaching Syrianness-as-war as an unnecessary, potentially-threatening appendix.

Conclusion

Despite their efforts and rehearsals, their affective attunement to the dynamics of interviews, and continuous dissociation of the war as a significant part of their queer refugeeness, Jaafar and Hasan were also denied resettlement. This should not be seen as a contradiction to Hussam's case, but rather as another manifestation of the affective "technologies of security"[41] that characterize third-country resettlement and its mandate of producing disciplined and secure humanitarian subjects. Whereas Hussam more clearly failed to articulate a discursive separation of sexuality from war through his utterances/testimonies, Jaafar and Hasan speculated that their emphasis on providing neutral, apolitical and unsuspicious answers to questions surrounding military service, the uprisings, and the regime versus Daesh failed to produce them as subjects who are detached from Syrianness-as-war. While Jaafar and Hasan's speculations about having failed to be legible as "secure" gay subjects were concretized through receiving the notice of ineligibility, Hussam has not received such a notice; he learned later in 2016 that his case was indefinitely suspended. Growing impatient with having his flights to the United States inexplicably canceled for the second time, Jaafar risked his life and attempted to cross to Europe by sea, and failed; his boat was captured by the Turkish Coast Guards, he was mistreated and jailed temporarily, and his status in Turkey was thus threatened. Hussam, out of despair, crossed to Greece in 2016 and continued to suffer the—sometimes life-threatening—consequences of the suspension of his case until receiving reassuring news from his lawyer in 2019 that he might finally be recognized as a refugee in Germany.

In their different dynamics and complexities, all cases reiterate and are different manifestations of the arbitrariness that inheres in UNHCR's third-country resettlement paradigm, especially when the resettlement country is the United States. The ultimate manifestation of the U.S. security mandate when it comes to Syrians, among other nationalities, can be seen in Trump's executive order of January 2017, also known as the "Muslim ban," which indiscriminately lumped the populations of seven Muslim-majority countries together, including refugees already admitted to the United States.[42] This ban, although heavily contested and challenged, was an unapologetic, material manifestation of the "Syrianness-as-war" logic governing resettlement as an essential part of the U.S. foreign politics and its offshore war on terror. Whereas third-country resettlement seemingly foregrounded Syrian LGBT refugees as exceptional through emphasizing/enforcing certain narratives of sexual injury as their only hope of arriving in the United States and attaining its citizenship, the ban shifts this hierarchy, unapologetically reinstating an understanding of Syrianness-as-war at the heart of its resettlement and asylum politics and thus exposing the instrumentalization of, rather than genuine care for, Syrian LGBT refugees over the years. As I demonstrate in this chapter, resettlement policies and processes that fail to acknowledge the intersecting identities shaping the LGBT applicants' sexual subjectivities and their narratives of persecution and flight run the risk of endangering the lives of the very populations they claim to protect. Therefore, further critical, theoretical, and ethnographic interventions into resettlement need to maintain an intersectional analytical lens that allows for different migration/flight narratives to emerge, other queer histories to be heard, and resettlement policies to achieve what they were meant for: protection, not exclusion.

Notes

1. Throughout the chapter, and following the wishes of the participants in this study, I use their real first names.

2. For the purposes of this chapter, I use LGBT, queer, and gay to denote different things. I use LGBT to refer to the ways Syrian queer refugees are spoken of by media outlets, INGOs, and humanitarian institutions. But much like this chapter demonstrates, LGBT as a homogenizing identity marker is mostly used to refer to gay male refugees and their experiences. I use "queer" to emphasize those elements of Syrian queer refugees' self-understanding that are prior to their encounter with the humanitarian-asylum complex and that are not seen as fitting UNHCR's or resettlement country's LGBT framework. I use "gay" to describe the asylum applicants in order to emphasize the asylum aspect and that this is how they present themselves at UNHCR. However, their actual identifications are

much more nuanced and follow various systems of identification that are not restricted to a Western LGBT identitarian framework.

3. U.S. Citizenship and Immigration Services, "Notice of Ineligibility for Resettlement," letter in an email message to Jaafar and Hasan, November 8, 2016. The notice was sent as an attachment to the email. Although the email was sent on November 8, 2016, the attached notice itself was curiously dated November 9, 2016.

4. In my use of "so-called" to describe the "Syrian refugee crisis," I draw on activist counter-discourses that argue that calling the movements of Syrians escaping war and seeking asylum in Europe a "crisis" produces "Europe" as a continent without complex migration histories and distracts from the strict EU migration policies that are the main cause of this "crisis." For more on this issue, see Daniel Trilling, "Five Myths about the Refugee Crisis," *The Guardian*, June 5, 2018, https://www.theguardian.com/news/2018/jun/05/five-myths-about-the-refugee-crisis.

5. Stephan Scheel and Phillip Ratfisch, "Refugee Protection Meets Migration Management: UNHCR as a Global Police of Populations," *Journal of Ethnic and Migration Studies* 40, no. 6 (2014): 926. For an excellent, critical account of UNHCR's expanding involvement in state affairs and refugee politics and its transformation into a potential "agent for a policy of containment and a threat to refugee rights" (244), see Michael Barnett, "Humanitarianism with a Sovereign Face: UNHCR in the Global Undertow," *IMR* 35, no.1 (Spring 2011).

6. Scheel and Ratfisch, "Refugee Protection," 928.

7. There is a considerable amount of literature that focuses on the imposition of Western narratives of sexuality and gender identity that are grounded in Western, essentialist notions and stereotypes of (both Western and non-Western) sexual and gendered identity; these are narratives of progress and civilization that produce the West as progressive and the rest of the world as backward, and expectations of specific stories of sexual injury and persecution, among various other outcomes. For recent work on these topics see, for example, Laurie Berg and Jenni Millbank, "Constructing the Personal Narratives of Lesbian, Gay, and Bisexual Asylum Claimants," *Journal of Refugee Studies* 22, no. 2 (2009); Rachel A. Lewis, "'Gay? Prove it': The Politics of Queer Anti-Deportation Activism," *Sexualities* 17, no.8 (2014); David A. B. Murray, "The (Not So) Straight Story: Queering Migration Narratives of Sexual Orientation and Gendered Identity Refugee Claimants," *Sexualities* 17, no. 4 (2014); and Senthorun Raj, "Affective Displacements: Understanding Emotions and Sexualities in Refugee Law," *Alternative Law Journal* 36, no.3 (September 2011).

8. There is a dearth of literature on the relationship between UNHCR's third-country resettlement and LGBT refugees in general, and Syrian LGBT refugees in Turkey in specific. In fact, most literature on issues of queer migration, asylum, and refugeeness has focused on asylum-seekers and refugees who have crossed borders and made it to the country where they requested their asylum. In addition to the sources already mentioned in the previous note, see, for example, Eithne Luibhéid and Lionel Cantú Jr., eds., *Queer Migrations: Sexuality, U.S. Citizenship, and Border Crossings* (Minneapolis: University of Minnesota Press, 2005); Eithne Luibhéid, *Entry Denied: Controlling Sexuality at the Border* (Minneapolis: University of Minnesota Press, 2002); and Lionel Cantú Jr., *The Sexuality*

of Migration: Border Crossings and Mexican Immigrant Men, eds. Nancy A Naples and Salvador Vidal-Ortiz (New York: New York University Press, 2009). An exception is Sima Shakhsari's insightful and critical work on UNHCR, refugee resettlement, and Iranian queer and transgender refugees in Turkey, most prominently in Sima Shakhsari, "The Queer Time of Death: Temporality, Geopolitics, and Refugee Rights," *Sexualities* 7, no.8 (2014); and Sima Shakhsari, "Killing Me Softly with Your Rights: Queer Death and the Politics of Rightful Killing," in *Queer Necropolitics*, eds. Jin Haritaworn, Adi Kuntsman, and Silvia Posocco (New York: Routledge, 2014). However, in both pieces, Shakhsari focuses on exposing the gaps and failures of UNHCR as a system on the one hand, and the paradoxes inherent in its constitution as a "rights-granting" paradigm that both fails to fulfill that promise and produces a hierarchy of more mournable versus less mournable bodies of queer and trans* asylum-seekers in Turkey. In that sense, her work still falls short of touching upon or understanding UNHCR's resettlement paradigm as a security-humanitarian assemblage that is invested in the surveillance and securitization of Syrian applicants, regardless of queerness. This might be because Syrian queer refugees emerged during the war, a factor that is missing in the case of Iranian queer and trans* refugees.

9. Jasbir Puar, *Terrorist Assemblages: Homonationalism in Queer Times* (Durham, N.C.: Duke University Press, 2007), 77.

10. Asylumineurope, "Introduction to the Asylum Context in Turkey," https://www .asylumineurope.org/reports/country/turkey/introduction-asylum-context-turkey.

11. The temporary protection regime governing Syrians and stateless persons originating from Syria is based on article 91 of Turkey's first asylum and migration law, *The Law on Foreigners and International Protection* (fully enforced in April 2014) and the *Temporary Protection Regulation* (issued in October 2014). See Asylumineurope, "Introduction."

12. Asylumineurope, "2011–2014: Temporary Protection Based on Political Discretion and Improvisation," http://www.asylumineurope.org/reports/country/turkey/temporary-protection-2011-2014-political-discretion-and-improvisation.

13. Marjoleine Zieck, "UNHCR and Turkey, and Beyond: of Parallel Tracks and Symptomatic Cracks," *International Journal of Refugee Law* 22, no. 4 (2010): 593–594.

14. Ibid.

15. Elif Sarı and Cemile Gizem Dincer, "Towards a New Asylum Regime in Turkey?" *Movements: Journal for Critical Migration and Border Regime Studies* 4, no. 2 (2017): 59–60.

16. Asylumineurope, "Introduction."

17. Zeynep Kıvılcım. "Lesbian, Gay, Bisexual and Transsexual (LGBT) Syrian Refugees in Turkey," in *A Gendered Approach to the Syrian Refugee Crisis*, eds. Jane Freedman, Zeynep Kıvılcım, and Nurcan Özgür Baklacioğlu (London: Routledge, 2017), 28. According to UNHCR, categories of highly vulnerable groups include, among others, women and girls/adolescents and children at risk, people with medical needs not available in the asylum country, and survivors of torture/violence. For a full list, see UN High Commissioner for Refugees, *UNHCR Resettlement Handbook*, July 2011, 37, http://www.unher .org/46f7c0ee2pdf. While Syrians in general cannot seek asylum based on war, those categories/groups enable a very small number of people to apply for asylum at UNHCR for reasons that can be seen as direct results of war. Syrian LGBT refugees' need for protection

and asylum claims, unlike Syrians who can or cannot apply for international protection at UNHCR, are expected to be completely detached from war.

18. UNHCR released the first Guidance Note formally and systematically tackling the question of refugee asylum claims based on sexual orientation and gender identity in November 2008. UN High Commissioner for Refugees, "UHCR Guidance Note on Refugee Claims Relating to Sexual Orientation and Gender Identity," November 21, 2008, http://www.refworld.org/docid/48abd5660.html. For a critical commentary on the guidance notes and its stipulations, see Nicole LaViolette, "'UNHCR Guidance Note on Refugee Claims Relating to Sexual Orientation': A Critical Commentary," *International Journal of Refugee Law* 22, no.2 (2010).

19. On this point, my argument throughout this chapter is heavily structured around Luibhéid's insight that migration scholarship must equally interrogate the processes that produce queer subjects, on the one hand, and "those who become defined as normative or 'normal' within a binary structure." Eithne Luibhéid, "Queer/Migration: An Unruly Body of Scholarship," *GLQ* 14, nos. 2–3 (2008): 171–172. However, in my employment of this insight, I argue that there is a reversal of the terms aligned with "queerness" and "heterosexuality" with UNHCR's resettlement paradigm, whereby "normality" becomes aligned more with queerness and "deviance" more with heterosexuality.

20. In her own rephrasing of Butler's formulation of the notion of the subject "before the law," Shakhsari succinctly points out the performative dimension of the "regulatory practices of the nation-state and human rights discourses," which "conceal the process of the construction of refugee subjects, by portraying them as prior to discourse." Shakhsari, "Killing Me Softly," 100. Yet, in my formulation of the construction of Syrian LGBT refugee subjects, I contend that there is another layer that not only involves *a priori*-given discourses through which subjects are produced: this layer, as in Karam's case, is still unknowable, in the process of being produced as a discourse, and its (co)construction, successful repetition, and embodiment are the responsibility of the emerging, gay refugee subject.

21. Wendy Brown, *States of Injury: Power and Freedom in Late Modernity* (Princeton, N.J.: Princeton University Press, 1995), 27.

22. Brown, *Politics Out of History* (Princeton, N.J.: Princeton University Press, 2001), 39.

23. Brown, *States of Injury*, 73.

24. Ibid., 53.

25. As Brown aptly puts it: "To make the past into the subjective and objective present, one has to reiterate the injury discursively, emotionally, as bodily and psychic trauma in the present." See *Politics Out of History*, 53.

26. To avoid switching between the different names the terrorist group has in the media, I consistently use its Arabic acronym "Daesh" throughout this chapter. For a commentary on the various names used, see Zed Khan, "Call It Daesh, not ISIL (or ISIS)," *CNN*, October 7, 2016, http://edition.cnn.com/2016/10/05/opinions/daesh-not-isil-or-islamic-state-khan/index.html.

27. Michelle Garcia, "ISIS Executes Two Gay Men in First Antigay Attacks in Syria," *The Advocate*, November 30, 2014, https://www.advocate.com/world/2014/11/30/reports-isis-executes-two-gay-men-first-antigay-attacks.

28. Caterina Franchi, "Resettlement Programme Is Letting Down Vulnerable Syrian Refugees, Warns Report," *The Justice Gap*, January 7, 2016, http://thejusticegap.com/2016/01/12208/.

29. Chris Johnson, "White House: No Quota, but Priority for LGBT Syrian Refugees," *Washington Blade*, December 8, 2015, http://www.washingtonblade.com/2015/12/08/white-house-no-quota-but-priority-for-lgbt-syrian-refugees/.

30. Kevin Ozebek, "Meet the LBGTI Refugees Who Are Fleeing Syria for the U.S.," *Time*, September 29, 2015, http://time.com/4048421/meet-the-lgbti-refugees-who-are-fleeing-syria-for-the-u-s/.

31. Oliver Wheaton, "David Cameron: We Will Resettle LGBT Refugees from Syria and Iraq," *Metro*, December 9, 2015, http://metro.co.uk/2015/12/09/david-cameron-we-will-resettle-lgbt-refugees-from-syria-and-iraq-5555194/.

32. Zi-Ann Lum, "How Canada Will Screen Gay Syrian Refugee Men," *Huffington Post*, November 25, 2015, http://www.huffingtonpost.ca/2015/11/25/syrian-refugees-canada-gay_n_8650582.html?utm_hp_ref=ca-gay-syrian-refugees.

33. Puar, *Terrorist Assemblages*, xiii.

34. Luibhéid, "Queer/Migration," 169.

35. Puar, *Terrorist Assemblages*, 148. In this sense, Luibhéid's formulation is reversed, for the promise of becoming a citizen is conferred upon "queers," whereas second-class citizenship becomes attributed to non-queers.

36. Discussion, September 2015.

37. For an excellent insight on this point, see Maya Mikdashi and Jasbir K. Puar, "Queer Theory and Permanent War," *GLQ* 22, no.2 (2016), 219–220.

38. In Syria, the practice of religious-profiling based on hometown villages—of one's parents or grandparents if one was born in the city—is quite common.

39. Discussion, November 2015.

40. Ibid.

41. Puar, *Terrorist Assemblages*, 115.

42. "Full Text of Trump's Executive Order on 7-Nation Ban, Refugee Suspension," *CNN*, January 28, 2017, https://edition.cnn.com/2017/01/28/politics/text-of-trump-executive-order-nation-ban-refugees/index.html.

6

Unsafe Present, Uncertain Future

LGBTI Asylum in Turkey

ELIF SARI

Due to the discrimination and the abuse they experience in Iran, each year many lesbian, gay, bisexual, transgender, and intersex (LGBTI)[1] people leave their home country and arrive in Turkey. They thus join the multitude of displaced refugees who are trying to make their way West. Although Turkey is party to the 1951 Convention Relating to the Status of Refugees, it does not provide long-term integration or settlement for refugees coming from outside Europe. Rather, non-European refugees temporarily reside in Turkey until the United Nations High Commissioner for Refugees (UNHCR) resettles them into a third country that would be willing to accept them.[2]

Until recently, the UNHCR and the third countries, such as the United States and Canada, had prioritized LGBTI asylum applications by expediting their assessment and reserving prioritized resettlement quotas for the victims of sexual- and gender-based violence. For instance, unlike many other refugee groups who were assigned their first refugee status determination interviews with the UNHCR after an average of ten months or much longer, LGBTI refugees were provided a date for the first interview in forty-five days. Similarly, the third countries had conducted resettlement interviews and visa processes of LGBTI refugees much faster and with lower rejection rates than of other, non-LGBTI, refugee groups. Thus, their particular "vulnerability" had rendered LGBTI refugees the "golden cases of the refugee pool in Turkey."[3]

This picture in which LGBTI refugees receive prioritized status and expedited mobility, however, has been drastically changing with the recent asylum policies of the UNHCR and the third countries. Since 2015, the average processing time of the UNHCR for LGBTI asylum applications has increased from eighteen months to forty months.[4] Moreover, since late 2015, Canada has begun to implement new resettlement programs for refugees from Syria, and simultaneously, the resettlement of other refugee groups, among them Iranian LGBTI refugees waiting in Turkey, has slowed down, if not completely stopped. On the other hand, U.S. President Donald Trump's executive orders, the first of which was issued in early 2017, have left Iranian refugees in a limbo situation in Turkey, suspending their resettlement processes indefinitely.

This chapter explores how these recent developments have affected the lives and experiences of Iranian LGBTI refugees in Turkey. As the United States and Canada have cut their refugee quotas and tightened their asylum policies, the prospects for LGBTI refugee resettlement have grown increasingly dim. Even applicants who have completed necessary asylum procedures and have been formally eligible for resettlement for years are still stranded in Turkey with insecure legal status. As they face an uncertain future, LGBTI refugees also have to live difficult lives in Turkey. Like other refugee groups, they dwell in small Turkish towns located mostly in the interior of the country, where they have restricted mobility: they have to "sign-in" regularly at the local immigration offices, and even a small trip to a nearby town puts them under the risk of deportation unless they secure a "travel permit" from the local immigration authorities. While living and waiting in small Turkish towns, they face multiple forms of violence and discrimination: the incessant verbal and sexual harassment from local townspeople and other refugees, the difficulty of finding housing and employment because of discrimination, and the perpetual vulnerability to labor exploitation and sexual harassment in the "informal" economy. Furthermore, the recent sociopolitical circumstances in Turkey—the deadly bombings and gun attacks since 2015, the military coup attempt in July 2016, and the following state of emergency—have turned Turkey into an increasingly unstable place for refugees.

The findings of this chapter draw on six months of preliminary research (2015–2017) and two years of ethnographic fieldwork (2017–2019) with Iranian LGBTI refugees who lodged their asylum claims in Turkey, waiting for resettlement to the United States or Canada. Fluent in Turkish and Farsi, I immersed myself in my interlocutors' everyday lives; worked with them at a textile factory; joined their community meetings and political demonstrations; accompanied them to various public offices where they sought legal, medical, and financial aid; and helped them draft emails and submit petitions to numerous embassies, international humanitarian organizations, and Turkish and North American NGOs. I also interviewed refugees, asylum adjudicators, lawyers, police officers, medical authorities, and aid providers in three Turkish towns (Denizli, Kayseri, Eskişehir) where the Turkish state has relocated most LGBTI refugees.

In the next section, I examine the legal processes of asylum in Turkey, examining how unpredictabilities embedded in refugee status determination and resettlement processes leave LGBTI refugees in a constant state of uncertainty. I also explore how the restrictive resettlement policies of the United States and Canada have exacerbated these uncertainties as well as how refugees have responded to these restrictions. The following section explores everyday life in Turkey, examining how the lack of established rights and effective protection generates multiple forms of violence in LGBTI refugees' lives. Finally, I offer an analysis of how the contemporary sociopolitical environment in Turkey has expanded the securitization of asylum and put refugees at greater risk of detention and deportation.

No Guaranteed Refuge: Refugee Status Determination and Resettlement

Refugees in Turkey need to follow a parallel asylum system, in which they must lodge two asylum applications—one with the UNHCR and one with the Turkish Directorate General of Migration Management (DGMM).[5] Both agencies conduct their own refugee status determination (RSD) interviews, investigating the reasons of asylum and assessing the "credibility" of refugees' claims.[6] The RSD interviews often last for years, and cases are not followed up on a regular basis. I have observed many times that the UNHCR and the DGMM notified refugees only a few days before their RSD interviews. "I check my phone every 5 minutes to make sure it has power and it's not on silent mode. I don't know when UNHCR would call me to give me a date for my interview," Farzad, a gay refugee, told me. When I met him in 2017, he had lodged his asylum application ten months ago and was still waiting for an interview date. In this context of long and unpredictable waiting times, it is important not to miss these calls because, as Farzad contended, "God knows how many more months I would have to wait if I miss the phone call. I even take my phone to the restroom with me."

During their RSD interviews with the UNHCR and the DGMM, LGBTI refugees need to prove their gender identity or sexual orientation in order to establish their "membership of a particular group" and to demonstrate that they cannot return to their countries of origin because of a "well-founded fear of persecution."[7] The UNHCR's special Guidelines advises against the use of stereotypical images of sexual minorities in determining refugee status, stating that self-identification as LGBTI should be sufficient to indicate one's sexual orientation and gender identity.[8] Furthermore, after the publication of Guidelines in 2008, some training workshops are said to have taken place for increasing sensitivity among UNHCR and DGMM officers in Turkey. However, many refugees described the interview questions as invasive and extremely prurient, as they were interrogated explicitly about their sexual lives, partners, and even their preferred sexual positions. Zahra left Iran in 2010 after being severely beaten up by her ex-husband, father, and brother for dating a woman. Five months after her arrival, she brought her ten-year-old son to Turkey with human smugglers. Zahra's RSD interview lasted five hours, because, as she said, the UNHCR found that it was unlikely for her to be lesbian because she had been married to a cisgender man in Iran and has a son. "I am very much offended by one of their questions. They asked me 'Do you have sex with your girlfriend in front of your son?' It pissed me off. I said to her [the officer] 'You have a kid, too. Do you have sex with your husband in front of your kid?' I did not care if she was angry with me or not. Her question broke my heart. Who do they think we are?"

Once the RSD process is completed successfully, the UNHCR refers refugees' files to the third countries' embassies and resettlement agencies. Thus, asylum applicants who are finally granted "recognized refugee" status enter yet another lengthy and ambiguous period of waiting, this time for their resettlement to a third country. Since the third countries are not legally obliged to accept refugees for resettlement, and are free to apply their own criteria for selection, refugees have to undergo additional interviews, medical examinations, and security screenings conducted by embassies and resettlement agencies in order to become eligible for resettlement. Like RSD, the resettlement process also lasts for years, during which time refugees do not know how long they have to wait, when their next interview would be, and when and where exactly they would be resettled. It is important to note that even after completing the third countries' cumbersome vetting processes, refugees might *still* not be eligible for resettlement, as the third countries often emphasize that "resettlement is not a right." The most worrisome example of this is the recent resettlement policies of the United States and Canada, which have stranded Iranian LGBTI refugees in Turkey for an undetermined period of time.

When I met Ehsan in the summer of 2016, he was waiting to be scheduled for his resettlement interview: he had lived in Turkey for twenty-five months, completed the parallel RSD procedures, and the UNHCR referred his file to the Canadian embassy. Ehsan already had two suitcases packed, which he stuffed with wool sweaters, down jackets, and gifts for his boyfriend who was a former refugee in Turkey and resettled to Canada in 2015. When I left Turkey for my studies in the United States at the end of the summer, we thought—hoped—that our next meeting would be in Canada. However, in late 2016, Ehsan and other LGBTI refugees waiting for resettlement in Canada began to receive phone calls from the UNHCR; they were advised to consider changing their resettlement country to the United States. While the exact reasons were not explained, the UNHCR told them that Canada would suspend the resettlement of Iranian LGBTI refugees until the end of 2017 and, thus, they would have to wait for one more year if they do not alter their resettlement country to the United States.

Ehsan had no choice but continue waiting for Canada in order to reunite with his boyfriend. Ali, a trans man in Denizli, received a similar phone call: "It has been thirteen months since I gained refugee status. Now I'm told that Canada is not open anymore, that its resettlement quotas are full. The UNHCR officer said, 'If you are in a hurry, we can send your file to America. If you want Canada, you will wait.' I said I can't go to America, because getting hormones is so difficult there." As with Ali, most of the trans refugees decided to continue waiting for Canada, since they thought Canada's refugee health care system would cover their expenses for hormone therapy and sex reassignment surgery.

In addition to their concerns about health care, many people also thought that Canada has better education and employment opportunities for refugees and greater tolerance for sexual and gender nonnormative people. Rosha, a lesbian refugee in her mid-thirties, explained to the UNHCR officer that she is afraid of xenophobia and homophobia in the United States, especially after the Pulse nightclub shooting in Orlando. "I told her, 'I was discriminated in Iran, and I am discriminated in Turkey. I suspect the situation would not be so different in America. I have been waiting for Canada for twenty-three months, and I don't mind waiting for a little bit longer. Because I don't want to live in fear in the next chapter of my life.'"

Some others, however, took the advice and changed their third country to the United States. Only a few weeks later, U.S. President Donald Trump issued an executive order titled, "Protecting the Nation from Foreign Terrorist Entry into the United States," which suspended entry into the United States of nationals from seven predominantly Muslim countries, among them Iran, where the vast majority of LGBTI refugees in Turkey are from.[9] The executive order immediately affected LGBTI refugees' resettlement: in the blink of an eye, the International Catholic Migration Commission (ICMC), a nongovernmental organization that conducts the vetting and resettlement of refugees to the United States, postponed all prescheduled interviews and canceled the airline tickets of those who were already authorized to be resettled. With the revised order, issued in March 2017, the cases of the latter group—those who were previously scheduled to be resettled to the United States—were suspended for 120 days, while those who were waiting for interview appointments had to continue waiting for an indefinite period of time.[10]

When I met a group of LGBTI refugees in Istanbul during the 2017 LGBTI Pride Week, the 120-day freeze on refugee settlement was coming to an end. Moein, a gay refugee and activist, was explaining to me that "the last year was the worst year for the LGBTI refugee community" and that "they all became suicidal after their cases were cancelled." Sarah, a lesbian refugee, interjected: "Suspended, not cancelled." Sarah thought that once the 120-day order is over, Moein would leave Turkey and she would continue her resettlement interviews with the ICMC. When I talked to Sarah three months later, in September, she was much less optimistic about her case: "It was easier to wait for those 120 days. Now it ended, but nothing has changed. ICMC called me to schedule an appointment for August, and I thought 'Here we go! Resettlement is starting again.' But two days later, they cancelled it without any explanation."

Executive orders have left Iranian LGBTI refugees in a legal limbo: although they had completed the cumbersome RSD and resettlement procedures and endured years of waiting, now they are suddenly denied entry to the United States. Remaining in a state of fear and uncertainty, with no assurances of how recent events would affect their resettlement, LGBTI refugees have also responded to the ban in various and creative ways. They have organized political protests, sit-ins, and press releases. Some of them have begun to establish connections with church groups in their satellite cities, so that as LGBTI *and* Christian refugees, they would be less affected by the Muslim ban. Those who have family members in the United States have requested a reassessment of their cases after the U.S. Supreme Court ruled that individuals who have "any bona fide relationship with a person or entity in the United States" can be exempted from the ban.[11] However, the Trump administration's heteronormative interpretation of a "bona fide relationship" has prevented unmarried queer refugees, whose partners reside in the United States, from requesting an exemption.[12]

Some refugees have also attempted to change their resettlement country to Canada, especially after Prime Minister Justin Trudeau announced that Canada "welcomes" those refugees who are not allowed to the United States.[13] This, however, has proved futile for two reasons: First, in order to benefit from this recent move of the Trudeau administration, refugees actually need to be rejected by the United States. However, none of the refugees waiting in Turkey have received an official rejection. Quite the contrary, most of them were already approved by the UNHCR and were due to be resettled in the United States.

Second, and more importantly, before Trump's executive orders came to force, the United States was swiftly becoming the only viable resettlement option for Iranian LGBTI refugees, since, as I mentioned before, Canada had begun to halt their resettlement. Ironically, after Trudeau's "#WelcomeToCanada" message, Canada's resettlement policies for Iranian LGBTI refugees have become even more restrictive. Those who had expressed their will to continue waiting for Canada, when the UNHCR advised them to change their resettlement country to the United States, received a second phone call in the summer of 2017, approximately ten months after the first phone call. Rosha recorded this conversation and graciously shared it with me:

> "We asked you to choose the United States for resettlement, and you refused to accept it, correct?" asked the UNHCR officer.
>
> "Yes, correct," said Rosha.
>
> "It has been ten months since then, and you are still waiting for Canada. Do you want to continue waiting like this?"
>
> "No, of course I don't want to wait any longer. Which country is open right now?"
>
> "Unfortunately, none of the countries are open now. But the US may open in two months [referring to the end of 120-day order]. If it opens, we can refer your file there."
>
> "I see," said Rosha after a slight pause, "If all countries are closed now, I'd prefer to continue waiting for Canada, since I have already waited for ten months."
>
> "Very well!" said the UNHCR officer, impatiently, almost threateningly, "If this is the case, please don't call us anymore to ask about your resettlement. If you don't choose the US now, we will also alter the resettlement status on your UNHCR page. Once it changes, you won't have the right to lodge a complaint, and your case will lose its priority."

Toward the end of the UNHCR officer's response, Rosha became visibly irritated and turned off the recording without waiting for the rest of the conversation. Then she opened her online UNHCR page, where her resettlement status read "not willing to be resettled." Next to "country for resettlement," there was only a dash, followed by the date of the call with the officer. Indeed, all LGBTI refugees, who refused to change their resettlement country to the United States, mentioned that their resettlement status and country information changed less than half an hour after the UNHCR's second phone call. Those who are marked as "not willing to be resettled" frequently send emails, write petitions, and make phone calls to the UNHCR. However, each time they are reminded that they have to wait indefinitely, since "they refused to choose a country when they were given the opportunity."

This is, of course, a deliberate misinterpretation and manipulation of the situation. First of all, as opposed to the discourse of "giving the opportunity of choosing a country," the UNHCR indeed forced refugees to choose the United States at a time when it halted Iranian refugees' resettlement and when it was not clear when its so-called travel ban would be over. Second, although refugees refused to be resettled to the United States, they did not reject the possibility of resettlement to another country. Quite the contrary, most of them expressed their willingness to go to *any* country that would accept them. For instance, Kiana, a lesbian refugee and mother of a 13-year-old daughter, had explained to the UNHCR officer that she cannot go to the United States because she is afraid that her ex-husband's family members, who live there, might try to take her daughter away from her. Kiana emphasized that she would accept any country other than the United States. However, similar to the conversation between Rosha and the UNHCR officer I quoted earlier, the UNHCR told her that none of the third countries were "open."

On a Thursday afternoon in March 2018, we were sitting in a café in Denizli, chatting, drinking tea, and smoking, while also listening to the UNHCR's on-hold piano music from Kiana's cell phone, which she put on the table in speaker mode. Kiana had waited on hold for hours, listening to the hold music's insipid piano track looping over and over again. Finally, she reached a UNHCR officer on the line, only to be advised to "stop sending emails" since, after all, "the UNHCR does not even open the emails of those who refused to choose a country, because their cases lost their priority." The all too familiar feelings of anger, frustration, and disappointment were vented into sarcastic jokes and dark humor. "Excuse me ma'am, which country are you waiting for?" asked Arman, a gay refugee, in a mockingly high-pitched voice. "I'm waiting for dash country. What about you?" said Kiana. "Me too. I've heard dash country is beautiful." I jumped into the conversation, "I've heard you guys don't want to be resettled. You must have liked Turkey so much." "Yeah, it's all good here. We love waiting in this café. The desserts are delicious, and the piano music is relaxing," said Rosha.

Experiences of those whose country for resettlement is reduced to a dash call into question Canada's supposedly progressive asylum laws and policies. As I am revising this chapter for publication three years after Trudeau's "#WelcomeTo-Canada" message, Ehsan, Ali, Rosha, Kiana, and Arman, among many others, are still waiting for a resettlement appointment from the Canadian embassy. Indeed, having realized that Canada has "unspokenly" retrenched the prospect for government-sponsored resettlement, Iranian LGBTI refugees have begun to increasingly reach out to Canadian queer NGOs and individuals, seeking "private sponsorship" as the only other available resettlement path. In this vein, I argue that Canada's recent "open-door" policy, at least in the context of Iranian LGBTI refugees, seems to be nothing more than lip service to recognizing Canada's commitments to the protection of refugees, international human rights, and sexual rights and freedoms. Practically speaking, Canada's doors are open only to a small minority consisting of rich, highly-educated, English-speaking, and well-connected refugees who could find "private sponsors" who would be willing to pay thousands of dollars for facilitating their resettlement to the country.

International asylum law is not a consistent and legally binding system of law. Rather, similar to Sally Engle Merry's description of international human rights law, it is a fragmentary mechanism that is "embodied in international conventions, but these take effect only when ratified by states."[14] The predicament of LGBTI refugees stranded in Turkey is exemplary of this fragmentary and inconsistent nature of the asylum system, which operates through constant negotiations with nation-states' immigration laws and geopolitical agendas. Since Turkey denies full refugee status to non-Europeans, Iranian LGBTI refugees have to navigate multiple asylum authorities, their sophisticated vetting procedures, and their shifting asylum policies and heightening border regulations. Furthermore, because the United States and Canada are increasingly reducing, or entirely cutting, the possibilities for their resettlement, refugees are stuck in Turkey for an undetermined time. Of critical importance here is that these lengthy and unpredictable asylum procedures leave LGBTI refugees vulnerable to multiple forms of violence. While waiting for an uncertain future, refugees also have to live difficult lives in small Turkish towns, where they do not have access to basic rights and protections.

Waiting/Living in Satellite Cities

Upon their registration, the Turkish state assigns refugees to one of the small Turkish towns, known as "satellite cities," located mostly in the interior of the country. Refugees have restricted mobility in satellite cities: they have to "sign-in" regularly at the local DGMM offices via iris recognition and fingerprint scanning, and any departure from their satellite city without travel permits issues by the DGMM puts them at the risk of deportation. Although Turkey does not confine refugees in camps or detention centers,[15] compulsory sign-ins, biometric identification technologies, and travel permits serve to police and control refugees' bodies and mobilities, blurring the boundary between the camp and the city.[16]

Although refugees have the right to work in Turkey, obtaining the necessary work permits is a costly and burdensome process, because they need an official job offer from an employer who would also be willing to pay for their health insurance. Thus, the vast majority of refugees work as day laborers in construction, manufacturing, and textile industries without work permits. Similar to the lack of basic rights and protections for unauthorized immigrant workers elsewhere, they are often exploited by their employers, work under inhumane conditions without any health insurance, and receive lower wages than citizens.[17] In addition to financial exploitation and physical insecurity, LGBTI refugees are doubly marginalized in the workplace due to their gender identity and sexual orientation. They are subjected to sexual harassment by their employers and coworkers and fired from their jobs when their LGBTI status becomes known. In both cases, they are left with no legal ground to file complaints because of the "informal" terms of employment. Ziba, a young lesbian woman, worked in a hotel in Kayseri for three months, where she was consistently harassed by her supervisor. In her second job in a furniture factory, she introduced herself as male in order to avoid sexual abuse. "Imagine you wear men's clothes, and they treat you as a man. But I am not as physically strong as a man. I carried heavy stuff, like 60–70 kilos [roughly 130–150 pounds]. It was very difficult. I got sick afterwards." When Ziba suffered a severe genital hemorrhage that prohibited her from working anymore, her employer refused to provide any compensation or medical care and instead, withheld her last monthly salary.

Because they do not have work permits or stable jobs in Turkey, and because most of them do not receive any help from their families, finding and maintaining housing constitutes a significant problem for LGBTI refugees. Neither the UNHCR nor the Turkish state provides any support for housing; refugees are expected to find a place on their own. In satellite cities, landlords often refuse to rent out their properties to "foreigners" or they take advantage of refugees' circumstances and demand nearly twice as much as the normal amount of rent. Furthermore, refugees often have to hide their gender identity or sexual orientation since they are denied housing or evicted from their apartments when their LGBTI identity is disclosed. Needless to say, these circumstances disproportionately affect trans refugees and refugees from working-class backgrounds. Sahar, a trans woman who is now resettled in Canada, told me that when she was first assigned to her satellite city, Kayseri, she could not afford to rent a room and had to sleep in a park for three weeks. "There were a lot of refugees sleeping in the park. I was afraid that they might rape me if they understand I am trans. I always slept with one eye open." She recalled those three weeks as "the most frightening and humiliating time of [her] life," and mentioned that each time she has to pass through that park she feels sick.

Finding housing and employment is relatively easier in bigger cities, such as Istanbul, Ankara, and Izmir, especially with the help of queer community networks and refugee rights and advocacy groups. Settling LGBTI refugees in remote satellite cities cuts them off from such support mechanisms and social networks. Indeed, instead of providing financial support, housing, employment, and access to adequate health care, the asylum system in Turkey forces refugees to fall back on informal means to solve "their own problems." In the almost entire absence of the Turkish state except as a policing force and the UNHCR except as a bureaucratic body that drags out the waiting process, LGBTI refugees often develop alternative support and solidarity networks to create more livable lives for themselves. Most of them stay with other LGBTI refugees, establish alternative families through queer rearticulations of heteronormative kinship ties, and form their own financial and emotional support mechanisms. Those who have been waiting for a significant period of time help the newcomers find housing and employment, inform them about complex asylum procedures, and prepare them for RSD interviews. These communal forms of sociality and solidarity, queer kinship ties, and everyday relations of love, care, and support seem to prove the truth of a Turkish immigration officer's bitter remark: "At the end of the day, a refugee's problems are solved by other refugees."

The predicament of LGBTI refugees caused by precarious housing and employment is often coupled with xenophobic, homophobic, and transphobic violence that they face in their everyday lives. In my long-term engagement with LGBTI refugees living in different Turkish towns, I have heard of numerous cases of verbal and physical harassment, sexual abuse, and even rape both by local townspeople and other refugees. Most of the time, refugees were afraid to approach the police for protection. When they reported sexual assault to the police, they rarely received an adequate response. Rather, the police turned a blind eye to their complaints, refused to investigate the reported crimes, or mocked and humiliated the refugees. In 2016, a trans woman was raped in Denizli. When her friends tried to report the rape, they were turned away by the police, because, as they contended, "she was both trans and refugee."

Although being LGBTI is not illegal or criminalized in Turkey, there is an institutionalized pattern of legal impunity and leniency for violence against women, queer and trans people, and sex workers.[18] Perpetrators who are charged with a violent act often benefit from the "unjust provocation" clause in Turkish Penal Code, which states that punishment will be reduced if a person commits an offense "with an affect of anger or asperity caused by the unjust act."[19] While the interpretation of what counts as "unjust provocation" is arbitrary at best, there are numerous cases in which judges considered proposing or initiating same-sex intercourse and sex work as unjust acts and, thus, reduced the sentences of those who killed gay men, transgender women, and sex workers.[20] Muhammed Wisam Sankari,[21] a Syrian gay refugee living in Istanbul, was kidnapped, raped, and violently murdered in July 2016. The court decided that the murderer committed the crime under "unjust provocation," since Wisam had sex with him without disclosing his positive HIV status.[22] In addition, because of the murderer's "good conduct" in the courtroom, the judge applied an extra "discretionary mitigation," reducing his penalty from life imprisonment to eighteen years.[23]

These acts of violence, coupled with institutionalized legal impunity and leniency, raise important questions: Who is worthy of protection by states, international human rights organizations, and the transnational asylum system? Which bodies are rendered vulnerable to violence? Whose lives and safety matter, and whose lives are cast as disposable and undeserving of protection? LGBTI refugees in Turkey occupy a precarious place that exists not only at the margins of citizenship, but also at the margins of a binary gender system and compulsory heterosexuality. While waiting, many of them continue to be subjected to the same violence and discrimination from which they fled. Their noncitizen status often exacerbates and justifies such violence and discrimination, whereas neither the UNHCR nor the states—Turkey, the United States, and Canada alike—offer effective rights and protections.

Being LGBTI *and* Noncitizen under the State of Emergency

The night the military coup attempt broke out in Turkey, Afsaneh, a trans woman who had gone to Istanbul for her resettlement interview, was stuck there amidst deadly armed conflicts. She was panicked, as she did not speak Turkish and had nowhere to go since all buses and flights from Istanbul were canceled. After her numerous attempts to reach out to the police for shelter and protection proved futile, she spent the night and the following day in the bus terminal until the buses started working again. The long and frightening hours Afsaneh had to spend in Istanbul is exemplary of how the recent political turmoil has rendered Turkey an unstable and insecure place for refugees, on the one hand, and how LGBTI refugees in Turkey are consistently denied effective protection, on the other.

As city centers of Ankara, Izmir, and Istanbul have endured a wave of bomb explosions and gun attacks since 2015, and military tanks rolled across streets during the coup attempt in July 2016, many refugees in Turkey, not unlike Turkish citizens, have been experiencing an unprecedented fear and sense of insecurity. "I am afraid of leaving my apartment. The idea of taking public transportation sends shivers up and down my spine," said Mehdi, a gay refugee who commutes from his satellite city to Istanbul for work. "It is not a safe place for you either [referring to me], but, at least, it is your home. Why are we here? Why does the UNHCR still keep refugees in Turkey?" Mehdi's question is indeed increasingly being shared by others: as Turkey has been failing to qualify as a "safe country," refugees have expressed frustration at the UNHCR and the third countries for stranding them in a country where their lives are at risk.

As Jasbir Puar rightly argues, the boundary that distinguishes those who are worthy of protection from those who are not becomes more legible at the times of crisis when nation states need to consolidate their borders by marking certain bodies as outsiders and excluding them from the nation and citizenship.[24] While LGBTI refugees in Turkey have always been at the margins of protection and recognition by the state, their lives have become more precarious in the wake of the 2016 coup attempt and the following state of emergency regime that lasted until 2018.[25] Most of them cautiously keep a low profile in satellite cities, worrying that the rising anti-immigrant hatred in Turkey would make them targets of xenophobic and homophobic attacks. They are also deeply concerned that the sharpening political divisions in Turkey's domestic and international politics would put them at risk of deportation.

Not an unreasonable worry at all. Although Turkey's asylum law recognizes the principle of *non-refoulement,* and thus guarantees the protection of refugees from being expelled to places where their lives are in danger, it also retains legally ambiguous definitions of the conditions for deportation. For instance, Article 54 states that those who "pose a threat to public order or public security or public health" will be subject to deportation, while leaving what counts as such threat open to the interpretation of administrative and law enforcement units.[26] With an emergency decree law established after the military coup attempt, the government has further expanded the scope for detention and deportation of refugees.[27]

In April 2017, Mitra, a trans woman who was working in a massage parlor in Denizli, was arrested by the police on the grounds of working without permission and "disrupting public order and safety." In response to the police charges, the Turkish DGMM ordered her to be deported to Iran.[28] After being held at the police station for three days, the DGMM sent Mitra to the Silivri deportation center in Istanbul, while rejecting her lawyers' request to obtain information on her case and whereabouts. After days of pressure from lawyers, national and diasporic queer organizations, and refugee rights and advocacy groups, the Constitutional Court ultimately suspended the deportation order. Since her release, however, Mitra's life has become a nightmare of bureaucracy, regulation, and surveillance. For two months, she had to make the 10-hour journey to Istanbul every two weeks in order to sign in at the police station. During this time, obtaining the necessary travel permits from the local DGMM office in her satellite city proved particularly difficult. And further, Mitra had trouble paying the bus fare for those biweekly commutes, especially given that she was no longer able to work.

Eventually, her lawyers managed to change Mitra's sign-in location from Istanbul to her satellite city, Denizli. But once they did this, the local DGMM increased her sign-in requirement to twice *per day*—a demand that did not allow Mitra the time to do anything aside from the commutes between her home and the DGMM office. Only after her lawyers' repeated requests, the DGMM reduced Mitra's compulsory sign-ins to once per day, indefinitely. I am writing this chapter almost a year after the Constitutional Court suspended Mitra's deportation order. In the meantime, she has had to move to a cheaper apartment at the outskirts of the city in order to afford rent without an income. Still, every day, she cycles for forty minutes from her new home to the local DGMM office, spends a few seconds before the iris scanner, and turns around to cycle the forty minutes back home.

Mitra's story points us to numerous inconsistencies embedded in the transnational asylum system. Refugees are stranded in Turkey for a long and indeterminate period of time, during which they do not have access to basic rights and services. They are expected to pay for their accommodation, food, health care, and travel expenses, but illegalized and criminalized for working. They need to travel to other cities for official paperwork, security checks, or resettlement interviews, but they cannot easily obtain necessary travel permits from the local authorities in their satellite cities.

Mitra's story also reveals the Turkish authorities' discretionary power in detaining and deporting refugees and the lack of effective judicial supervision over these decision-making processes. Indeed, the use of the "public order," "public safety," and "public health" discourses under the emergency rule has increased the discretionary power the administrative units hold and exacerbated their unlawful and arbitrary practices of detention and deportation. Although the government ended the state of emergency in 2018, many laws passed during the emergency rule have remained intact and effectively institutionalized the criminalization of LGBTI refugees. For instance, lesbian, bisexual, and trans women who work in nightclubs are being increasingly arrested for allegedly engaging in sex work and ordered to be deported for "disrupting public order and public health." Furthermore, social workers with whom I conducted follow-up interviews in 2020 remarked that police have begun to detain refugees living with HIV on the grounds of "threatening public health and public safety" and force them to sign "voluntary return" documents.

Indeed, experiences of LGBTI refugees waiting in Turkey call into crisis the liberatory promises of the international asylum system. The humanitarian organizations and North American countries depict LGBTI asylum as a continuous journey from home country to host country, past to future, and oppression to freedom. However, against the backdrop of the heightened securitization of borders of the Global North and the externalization of asylum that aims to keep asylum seekers offshore, even those LGBTI asylum applicants, who are granted recognized refugee status, wait in long-term limbo in so-called "transition countries" in the Global South.[29] Furthermore, while waiting, they face multiple forms of economic, sexual, and physical violence and live under the shadow of criminalization, detention, and deportation.

As the discriminatory policies of the United States and Canada have retrenched the prospect for resettlement, and as Turkey has been failing to qualify as a "safe country," Iranian LGBTI refugees are overwhelmed by the unsafe conditions of their present and uncertainty of their future. Yet, as I demonstrated in this chapter, they have also responded to these forms of violence and uncertainty in various ways, through humor and sarcasm, political and communal organizing, and alternative support and care networks. In this vein, while waiting serves to govern, demoralize, and demobilize refugees, LGBTI refugees have also turned it into an active time-space of emerging queer socialities and solidarities.

Notes

1. In this article, I use the term *LGBTI* as it is articulated by the UNHCR and refugees to refer to the people who lodge asylum claims on the grounds of sexual orientation and gender identity.

2. Kristen Sarah Biehl, "Governing through Uncertainty: Experiences of Being a Refugee in Turkey as a Country for Temporary Asylum," *Social Analysis* 59 (2015): 57–75; Elif Sarı and Cemile Gizem Dinçer, "Toward a New Asylum Regime in Turkey?" *Movements* 3, no.2 (2017).

3. Sima Shakhsari, "The Queer Time of Death: Temporality, Geopolitics, and Refugee Rights," *Sexualities* 17, no. 8 (2014): 1010.

4. Iranian Railroad for Queer Refugees, Annual Report 2017, http://irqr.net/2016/wp-content/uploads/2018/01/AnnualReport2017.pdf, 6.

5. The DGMM was founded in 2013 in line with Turkey's European Union accession negotiations. For a detailed analysis of the DGMM, see Sarı and Dinçer, "New Asylum Regime."

6. In September 2018, the UNHCR stopped its registration and RSD activities in Turkey. Since then, the DGMM has become the sole authority in registering and interviewing refugees. This chapter, however, examines the experiences of refugees who filed their asylum claims with both authorities prior to September 2018.

7. Convention and Protocol Relating to the Status of Refugees, Geneva, 2010, http://www.unhcr.org/en-us/3b66c2aa10, 14.

8. "Guidance Note on Refugee Claims Relating to Sexual Orientation and Gender Identity," *Geneva*, November 21, 2008, http://www.refworld.org/pdfid/48abd5660.pdf.

9. Exec. Order No. 13,769, 82 Fed. Reg. 8977 (Jan. 27, 2017).

10. Exec. Order No. 13,780, 82 Fed. Reg. 13209 (March 6, 2017).

11. *Trump v. Int. Refugee Assistance Project*, 582 U.S. (2017), 12.

12. Although unmarried same-sex couples can declare partnership before the UNHCR and the U.S. resettlement agency in order to expedite their resettlement and reunion, their partnership is not legally binding, and thus, it does not qualify as a "bona fide relationship." On the other hand, because one of the partners still waits in Turkey, where same-sex marriage is not legal, the same-sex couple in question cannot get married either, and thus, cannot benefit from the Trump administration's exemption.

13. Justin Trudeau, January 28, 2017 (12.20 pm), *Twitter*, https://twitter.com/justintrudeau/status/825438460265762816?lang=en.

14. Sally Engle Merry, *Human Rights and Gender Violence: Translating International Law into Local Justice* (Chicago: University of Chicago Press, 2006), 227.

15. Unlike all other refugees who wait in Turkey as "conditional refugees" to be resettled to a third country, the Turkish state applies a "temporary protection" regime to Syrian refugees. Accordingly, Syrian refugees can live in any city that they like, or they can settle in camps run by the Turkish Disaster and Emergency Management Presidency.

16. Sarı and Dinçer, "New Asylum Regime," 63.

17. Shakhsari, "Queer Time of Death," 1006.

18. Elif Sarı, "In Memory of Ozgecan Aslan: Sexual Violence and the Juridical System in Turkey," *Jadaliyya*, February 18, 2015, http://www.jadaliyya.com/pages/index/20876/in-memory-of-ozgecan-aslan_sexual-violence-and-the.

19. Turkish Penal Code, Law No. 5237, September 26, 2004, http://www.refworld.org/docid/4c447a5f2.html.

20. Meltem Ince Yenilmez, "Socio-Political Attitude towards Lesbians in Turkey," *Sexuality & Culture* 21, no. 1 (2016): 296; Aslı Zengin, "Sex under Intimate Siege: Transgender Lives, Law and State Violence in Contemporary Turkey" (PhD diss., University of Toronto, 2014), 223.,https://search-proquest-com.proxy.library.cornell.edu/docview/1810434770?accountid=10267.

21. In this chapter, I use only Wisam's original name and employ pseudonyms for other refugees.

22. Yıldız Tar, "Syrian Gay Refugee Killed in Istanbul," *Kaos GL*, August 4, 2016, http://kaosgl.org/page.php?id=22071.

23. Turkish Penal Code, Article 62 states that "In the evaluation of discretionary mitigation the following matters shall be taken into account: background, social relations, the behavior of the offender after the commission of the offence and during the trial period, and the potential effects of the penalty on the future of the offender."

24. Jasbir Puar, *Terrorist Assemblages: Homonationalism in Queer Times* (Durham, N.C.: Duke University Press, 2007), 3, 81.

25. Turkey ended the state of emergency in July 2018, two years after the coup attempt. The emergency decrees have resulted in the restriction of rights and freedoms, the arrest of over 40,000 people, and the shutdown of hundreds of media outlets and civil society organizations.

26. Law on Foreigners and International Protection," no. 6, April 2014, http://www.goc.gov.tr/files/files/eng_minikanun_5_son.pdf.

27. Decree Law 676, no. 29,782, *Official Gazette*, October 29, 2016, http://www.resmigazete.gov.tr/eskiler/2016/10/20161029-5.htm.

28. Aslı Alpar, "Deportation of Iranian Refugees Suspended Temporarily," *Kaos GL*, April 25, 2017, http://www.kaosgl.org/page.php?id=23613.

29. On refugees' experiences of waiting, see Melanie B. E. Griffiths, "Out of Time: The Temporal Uncertainties of Refused Asylum Seekers and Immigration Detainees," *Journal of Ethnic and Migration Studies* 40 (2014): 1991–2009; Ghassan Hage, ed. *Waiting* (Melbourne: Melbourne University Press, 2009); Antje Missbach, *Troubled Transit: Asylum Seekers Stuck in Indonesia* (Singapore: ISEAS-Yusof Ishak Institute, 2015). On the use of waiting as a governmental technology, see Biehl, "Governing through Uncertainty"; Juliet Peteet, "Camps and Enclaves: Palestine in the Time of Closure," *Journal of Refugee Studies* 29, no. 2 (2016): 208–228. On how refugees interpret and respond to waiting and uncertainty, see Michel Agier, translated by David Fernbach. *Managing the Undesirables: Refugee Camps and Humanitarian Government* (Cambridge, U.K.: Polity Press, 2011); Heath Caboth, *On the Doorstep of Europe: Asylum and Citizenship in Greece* (Philadelphia: University of Pennsylvania Press, 2014).

7

Welcome to Cuban Miami

Linking Place, Race, and Undocuqueer Youth Activism

RAFAEL RAMIREZ SOLÓRZANO

On Friday, January 1, 2010, Gaby Pacheco, Felipe Matos, Juan Rodriguez, and Carlos Roa laced up their new pairs of walking shoes at the foot of the Freedom Tower, a landmark building in downtown Miami. They were ready to embark on the Trail of Dreams. These four Miami Dade College students had spent their college years challenging the U.S. deportation machine and advocating for immigration reform. Except for Juan who had attained legal residency in 2008 after being undocumented for thirteen years, all were undocumented.[1] Gaby, Felipe, Juan, and Carlos walked for 120 consecutive days (four months), 16 to 24 miles per day, across several highways, and through more than 100 cities. They stopped at churches, family homes, and community centers. The walkers' hosts and supporters varied, depending on the space and place (i.e., rural, suburban, urban). Some days, they were joined by high school and college students, families, and immigrant and queer rights organizations; other days it was farmworkers, Maya day laborers, and Black Christian leaders. In Florida, many of the walkers on the Trail of Dreams were part of the statewide Florida Immigrant Coalition (FLIC). With only two months of planning and a dilapidated truck for storing food, water, first aid, clothes, and shelter, the walkers built a multiracial support network across the southeastern United States that would help them reach Washington, D.C.

South Florida is home to nearly half a million undocumented migrants. It is not surprising, then, that there has been a rise in undocumented youth resistance.[2] Using the Trail of Dreams as a starting point to explore the movement building of undocumented migrants in the South, this chapter demonstrates how the precise nature and content of their resistance is shaped by the history of their region. Undocumented/undocuqueer migrants, coalition partners, and allies risked their lives to walk across the U.S. South, protesting President Obama's lack of action on legislation granting legal status to undocumented migrants.[3] The walkers challenged the Obama administration's renewed commitment to the expansion of immigration enforcement, proliferation of immigrant detention sites, increased deportation and criminalization of migrants and communities of color, and repeated failures to pass the DREAM Act.[4]

What motivated Gaby, Carlos, Felipe, and Juan to walk across the southeastern United States into hostile anti-immigrant territory? In the summer of 2015, I interviewed migrant rights activists who participated in the Trail of Dreams and who were doing migrant rights activism at that time. By sharing their "story of the self" as they made their way north one city at a time, the walkers not only dispelled myths and stereotypes of migrants living in the United States, but they also revealed how racism structures and is structured by various landscapes and places.[5] Migrant rights advocates illustrate how Cuban Americans in Miami enact a Cuban immigrant power structure that upholds a regional racial hierarchy. As longtime migrant rights advocate, Maria, describes, this patriarchal Cuban immigrant power structure subordinates and racializes other people of color, particularly African Americans, undocumented/undocuqueer migrants, and Afro-Caribbean migrants, like Haitians and Afro-Cuban Americans. Drawing on a larger four-year multisited study of the Trail, which included 42 face-to-face interviews with undocumented/undocuqueer activists in the South, I demonstrate how place-based race dynamics inform activists' political protests and selves. Moreover, I show how the geography of the South has shaped the lived experiences of undocumented youth activists in Miami. As a social movement scholar, I argue that these dynamics have to be analyzed at a local scale. I begin this case study by illustrating the importance of racial legacies of Jim Crow, the Civil Rights Movement, Cuban incorporation, and migrant resistance in South Florida.

Regional Racial Formations and Intersectionality: My Analytic Modes

Few scholarly discussions of undocumented youth have examined how race, gender, sexuality, il/legality, and global histories of colonialism exacerbate experiences of racialization in the South. My approach is centered on a theoretical understanding of "race as socially constructed in relational ways, that is, in correspondence to other groups."[6] Here I turn to historian Natalia Molina, who describes a relational approach to the study of race as attending to how, when, and to what extent groups interact. She describes this method as a zooming-out process. Molina asks, "who else is (or was) present in or near the communities we study?"[7] Molina argues that examining Latinas/os/xs in relation to other racialized groups helps us develop a fuller understanding of how racial categories form and operate. I extend Molina's analysis to explore how we understand the cumulative experiences of the diverse present-day residents of Miami; how do their experiences and perspectives constitute a place-specific state of mind—a regional worldview that is grounded in a spatialized racial history of an area?[8] To answer this question, I draw on Wendy Cheng's regional racial formation framework, which pays attention to everyday actions and movements, as well as to localized knowledges within a specific place.

A place-specific racialization process requires a focus on gender and sexual difference. In *Race, Space, and the Law*, Sherene Razack shows not only how racial geographies are built but also how racial logics produce heterosexist and patriarchal spatial arrangements. Within critical race theory, Kimberlé Crenshaw articulates this analytic as intersectionality, the recognition of systems of domination (capitalism, white supremacy, patriarchy, heterosexism) as interlocking and mutually constitutive. By adopting an intersectional framework, I, too, "engage in a complex historical mapping of spaces and bodies in relation," identifying the interrelatedness of multiple systems of domination.[9] In the next section, I consider how Black migration and the demographic, political, economic, and social changes at the turn of the 20th century affected communities of color and provided the backdrop for a shifting color line in Miami.

Toward a Black/Non-Black Color Line in South Florida

Florida's colonial past, specifically the expanding U.S. economy, helped shape regional concepts of race. Florida's Indian country experienced numerous co-lonial transfers of power, including Spain, who claimed power over the region between 1513 to 1821.[10] By the time of the American Revolution (1776), the region had accumulated a population of multiethnic Creeks, known as Seminoles, who migrated to Florida to escape U.S. policies of removal and extermination.[11] Af-rican slaves fleeing enslavement soon joined them and coalesced into Seminole culture.[12] Moreover, South Florida has been linked to the Caribbean for centuries, and historian Julio Capó describes this relationship as evolving and changing throughout time, but never ceasing.

At the turn of the twentieth century, Miami was populated by a significant num-ber of African American and Afro-Caribbean migrants; hence, it has never seen itself as a typical southern city.[13] Between 1910 and 1920, the extension of a railroad system from Miami to the Florida Keys dramatically increased the number of Black Bahamians, who came to work in the burgeoning construction industry and service jobs in the emerging tourist city.[14] By 1920, Afro-Caribbean migrants constituted 52 percent of the city's Black population, which was 30 percent of Miami's total population (29,000).[15] Black migrants paved the way for future hotel and resort projects, laboring as skilled workers, maids, carpenters, laundresses, cooks, plasterers, hotel porters, tailors, and hack men at the railroad station.[16]

After the completion of the railroads and hotels and the arrival of tourists in the early twentieth century, racial disputes over spaces and places became a source of social unrest.[17] As Miami boosters praised Miami's beaches, attractions, weather, and progressivism, they simultaneously adopted a New South creed that promoted a new order "for whites only."[18] In *Black Miami in the Twentieth Century*, Marvin Dunn vividly describes the rise of white extremism that engulfed much of the South in the 1920s and 1930s.[19] The Klan led parades in full regalia through downtown Miami in 1926; Dunn notes that white extremists launched a campaign to discourage Black people from participating in an election in 1939.[20] Afterward, city officials chose to harden the racial boundaries between Black and white communities to lessen the city's hostile racial climate.[21] As a result, Black Miamians were crowded into a fifty-block area in the older historic neighborhoods outside the original city, which later became known as "Colored Town."[22] A look at the New Deal era of the 1930s where Blacks and whites worked together reveals how Colored Town became a geographical place and paradox that was part of the city's power equation that defined Blacks through labor inclusion, residential regulation, and racial exclusion. Moreover, the Black quarter was afflicted by poor sanitation facilities that later caused epidemics of influenza, yellow fever, and small pox.[23]

In spite of violence generated toward those who fought against racial segregation and anti-Black participation in the political process, racial coalitions still materialized. During the post–World War II period, an emerging new Black middle class, Black associations, and Black-Jewish coalitions indirectly confronted Jim Crow segregation by demanding equal access to the city's public leisure sites.[24] On November 25, 1959, a group of National Association for the Advancement of Colored People (NAACP) and Congress of Racial Equality (CORE) leaders led a wade-in at Crandon Beach—Miami's largest and most popular public park on the northern half of Key Biscayne.[25] Encircled by spectators, local media, and fifty police officers, a multiracial coalition of activists entered the water, swam, sunbathed, and peacefully integrated Crandon Beach through direct action. As Chanelle Rose argues, Miami's traditional Black leadership, during the Civil Rights Movement, strategically employed a "booster rhetoric of good race relations among the city's image-conscious white civic elite" to win racial concessions.[26] In tracing Miami's Black migration, burgeoning tourist industry, and Jim Crow segregation, not only do I reveal the city's official role in both hardening and loosening racial geographic boundaries, but I also show that historical context must be taken into account to understand the city's move toward a Black/non-Black color line.

Latinization and the Birth of the Pan-American Idea in Miami

To understand how Cuban Americans "made it in Miami" more quickly than any other Latino migrant community, one must understand Miami's early Pan-American vision of the city before the arrival of Cuban exiles. In exploring the long fight for civil rights and the evolution of race relations in one of the country's most popular tourist destinations, Rose reveals how the white establishment made changes to the established racial order to accommodate foreign tourists and trade with Latin America.[27] Since the early 1920s, white civic and business leaders had begun envisioning the City of Miami as a Pan-American metropolis. To better facilitate the transition from serving white, northern, and middle-class tourist clientele to Spanish-speaking visitors, white civic elites created multicultural programs and advertising that attracted new tourists. As early as 1926, the University of Miami, the largest private institution in the southeastern United States, promoted itself as the "Pan-American University" at its official opening on April 1st. The university created scholarships for Latin American students and offered English-language classes. Moreover, in 1930, the Pan American League (PAL) advocated locally and nationally for the City of Miami to improve international relations with Latin America. And, the chamber of commerce began promoting Miami as the "gateway to the Americas."

At this time, it became a financial liability for city leaders to maintain Jim Crow practices or arrest and jail civil rights leaders in a burgeoning southern metropolis that promoted itself as an exemplary city of cultural tolerance. These challenges influenced various white business leaders to modify Jim Crow practices for Spanish-speaking vacationers, which paved an alternative path in race relations, one that posited Spanish-speaking migrants as desirable unless they were Afro-Latina/o/x. Consequently, the state and civil society promoted a triracial order; one where Cuban exiles benefited from the city's Pan-American vision, economic opportunities, and the start of the civil rights movement, while African Americans continued to fight against racial discrimination. Thus, Cuban migration moved Miami into a new racial order.[28] Sociologist Eduardo Bonilla-Silva describes this order as a loosely organized racial stratum that is made up of white, honorary white, and the collective Black, or what some scholars would call a Latin American–like racial order.[29] For instance, in their highly nuanced account of how migrants have remade Miami, Alex Stepick, Guillermo Grenier, Max Castro and Marvin Dunn document that the city emerged as a de facto capital of Latin America; Miami became a city where light-skinned, immigrant, and Spanish-speaking residents dominate.[30] Beginning with the city's increasing number of Spanish-speakers after the Second World War, particularly tourists from the Caribbean and Latin America and continuing with the arrival of upper- and middle-class Cuban exiles in 1959, *los Marielitos* in 1980, and *los Balseros* from 1990 to 1994, Miami's racial landscape evidenced a triracial stratum.[31]

The expanding U.S. economy that recruited Miami's Black migrants remained, but the Latinization of Miami's post–Cuban Revolution of 1959 tells another story of incorporation and racialization of people of color. After Fidel Castro assumed power in Cuba in 1959, the U.S. government took a keen interest in providing financial assistance to early Cuban exiles, who tended to be white, well-educated, and from upper- and middle-class families. As an attempt to bolster its fight against communism, the U.S. government authorized the establishment of the Cuban Refugee Program (CRP) that included training for professionals, scholarships, and business loans for refugees.[32] In *Miami's Forgotten Cubans*, Alan Aja argues that Cuban engagement in direct acts of policy making would not only serve "as historical determinant in American racial formation and racialization," but also would support the structural scaffolding of Cuban lateral mobility, thus protecting the Cuban exiles from the type of racialization that other Latinas/os/ xs historically endured.[33] Unlike Mexican Americans and Puerto Ricans, who were subject to segregation and exclusion, the Cuban community benefited from direct government assistance and the start of the civil rights movement.[34] Stepick et al. note how, through the CRP, first-generation Cuban families in Miami "took advantage of it all," and would eventually exercise political control of the city of Miami.[35]

The increasing postwar Latinization of the city would have a profound impact on the evolution of Miami's race relations. Rose writes that the honorary white status accorded to some Spanish-speakers and Latina/o/x migrants, specifically light-skinned Cubans, would not change the racial oppression of African Americans, English-speaking Black Caribbeans, *los Marielitos*, and, later Haitian migrants. In fact, early Cuban exiles not only diminished the spotlight on local civil rights activities and attained various citizenship rights that were denied to Black Miamians but also fast-tracked the Latinization of the city. Cheng names this upward mobility as a racialized privilege—the ability to enjoy greater opportunity and expectations than Black Miamians as a racialized group.[36] In her revealing work on Cuban American gay culture in Miami, Susana Peña illustrates how dark skinned, queer migrant presence was silenced within the Latinization of the city.[37] The presence of gay men who came during the 1980 Mariel exodus from Cuba was delegitimized and met with much hostility from prominent Cuban Americans. Peña maintains that "the 1980 Mariel migration challenged the image of Cuban success and Cuban whiteness," and most likely challenged a homogeneous Cuban American heterosexist privilege.[38] Plotting out how Miami's racial relations and spatial arrangements have formed, mutated, and been maintained serves as an historical background that contextualizes the present racialization of undocumented Latinas/os/xs, Afro-Latina/o/x migrants (Afro-Cubans, Dominicans, Puerto Ricans), African Americans, and Afro-Caribbean migrants (Haitians, Bahamians).

In this cultural, social, and physical space, I encountered many youth and adults who were geographically far from their country of birth (Brazil, Colombia, Ecuador, Guatemala, Honduras, Mexico, Venezuela, to name a few). Their families migrated to the United States seeking physical, economic, and social security. They are part of Miami's high proportion of foreign-born residents, as is common in many major metropolitan areas in the United States.[39] Over 70 percent of the city's population are either first- or second-generation immigrants. In their book, *Making a Life in Multiethnic Miami*, Elizabeth M. Aranda, Sallie Hughes, and Elena Sabogal note that "Haitians [were] seeking political stability and economic security; and Mexicans and Central Americans fleeing both physical violence and economic insecurity. Venezuelans, some of whom describe themselves as political exiles, flee all the above."[40] For instance, in the 1980s, Nicaraguans, first fleeing the Sandinista regime and then the Contra War against the Sandinistas made Miami the largest Nicaraguan settlement in the United States. In the 1990s, Venezuelans sought refuge from political uncertainty and Colombians fled to Miami due to the drug war. Historically, Miami also has a significant influx of Caribbeans, primarily Black migrants.[41] Florida's Haitian population is the largest in the United States, surpassing the number of Haitians in the New York Metropolitan area.[42] All of the growth in the Black population in Miami-Dade County between 1980 and 2000 came from Black migration. As noted in a History of Miami Museum epigraph, titled "Miami: Gateway of the Americas," Miami is constantly reinventing itself through its racially diverse arrivers, and this "city of the future" would therefore provide us with an alternative racial relations paradigm that nurtures the ideology, materiality, and dreams of all its inhabitants and migrants.[43] In the next section, we shall see to what extent this major gateway to the United States incorporates undocumented/undocuqueer activists, known to many as DREAMers.

The Racialization of Undocuqueer Migrants in Miami in the 21st Century

In the summer of 2015, I interviewed FLIC partners and allies in order to understand how undocumented/undocuqueer activist resistance to detention and deportation in 2010 was connected to place-based racial dynamics. Sitting at dining room and conference room tables, and over Skype video calls, I listened to *testimonios* of how difficult it was growing up undocumented, queer, poor, and vulnerable to detention and deportation while organizing for migrant rights in Miami-Dade County. Over the course of five years, I have learned about the multiple ways undocumented Latinas/os/xs were experiencing and organizing for migrant rights and how deeply geography would figure into these accounts. Migrant rights organizers were affected by those with whom they shared space. In their interviews, they reflected on these moments and shared how it was difficult to advocate for all migrants, especially those who were undocumented, queer, poor, and Black.

That summer, I had the opportunity to interview Felipe Sousa-Rodriguez and Isabel Rodriguez, both migrant rights activists, who were queer and the only couple on the Trail of Dreams. Felipe was born in Rio de Janeiro, Brazil, and arrived in the United States at the age of two; Isabel was born in Bogota, Colombia, and came in 1996 when ze was six. In 2009, both Felipe and Isabel were living in Little Havana and attending Miami Dade College.[44] During the interview Isabel recalls their elementary school years and learning how to speak English: "It was not a difficult transition for me or my family because Miami has a majority Hispanic population. We were surrounded by Peruvian, Venezuelan, Mexican, Colombian and other immigrant communities." Isabel, a light-skinned migrant, was able to smoothly transition into school and learn English because ze was able to benefit from the Latinization of Miami and its bilingual culture. Similarly, Felipe shares how he assimilated into Miami, which he describes as a unique place:

So, I just integrated myself in an interesting way. Spanish is not my first language. I speak Portuguese as my first language. I learned Spanish really quickly to be like everyone else. It's sort of a weird experience compared to most people, because most people go to a place that is English dominated. I went to a place that Spanish is a dominant language.

Both Isabel and Felipe describe Miami's bilingual culture as a positive experience. They also note that the dominance of Spanish over English in Miami produces racial dynamics distinct from other urban cities in the United States. Isabel and Felipe did not experience linguistic stigmatization that most Latinos confront in the United States.[45] In fact, for Felipe, it was a priority to learn Spanish quickly over English in order to fit in to Little Havana. Having made an investment to learn Spanish also speaks to Felipe's various survival strategies:

You know something that happens that is a very Miami thing. I've been doing immigrant rights for a long time, and I've noticed, what people try to do is to assimilate. Assimilation is a process of survival, you assimilate so you can survive so you can go under the radar so you don't get caught as an undocumented person. In Miami people try to be Cuban or try to look Cuban. Because if you're Cuban you have papers. . . . For many years, people would just call me Cuban, and I would be like, "yeah, that's totally, who I am," that's how was able to, you know, not be get caught by the police.

Complicating theories of immigrant incorporation and assimilation that involve a "default to whiteness," the adoption of customs and ways of white American culture in order to pass as a U.S. American citizen, Felipe's strategy reveals the advantages of accessing the honorary white racial privilege accorded to light-skinned Cubans. In Miami, light-skinned Cubans "have papers," legal status and are fully recognized within society as white.[46] Aware of Cuban legal status in Miami-Dade County, Felipe admits to identifying himself as Cuban as a survival tactic when coming into contact with police. Additionally, during his interview, he shares how he learned to emphasize his last name, Matos, because it was a common Cuban surname. Although Isabel and Felipe can circumnavigate Miami's triracial stratum through surname, language, and light-skin privilege, there are limits. In the following conversation, Felipe shares how his "Latinidad was embraced, but my undocumented status and my queerness was not:"

> If you ever go to Miami, it is basically all Latinos right, because it's run by Cubans. The city has had several Cuban leaders, even the mayor is Cuban, it's always like that right. Being an immigrant was not a big deal, being an undocumented immigrant was a big deal but no one knew that I was undocumented because I look like most people. Being queer was different, it felt different to me. I had a real hard time coming out as a queer person, because Miami is a conservative city, people talk about LGBTQ people in Miami all the time but really that's a misconception. I think people could be free to be queer in South Beach, but most of them are tourists. I was living and breathing in the real world, living in a low-income neighborhood, whatever.

The security of being Latino in Miami has its physical boundaries, especially for those advocating for undocumented/undocuqueer youth within Miami's power structure. As someone who has "been doing immigrant rights long time," Felipe quickly learned the strategies undocuqueer youth needed to adopt to "pass" and organize within Miami's conservative political landscape. Additionally, he reveals Miami's fabricated myth of an international tourist hub that embraces gender and sexual difference. For Felipe, the freedom to be queer is highly spatialized— it exists in South Beach and is only accorded to tourists. As he states, for those "living and breathing in the real world, living in a low-income neighborhood [Little Havana]," coming out as undocumented and queer was not acceptable. For undocumented/undocuqueer activists, the dynamics of illegality are not tied to race and legal status only, but also to spatial and living arrangements. Felipe's feelings of difference and adversity living in Little Havana is telling of the complex mapping of spaces and bodies in relation to one another. It reflects how Miami, specifically Little Havana, was also a contested migrant enclave at the intersection of the city's investment in whiteness, heterosexism, and patriarchal spatial arrangements.

The Undocumented Youth Movement and the Cuban Immigrant Power Structure

When undocumented/undocuqueer activists reflect on their successes within the fight for migrant rights in South Florida, they disclose how growing up in a hostile environment—confronting a place-specific U.S. racial structure—became the impetus to fight against the deportations and detention of undocumented migrants. The U.S. South has a long history of abusive federal immigration enforcement that has produced a hostile political climate in which many Latino immigrants live and work.[47] In fact, next to California, Florida is home to some of the most militant nativist activists (Neo-Nazi, White nationalist, Neo-confederate, Ku Klux Klan, anti-LGBT, -Muslim and -immigrant groups) in the country and even has its own anti-immigrant political party.[48] Undocumented youth activists in Miami face similar distresses caused by their undocumented status as their counterparts across the United States; their lives are also increasingly marked by a "juridical status and a sociopolitical condition that carries exclusionary and stigmatizing consequences."[49] Yet, as I have demonstrated, undocumented/undocuqueer youth face specific histories of incorporation that have shaped their otherness and, thus, their deportability in relation to other racialized groups. Those whom I met in Miami—coalition leaders, youth, and political activists who were undocumented/undocuqueer—did not passively give into Miami's patriarchal Cuban immigrant political structure. On the contrary, most of them did what they could to navigate and push back against interior immigration enforcement and racial and heteronormative logics that restricted their mobility and kept them apart.

Latina/o/x resistance in Miami is neither unusual nor unexpected but for undocumented/undocuqueer Latina/o/x youth to walk 1,500 miles across the South, afraid of detention and deportation but doing it anyway was especially historic locally, regionally, and nationally. I met with Maria, executive director of FLIC, at her office, which overlooks Biscayne Bay. Maria has been FLIC's executive director for over twelve years and has facilitated a statewide coalition of more than sixty-five–member organizations and over one hundred allies who envision a new Florida based on inclusion and equality, without racism and exclusion, where immigrants can live and love without fear.[50] It was at Students Working for Equal Rights (SWER), FLIC's youth organizing arm, where Carlos, Felipe, Gaby, and Isabel met. During my visit, Maria shared her experience of what it means to fight for migrant rights in Miami:

> We can talk about Miami, it's a different story. Doing immigrant rights in Miami is very challenging because there is an immigrant power structure, a Cuban immigrant power structure. . . . Either white or Black people feel displaced by immigrants so it's a very different dynamic, it's not Black or white, like it might be on other parts of the South, [where] it's a white power structure and a Black resistance. . . . Miami is very different. But, Miami is very different from the rest, every county has its own context, it varies a great deal.

Maria's description of Miami's political power structure echoes Felipe's experience— a city run by privileged, largely light-skinned Cuban Americans. Cuban Americans have gained political power; hold federal, state, county, and citywide elected offices; and have largely embraced the city's conservative heterosexist political landscape. As Capó notes, Miami Cubans joined forces with other conservatives advocating for "prayer in schools and against busing, abortion, gun control, and what we now associate with lesbian, gay, bisexual, and transgender rights," and have played a key role in the emerging "New Right."[51] Therefore, for Maria, who has been organizing in Miami since the 1990s, Cuban political enfranchisement has built a dynamic, which she also calls a "Cuban immigrant power structure." Maria maps power relations, explaining who is on top, below, and in-between, and how they are related. As a result of this structure, she describes Miami as very distinct from the rest of the Deep South, which has been studied as having a Black and white racial binary. So, how do undocumented/undocuqueer youth organize within Miami's Cuban immigrant power structure? How are they successful in challenging and reconfiguring what Aja calls "the state's encouragement of the reproduction of whiteness and anti-Blackness in the Miami Cuban community"?[52]

During our interview, Maria discloses the underside of bipartisan political organizing within the migrant rights movement in Miami. When discussing immigrant youth issues, Maria admits that activists in Miami have created "a lot of political space" by adopting a narrative that posits "immigrant youth [as] deserving immigrants." Migrant rights leaders in Miami are not alone: several migrant rights organizations across the United States have adopted campaign frames that describe immigrant youth as DREAMers. This local DREAMer narrative, which lauded undocumented youth as ideal protocitizens—good, hardworking, competitive, self-sufficient, entrepreneurial, and deserving—allowed them to reach across the political aisle and access Miami's political "conservative mindset."[53] Indeed, for undocumented/undocuqueer Latina/o/x migrants to achieve personhood in

Miami, they had to perform a racial model-minority identity along neoliberal, racial, and gendered lines. Although these tactics may be opening political space, political scientist Amalia Pallares argues that these racial model-minority narratives, as political frames, are troubling because they privilege human capital and ignore the state's role in promoting the integration of some migrants over others.[54] Similarly, Maylei Blackwell and Edward J. McCaughan illustrate how within the migrant rights movement, "we see moves with the limited acceptance of undocumented youth as DREAMers, while the US government rejects their parents or other members of the undocumented migrant communities."[55]

In addition, when I interviewed Isabel, ze revealed a Cuban immigrant power structure that supported a merit-based system of immigration and punishment, "such as anyone that has committed a crime needs to be punished and they don't deserve to be Americans." Isabel further describes the sociopolitical condition that undocuqueer youth activists have to confront in Miami:

> You have to negotiate a space with conservative Latinos [Cubans], because they believe in immigrant rights but they believe in legal migration and so they want to create legal processes for people to follow and they also believe in a lot of punitive stuff. Such as anyone that has committed a crime needs to be punished and they don't deserve to be Americans. So a lot of those conservative mindsets, you kind of wrestle with it; I think the DREAMer movement was successful in Miami because across party lines a lot of people love supporting the bright overachievers in the family.

For Isabel, the values and immigration policy stances of Miami's leaders suggest a punitive model. For instance, those who entered the United States without being inspected and/or admitted are not fit or deserving enough to be U.S. citizens because they committed a criminal act. Consequently, ze narrates how undocumented/undocuqueer activists in Miami had to uplift "the bright over-achievers in the family," aligning with mainstream strategies being implemented at the national level. Isabel's narration of inclusion for undocumented/undocuqueer activists in Miami marks a regional difference that intersects with its triracial landscape while others navigated a biracial order. Unlike their West Coast counterparts in California, who drew support from Latina/o politicians, Cuban Republican politicians shifted their stance on immigration to win consensus within the Republican party in Washington D.C. In addition, Isabel describes a move toward an "in-between" status as honorary whites that subordinates a collective Black community (African Americans, and Afro-Caribbeans). In fact, this dominant narrative within the migrant rights movement rendered the Black and non-Latina/o/x migrant experience invisible.[56] To counter their invisibility, however, a multigenerational network of undocumented Black people, called the UndocuBlack Network, held a first-of-its kind convening of undocumented Black people in Miami, Florida, in 2016.[57]

Additionally, within the context of my interviews, Isabel and Felipe shared how these narratives also led to the silencing of queer bodies at different moments within organizing campaigns, such as the Trail of Dreams. On this occasion, they discussed and were encouraged to keep their relationship discreet because it would be distracting to the overall strategy and draw more violence toward them. As I have noted, the freedom to be a queer Latina/o/x was a highly spatialized experience, not only residentially but politically in Miami. For undocumented/undocuqueer activists living and organizing in Little Havana, the convergence of migrant rights and queer rights was not acceptable. Isabel's reflection on the DREAMer narrative must be situated within Miami's legacy of white supremacy, which not only privileges new and emerging whites (Cubans, light-skinned, privileged Latinxs) but also perpetuates historical racial segregation of places and spaces by supporting discriminatory policies and practices that advantage only whites. Research by Aranda et al. documents that "Cuban discrimination" or intra-ethnic animosity might be linked to patterns of residential and occupational segregation within the city.[58] Since Cubans benefit from an honorary whiteness, their immigrant power structure is upheld through its alignment with the state's reproduction of whiteness, legality, heteronormativity, and anti-Blackness in Miami.

Scholars and Activists Must Place an Importance on Space and Place

Despite activists' criticism of the DREAMer narrative and Miami's Cuban immigrant power structure, the fight for migrant rights has exhibited contradictions when organizing community and bipartisan support. As Isabel and Maria have demonstrated, organizations and leaders have made campaign errors and have had to backpedal. This being said, there also exist key moments where political campaign moves and coalition-building aim not to exacerbate racialized experiences between communities of color but rather to undermine place-specific systems of domination-subordination. For instance, FLIC's youth organizing campaigns and statewide coalition are grounded in inclusion and equality. Moreover, we see it within migrant rights activists' adoption of a political frame to build local bipartisan support for undocumented youth, and undocumented/undocuqueer youth participation in the Trail of Dreams. Indeed, we even see this in the first convening of the UndocuBlack Network that centered an intersectional approach within the fight for migrant rights that centers Blackness, and queerness.

When I began my research, I was interested in how undocumented/undocuqueer youth were redefining the migrant rights movement in the 21st century. I discovered that these testimonios illuminated lived experiences and political activisms that spoke to a place-specific racialization and heteronormative project that nurtured the incorporation of some Latina/o/x migrants over others. For example, I understand now that Miami's Cuban immigrant power structure cannot be understood along a Black and white color line. As I have demonstrated, Miami's triracial order—also known as Latin American–like racial order—complicates how race, gender, sexuality, and legal status work in the United States. In the cases of Maria, Felipe, and Isabel, their experiences of negotiation with the political climate of Miami must then be understood in relation to the city's legacy of upholding white supremacy by offering light skinned, upper- and middle-class Cuban Americans and DREAMers honorary white status, while simultaneously rendering migrants from the African diaspora and African Americans invisible. Moreover, we must keep in mind that the processes through which people became white, Black, undocumented, and Latina/o/x in the United States is intricately tied to the ongoing dispossession of Indigenous peoples.[59]

Second, not only do I agree with ethnic studies scholars and cultural geographers whose research is devoted to writing a thorough account of the history of people of color, but I would make the case that we must continue to write histories of resistance that privilege a relational and regional approach to studying racialization.[60] Doing so allows us to understand how the fight against deportation and detention is shaped by local history and localized knowledge. Unquestionably, recognizing who migrant rights activists meet and encounter is critical to grasping their political consciousness and activism. Based on the experiences and perspectives of activists in Miami, this chapter argued the need to recognize everyday landscapes as crucial terrains through which racial hierarchies are challenged. In future work, scholars must study how Latina/o/x resistance—like the Trail of Dreams—emerges from, reflects, and challenges racial formation dynamics.

Finally, I not only encourage alternative approaches that study social movements and undocumented/undocuqueer racialization as deeply spatial, but I also show the need for building movements and political tactics and strategies that are cross-sector, multi-issue, and place-based. This not only means the need to direct migrant rights activism to local and state contexts, which was the case after the inability to pass the DREAM Act in 2010, but also a commitment to develop local campaigns that address the spatialized racial history of an area. Indeed, this means incorporating local knowledges within a specific place-based activism. Put another way, I wish to underscore how we need to avoid exacerbating racialized experiences of erasure of Indigenous communities and Blackness within migrant rights activism. Addressing the multiplicity of histories as a key aspect within developing political campaigns pushes social movement scholars and activists to center ways of knowing that offer alternative worldviews to resist white supremacy.

Notes

1. Since 2010, Felipe Matos now goes by Felipe Sousa-Rodriguez and Juan Rodriguez has changed their name to Isabel Souza-Rodriguez. During an interview, Isabel shared how hir name change was part of affirming hir gender nonconforming identity. We agreed that it was ok to use hir previous name in order to document their involvement in the Trail as Juan or when others cite them as Juan. As for pronouns, it was agreed to the following self-identification pronouns—she, he, ze, hir, they. This research was funded by the University of California, Los Angeles's Institute of American Cultures and the Chicano Studies Research Center, and the James Weldon Johnson Center at Emory University.

2. According to a report by the Pew Research Center about 450,000 undocumented migrants reside in the greater Miami–Fort Lauderdale–West Palm Beach area and about 55,000 live in the city of Miami alone: "20 metro areas are home to six-in-ten unauthorized immigrants in U.S." Pew Research Center, http://www.pewresearch.org/fact-tank/2017/02/09/us-metro-areas-unauthorized-immigrants.

3. I use the category of *undocumented/undocuqueer* to denote the variety of queer identities included in the category of undocumented migrant. It signals the sexuality, gender queer, and multiplicity within people's lives, and captures a potent network of queer migrant leaders. I also use the word *migrant* because it draws attention to a mobile relationship in which people have embodied within their host country—they plan on returning to their host country or come from families in which people have migrated between two nation-states for generations. I use the word *immigrant* when citing others who use this term, or as a generic reference to all people who have immigrated to the United States. Eithne Luibhéid and Lionel Cantú Jr., *Queer Migrations: Sexuality, U.S. Citizenship, and Border Crossings* (Minneapolis: University of Minnesota Press, 2005); Ramon Grosfoguel, Nelson Maldonado Torres, and Jose David Saldivar, *Latin@s in the World-system: Decolonization Struggles in the Twenty-first Century U.S. Empire* (New York: Routledge, 2006); Alfonso Gonzales, *Reform without Justice: Latino Migrant Politics and the Homeland Security State* (New York: Oxford University Press, 2014); Julia Preston, "To Overhaul Immigration, Advocates Alter Tactics," *New York Times*, January 1, 2010.

4. In a *New York Times* op-ed, Gaby Pacheco describes how the Trail was in part inspired by the Civil Rights Movement and was "a memorial to the Native Americans who died in the Trail of Tears." Gaby Pacheco, "What the Dreamers Can Teach the Parkland Kids," *New York Times*, March 17, 2018.

5. In multiple interviews, organizers spoke about attending trainings where they learned "the story of the self." Developed by sociologist Marshall Ganz, "The Power of Story in Social Movements," centralizes storytelling in political activism because it constructs agency, shapes identity, and motivates action.

6. Natalia Molina, *How Race Is Made in America: Immigration, Citizenship, and the Historical Power of Racial Scripts* (Berkeley: University of California Press, 2014), 3.

7. Natalia Molina, "Examining Chicana/o History through a Relational Lens," *Pacific Historical Review* 82, no. 4 (2013): 522.

8. Wendy Cheng, *The Changs Next Door to the Díazes: Remapping Race in Suburban California* (Minneapolis: University of Minnesota Press, 2013), 3, 21; Perla M. Guerrero, "Chicana/o History as Southern History: Race, Place, and the US South," in *A Promising Problem: The New Chicana/o History*, ed. Carlos Kevin Blanton (Austin: University of Texas Press, 2016), 94–98.

9. Sherene H. Razack, "Introduction: When Place Becomes Race," in *Race, Space, and the Law: Unmapping a White Settler Society*, ed. Sherene H. Razack (Toronto: Between the Lines, 2002), 5; Kimberlé Crenshaw, "Mapping the Margins: Intersectionality, Identity Politics, and Violence against Women of Color," *Stanford Law Review* 43, no. 6 (1991): 1245–1246.

10. Julio Capó Jr., *Welcome to Fairyland: Queer Miami Before 1940* (Chapel Hill: University of North Carolina Press, 2017), 27.

11. Ibid.

12. Patrick Riordan, "Finding Freedom in Florida: Native Peoples, African Americans, and Colonists, 1670–1816," *Florida Historical Quarterly*, 75, no. 1 (1996): 35. Equally important, the Seminole wars of the 19th century would result in the violent relocation of thousands of Indigenous people to Creek territory west of the Mississippi River. Capó, *Welcome to Fairyland*, 28.

13. Chanelle Rose, *The Struggle for Black Freedom in Miami: Civil Rights and America's Tourist Paradise, 1896–1968* (Baton Rouge: Louisiana State University Press, 2015). *The Struggle* represents one of the most recent studies of Blacks and the civil rights movement in South Florida.

14. Ibid., 19.

15. Ibid. 28.

16. Ibid. 19.

17. Ibid.

18. Paul Gaston, *The New South Creed: A Study in Southern Mythmaking* (Montgomery, Ala.: New South Books, 1970).

19. Marvin Dunn, *Black Miami in the Twentieth Century* (Gainesville: University Press of Florida, 1997).

20. Ibid., 117, 193.

21. Dunn details how residential conflicts became progressively common when Black neighborhoods grew. To avert clashes, whites called for more residential restrictions and proposed a physical color line—segregation laws that kept neighborhoods segregated from each other. See also: Rose, *The Struggle for Black Freedom*, 59.

22. Colored Town was originally founded during the Jim Crow era of the late nineteenth through the mid–twentieth century. It was once the preeminent and historic center for commerce for the Black community. Presently the neighborhood is called Overtown. Raymond A. Mohl, "Whitening Miami: Race, Housing, and Government Policy in Twentieth-Century Dade County," *Florida Historical Quarterly* 79, no. 3 (2001): 319–345.

23. Dunn, *Black Miami in the Twentieth Century*, 61.

24. Ibid., 171.

25. Rose, *Struggle for Black Freedom*, 75.

26. Ibid. 77.

27. *Ibid.*, 75.

28. Several other scholars document how Miami's new racial order between the late 1960s and the 1980s caused Black discontent and racial uprisings. See Rose, *Struggle for Black Freedom*, 64; Alex Stepick, Guillermo Grenier, Max Castro, and Marvin Dunn, *This Land Is Our Land; Immigrants and Power in Miami* (Berkeley: University of California Press, 2003); Alan A. Aja, *Miami's Forgotten Cubans: Race, Racialization, and the Miami Afro-Cuban Experience*, (Brooklyn: Palgrave Macmillan, 2016); Louis Marcelin "Identity, Power, and Socioracial Hierarchies Among Haitian Immigrants in Florida," in *Neither Enemies Nor Friends*, ed. Anani Dzidizienyo and Suzanne Oboler (New York: Palgrave Macmillan, 2005).

29. Eduardo Bonilla-Silva, "From Bi-Racial to Tri-Racial: Towards a New System of Racial Stratification in the USA," *Ethnic and Racial Studies* 27, no. 6 (2006): 931–950. Moreover, Aja describes this tri-racial as dominated by emerging whites (Cubans, light-skinned, privileged Latinx), a collective Black community (African Americans, Afro-Caribbeans, and earlier Afro-Latinx arrivals), and the other a middle groups of mixed-race, racialized communities of color. *Miami's Forgotten Cubans*, 13.

30. Stepick et al., *This Land Is Our Land*, 20.

31. Los Marielitos were a new wave Cuban refugees from 1979 to 1980, mostly Blacks and of mixed race. Los Balseros came in rafts from 1990 to 1994 and under new immigration law, signed in 1995, known as the "wet foot/dry foot" policy were allowed to apply for refugee status if they reached the U.S. shores. See also: Dunn, *Black Miami in the Twentieth Century*; Rose, *The Struggle for Black Freedom*; Stepick et al., *This Land Is Our Land*.

32. Stepick et al., *This Land Is Our Land*, 39.

33. Aja, *Miami's Forgotten Cubans*, 7. See Roman Grosfoguel, "Race and Ethnicity or Racialized Ethnicities? Identities within Global Coloniality," *Ethnicities* 4, no. 3 (2004): 315–336; Michael Omi and Howard Winant, *Racial Formation in the United States* (New York: Routledge, 2015).

34. Lisa García Bedolla, *Latino Politics* (Cambridge: Polity, 2009), 148–150.

35. Stepick et al., *This Land Is Our Land*, 9.

36. Cheng, *The Changs Next Door to the Díazes*, 16.

37. Susana Peña, *Oye Loca: From the Mariel Boatlift to Gay Cuban Miami* (Minneapolis: University of Minnesota Press, 2013).

38. Ibid. xxv–xxvi.

39. Stepick et al., *This Land Is Our Land*, 19.

40. Elizabeth Aranda, Sallie Hughes, and Elena Sabogal, *Making a Life in Multiethnic Miami: Immigration and the Rise of a Global City* (Boulder, Colo.: Lynne Rienner Publishers, 2014), 22.

41. Dunn, *Black Miami in the Twentieth Century*, 51.

42. Stepick et al., *This Land Is Our Land*, 22.

43. This epigraph is part of a permanent exhibit, "Tropical Dreams: A People's History of South Florida," at the History of Miami Museum, which explores South Florida history from prehistoric times to the present day.

44. In an interview with Felipe, he shares how Miami Dade College "in many ways still is the hub of undocumented youth," and was a place where their organizing efforts were supported.

45. Flores-González notes how Latino millennials confront racial linguistic aggressions, which casts them as linguistically incompetent. Nilda Flores-González, *Citizens but Not Americans: Race and Belonging among Latino Millennials* (New York: New York University Press, 2017), 38.

46. Omi and Winant, *Racial Formation in the United States*, 29.

47. Chris Zepeda-Millán, "Weapons of the (Not So) Weak: Immigrant Mass Mobilization in the US South," *Critical Sociology* 42, no. 2 (2016): 1–19. Julie M. Weise, *Corazón de Dixie: Mexicanos in the U.S. South since 1910* (Chapel Hill: University of North Carolina Press, 2015), 156–165. Guerrero, "Chicana/o History as Southern History," 98.

48. Zepeda-Millán, "Weapons of the (Not So) Weak," 4; Heidi Beirich and Susy Buchanan, "2017, The Year in Hate and Extremism" *Intelligence Report* (Montgomery, Ala.: Southern Poverty Law Center, 2018), https://www.splcenter.org/fighting-hate/intelligence-report/2018/2017-year-hate-and-extremism.

49. Roberto Gonzales, *Lives in Limbo: Undocumented and Coming of Age in America* (Oakland: University of California Press, 2016), 99.

50. On their organization website, FLIC describes their organization as a hub for a bold, agile, and strategic multiracial, intergenerational social movement. "Mission and History," Florida Immigrant Coalition, http://www.floridaimmigrant.org/mission-history.

51. Capó, *Welcome to Fairyland*, 288.

52. Ibid., 7. Aja, *Miami's Forgotten Cubans*, 7.

53. For discussions on undocumented migrants as neoliberal subjects, see Amalia Pallares, *Family Activism: Immigrant Struggles and the Politics of Noncitizenship* (New Brunswick, N.J.: Rutgers University Press, 2014); Leo Chavez, *The Latino Threat: Constructing Immigrants, Citizens, and the Nation* (Redwood City: Stanford University Press, 2013). For discussion on how migration politics and queer politics meet in ways that challenge neoliberal projects of inclusion, see Karma R. Chávez, *Queer Migration Politics: Activist Rhetoric and Coalitional Possibilities* (Urbana: University of Illinois Press, 2013).

54. Pallares, *Family Activism*, 105.

55. Maylei Blackwell and Edward J. McCaughan, eds., "Editors' Introduction: New Dimensions in the Scholarship and Practice of Mexican and Chicanx Social Movements," *Social Justice* 42, nos. 3–4 (2015): 1–9.

56. In many accounts, the DREAMer narrative as a national political frame, centered the young undocumented migrant as a Latina/o youth from Mexico or Central America.

57. On January 15–17, 2016, the UndocuBlack Network (UBN) held their first Undocumented and Black Convening in Miami, Florida. Over 65 Black undocumented persons participated in establishing a network that would advocate for the undocuBlack com-

munity and uplift its stories. There are a reported 619,000 undocumented Black migrants in the United States mostly from the Caribbean, and Northern and sub-Saharan Africa. "About Us," UndocuBlack Network, http://www.undocublack.org/asdasd.

58. Aranda et al., *Making a Life in Multiethnic Miami*, 199–238.

59. Laura Pulido, "Geographies of Race and Ethnicity III: Settler Colonialism and Nonnative People of Color," *Progress in Human Geography* 42, no. 2 (2017): 1–10.

60. For discussions on the relational and regional formation, see Laura Pulido, *Black, Brown, Yellow, and Left: Radical Activism in Los Angeles* (Berkeley: University of California Press, 2006); Perla M. Guerrero, *Nuevo South: Latinas/os, Asians, and the Remaking of Place* (Austin: University of Texas Press, 2017); Cheng, *The Changs Next Door to the Díazes*; Molina, *How Race Is Made in America*.

8

O Canada

HIV Not Welcome Here

RYAN CONRAD

I'm sitting in the examination room of a medical clinic in suburban Ottawa, awkwardly fumbling with a laminated sheet of paper. I'm anxious. I never go to the doctor, a likely result of not having health insurance most of my adult life before coming to Canada to study at nearly 30 years old. I'm convinced the patch of psoriasis on my elbow or the unmistakable vitiligo on my face will give away that I have immune system problems. And then there's the ten-inch scar on my stomach—how do I prove I was the live donor in a liver transplant operation when I was 21 and not the sick patient who needed the life-saving operation because of an undetected genetic disorder? I'm about to receive a medical examination by a doctor approved by the federal government to determine my admissibility for permanent residence in Canada. Would all of these visible markers of illness mark me unfit to become a full-time resident in the country where I've already been living the last six years as a graduate student? Or perhaps there's something in my blood not visible to the unaided eye? The document in my hands is a wordy flow chart mired in '90s aesthetics, and worse, '80s language. The document is titled *Blood test for AIDS* and declaims: "For people *over 15 years of age*, AIDS testing is a *mandatory* part of the Canadian immigration examination" (emphasis original).

I knew before I arrived at the clinic that I would be undergoing a mandatory and explicitly not anonymous HIV test—there's no such thing as an AIDS test—and that it would be grounds for barring me from immigrating as "medically inadmissible" if I tested positive. Would-be HIV-positive immigrants to Canada are considered too great a financial burden based on a macabre administrative formula that deems anyone requiring annual care (medication, doctor's appointments, blood work, hospitalization, social services, etc.) in an excess of $6,655 to be inadmissible. Being a vocal queer activist and scholar, the ban on

HIV-positive immigrants as medically inadmissible was one of the first things I learned about the immigration process from an acquaintance that worked at Immigration Québec. When he learned I was exploring the process of becoming a Permanent Resident (the Canadian equivalent of a U.S. Green Card), my serostatus was his first question. He was aware of my activism advocating for queer youth, rural queers, sex workers, prisoners, and people living with HIV/AIDS in Maine, and he knew that I taught HIV/AIDS-themed courses in my university's burgeoning Sexuality Studies program in Montréal. It was a fair question to ask given his context for me as a loud and proud sexual liberationist, and it would have saved me a lot of time wasted had I been HIV-positive. Up to that point, I had never tested positive, so I sit in the doctor's office, prepared but anxious, mentally reviewing my sexual encounters over the previous six months and how "safe" each encounter had been.

The doctor is kind and friendly. She ignores my skin conditions, remarks how unusual it is to meet a live organ donor, and then explains the blood tests and X-rays I need to take to prove my good health. She asks if I have any high-risk factors for HIV and I hesitate. She then asks if I use injection drugs or if I am a homosexual. I chuckle a little at the medical language and roll my eyes at the conflation between sexual identity and risk-taking behaviors. I tell her I'm gay, although for the most part I self-identify as a fag. I'm just trying to manage the situation as amiably as possible as my future is in her hands. We share more friendly banter before she sends me off to do my blood tests and to pay the $200 fee for the ten-minute physical exam. While the provincially administered health care system in Canada is public and universally covers its citizens and permanent residents, temporary foreign workers like me pay for everything.

The United States, on the other hand, has no public health care system to speak of, thanks to the handiwork of plutocrats, spineless politicians, and a unique brand of hyper-individualism I am glad to have left behind years ago. Strangely enough, because of the moralistic approach to health care in the United States where everything is maximally privatized and contingent on employment status, the change President Obama made in 2010 lifting the more than two decades long ban of HIV-positive immigrants had no fiscal implications for a nonexistent public health care system.[1] Simply because the United States does not hold the health of its citizens as a common public good, the serostatus of immigrants is no longer of any immediate consequence. Once you arrive, you can either pay for your prohibitively expensive medical care yourself or go die somewhere, preferably out of sight. The wonders of individual choice in the United States.

Canada too, has gone through variations of its current HIV immigration ban since it began "common-sense" testing of all applicants in 2002.[2] The most recent change was brought about in 2018 when the Liberal government made a procedural adjustment to temporarily increase the medical inadmissibility cap from

$6,655 to $19,965 annually. This allows some immigration applications to proceed but only at the discretion of the immigration officer reviewing the file because many medications alone still cost upward of $15,000/year in Canada.[3] This was preceded by HIV/AIDS activists in 2005 who challenged the federal government to change its policies requiring the disclosure of HIV status when applying for an entry visa, even if only entering the country for short-term temporary visits. The catalyst for this change was the upcoming XVI International AIDS Conference that was to be held the following year in Toronto and the need to ensure no participants would be barred from attending.[4] The banning of HIV-positive people from entry prior to the 2010 change under the Obama administration was the reason that the International AIDS Conference, which began in Atlanta, Georgia, in 1985, had not been hosted in the United States for more than two decades. Despite these changes over the last two decades, the only way to ensure that HIV-positive immigrants are not discriminated against at the border is to end mandatory testing as part of the immigration process.

Beyond the barring of HIV-positive immigrants in Canada, there are other historical and present-day laws regulating the movement of HIV-positive people—namely HIV quarantine laws debated by state and provincial governments and the criminalization of HIV nondisclosure, exposure, and transmission. Bill 34, a piece of quarantine legislation that sought to intern people living with HIV/AIDS on an island off the coast of Vancouver, of the then-Social Credit Government of British Columbia spurred numerous demonstrations by the People with AIDS Society and the Coalition for Responsible Health Legislation in the late '80s Vancouver, which set the stage for the emergence of ACT UP/Vancouver shortly thereafter. The province of Ontario's Chief Medical Officer of Health (1987–1997), Richard Schabas, also became a frequent target of Toronto's AIDS ACTION NOW! and the Prostitutes' Safe Sex Project in the early '90s after recommending the reclassification of HIV as a virulent disease in order to more easily quarantine sexually active HIV-positive people through Section 22 of the *Ontario Health Promotion and Protection Act*.[5] The criminalization of HIV nondisclosure, where an HIV-positive person does not share their serostatus with sexual partners regardless of actual risk of transmission, has been ongoing in Canada since the early '80s. Unlike the United States where there are HIV-specific laws that specifically criminalize nondisclosure, exposure, and transmission in more than half of U.S. states, Canada uses sexual assault law to prosecute most cases.[6] Today, Canada is a global leader in prosecutions and convictions for HIV nondisclosure that have disproportionately affected racialized people and recent immigrants.[7] Furthermore, criminal convictions in both the United States and Canada, whether serostatus-related or not, are grounds for labeling immigrants as "criminally inadmissible" and deporting them.[8] While quarantine and nondisclosure laws targeting citizens are not the same as laws targeted at would-be immigrants, they represent the lengths to which the state has gone and continues to go in order to regulate the movement of HIV-positive people within and at its borders.

In Canada, the matter at the heart of the present-day ban on HIV-positive immigrants is the "excessive demand" they would supposedly place on the publicly funded health care system. Yet the policy is incoherent as it applies only to certain classes of immigrants in Canada's increasingly privatized immigration system.[9] Accepted refugees and spouses of citizens or permanent residents can be HIV-positive and immigrate to Canada without being considered an "excessive demand" on the health care system. But economic immigrants coming through Canada's much-admired Express Entry program—the vast majority of immigrants to Canada today, including myself—are still subject to the "excessive demand" provision of the *Immigration and Refugee Protection Act*.

While I support the wholesale abandonment of the ablest and discriminatory "excessive demand" provision that frames people with illnesses and/or disabilities solely as non-contributing leeches, we are at a unique juncture where the specific demand to drop HIV from the list of diseases that bars one from immigrating to Canada seems plausible. HIV medications, the life-saving and prohibitively expensive protease inhibitors that have been on the market for twenty years, are finally losing their patent protections and cheaper generics are beginning to enter the market. While I'm not callous enough to claim pills are the only health care needs of people living with HIV, it is one of the most expensive components of care and often cited as the "excessive burden" on the health care system. Furthermore, nearly all provinces where almost 90 percent of Canadians reside, are offering low to no-cost Pre-Exposure Prophylaxis (PrEP) to their residents as part of their provincially administered public health care.[10] It is hard to argue that HIV-positive people constitute an "excessive demand" on the health care system when the very same drugs prescribed to keep HIV at undetectable levels in the blood of HIV-positive people are now being prescribed to HIV-negative people through a growing number of the publicly funded provincial health care systems as a prevention strategy. In fact, the *Canadian Medical Association Journal* published guidelines for PrEP nationwide in November 2017, encouraging its use across the country as an additional biomedical tool for reducing seroconversion among those at high risk.[11] How can we continue to justify barring HIV-positive would-be immigrants because they're too expensive to treat, while encouraging the widespread use of the very same treatments for HIV through the publicly funded health care system on HIV-negative Canadians? It's not only incoherent, but discriminatory and unethical.

While the Canadian HIV/AIDS Legal Network and other groups like the HIV/AIDS Legal Clinic Ontario have done the impressive work of doing research, creating reports, lobbying government, and holding press events to challenge the neoliberal logic of the "excessive demand" provision in Canadian immigration law, I still yearn for the direct action tactics that these groups do not engage. When do we occupy the offices of the Minster of Health and the Minister of Immigration, Refugees and Citizenship? When do we dog the Prime Minister at every public event for upholding stigmatizing serophobic immigration laws while accepting international recognition for being immigrant- and refugee-friendly? When do we confront HIV/AIDS service organizations about prioritizing PrEP for HIV-negative Canadians while remaining silent on the exclusion of HIV-positive immigrants? When do we ransack the offices of AIDS profiteers over the extension of intellectual property rights regarding life-saving medications in trade deals like the Trans-Pacific Partnership (TPP) and the Canada-European Union Trade Agreement (CETA)? And is there a place for HIV/AIDS justice work in the thinly stretched migrant justice movement already under attack by newly emboldened anti-immigrant white supremacists like the Cultural Action Party of Canada, Canadian Coalition of Concerned Citizens, Storm Alliance, The Northern Guard, and La Meute?

I'm still trying to find my activist footing in a new city while I wait for my permanent residency application to wind its way through the six-to-nine-to-twelve months of bureaucratic hell it must clear. In the United States, my activism was bombastic and in your face, landing me in jail twice on minor charges—but in my precarious position as a temporary foreign worker in Canada (and even as a future-permanent resident who can still be stripped of legal status and deported for criminal convictions), my activism is more cautious. This has made it challenging to find the kind of all-in activist community I was a part of back in Maine, let alone engage in the kind of collective direct action for which I yearn. Furthermore, the nation's capital is notoriously professionalized, where activists and activist work are co-opted by the state and nongovernmental organizations at a record pace—or worse, before it even starts. The recent relaunching of the Ottawa chapter of No One Is Illegal gives me hope that I'll still find my people here, but HIV/AIDS justice work appears nonexistent in a city where service provision rules the day. And queer organizing work in Ottawa? Let's just say with an estimated 26,400 dead from HIV-related illness in Canada,[12] dance parties are not enough.

Notes

1. For a brief overview of the fight to lift the ban on HIV-positive immigrants in the United States, see Karma R. Chávez, *Queer Migration Politics: Activist Rhetoric and Coalitional Possibilities* (Urbana: University of Illinois Press, 2013), 1–4. For a longer take on race, gender, sexuality, disease, and immigration in the United States, see Erica Rand, *The Ellis Island Snow Globe* (Durham: Duke University Press, 2005).

2. Emily McBain-Ashfield, *"Generosity Has Its Limits": Debates on HIV/AIDS and Medical Inadmissibility in Canada during the 1990s* (Master's Thesis, University of Ottawa, 2018).

3. Deborah Yoong et al., "Public Prescription Drug Plan Coverage for Antiretrovirals and the Potential Cost to People Living with HIV in Canada: A Descriptive Study," *CMAJ Open* 6, no. 4 (November 27, 2018).

4. Canadian HIV/AIDS Legal Network, "Recent Changes to Visitor Visa Process Affecting Entry into Canada for People Living with HIV/AIDS" (Toronto), June 23, 2005.

5. To learn more about the activist response to HIV quarantine legislation in Canada, see the Vancouver and Toronto transcripts from the AIDS Activist History Project's oral history archive: https://aidsactivisthistory.ca/interviews/vancouver-interviews/; https://aidsactivisthistory.ca/interviews/toronto-interviews/.

6. For a more detailed overview of HIV nondisclosure laws and related activism in the United States, visit the Sero Project: www.seroproject.com. For a more detailed overview of sexual assault law and HIV criminalization in Canada, visit the Canadian HIV/AIDS Legal Network's documentary *Consent: HIV Non-Disclosure and Sexual Assault Law* (2015), www.consentfilm.org.

7. Eric Mykhalovskiy, Colin Hastings, Chris Sanders, Michelle Hayman, and Laura Bisaillon, "Callous, Cold and Deliberately Duplicitous: Racialization, Immigration and the Representation of HIV Criminalization in Canadian Mainstream Newspapers," November 22, 2016. Available at SSRN: https://ssrn.com/abstract=2874409; Colin Hastings, Cécile Kazatchkine, and Eric Mykhalovskiy, *HIV Criminalization in Canada: Key Trends and Patterns*, report (Toronto: HIV/AIDS Legal Network, 2017).

8. Amira Hasenbush and Bianca D. M. Wilson, *HIV Criminalization against Immigrants in California*, publication (Los Angeles: Williams Institute, 2016); *Immigration and Refugee Protection Act*, SC 2001, c 27, s 36.

9. For a brief overview of privatization in Canadian immigration policy, see Audrey Macklin, "European Politicians Envy Canada's Points System for Migrants. But How Well Has It Worked?" *The Guardian*, March 24, 2015, theguardian.com/commentisfree/2015/mar/24/european-politicians-envy-canada-immigration-points-system.

10. Vik Adhopia, "Ontario to Cover HIV Prevention Pill under Public Health Plan," *CBC News*, September 22, 2017, www.cbc.ca/news/health/hiv-prep-coverage-1.4302184; Cherise Seucharan, "'We've Been Waiting for This for a Long Time': B.C. to Fund HIV-Prevention Drug," *CBC News*, December 28, 2017, www.cbc.ca/news/canada/british-columbia/province-announces-hiv-drug-coverage-1.4467003.

11. Darrell H. S. Tan et al., "Canadian Guideline on HIV Pre-Exposure Prophylaxis and Non-occupational Post-Exposure Prophylaxis," *Canadian Medical Association Journal* 189, no. 47 (November 26, 2017), http://www.cmaj.ca/content/189/47/E1448.

12. Public Health Agency of Canada. *Summary: Estimates of HIV Incidence, Prevalence and Proportion Undiagnosed in Canada, 2014.*

(A) Untitled by Rommy Torrico

(B) Differed/Action by Myisha Arellanus

Immigrants' rights are human rights:
End the criminalization, detentions, and abuse!

Los derechos de los inmigrantes son derechos humanos:
¡Ya basta con las detenciones, los abusos, y la criminalización!

Les droits des immigrants sont des droits humains:
Mettez fin à la criminilisation, aux détentions, et aux abus!

حقوق المهاجرين من حقوق الإنسان
إنهوا التجريم والحجز والظلم!

移民权利就是人权:
停止犯罪化,拘留,和滥用!

(C) Immigrants' Rights Are Human Rights by Molly Fair

(D) re triptych by Adela C. Licona and Greg Bal

(E)

(F) They Don't Deserve This by Matice Moore

UNDOCUMENTED QUEER
UNAFRAID UNASHAMED

THE BATTLE FOR LGBTQ RIGHTS OR IMMIGRANT RIGHTS IS NOT JUST A GAY ISSUE OR AN IMMIGRANT ISSUE, IT'S A HUMAN RIGHTS ISSUE!

(G) Untitled by Felipe Baeza

(H) Untitled by Maria Inés Taracena

Artist Statements

ROMMY TORRICO

(A) Title: Untitled

Most of my sentiment throughout the process of creating this piece was urgency and raw, powerful emotion. I realized it was necessary for me to reach beyond ache in order to truly uplift our divine trans siblings; those with us, those detained and those watching over us, and depict a world that they, and all of us, could be proud of. We own this resilience as part of the journey toward liberation, and this is my way of recognizing that that journey is anything but quiet; it's fiery and dynamic and shameless and angry and hopeful and beautiful.

MYISHA ARELLANUS

(B) Title: "Differed/Action"

This painting reflects the huge risks and efforts that undocumented youth took in order to achieve an impermanent sense of protection, known as DACA. Its many symbolisms also serve to remind beneficiaries of DACA that the entire immigrant community continues to be criminalized.

MOLLY FAIR

(C) Title: "Immigrants' Rights Are Human Rights"

With the proliferation of laws and enforcement policies that criminalize immigrants in the United States, detention centers have become a ubiquitous form of incarceration. This for-profit industry is growing, separating families, and subjecting people to physical, psychological, and sexual abuse. This graphic was created in solidarity with all those who continue to resist and struggle to survive. It was created for the project Migration Now! a collaboration between Justseeds Artists' Cooperative and Culture/Strike.

ADELA C. LICONA AND GREG BAL

(D) (E) Title: "re triptych"

These photos were taken on our recent photo-tour of the Sonoran borderlands, which included visits to Sasabe, Lochiel, and both Nogaleses. We joined our photos in triptych style to highlight the ways the crudest borderlands technologies of control and containment are regularly used by the U.S. Border Control in ways that inhibit mobility and constrain movement and migration. We want to provoke ways of looking and seeing that contend with the many and multiple ways borders and borderlands technologies scar the landscape and also erase embodied, living histories. Edited together, our photos depict, too, the embodied implications of such mundane technologies of constraint and control. We mean for viewers to confront the contrasting sets of images with a degree of uncertainty.

The shrouded wandering figure is one that symbolizes displacement and dispossession. The repetition of this diasporic figure here suggests not only the broad reach of neoliberal and neocolonial policies but also is meant to have viewers consider the consequences of continuing to work to contain all who are being presently dispossessed and otherwise displaced. What would the world be, and become, if all but 1 percent of its human inhabitants were detained and constrained?

Our use of the black-and-white stark contrast photographs (photo credit, Licona), and especially the negative space that gets produced through this stylized contrast and purposeful overexposure, means to move viewers to see the border as an imposed and arbitrary division and also to imagine the possibility of no border . . . a borderless world. In other words, the void produced by the black and white contrast is meant to be a productive space of the unknown and the imagined.

Our use of vivid color photography (photo credit, Bal) is meant to depart from the black-and-white exposed contrast to suggest that these diasporic figures are vital beings, life forces who, while marked and constrained by mundane borderlands technologies, cannot be forever contained. Moreover, these figures (whose bodies and faces we cannot see but who are proliferated in our collaboration) may be imagining other worlds and ways of being as well as other uses for these technologies—collectively and individually.

MATICE MOORE

(F) Title: "They Don't Deserve This"

This piece was completed in 2016 for the Visions from the Inside project organized by Culture Strike. I collaborated on the piece with a transgender identified woman named Christina.

"My hope is that they close that place. That the people in charge of taking care of detained immigrants treat us like human beings . . . I hope to God that he also frees the many trans girls in there because they don't deserve this."—excerpt from Christina's letter

Christina's testimony about the cruel guards, the denial of hormones and basic medical treatment, and of having to hide her trans identity exemplified the ways our immigration laws and policies constantly oppress, dehumanize, and require an extraordinary degree of resilience, particularly from those who already face extreme marginalization within our cultures.

Whenever I carve a piece of linoleum, I am reminded of how light helps us make sense of the dark. As such, Christina's story inspired me to imagine a God born from despair and perseverance, a God who transcends gender, who listens and frees us all.

FELIPE BAEZA

(G) Title: Untitled

MARÍA INÉS TARACENA

(H) Title: Untitled

Joselyn (left), from the Nicaraguan Miskito Coast, and Estefany (right), from Honduras, are members of Arcoíris 17, the first caravan of transgender and gay asylum seekers from Central America. This photograph was taken in front of the border wall in Nogales, Sonora, in August 2017, moments before Joselyn and Estefany marched to the port of entry to apply for asylum. I wanted to capture their expressions up close as a way to highlight their confidence and resistance—two virtues that are often ignored in the coverage of LGBTQI resistance in Central America and at the U.S.-Mexico border. Joselyn and Estefany were sent to immigrant detention, from which they were released on humanitarian parole one month later. Joselyn resettled in New Mexico and Estefany now lives in the Bay Area. Joselyn won her asylum case. The status of Estefany's asylum claim is unknown.

PART III

Resisting/Refusing

9

Bridging Immigration Justice and Prison Abolition

JAMILA HAMMAMI

I first got involved in this work because my father is a North African migrant from Tunisia, and I recognized that if I were to have been born in Tunisia and not the United States, as a nonbinary queer person, I would have been seeking asylum and likely would have been caught up in the migrant detention system. I also come from a family that has dealt with incarceration, and I have my own experiences with the justice system.

The Queer Detainee Empowerment Project (QDEP), located in New York City, started out as an alternative-to-prison program, but with the co-optation of this language and approach by the state, QDEP shifted our model.[1] Our mission is not only focused on post-release support, but also support while folks are locked in cages. Thus, QDEP is a prison center visitation, post-release support, direct service, and community organizing project that works with lesbian, gay, bisexual, two spirit, queer, intersex, asexual, gender nonconforming, transgender LGBTQIA* GNC TG), and HIV+ migrant prisoners and their families currently in immigrant prison nationally, those that have been recently released from immigration prison, those at the border that need to cross and seek asylum, and those at risk of entering immigrant prisons in the Tri-State Area (Connecticut, New Jersey, New York). QDEP assists folks coming out of immigrant prisons to secure health/wellness, educational, legal, and emotional support and services. QDEP works to organize around the structural barriers and state violence that LGBTQIA* GNC TG and HIV+ detainee/undocumented folks face related to their immigration status, race, sexuality, and gender expression/identity. QDEP is committed to assisting folks in building lives outside of immigration prisons, to breaking down the barriers that prevent folks from building fulfilling and productive lives, and to keeping queer families intact by demanding an end to deportations/immigration prisons/policing. QDEP works to create a world where LGBTQIA* GNC TG and HIV+ detainees/undocumented/migrant folks can pursue their own vision and dreams in their lives without fear of structural violence or violence due to their race, status, sexual orientation, and/or gender identity/gender expression. QDEP believes in creating a narrative of thriving, not just surviving.

QDEP fights for the rights of queer and trans migrants inside and outside of immigration prisons through community organizing, advocacy, policy change, and direct services. QDEP organizes folks in the community through base building, political education, training, and more, in order for folks to fight for themselves. QDEP's process is long and always in development but with the end goal of collective power to fight against the deportation machine.

One major issue that motivates the work of QDEP is the fact that only 14 percent of individuals in immigration prison have legal representation. This differs from the U.S. criminal justice system, in which folks have rights to legal representation. In addition, migrants are subjected to prolonged, arbitrary "detention" (incarceration), masked as "mandatory detention laws" (prison). They are jailed in local and state jails and prisons as well as in federal and private prisons, in beds purchased by Immigration and Customs Enforcement (ICE), where there is minimal oversight. Folks are picked up at ports of entry, as well as on the streets, through home raids, and more. ICE's collaboration with local police departments allows this process to flourish—even in cities that have adopted "sanctuary" status. "Sanctuary" cities are not real. End of story. As long as the federal government has reign over Constitutional-Free Zones (any place within 100 miles of the border, or the ocean, are zones that ICE has free ability to raid, arrest, and detain migrants), and local police departments are collaborators, the term *sanctuary* is not real and the theory is completely irrelevant. We must rely on community control—block watches, cop watches, hate-free zones, and more, in order to fight for the safety of migrant communities, especially the most marginalized—queer and trans migrant communities.

Without bridging the immigration and prison abolition movement, while centering the folks that are the most disproportionately impacted by state violence, we will never win. Prison abolition is often thought of through a criminal justice system lens, but it should be expanded to address the incarceration of migrants—for often indefinite lengths of time under atrocious conditions, which jeopardize their safety, health, and well-being.

Trans and queer migrants fall between the cracks in the migrant prison system, experiencing elevated levels of sexual violence, physical violence, psychological torture (at the hands of their peers and the guards alike), placement in solitary confinement for their own "protection," denial of medical care, refusal of hormone therapy and HIV care, and more. It's absolutely critical to address these issues in tandem, rather than siloed, as it currently stands. The system of criminalizing queer and trans migrants, and then punishing them again through the migrant incarceration system while denying them adequate legal representation, and requiring unattainable bonds, combines to form "the deportation pipeline." Movements to end prison abolition are often so isolated from movements to end migrant detention, that folks don't know that these are the realities of the migrant community. That's part of why QDEP came to exist: to unite these movements and create collective effort to fight for queer and trans migrants.

In order for queer and trans migrant folks to be free, we have to stop ICE from expanding and we have to push for divestment from federal programs that collaborate with local law enforcement to harm queer and trans migrant communities. Furthermore, we need to call "immigration detention" what it is: migrant prison. It is important to understand the reality of extensive immigration prison and deportation systems within the prison industrial complex. Violating immigration law is a civil violation, for which, migrants must go through a process, overseen by the Department of Homeland Security, to determine whether they can remain in the United States. But, as a community, we need to work harder not to create a good migrant/bad migrant narrative (the binary belief system that all migrants are "bad," until they receive some sort of legal status in the United States), in the context of explaining the realities of what queer and trans migrants face in the migrant prison system.

QDEP works not only to queer the migration narrative, but also shift hearts and minds around the migrant community. While migrant rights work often claims to be intersectional, it has become clear that this is not the case. The migrant movement has been very heterosexist, claiming strength in the heteronormative, monogamous, nuclear family, while erasing the identities of those that exist as LGBTQIA* GNC TG folks who experience family in tremendously different ways. QDEP works to ensure the inclusion of trans and queer migrant incarceration in the anti-carceral movement. Without bridging these two movements and centering the folks that are the most disproportionately impacted by state violence and marginalization, we will never win.

Living in a world where folks are truly free to live their truest selves and lives is something of a pipe dream to me in so many ways. The end of mass incarceration, racial profiling, Islamophobia, and state surveillance sounds like an incredible world. But it also has to come with critical pieces that feed into the thriving of our people: housing, mental health care, physical health care, substance use support/care, food access, trans health care, wrap-around social services to provide legitimate support to those that need it, and more are absolutely a part of this ideal world that I imagine.

Notes

1. Jamila Hammami served as the founding executive director of QDEP for five years and was in that position at the time they initially drafted this chapter. Since then, Hammami has left that position and enrolled in a PhD program. Although the editors made the decision to keep this written in present tense, Jamila does not intend to speak for QDEP's current work or leadership.

10

Facing Crisis

Queer Representations against the Backdrop of Athens

MYRTO TSILIMPOUNIDI

AND ANNA CARASTATHIS

In July 2017, in Athens, we ran a photography workshop with a group called LGBTQI+ refugees, comprised of international and local activists, which we called "Facing Crisis." The initial aim of the workshop was to engage people in collective acts of self-representation through portraiture. Participants in the workshop were people who have been rendered entirely invisible in hegemonic and social movement discourses of the "refugee crisis" in Greece, Europe, and globally, because their lives, desires, and embodiments do not fit the narrative of the "deserving refugee," understood in terms of what Gayatri Chakravorty Spivak has called "reproductive heteronormativity."[1] In other words, they trouble the naturalized assumption that human lives and relationships gain value, significance, and meaning through ostensibly universal, heteropatriarchal structures of kinship and reproduction. In that sense, they trouble a fundamental condition of citizenship—and refuge. As Eithne Luibhéid has argued, sexual normativity is crucial to nation-state projects of "biological and social reproduction of the citizenry, but also for the cultivation of particular kinds of social, economic, and affective relationships."[2] Yet, sexual normativity also structures affective and social relationships in counterhegemonic social movement discourses and endeavors, in which LGBTQI+ refugees also found themselves violently marginalized.

Workshop participants were survivors of war and racialized gendered violence, in their intersecting manifestations, understood not as "exceptional crises," but as the systemic underpinnings of global capitalism. Rather than simply offering a counter-narrative of inclusion to hegemonic and activist representations of "deserving refugees," the workshop sought to intervene in the ways that inclusionary responses reproduce representational violence in rendering certain subject positions unthinkable, untranslatable, and, ultimately, unlivable. Our motivation in offering the workshop was a desire to enact "queer coalitions,"[3] that is, to find embodied ways of living and working together across and against axes of power and lines of belonging constituting our bordered reality, in which movements across space that contest the nation-state system are criminalized, and those that threaten its foundational institutions, including the heteropatriarchal family, are violently punished.

The continental project of securitization and the transnational politics of migration management that have produced Europe as a "Fortress" are, by now, well documented, as is the death toll of these necropolitical regimes, constituting the Mediterranean Sea passage the deadliest border in the world, while constructing surveillance, detention, and slavery economies. Migration management is therefore a euphemism for the militarization of the borders of Europe, but also its interior, since the border is everywhere.[4] For many refugees attempting to cross the eastern Mediterranean and Aegean seas, particularly given the conditions of extreme austerity that have been imposed on its populace, Greece was viewed as a space of transit into "Europe."[5] Yet, with the institution of the hotspot mechanism[6] and the closure of the northern borders (with Albania, Bulgaria, and Macedonia, entry points into the so-called "Balkan Route") at the behest of central European powers, Greece has been transformed into a site of containment, trapping more than 60,000 refugees and asylum seekers on its islands and mainland, the majority of whom are made to live in segregated camps outside urban centers and in detention centers awaiting their relocation to "Europe" or their deportation to Turkey. Turkey is declared to be a safe third country,[7] despite being an antidemocratic regime, waging wars, and persecuting dissidents, many of whom are now seeking asylum.

At the same time, a housing occupation movement emerged, particularly in the urban centers of Athens and Thessaloniki, contesting the state policy of segregating refugees and demanding, instead, their integration into the urban social fabric. Yet, conditions—not only in state camps and detention centers but also in housing squats—have proven hostile to LGBTQI+ people who are seeking refuge. The Greek police, military, but also religious NGOs, certain solidarians,[8] and some members of their "own" communities "replicate the persecution [LGBTQI+ refugees] fled in the first place."[9] Against this "backdrop" of intersecting crises—that is, multiple, overlapping, declared, and undeclared crises, the targets of which are pitted against each other—LGBTQI+ people of various origins and trajectories struggle for their survival in the urban space of Athens.

Facing crisis, then, means turning our attention to what usually remains in the background, what is unsaid, or what remains unheard while our attention is focused on the spectacular and hegemonic representations of an urban environment in crisis, such as Athens. Facing crisis engages with different ways of seeing the soft, lived, every day, and banal manifestations of crisis on the social fabric/

body. This essay reflects on the "Facing Crisis" photography workshop, on the politics of "representing refugees," and on our own struggle of engaging with these representations. Conceived as a *photografía—as the act of gráfo*/writing *with fos*/light—it is a dialogue between the images and the text that accompanies them, between visual representations and social theories. In doing so, it attempts to treat them both as equal partners in the knowledge-producing process and as such to dissolve scientific over-reliance on text.[10]

Refugees Welcome

Our point of entry into this discussion is by now a globally familiar image that, in the summer and fall of 2015, became the trademark of the "Refugees Welcome" movement in Europe. The image was reproduced on banners and placards at demonstrations, stenciled on walls in many cities, worn on T-shirts, and displayed on stickers to mark spaces "friendly" toward refugees (Photo 10.1).

In the image that has become iconic of the "Refugees Welcome" movement, we see a man leading a woman who holds a female child by the hand, all of them running (the child almost being dragged off her feet). The caption urges: "bring your families."

Despite its reappropriation by a movement that called (to lesser or greater degrees, given its heterogeneity) for open borders or no borders, it is important to acknowledge the origins of the image: it is the nation-state. And not just any nation-state, but the United States of America, where at one of the most violently policed

Photo 10.1. #RefugeesWelcome, photograph by Hossam el-Hamalawy, 2018 (Used with permission, CC BY-SA 2.0)

borders in the world, between the United States and Mexico, after hundreds of people were killed by cars from 1987 to 1990 while crossing along interstate 5, the U.S. transportation authorities commissioned John Hood to design a highway sign warning drivers of "border crossers." Hood, a Navajo artist, has stated that he wanted to elicit U.S. citizens' empathy with migrants crossing the borders, hence choosing to represent them, in his design of the *Immigration Sign*, as a fleeing family in whose place any Americans could substitute their own.[11] The sign was placed near the border fence that was, by the mid-90s, still under construction, and that now seals the U.S.-Mexico border. Despite/because of this fencing and current calls to "build a wall," making it less porous and the crossing more hostile, this border remains, in the words of Gloria Anzaldúa, "una herida abierta [an open wound] where the Third World grates against the first and bleeds."[12] Used widely in the United States by pro-immigration movements, the image was popularized globally through a stencil by the street artist Banksy, which meant to subvert the negative connotations of the warning sign by emphasizing the hopefulness and agency of those undertaking migration trajectories.[13] By 2015, the iconic image was lifted from the *Immigration Sign* and used as the trademark of the "Refugees Welcome" protest movement across Europe in the wake of the so-called "refugee crisis" (Photo 10.2).

This image, its circulation, and its political underpinnings, illustrate the heteronormalization of the "refugee crisis." The term *heteronormalization* means the construction of the figure of the refugee—whether as a victim or as a threat—as presumptively heterosexual and as reproductive. Refugees are constructed as displaced reproductive citizens deserving or undeserving of moral concern. We discern two dominant representations: one that promotes their induction or

Photo 10.2. Kite-2. Photo-credit: Banksy, series outside: Los Angeles. Permission: Banksy Creative commons

"welcoming" into an affective economy as it articulates nationalized space; and, conversely, a construction by nationalist and fascist ideologies as a demographic threat. "Sympathetic" representations rely on the heterosexualization of refugees, which secures a transcultural legibility of their participation in family and kinship structures, and on their gendering—as imperiled patriarchs, courageous but desperate fathers, or as inherently vulnerable women and innocent children. In "hostile" representations, refugees are made to embody what in another context Cathy Cohen has termed queer heterosexualities: that is, forms of reproductive agency that are seen as dangerous to the continuity and coherence of a racialized national subject, understood in biological terms.[14]

By offering this provocation, we want to problematize the multiple forms of bordering in the countries of departure and arrival, while at the same time unpack the possibilities for queer responses to forced migrations. We suggest that, through the hetero-normalization of refugees, the survival trajectories of refugees are perceived through framings not only of their own reproductive histories and futures (figurations of "family," "childhood," "maternity," and "paternity") but also of their (in)capacity to reproduce institutions—family, religion, nation—as a precondition of their social belonging. Survival and fugitivity as such become framed as questions of reproductive justice or reproductive danger, conditioning empathy, hospitality, and social integration, on the one hand, and indifference, hostility, and social exclusion, on the other.

In short, the survival of refugees is framed in reproductive terms—both in fascist discourses, which view them as a demographic threat, and in solidarity discourses urging their integration. The latter, while challenging the legitimacy of nation-state borders, nevertheless reproduce one of the most important institutional logics that constitute nation-states. Recall our earlier discussion of Spivak's term *reproductive heteronormativity*: the "assumption that producing children by male-female coupling gives meaning to any life" and is "the oldest, biggest sustaining institution in the world, a tacit globaliser," which reproduces itself through "war and rape."[15] The effects of normalizing heterosexuality as the natural bond that affectively connects all human beings or as a universal cultural trait inherent in societies in so-called "refugee-producing countries" are many. For one, this raises the question of who is the subject of solidarity within the antiauthoritarian movement, which reproduces (state and supranational) institutional categories of migration (the family, the unaccompanied minor, the single man, the pregnant woman, and so forth) that are all based on reproductive heteronormativity in order to construct hierarchies (on the representational and material levels) of respectability, deservingness, and belonging. If heteronormalization structures the state of emergency (the humanitarian crisis) to which social movements then seek to respond with socially reproductive and discursive interventions, then part of what such movements are reproducing is heterosexuality. To be clear, heterosexuality in this sense is not a sexual preference, but an institution, and—in most places in the world—a compulsory form of social life, which is violently enforced: in war-zones, on the route of escape, in detention centers and camps, on food lines run by Christian nongovernmental organizations (NGOs), and in housing squats occupied by solidarists. With respect to the latter, but also to refugee activism more broadly, one cannot—without tragic contradiction—oppose nation-state borders and then erect or defend borders that constitute nation-states, that is, borders of a gendered order that heteronormativity naturalizes.

If the highway sign became iconic of the Refugees Welcome movement in Europe, that movement arguably would not have emerged or grown to the extent that it did were it not for images of arrival taken on the shores of the Aegean islands, particularly Lesvos. The "refugee crisis" has been, perhaps, the "most photographed humanitarian crisis in history."[16] Ironically, the arrival becomes iconic of the crisis, because after all what has been called the "refugee crisis" in/of Europe begins with the arrival of people on the shores of what is—at least nominally—Europe. Lesvos is the most iconic and well-documented site of arrival by press photographers; for this reason, it was also chosen as the backdrop/horizon of crisis by international superstar artists such as Ai Weiwei. This mediatized construction of the "crisis" does not allow us to fix our gaze on the destruction of bodies, spaces, and cities by a war-machine that is mainly driven by a fixation on power, profit, and Western ideologies. On the contrary, this representation of the "refugee crisis" habituates us into perceiving as the starting point of the crisis the arrival of displaced bodies on the shores of Europe. Not a word for the unseen bodies who never made it through the journey and whose killings have transformed the Aegean Sea into an aqueous cemetery.

We want to juxtapose these widely circulating images—of fathers, mothers, children, grandparents—with a narrative of the kind of incident no one was there to photograph. This is Souma's story, a trans woman from Cairo, as she told it to a Greek journalist:

> We arrived in Chios by boat having each paid 700 euro. All four of us LGBT people who had boarded the boat were for the entirety of the journey very discreet; in fact, I had covered myself almost completely in a niqab—it seems funny but I was afraid to meet the same fate as another trans refugee; once her travelling companions realised she was trans, they threw her in the sea. Hours later the Turkish coastguard collected her, but this whole torment, I learned later, made her go mad.[17]

Who gets pushed overboard when survival becomes a question of reproduction?

What we are trying to challenge in this paper are our ways of seeing in the milieu of crisis, the notion of perspective in an era characterized by the proliferation of images and the ways these affect our imagination, and thus, our reactions to the crisis. Representations of refugees are dangerous images, not only in the sense that the risk of objectification inheres in them but also because the material conditions that give rise to them are necropolitical ones. That survival—framed as reproduction—is apparently the subject of these images only means that the backdrop remains out of focus: the sea, the fear, the war, everyone left behind, everything destroyed, everyone fallen or pushed overboard.

Imagine you are standing on the shore of a sea staring across at a landmass opposite, which forms your horizon. You know, although they are not visible to you, that beneath the surface of this sea are the corpses of thousands of people who tried to cross it in order to arrive where you are now standing. Your horizon, then, is a border. This sea has long been viewed as a threshold, and yours is not the first epoch during which it has been crossed by masses of people in a rising tide of desperation, propelled by unspeakable violence. But crossing it has, in your epoch, become a crime. It is the liquid border between what is called "Greece" and what is called "Turkey"; and the solid ground on which you are standing is the "entrance gate to Europe." That you are standing here at all depends on prior crossings of people who, many years later, contributed to this threshold nation the semblance of solidity, even as they kept gazing across to a place they never ceased to remember as "home." Recently, this border has been multiplied; metaphorically and discursively, it travels; it exists in the imagination as far away as that "island nation" eager to "Brexit" from the continental project of Europe; it's being walled up and razor-wired shut, patrolled by border hunters chasing equally imaginary refugees. Your horizon has become a wall; a multilateral bargain; an aqueous cemetery. Staring at this horizon, things stop making sense. So you turn away. You stop imagining.[18]

Facing Crisis

Our initial aim in conducting the Facing Crisis workshop was to engage people who have been marginalized in this economy of representation, but also in the solidarity economy, in a collective process of self-representation.[19] Confronted with a horizon against which things stop making sense, we selfishly wanted to find ways to keep imagining. Based on the premises of participatory photography methodologies, the workshops were designed around a series of talks about issues of representation, intersectionality, identity, and belonging, and aimed to give participants technical knowledge of framing, composition, visual language, and visual stereotypes. We chose portraiture because it was the most obvious inroad to self-representation, even though we wanted—and urged participants—to move from the stereotypical notion of the "face" (noun) to "facing" (verb): that is, through taking a stance, to claim the visual as a space of resistance.[20] Against and behind hegemonic representations of "crisis," we wanted to question who becomes the normative subject of crisis, and who gets pushed out of the frame. Portraiture was thus the medium for bridging the metaphorical "social body" with the literal experiences and representations of embodiment of our participants, dwelling in the margins and contesting their marginalization against the backdrop of "crisis." Our idea was to lead a series of practice sessions in various places in the city, giving each participant a disposable camera, and, at the end, to curate an exhibition of the works produced by the participants.

In the end, the photographs were taken not with disposable cameras, but in a much more painstaking way using a professional digital camera, a collaboration between the "students" and the "teachers." This was because the workshop participants were keen to learn photographic skills that necessitate more sophisticated equipment. This took them out of the habit of taking snapshots and resulted in thoughtful framing, lighting, and other compositional choices. In the end, there was no exhibition (although we printed the photographs and the photographers shared them with each other). Indeed, in this article, we are not including any of the photographs that were taken during the workshop. In fact, as we reflect on the workshop, we want to problematize the ubiquity of projects that give cameras to "refugees" and exhibit photographs they take (of themselves, other "refugees," and so forth). What anxieties do we mask in seeking to make the subaltern visible? Make the subaltern show its face? Asking the "subaltern to take a selfie" perhaps is an attempt to resolve on the level of representation the violent hierarchy that exists by virtue of the nation-state system. Do we have a romantic investment in a subject of struggle? We want representations that make us feel that this hierarchy can be eliminated in our personal relationships and in the perceptual and affective relationship of the viewer to an image, particularly an image of a suffering other.

The primary way in which the suffering other becomes relatable in the image is through familiality: they become familiar by being familial. This is because our primary way of understanding relationships as such is through the institution of reproductive heterornormativity. This is a question of violence. But we realized that, while they refused this visual discourse of suffering, and the subject positions and affects assigned to "refugees"—gratitude, despondency, resilience—the photographs that were taken during the workshop engaged in a stereotypical counter-discourse, of camp gayness, replete with hegemonic standards of beauty. In that sense, they were all too relatable, familiar if not familial, homonormative if not heteronormative. But the point is not to replace one normativity with another: to create an ideal model of the LGBTQI+ refugee to counter the "bring your families" narrative.

Facing Crisis, then, comes to mean something else as we consider the dynamics of power that center a subject, constructing her/him as an exemplar or even seeking to capture their individuality. Portraiture has always oscillated between these seemingly contradictory aspects of the subject. The refugee is not a subject, it is a state category. And as such, it cannot show its face. In this light, what would the face of the refugee look like? How is the refugee seen? Well, in this era and on our corner of the Aegean Sea, the sympathetic refugee is Syrian (preferably Christian) and comes in the size of a family.[21] The "refugee" is not simply someone seeking refuge or fleeing violence; it is someone who qualifies for what is called "international protection," someone recognized by a state as a legitimate supplicant. The obverse of the refugee is the "economic migrant," and, indeed, what constitutes the "refugee crisis" for Europe is the logistical difficulty that ostensibly large numbers of people arriving present to the procedures designed to distinguish between the two. For example (at the time of writing), on the logic of "refugee producing nations," people arriving from Afghanistan, Yemen, Somalia, and Nigeria are not considered refugees and as such not given the opportunity to claim asylum in Europe. Whose crisis is declared and visible and whose remains undeclared and invisible? The category of the "refugee" is a crystallization of normative ways of viewing crisis, which makes people's experiences of fleeing violence legible only to the extent that they converge with state and supranational interests. Under this light, we cannot possibly produce or reproduce portraits of refugees.

So, the second stage of the Facing Crisis workshop was to reproduce the reproductions, returning to stage the same photographs that we had collectively decided were "the best ones" but with their subjects absent. The images were restaged against the same backdrop: Athens, an urban landscape itself a decade into the financial crisis in Greece. We could have photo-shopped the images in order to remove the subjects, but our aim was not to aestheticize; we could have laid a censor bar over the eyes or pixelated the faces of the subjects to anonymize them (as is commonly done in photographs of demonstrators or of children to protect their identity), but our aim was not to be grotesque, either. Taking the photographs again seemed important, not least of all because it required us to meticulously reproduce the photographer's perspective—to set the same frame, to set the camera just as they had, to remember the reasons they gave for their choices, what they had sought to make visible. But, further, the choice to revisit the sites of these photographic situations and restage the images was motivated by our own desire to make visible the structures of substitutionality—the familial and the familiar—that condition empathy (or its lack thereof). We wanted to underscore that the subject is always absent in reproductions of "refugees." Not only in the sense that viewers of a photograph will always project their own categories of perception on an image, framed by that label, but, also, in the sense that the category is dehumanizing, and desubjectifying, whether one is made to wear it or is denied its protection.

Thus, in what follows we engage in the technique of *photografía*, writing with light, in order to provide an account of the workshop that is accurate to the main premises of the work. Our participants did not aspire to be represented as "refugees," nor, in that sense, to become exemplars of queer refugees in Europe.

Although we had their consent to use the photographs they took, we believe that circulating these dangerous images—by reproducing them in this chapter in what is a highly regulated visual economy—we would be contributing to an exoneration of Europe, its colonial history, and the continuity of that history into the present. On the one hand, European states are selling munitions and waging wars that produce refugees; on the other hand, Europe (and supranational organizations such as the UNHCR and the IOM) congratulates itself for "welcoming" refugees, by circulating celebratory images of their survival and resilience (even as it obfuscates the material conditions to which they are subject and attempts to quash their resistance).

In this context, giving "refugees" cameras to represent themselves elides the process of representational and political violence that congeals in the category of the refugee. Moreover, we want to move away from the discursive violence that refugees are facing on a daily basis as they become the subject of scholarly research and of artistic representations. We are disciplined into circulating these kinds of images, not only in research and art practice but also in social media, as evidence of our moral concern for refugees. While a thorough discussion of the ethics of representing violence lies beyond this paper, we invite the viewer to face it with the photographs below (Photo 10.3).

Instead of "them" facing "us," their faces being literally exposed, we want to destabilize the comfort of the viewer and eliminate any possibility of celebratory consumption of these images. In this sense, the images are banal and everyday and may even seem boring, portraying only the backdrop of Athens, apparently with no subjects present. Yet by choosing to remove the subjects from the frame, our intent is to bring subjectivity into the light—both that of the viewer whose desire to see the "refugee" (in this case the "LGBTQI+ refugee") is frustrated, but also that of our participants through whose eyes these frames were initially constructed.

We are at the National Technical University of Athens on a very warm summer day of 2017. In this space, right in front of this building, the Polytechnio, in 1973, the revolution against the junta took place. We share these stories as we walk around the space of the university, we add layers of stories, and we interview walls, as the space is saturated by street art and political slogans. We chose this space as the main site of the Facing Crisis workshop, as universities are asylum spaces in Greece, after the murder of students revolting against the fascist regime in 1973, which took place in this very place. Our participants tell us they feel unsafe in most places in the city, even those claiming to "welcome refugees" because they are being harassed by Greeks and other "refugees."

Photo 10.3. Photografía 1. Photo-credit: Anna Carastathis & Myrto Tsilimpounidi

On the top stair, lying in front of the imposing door of this building, imagine a topless man smoking his shisha, enjoying the play between sun and shade. The frame was chosen as we discussed the traps of Hellenist representations of "Greece"—with Doric columns and whitened marble making for small Acropolises everywhere— while the subject plays with Orientalist representations of "Syria" as he blows smoke circles. As a cloud of smoke obscures his face, the photographer captures his image. Can we ever dissociate ourselves from the myths of our national heritage and the hegemonic representations that build national identities (Photo 10.4)?

One of the participants shares the story of his journey to Athens, the crossing, the violence, the discrimination against his—according to him—obvious homosexuality. With the help of the other participants, he paints this violence on half of his face, while the other half he decorates with vibrant makeup. He stands some distance down the path from the camera and stares directly at it, almost facing it down. Where there is oppression there is also resistance, he tells us; this photograph is meant to inspire people to get out of abusive situations. He says that there is always a light at the end of the tunnel; you can see this light illuminating his figure (Photo 10.5).

A trans woman gets inspired by this street art piece on the walls of the university. She places her body in a pose drawn from a fashion magazine between

Photo 10.4. Photografia 2. Photo-credit: Anna Carastathis & Myrto Tsilimpounidi

Photo 10.5. Photografia 3. Photo-credit: Anna Carastathis & Myrto Tsilimpounidi

Photo 10.6. Photografia 4. Photo-credit: Anna Carastathis & Myrto Tsilimpounidi

these two figures. Posing in front of them, she says she wants to highlight the contradiction between the two serious, stiff, male figures and her own self. She talks about capitalist exploitation and the financial crisis in Morocco and Greece; she identifies these two figures as bankers or politicians fixated on money and profit making. As the image is taken, she is seductively staring at the camera, while a few seconds after the shot we discuss the "refugee economy" in Europe and how this sometimes becomes a new form of capital in the milieu of crisis. Our participants get angry: they say that they encounter such figures, whether in the form of border guards or politicians, who are responsible for the destruction of their homelands. This is a long conversation; the second image against this wall is shot after sunset, with no daylight. One of the participants dusts his hand with glitter and gives the graffiti the finger. Ai Weiwei would be proud (Photo 10.6).[22]

To take this photograph, the photographers struggle to get the right angle. The subject is lying down, his head amid the two hearts painted on the pavement. He is wearing a white tulle veil, which covers his face, affixed to his head by a plastic bejeweled tiara. Still, through the veil you can see that his eyes are closed. This is the last photograph we shoot that night; its meaning (from the point of view of the subject, who orchestrated it) is not discussed, as we were mainly focused on the formal challenge presented by taking a photograph when the subject is below us, not at eye level. As he stands up, he says he wants to title this photograph "Love Wins."

Photographs, Utopias, and the Need for Hope

Here I am, making another, bound to fail, attempt to position myself in a world characterized by mobility, liquidity, and speed, not the celebratory ones in which people, products, and ideas flow nicely as elaborated in the globalization studies mantra. The other one, in which you find yourself bumping awkwardly against walls, borders, fences, defenses, and hegemonic attitudes all the time. This is why I find it difficult to position myself, but for sure I know which side I am on. So, perhaps it is much more relevant to clarify this: I'm side by side with the ones who resist and revolt against dominant narratives, who fail and then join the collective depression, before they realize that they have to make room for queer failures and utopias, and, perhaps, then find the ways to resist again. At this very moment I'm struggling to make space again for hope and new utopias. Perhaps this is the most honest justification of the photographic workshop, accompanied by my training and my belief that, sometimes, theory has the capacity to dismantle and provoke certain reactions. Photographs have the capacity to capture the untold, the unspeakable, the untranslatable, all those delicate performances that are not registered in speech. Photography adds an invaluable layer to our logocentric qualitative data collection mechanisms. Perhaps this is another reason to use the medium of photography in order to invoke the soft, daily, omnipresent effects of crisis and the things yet to come. To quote Ursula Le Guin:

> *You cannot take what you have not given, and you must give yourself. You cannot buy Utopia. You cannot make Utopia. You can only be the Utopia. Utopia is in the individual spirit, or it is nowhere. It is for all or it is nothing. If it is seen as having any end, it will never truly begin. We can't stop here. We must go on. We must take the risks.*

So, utopia is a transforming force that plays with the limits of the human. Yet, as Susan Sontag says "humankind lingers unregenerately in Plato's cave, still reveling, its age-old habit, in mere images of the truth."[23] In this sense, most utopias are like photographs, offering glimpses at a moment or time that portrays the desirable outcomes of the utopian imagination. Utopia is a representation, evincing that which is not in itself present (this is the first meaning of the word "representation," its theatrical or politico-moral meaning); specifically, it puts on display and makes present the impossible itself. Yet, to return to Plato's cave, what limits and constitutes our understanding of utopian representations is the position of the guards.

I can't stop thinking of a graffiti slogan at the port of Lesvos underneath the stencil of faded, ghostlike figures of bodies arriving. We are an image from the future.[24]

Notes

1. Nayanika Mookherjee, "Reproductive Heteronormativity and Sexual Violence in the Bangladesh War of 1971: A Discussion with Gayatri Chakravorty Spivak," *Social Text* 30, no. 2 (2012): 123–131.

2. Eithne Luibhéid, *Pregnant on Arrival: Making the Illegal Immigrant* (Minneapolis: University of Minnesota Press, 2013), 4.

3. Cathy J. Cohen, "Punks, Bulldaggers, and Welfare Queens: The Radical Potential of Queer Politics?" *GLQ* 3, no. 4 (1997): 437–465.

4. Nicholas De Genova, "Spectacles of Migrant 'Illegality': The Scene of Exclusion, the Obscene of Inclusion," *Ethnic and Racial Studies* 36, no. 7 (2013): 1–19.

5. Georgios Agelopoulos, Elina Kapetanaki, and Konstantinos Kousaxidis, "Transit Migrants in a Country Undergoing Transition: The Case of Greece," in *Characteristics of Temporary Migration in European-Asian Transnational Social Spaces. International Perspectives on Migration*, eds. Pirkko Pitkänen, Mari Korpela, Mustafa Aksakal, and Kerstin Schmidt (New York: Springer, 2018), 121–138.

6. European Commission (EC), "Explanatory Note on the 'Hotspot' Approach," Statewatch, 2015, http://www.statewatch.org/news/2015/jul/eu-com-hotsposts.pdf.

7. European Union (EU), "EU-Turkey Statement, 18 March 2016," Council of the European Union, 2016, www.consilium.europa.eu/en/press/press-releases/2016/03/18/eu-turkey-statement/.

8. In the context of the multilingual, international solidarity movement with refugees converging in Athens, the Greek noun «αλληλέγγυος»/«αλληλέγγυη» describing a person who stands in solidarity (αλληλεγγύη) is translated into English as "solidarian." People coming from elsewhere to participate in refugee welcoming efforts are also commonly referred to as "international volunteers," but for political reasons we prefer the language of solidarity to describe this choice.

9. Matt Broomfield, "Queer Refugees on Lesvos are Crying Out for Help," *The New Arab*, November 10, 2017, https://www.alaraby.co.uk/english/indepth/2017/11/10/queer-refugees-on-lesvos-are-crying-out-for-help?utm_source=twitter&utm_medium=sf; Lesvos LGBTQI+ Refugee Solidarity, "LGBTIQ+ Refugees at Grave Risk of Exposure, Violence and Death as Conditions Worsen on Lesvos: Statement from Lesvos LGBTQI+ Refugee Solidarity," November 4, 2017, https://www.facebook.com/permalink.php?story_fbid=309 129119494411&id=286931478380 842; LGBTQI+ Refugees, "Our Own Home: Fighting for Safety, Stability, and Choice as LGBTQI+ Refugees in Greece." *Arts Everywhere*, February 5,

2018, www.artseverywhere.ca/2018/02/05/lgbtqi-refugees/; Alexi Tsaggari, "Unsafe Refuge: Life and Death for the LGBTQI Refugees," *Baklan Inside*, January 23, 2018, https://balkan insight.com/2018/01/23/unsafe-haven-life-and-death-for-lgbt-refugees-12–14–2017/.

10. Myrto Tsilimpounidi, *Sociology of Crisis: Visualising Urban Austerity* (London: Routledge, 2017).

11. Scott Gold, "The Artist behind the Iconic 'Running Immigrants' Image," *Los Angeles Times*, April 4, 2008, http://www.latimes.com/local/la-me-outthere4apr04-story.html. Victor Morales, "Iconic Sign Evokes Connection to Long Walk," *Indian Country Today*, October 12, 2008, https://indiancountrymedianetwork.com/news/iconic-sign-evokes -connection-to-long-walk/.

12. Gloria Anzaldúa, *Borderlands/La Frontera: The New Mestiza* (San Francisco: Aunt Lute, 1987), 25. Some sections of the U.S./Mexico border are fenced or walled, and some sections are not. In 2019, 654 miles of the border were fenced and 1,279 were not, https:// www.businessinsider.com/us-mexico-border-wall-photos-maps-2018–5. An interactive map of the border and the different kind of barriers in place at different sections can be found at: https://www.usatoday.com/border-wall/us-mexico-interactive-border-map/.

13. Jorge Rivas, "Bansky Transforms Migrant Road Sign into DREAM Crossing," *Color-lines*, February 22, 2011, http://www.colorlines.com/articles/banksy-transforms-migrant -road-sign-dream-crossing.

14. Cohen, "Punks, Bulldaggers."

15. Mookherjee, "Reproductive Heteronormativity," 125.

16. Jerome Phelps, "Why Is So Much Art about the 'Refugee Crisis' So Bad?" *Open Democracy*, May 11, 2017, https://www.opendemocracy.net/5050/jerome-phelps/refugee-crisis -art-weiwei.

17. Our translation. Thodoris Antonopoulos, "Gay, Lesbian, Trans Refugees in Athens: One of the Most 'Invisible,' Dramatic but Also Heroic Sides of the Refugee Issue," [in Greek] *Lifo*, November 8, 2016, http://www.lifo.gr/articles/lgbt_articles/120527.

18. Extract from Research Diary (AC), July 2016.

19. A version of this chapter and the outcomes of the "Facing Crisis" workshop is presented in our book *Reproducing Refugees: Photographia of a Crisis*, (Lanham, Md.: Rowman and Littlefield, 2019).

20. Susan Sontag, *On Photography* (New York: Penguin, 1973).

21. The size of this family is understood through western European norms as a "nuclear" as opposed to an extended family.

22. This is a reference to Ai Weiwei's photography series, "Study of Perspective" (1995–2003), in which the artist is giving the finger to monuments and symbols of authority around the globe.

23. Sontag, *On Photography*, 5.

24. Extract from Research Diary (MT), July 2017.

11

Fantasy Subjects

Dissonant Performances of Belonging in Queer African Refugee Resettlement

AB BROWN

Reading soundtrack: Please search and play "Coucou" by Koffi Olomide while reading.

The tinkle of the synthesizer keys bounce, and Olomide's rich, throaty voice echoes in from the background, a call from the distance that comes closer and closer, *yeeaaaaaaaa eh!* Only to whisper, *il y a dans mon coeur un trouble, qui s'appelle l'amour.* (*There is a hole in my heart named love.*) Boldly announcing his presence only to pull back, drawing us toward him to listen more closely. Then, slowly bringing his voice back to fuller volume, this time singing into us. As Olomide's voice arrives more fully, sliding in from the distant background to reverberate in our eardrums, François dances in the center of the dance floor of Scarlet, a small, dark, ornate gay club on the main strip of Halsted Street in Chicago's gayborhood. His torso is elongated and languid, stretching to one side, his head following, float-ing behind as the singer's voice croons into his extend phrases only for François to jerk his head and shoulders in short, repeated snags back to the other side with the song's more punctuated lyrics. François' arms undulate from shoulder out to finger tips in all directions like underwater tendrils, moving everywhere and nowhere all at once. His eyes are closed, head tilted slightly back, mouth slightly open, swaying in the middle of the dance floor. Everyone has paused in a brief moment of exaltation, soft round eyes and bright smiles at this beautiful sight. Compelled, a few fellow dancers begin to move in rhythm toward François with both admiration and longing. And just as they are about to touch . . .

François snaps back to reality. Scarlet would never play Koffi Olomide. The fantasy dissolves and François is left swaying and humming to himself, alone, on the carpeted living room of his small apartment on the edge of the city. Every week or so he brings himself back to this reverie, dancing alone in his living room.

> *I put on my music, you know, and just like listen to the music that remind me of that side. Music from my country and dance here myself. And you can picture at like a nice bar or something the music playing and everyone dancing together, singing along. Maybe dancing with a nice man, how he holds you. But me, I am dancing with me, myself and I!* François laughs. *For me it can be frustrating going out because I don't really like to be alone. But at the bar, everyone is either a couple, with their group of friends, on their phone, you know. There I am sitting at the bar by myself. Here, like, in my mind I can be wherever. I am not alone. Here I can move.*[1]

François,[2] a gay refugee from the Democratic Republic of Congo, was recently resettled to Chicago by way of South Africa.[3] While he long-dreamed of coming to the United States, he now faces considerable isolation induced by systemic xenophobia, homophobia, and racism that inform both the social politics he confronts in everyday life and the legal politics, which are rooted in historically homophobic and racist asylum and immigration laws, that he navigates as he continues his journey to residency and citizenship. In this passage, I am interested in his use of imagination to resituate himself in relation to others that simultaneously hangs on to and reveals the failure of notions of belonging—in this case, in a particular location (a gay club), to a social setting (among other gay people), and to a nation. François critiques his current condition and offers a series of tools for reconstructing a sense of belonging, reorienting them toward self-articulation, pleasure, and fulfillment—even if only imagined. In this essay, I look at various configurations of imagination expressed by LGBTIQ African refugees who have been resettled to the United States. I use imagination to refer to the process of visualizing, sensing, and narrating external realities that do not yet fully exist. I use fantasy to refer to a heightened state of imagination in which what is visualized or sensed lives in stark, seemingly impossible contrast to what is or likely will be. At the same time, I pay deep attention to the significance of felt, embodied, and material (if partial) consequences and manifestations of imagination and fantasy. I am interested in the ways imagination makes multiple states of being and belonging possible at the same time, even in contradictory ways, without necessitating a utopian, liberatory, or unidirectional disavowal of present-tense, embodied, and structural particularities.

Throughout, I follow a trend in my collaborators' narratives in which imagination allows individuals to dilute conventional boundaries of linear temporality, space, and selfhood. These imaginations also trouble the validity of a singular reality and disrupt conventional hierarchies between lived, "real" and desired, "false" experience. In this regard, I invoke the notion of fantasy as a kind of imagination that calls our attention to discrepancy, contradiction, incongruity, dissonance. By advocating for these qualities of fantasy, the individuals represented here highlight the contradictory role imagination can play in constructing notions of belonging at the level of the individual, the social, and the national/geopolitical. In doing so, they propose ways of thinking about subjectivity and agency, community, and structures of citizenship within migration and refugee studies. I situate this inquiry within scholarship on imagination, fantasy, and subjectivity that emerges from women of color feminisms, queer theory, performance studies, philosophy, and political theory to contribute to an interdisciplinary examination of subjectivity in refugee and migration studies.

It is impossible to account for the extensive disciplinary and methodological approaches to refugee and migration studies, but I identify a few themes that emerge around the theorization of imagination within these fields. In the development of contemporary formations of globalization toward the end of the 20th century, political theory and history drew upon imagination to critique the highly constructed parameters of seemingly naturalized social formations or "bodies" from communities to legal structures to nation-states. This is often applied specifically to refugee and migration studies to show how refugees and migrants unsettle the previously unexamined imagined cohesiveness of nation-states and their ability to control cultures, groups of people, and geographic political structures.[4] Political philosophers have furthered these debates by drawing more explicitly on psychoanalytic theorizations of imagination and fantasy in which fantasy is often sexualized and pathologized and functions as a false origin that one is forever trying to "reattain" even though it never existed in the first place. Various structures of power, from the ego to governments, then propose routes toward realizing this fantasy, thereby conditioning behavior and beliefs. For instance, anthropologist Arjun Appadurai calls imagination a "social practice" to account for the ways that imagination is, "a form of work . . . a form of negotiation between sites of agency (individuals) and globally defined fields of possibility." Appadurai distinguishes between imagination as a shared resource for agency and fantasy as a "private" and "individualistic" experience, an "opium for the masses," or an "escape from a world defined principally by more concrete purposes and structures."[5] When this philosophical/psychoanalytic genealogy gets taken up in refugee studies, it often helps scholars argue for the role of imagination in shaping collectivity as migrant communities share dreams for their new lives or likewise imagine retrospectively, in the form of memory and nostalgia, about home or fantasies of return.

Slavoj Žižek offers a shift in the value of fantasy, suggesting that political and ideological systems themselves are built upon deep inconsistencies and therefore have their own fantasies of origin that prescribe their behavior as well.[6] Žižek expands fantasy to encompass social and political formations and suggests that part of fantasy's value might lie in its very contradictions or inconsistencies. Similarly, feminist anthropologist Neferti X. M. Tadiar develops the framework of fantasy-production to argue for the sexual politics of global capital circulation and how fantasy manifests itself in embodied actions from the individual level to the nation-state. This informs my valuation of the role of the body in performing and therefore partially manifesting fantasy, in what I call here neoliberal performances of self or neoliberal subjectivities, when I describe how my collaborators'[7] everyday behaviors index rich, complicated relationships to the state and the asylum system's collusion in neoliberal capitalist logics.

When these more recent theorizations of fantasy are used to analyze refugee subjectivity, they often and importantly attend to the multiple subjectivities of refugees held in extended states of displacement and desire through legally and socially drawn-out resettlement processes.[8] What I push against is the tendency to emphasize fantasy as a recuperative tool—a way to remain resilient in times of abjection until one can successfully integrate into a set of social, cultural, and economic parameters in their country of resettlement in a defined, attainable future moment. While fantasy, of course, refers to the future yet to be realized, its definition along with its quotidian connotations can also invoke a sense that what is imagined or desired is impossible or improbable, never to occur.[9] Where others take up the potentiality of fantasy, I am interested in its incommensurability, its improbability, and its dissonance and how these articulate a multiplicity in which many pasts, presents, and futures might exist at the same time without resolution.

In many ways this directionality is resonant with José Esteban Muñoz's configuration of queer futurity in which aesthetically imagining and approaching utopian worlds does not propose a future to be realized, but rather indexes the failure or negation of what is in the present while also acknowledging the existence, in that very present, of what could and should be.[10] I offer a queer performance studies critique of existing scholarship about imagination and fantasy in relation to refugee subjectivity and agency similar to Muñoz's notion of disidentification,[11] which founds his articulation of utopia. In this essay, my collaborators perform contradictory identifications in order to reveal the fragile construction of these identities and the structural power dynamics that enforce their boundaries. Where this essay diverges slightly is that my collaborators are not necessarily performing stereotypes with the intent of critique, but rather to secure genuine access. Their multiple conflicting identifications live unresolved alongside one another and do not always collapse or crack in ways that immediately reveal a subversion. Lastly, many of the performances I attend to here are themselves imagined, locating the subversive contradiction in the imaginary, perhaps expanding the sense of impossibilities bound up in the performances analyzed by Muñoz.

Informed by women of color feminisms, queer theory, and performance studies analyses of subjectivity and the body that encourage us to think of states of undecidability, of "possible-impossible"[12] subjectivity as perpetual and perhaps desirable states of being, this essay invites us to live in the disjuncture and to interrogate what this imposes upon and makes possible for our relationships to self, others, and power. Performance studies' attention to the simultaneous scripted and unpredictably live nature of everyday behavior also allows for a more complex consideration of agency in which individual behavior, including fantasizing, is highly conditioned by existing structures while also holding liberatory potential at the same time. Therefore, in addition to thinking of refugee fantasies as recuperative in a way that allows refugees to be resilient under the structural disavowal of the asylum system in order to work toward reintegration as a successful, stable, self and member of society, I want to "stay with the trouble"[13] in order to think of fantasy as a resistance to notions of resilience and integration as well as a potentially desired state of being for refugees. Fantasy's appeal to dissonance asks us to uncomfortably hold together the lived reality that refugees genuinely want to live whole, healthy, "productive" lives that in many ways assimilate into the neoliberal lifeways entrenched in the transnational asylum system while at the same time honoring the rich potential of the contradictory embrace of statelessness in its many forms: legal, geopolitical, psychological and material (bodily) articulated by the queer African refugees I theorize with in the following pages.

I name my collaborators' imaginations, behaviors, and stories as performances for many reasons, but for this argument particularly because performance, with its invocation of repetition through rehearsals and public restagings across time and place, allows us to think of the self and our relationships as a series of repetitions across time and space. This supports my focus on how the intersections of queerness, Africanness, and refugeeness argues for the dissolution of a single self and rather an insistence on the production of the individual as always already imbricated in and across other people, places, versions of the "single" self, histories, legal systems, and other structures of power. This line of thinking is informed by and parallel to poststructuralist theories of relational subjectivity.[14] My collaborators play with the cyclical or performative reproduction in ways that are both agentive and conditioned. In what follows, I hone in on a series of everyday tactics that could be read as ideal capitalist, neoliberal performances of self-emphasizing individuality, grittiness, and liberation or self-realization through consumption—but that paradoxically allow for queerness and non-geopolitically bound notions of self to flourish and work horizontally across national borders as well as individual selves.[15] In so doing, my collaborators postulate critiques of the givenness of neoliberal capitalist structures of subject formation within asylum systems and discourses. They begin to chart the edges, or perhaps the end, of our current political economic structure, particularly the ways neoliberal capitalism structures modes of citizenship, belonging, and subjectivity in the United States.

This research extends fieldwork during which I lived and worked for over seven years with a growing network of LGBTIQ African refugees seeking asylum in South Africa from across the continent. We collaboratively devised a series of staged and quotidian performances that sought to complicate contemporary representations and monolithic legal, political, and cultural framings of people who were simultaneously queer, African, and foreign (to South Africa). Throughout this fieldwork, almost all of my collaborators expressed dreams of resettling to the United States, articulating imaginations, perhaps even fantasies, of broad acceptance, economic opportunity, and liberal social protections. We had (and continue to have) regular conversations during which I would propose critiques of U.S. exceptionalism when it came to acceptance of queer, foreign, and Black bodies, particularly after the 2016 election. And they would challenge me by pointing out the already contradictory nature of their experiences in South Africa and that at least, by comparison, the United States had abundant resources, making even nominal acceptance more desirable. Nevertheless, what I witnessed in South Africa was a tightly knit, though amorphous, group of people working in less than ideal conditions to facilitate queer belonging, intimacy, and survival, and I was curious about how these tactics would translate in the process of resettlement, especially to the United States, especially after the 2016 election with xenophobic rhetoric and policy on the rise and civil rights eroding by the day.

I stayed in touch with these resettled friends, communicating regularly through various social media platforms, having extended video chat conversations and formal research interviews, and having been able to visit each in person over the one to five years of their resettlement (from 2014 to present). Through them, I have been introduced to a wider range of queer African refugees who have been resettled to the United States, some of whom had not arrived via South Africa. This writing draws only on my research with three of the refugees who have been resettled since my fieldwork in South Africa, though their insights and experiences are often parallel to a wider "sample" of individuals. The once close-knit community of LGBTIQ asylum seekers in South Africa are no longer bound by proximity, geographic journey, or loosely correlated history and cultural experience as "Africans."[16] For the most part, they were living alone, working to accumulate financial stability, and integrating their sense of self into the highly isolated, individualized culture and political economy.

Throughout our interviews and time together, my collaborators seemingly, if necessarily, embraced the privatized, commodity-driven lifestyle narrated by the United States as a land of opportunity as well as fantasies of a liberal, all-inclusive queer community often endorsed by mainstream representations of LGBT people and communities as well as liberal human rights discourse. François talked about actively using gay dating apps, going to the club to find men, attempting to train his body to appear more muscular and masculine. Juju, who I will introduce in a moment, discussed using Uber, intentionally wearing headphones with his iPhone to avoid public interactions, and his desire to get married. Were they assimilating? Adopting and reproducing all the trappings of the dominant paradigm of a gay, white, cis-male, able-bodied, consumer?

Performing Queer Fantasies of Belonging

In a casual Skype conversation, Juju and I are talking about connections back to South Africa and Uganda. Juju left Uganda in 2004 after his mother tried to kill him when she found out about his sexuality. After spending almost a decade in South Africa, struggling to hold down jobs and housing and attacked multiple times for his gender presentation and sexuality, Juju was successfully resettled to San Francisco in 2015. Juju is in his early 30's and identifies as gay, queer, and transgender in different contexts. He talks often of finding the right man to marry. While struggling to find affordable and reliable housing and employment in the Bay Area, he has successfully started paralegal courses at a local university in pursuit of his dreams of becoming a human rights lawyer. I ask Juju, *"has coming to the US changed your relationship to people back in Uganda?"*

He responds, focusing in specifically on his family,

> I think me coming to the US brought our relationship together. When I was in South Africa they were not even talking to me or anything, but coming to the US made them like come back. They start talking to me, calling me. The distance is still very far. But there's something I have to tell them about my health too because it's permanent. But I don't want to tell them because they're in Africa. They don't know like you can be healthy, you can be fine. So, in my mind I see if they get to come over here, that's when maybe they will just sit and I'll put all my medication on the table. "Do you guys see what you did?" You know. "This is homophobia, this is what it leads me to do. Because if I had your support, if I had family support, I don't think I would be in this situations [sic]. So you guys put me in this situation, but the good thing is I'm a survivor and I'm still around. And, I helped you, I made you come over here. So the lesson is you have to treat the next generation and no matter who the person is, they have to be treated with dignity and respect." That's going to be my message to them.[17]

Among many compelling insights into the role of distance in facilitating intimacy and the authority that access to and establishing a life within the United States lends to his gender identity and sexuality, Juju spends a majority of his time reflecting on this relationship in a moment of imagined interaction—talking to his family about his HIV status. Juju imagines and performs multiple selves and realities simultaneously: there is Juju telling the story, past Juju disowned by his family due to his sexuality, and Juju whose health is made vulnerable by the compounded homophobia and xenophobia of South Africa. There is also future, healthy Juju in the United States with his family and, arguably, Juju whose sense of self is bound up with and dependent on the materiality of antiretroviral medications, which feature as the central prop through which Juju punctuates his political message to his future, imagined family. These multiple selves live in conjunction and at times at odds with multiple contexts for Juju's narration: there is the hypothetical meeting with his family, the potential realization of a more radical politics made possible through this meeting, the past conditions of Juju's family's rejection, the present ambiguity as his relationship to them shifts along with his geographic location and his physical health, and of course the broader sociopolitical context of Juju's resettlement. Across many conversations, Juju has expressed—and I have personally witnessed—his struggles with racism within LGBTQ spaces, homophobia and xenophobia in the workplace and in securing housing, and the dualistic insistence on and suspension of Juju's ability to assimilate or even build a stable life due to the extensive bureaucratic timeline and loopholes of the U.S. immigration system, especially after the 2016 election. Given these multiple, contradictory conditions, we might call Juju's imagination a fantasy. Juju's fantasy does not singularly imagine an assimilated self, nor does he fondly reconstruct a relationship to family and place based on nostalgia or desired return, nor does he propose an isolated critique of U.S. nationalism, nor does he articulate a fluid, displaced, and therefore liberated sense of self.

At the same time, Juju points to how arrival in the United States and supposed access to its resources facilitates a closer relationship with and acceptance by his family. Juju has both experienced and further imagines how being accepted by the United States translates into acceptance from his family as well as giving him a sense of authority in shaping the terms of their relationship—a stark shift from being disowned because of his sexuality. As Juju states, "*I helped you, I made you come over here.*" On the one hand, Juju might replicate paradigms of U.S. imperial behaviors toward Africa, the very same paradigm that resulted in Juju's own relocation. On the other, this power dynamic does not singularly assert a selfish, improved relationship with his family, nor even an immediately improved future for Juju. Rather, through this intimate fantasy with his family, he maps complex circulations of power that target specific people for neglect and erasure while positing possible reframing of conventional narratives that assume seropositivity to be a singular, unidirectional condition.

Juju's HIV status is closely linked to his sexuality. His serostatus elucidates the structural conditions that produce and naturalize vulnerability among particular groups of people—in this case, LGBTIQ people in sub-Saharan regions of Africa. Juju's serostatus changed because he didn't have access to sustainable housing, employment, and social relations because the South African government failed to provide rights to those seeking asylum from gender- and sexual- orientation-based violence. In asking, "*Do you see what you guys did?*" he suggests his family plays an intimate role in these structural conditions. It is *through* and *upon* this very status that Juju builds (imagines) and demonstrates a successful, fulfilling life to his family and upon which he imagines their personal growth and acceptance as well as his broad political charge, no matter how unlikely. Juju's fantasy calls our attention to the ways that this imagination of U.S. exceptionalism results in cultural imaginations of other places as uncivilized or undeveloped that both critique and validate, for instance, their "inherent" homophobia. Juju's fantasy presents many discrepancies, such as praising his access to health care in the United States while he would later talk about his health being affected by not being able to maintain a steady job because of homophobic and xenophobic incidents. This disjuncture opens space for us to perceive and critique transnational circuits of homophobia as it manifests in different personal and policy levels. To be more specific, here, Juju's fantasy connects access to medicine to his family's reaction to and treatment of his sexuality and gender.

The fanciful imagination facilitates a doubling of assimilation and resistance. Juju's fantasy articulates a reality largely at odds with his lived experience that I have observed, that he has discussed openly on social media and that he describes elsewhere in our conversations in which he critiques the persistent racism, xenophobia, and homophobia he experiences in the United States. In embracing rather than trying to fix the dissonance of his fantasy, what emerges is a much more expansive politics in which contradiction is central. In fact, this inconsistency is internalized—in Juju's own relationship to himself. Subjectivity exceeds singularity and fixedness to be multiple and contrary. This happens not just in regard to Juju's intersectional identity, but between present, material Juju in this world and an imagined Juju of another time and condition. He is critical of his family and his experiences in Uganda, South Africa, and the United States, *and* he participates in performances that embrace and perpetuate the very relationships and conditions he critiques. This incommensurability between critique and assimilation suggests alternative ways of constituting evolutionary, unidirectional notions of progress for refugees or progressive politics more broadly wherein those with "bad politics" are left behind or unitary notions of community in which an individual with "problematic" worldviews or behaviors is excluded. By embracing contradiction, contradiction becomes part of the "better" future imagined, which, in this specific case, procures a political commitment beyond the individual. Juju moves from educating his family and establishing a fulfilling life for himself to a broad, generational assertion of respect and dignity. He critiques the difficulties he has experienced in the United States while upholding it as a place of wealth, human rights, and acceptance. By not resolving this contrariness, the temporality of progress or past trauma often affixed to imagination and fantasy for refugees is disrupted, which has implications for the ways non-refugees and refugees narrate, structure, and experience resettlement, displacement, assimilation, and structures of citizenship, the nation, and belonging.

Kaia, a lesbian from Malawi, echoes Juju's imagination when I ask her about changes in her relationships in her country of origin. Kaia was resettled to DC from South Africa. Despite having a good relationship with her family, members of her village in Malawi began to threaten her and her family, which she does not reveal to anyone except in her asylum interviews. So, she left in hopes of ensuring her and her family's safety. Kaia continues to work in informal economies in DC and has a long-term girlfriend who helps support them with housing and a reliable income. Kaia shares:

> My relationship with my mom was always good. Even when I was in South Africa. She was like a big support and yeah. She was really a big support. Compared to the other family members, my mom was. Even she not like, you know, okay with my lifestyle or whatever, but she always was support and continue to be the person you're supposed to be.
>
> And specially you know, the other thing, you know when I was in South Africa, I was like just feeling her voice. And, it's been like let's see, eight years now I didn't see her. And, you know, arriving here in my mind, I have this picture of her, you know, looking like a sixty-year woman, you know. I still saw that picture, you know. And 26th of July of this year, that's her birthday, so I did a video call. Oh my gosh I was so submerged. And I was like, oh my gosh. Cause, I could see how the time is passing, you know, she's getting old. She's 77 now years old. Yeah. And, I was like, oh my gosh, when we like were done, you know, with the communication, I started crying. I couldn't stop crying because it was like oh my gosh.
>
> It was something. It was something. And I think, maybe if I try again a second time she will see me too. It feel much better cause she could see how I looked like. See that I am healthy and I am strong. I don't want to tell her, you know, but at least maybe she can see and she will know. That's something.[18]

Kaia grounds the ways we can think about queer refugee fantasy and demonstrates how it can manifest through everyday practices, like using Skype. As for most obedient neoliberal subjects, technology expedites convenient ties across distance while allowing one to continue to pursue individualistic advancement. For example, for many people in the United States, video calls allow us to perform familial duties and maintain intimate communication while also pursuing personal, often career-oriented goals that might distance us from more regular, in-person relationships to home, family, and our past. Additionally, as has often been theorized around migration, technology both elicits and manages existing roles of memory and imagination in maintaining a connection to home.[19] Kaia's word choice, "submerged," describes the feeling of perhaps losing or sharing one's autonomy with time and with another. Kaia is submerged in the overwhelming experience of her mother's transformation over time. Kaia's uncontrollable crying signals an experience that exceeds herself. This is then reciprocated by the fact that Kaia wants to communicate her health through appearance, much like Juju, constructing a shared understanding of her health that relies more heavily on her mother's perception, her interpolation of her than, say, directly telling her mother about her health.

I am interested in how this openness of subjectivity to another is made possible by queerness in two ways. One, Kaia is also HIV positive as the result of a "corrective rape"—the name commonly used in South Africa for sexual assault intended to make a lesbian "straight"—while seeking asylum in South Africa. Kaia, like Juju, imagines demonstrating physical well-being, in this case to her mother. Because of widespread stigma around HIV-positive status which, for Kaia, is implicitly bound up in her sexuality, Kaia's imagined interaction with her mother is based upon being able to claim and demonstrate a future embodiment, a self that is "healthy and strong" and a self that does not need to tell, but can show. Therefore, her imagination is queer because it is founded upon performing an-other self that can be read as both physically healthy in relation to her serostatus and mentally and emotionally healthy in who she is as a queer woman. Additionally, Kaia enacts a queered version of the coming-out trope to her mother.[20]

The role of subjectivity and embodiment staged in her imagination further unravels conventional notions of an individual self that is produced in relation to digital technology. Kaia's experience of submersion in being confronted with her mother's aged body articulates a queer sublimation of self in relation to another—her mother and the power of the technology itself. Kaia is undone, allows herself to be undone, giving herself to the "something" that this digital connection imposes on her. Kaia does not bolster a notion of herself as a coherent individual using technology to communicate with a distant relative in order to prioritize her pursuit of an individually focused, self-fulfilling life separate from family. Instead, she gives herself up to another, to her mother scattered across time from the woman Kaia imagined to the woman projected onto the screen before her. Rather than technology solidifying individualism as François points out, Kaia's use of digital media sublimates her sense of self—of a contained body and identity—and her sense of another (her mother) as fixed in time and in a particular body. This intersubjectivity between herself and her mother, between herself and her past self and her mother and her mother's past self, and between both of them and the technology they are using ignites imagined interactions.

A final example focuses on performances of dissonant imagination that help demonstrate how these fantasies take place both in visualized images, self-narrations, *and* through the body. We return to Juju who, when I ask about the differences in homophobia he encountered in the United States compared to in South Africa or Uganda, says:

> Um . . . I think most of it yes, it's verbal abuse . . . on the streets. Since I came, I'm lucky, I've never been beaten up like it was in South Africa where even after two weeks or three weeks you get beaten up. That's why like most of the time if I want to go out I just make sure I put on my ear phones. Like if I'm using public transport, I don't have to hear what are the people saying and sometimes people, because they know what they say might be illegal, mostly people talk indirectly. Like I'll be talking about you, but I'll be talking like I'm talking about someone else. It affects you mentally more than physically. That's why they say if we cannot kill them physically, let's kill them mentally. So, they put you in a position where you start having mental health issues. Or instead of public transport maybe I will take an Uber, you know, so that way I don't have to talk to or hear those people what they have to say. Here that's how I live my life.[21]

On the surface, Juju appears to be brilliantly assimilating into U.S. norms that encourage and ensure our isolationist individuality: walking down the street looking at our phones with headphones in and using rideshare services in which we don't even have to talk to the driver if we don't want. It is the very same antisocial behavior that François critiqued at the opening of this essay. I kept coming back to this moment, fixated on what should have been the most mundane part of our conversation. It struck me that Juju's theorization of the way homophobic violence reconfigures itself in the supposedly liberal United States in order to perpetuate networks of difference and oppression resonated with a similar observation François made about the repertoire of queer sociality when he noted that in South Africa it was much more embodied and ubiquitous:

> In South Africa, at least, you know, there's this things of meeting outside. You know? Yes there are dating sites, but uh, when you outside, you know, in public the body language. It was no . . . you're looking at someone and then they. No much talking, but just the body language, you know. And then you could, you know, approach

someone. Then you could talk to someone. Then, yeah. And whatever. And that
was everywhere. It could be in the train station, it could be on the beach, it could
be, you know, everywhere in South Africa. But, here seems like it must be like a
specific place. And even when it's done in this specific place like in the . . . village,
the gay village, here, they still, uh . . . have like a problem to, to, to be approached or
to approach. Here everybody's it's like distance, you know. There is this kind of like,
uh, yeah. I don't know how the culture here because even in the, uh, metro. In the
subway, you could see those people avoiding to look at each other. Some of them on
they cell phone or there's really just a thing of avoiding looking at each other. It's, my
gosh, it's really really difficult.[22]

Juju identifies that in verbal homophobic violence there exists a less public, less identifiable effect, which might be internalized—one hears the threat, feels affected, and may then move, think, or behave differently in response to this attack. Internalization could be seen as a form of individualization in which the homophobic violence is taken within the individual and often invisibly reproduced therein, such that it becomes more difficult at times to both identify its source or even its existence. Physical homophobic violence renders two physical forms in an indelible moment of contact, an interpersonal relationality that can be evidenced in more material ways.

When Juju puts on headphones or takes a rideshare, he is not merely isolating himself in an individualistic pursuit of comfort in public spaces (that is, converting a public to a private, individualistic space), he is deflecting and denying access to his interiority. The repertoire, physical gestures, of individualism not only protects Juju, in some ways asserting an individuality, it also allows Juju to imagine he is elsewhere. He is transported physically and imaginatively to another place. In fantasy, Juju opens up an imagined alternative political and social structure in which his being is no longer threatened. But is this still an individualistic gesture and is that necessarily negative? Juju's actions do not immediately appear to make space for a collectivity in the ways the previous examples do. But, then again, Juju and other LGBTIQ African refugees are not *supposed* to be individuals. Rather, their rehearsals of self throughout the asylum application and resettlement process are supposed to posit and strengthen universal truths—the contradiction of proving individual harm through such a process that in the very moment of individual narration, one becomes utterly flattened, having to perform Westernized comportments of homosexuality, monolithic narratives of African homophobia and violence, inherent refugee victimhood, and unquestionable graciousness on behalf of the receiving country—in order to be legible to the asylum system.

Juju breaks from the universality scripted onto refugees, especially LGBTIQ refugees. There is an individual where there should be none. Through fantastic imaginations, Juju, Kaia, François, and others complicate a singular figuration of

LGBTIQ African refugees by situating themselves in direct performative inter-section with the repertoires and self-fashioning of neoliberalism in the United States. The everyday performances discussed here both reify and internally alter the shape and look these same political and economic structures impose on ev-eryday life, asking: can we imagine beyond a model of dichotomous inclusion/exclusion, self/other, assimilation/resistance?

The Expansive Politics of Fantasy

Paying attention to imagination forced me to think twice about romanticized accounts or expectations—fantasies in their own right—of refugee agency and resilience. My collaborators understand themselves as simultaneously attempt-ing to survive and build fulfilling lives in entirely new and often hostile settings with few—and rapidly disappearing—resources. In a way, they are committed to and demanding the actualization of U.S. exceptionalism and inclusion prof-fered by narratives of progressive LGBT civil rights and acceptance of (deserving) refugees. These everyday theorizations, these adaptive, if submerged, practices also reveal how potentially embracing dissonance, rather than trying to pin it down or disentangle its complexities, might in itself be a strategy of survival and world-making that maintains an (il)logic of contradiction as a way to manifest new relationships to self, others, and power.

For instance, when I ask François specifically about how the current president and his administration's xenophobic policies are affecting him personally, he rebuts, "It's not a Trump thing. It's a world ignorance. . . . What doesn't matter is him, what matters is us. One of the things I've learned from my journey, at times when I am almost on the streets, it is those in the worst place, worst off who offer a little help. They always had joy in their face. I really learned from them. I use that to get myself to go forward." These political attitudes demonstrate a more expansive set of concerns and experiences across multiple contexts and histories that go far beyond the individual and the United States. They also offer some conceptual guideposts for centering queer migrant experience as an analytical framework from which to think otherwise about political commitments, modes of activism, and everyday performances of self/collective within contemporary conditions in the United States in which regressive nationalism is emerging within a paradigm of heightened neoliberal individualism. In this way, rather than seeing the margins as something to which LGBTIQ African refugees are relegated, I am suggesting scholars and activists of refugee experiences might invert this logic to ask how LGBTIQ African refugees are mapping the edges of neoliberal capital-ist paradigms, reminding us that there is an edge, an end—that there always has been—and, allowing us to imagine beyond it.

My collaborators' seemingly assimilative adoption of individualistic every-day behaviors and relations extends existing analyses of how the asylum system compartmentalizes multiple, intersecting identities within an individual. The selective sliver of everyday tactics explored in this chapter reveals how a strategic redeployment of individuality and the falsely static identities (LGBTIQ, African, refugee) that produce queer African refugees in the first place carry over into the resettlement process. Creative redeployment of individualism and static identity categories facilitates access to resources and a livable life while subtly opening up fissures in our expectations about these supposedly fixed identities as well as the very Westernized, neoliberal expectation of individual, coherent selfhood. In doing so, my collaborators work to reshape what belonging to a nation or com-munity looks and feels like. These reshapings of singular subjecthood exemplify a set of tactics for survival as these LGBTIQ African refugees work to accom-modate a divergent set of selves across varying times, spaces, and relationships while existing within a set of conditions that continuously work for the exclu-sion and eradication of these hybrid subjectivities. At their broadest, then, the openings created by François, Kaia, and Juju offer ways to perceive and analyze structures of citizenship, community formation, and national imaginaries. And, importantly, they do so without reconciling the improbable, contradictory selves that they are or might be with the social and political structures that are or might be. In other words, the radical undoing of self, unself-making, unworlding that François, Kaia, and Juju experience and enact might allow us to see our current conditions as already a fantasy and to imagine what is already possible now and has already been possible.

Notes

1. François in conversation with the author, December 2017.

2. For anonymity, all collaborators have chosen pseudonyms.

3. Like many LGBTIQ people from across the continent, François originally fled his country of origin for South Africa—the only country on the continent to offer asylum in response to gender and sexual-orientation–based violence—before seeking permanent resettlement elsewhere.

4. For examples, see Renata Saleci, "The Fantasy Structure of Nationalist Discourse," *PRAXIS International* 13, no. 3 (1993): 213–223; Sonia Madgalena Tascón, "Refugees and Asylum Seekers in Australia: Border-Crossers of the Postcolonial Imaginary," *Australian Journal of Human Rights* 8, no. 1 (2002): 125–139.

5. Arjun Appadurai, *Modernity at Large: Cultural Dimensions of Globalization* (Min-neapolis: University of Minnesota Press, 1996), 31.

6. Slavoj Žižek, *The Sublime Object of Ideology* (London: Verso Books, 1989).

7. I use the term *collaborators* instead of the more common *interlocutors* to attempt to heighten the reciprocal nature of this scholarship.

8. Barbara Pinelli, "Fantasy, Subjectivity and Vulnerability through the Story of a Woman Asylum Seeker in Italy," in *Being Human, Being Migrant: Senses of Self and Well-Being*, ed. Anne Sigrid Grønseth (New York: Berghahn Books, 2013).

9. The Oxford English Dictionary's first definition for fantasy is "the faculty or activity of imagining impossible or improbable things." Sub-point two adds, "an idea with no basis in reality."

10. José Esteban Muñoz, *Cruising Utopia: The Then and There of Queer Futurity* (New York: New York University Press, 2009).

11. José Esteban Muñoz, *Disidentifications: Queers of Color and the Performance of Politics* (Minneapolis: University of Minnesota Press, 1999).

12. Jacques Derrida, *Of Grammatology* (Baltimore: Johns Hopkins University Press, 1998).

13. Donna Haraway, *Staying with the Trouble: Making Kin in the Chthulucene* (Durham, N.C.: Duke University Press, 2016).

14. E. Jeffrey Popke, "Poststructuralist Ethics: Subjectivity, Responsibility and the Space of Community," *Progress in Human Geography* 27, no.3 (2003): 298–316; David R. Howarth, *Poststructuralism and After: Structure, Subjectivity and Power* (London: Palgrave Macmillan, 2013).

15. My attention to paradox within what could be called everyday performances of subversive assimilation is deeply indebted to Michael Taussig's work on mimesis and Homi Bhabha's exploration of mimicry and hybridity in postcolonial contexts. Homi Bhabha, "Of Mimicry and Man: The Ambivalence of Colonial Discourse," *Discipleship: A Special Issue on Psychoanalysis* 28 (1984): 125–133; Michael Taussig, *Mimesis and Alterity: A Particular History of the Senses* (New York: Routledge, 1993).

16. My collaborators regularly refer to themselves as "Africans" denoting their shared experiences, especially in contexts of white domination. I try to attend specifically to each individual experience, though I occasionally use this term as they do to refer to queer "African" refugees when attempting to make a broader claim based on their experience and those shared with me by queer refugees from the African continent.

17. Juju in conversation with the author, August 2017.

18. Kaia in conversation with the author, October 2016.

19. See Victoria Bernal, *Nation as Network: Diaspora, Cyberspace, and Citizenship* (Chicago: University of Chicago Press, 2014); Anna Everett, *Digital Diaspora a Race for Cyberspace* (Albany: State University of New York Press, 2009).

20. Most recently thoroughly analyzed in C. Riley Snorton, *Nobody Is Supposed to Know: Black Sexuality on the Down Low* (Minneapolis: University of Minnesota Press, 2014).

21. Juju in conversation with the author, March 2016.

22. François in conversation with the author, December 2017.

12

Validation through Documentation

Integrating Activism, Research, and Scholarship to Highlight (Validate) Trans Latin@ Immigrant Lives

JACK CÁRAVES AND BAMBY SALCEDO

This chapter is a result of our collaborative work, dialogue, and reflections. Due to our own experiential knowledge and positionality, the use of two voices is central to the substance contributed here. In using our distinct voices in collaboration, we follow the model offered by the foundational article in *Gender and Women's Studies* by María C. Lugones and Elizabeth Spelman, "Have We Got a Theory for You! Feminist Theory, Cultural Imperialism, and the Demand for Women's Voices."[1]

Jack Cáraves is a scholar-activist and, at the time of writing, a PhD candidate in Chicana/o Studies at UCLA. Bamby Salcedo is an internationally known activist, advocate, community organizer, and president and CEO of TransLatin@ Coalition, a nationally recognized organization that advocates for the dignity and respect of Trans Latin@ lives.

Bamby: The TransLatin@ Coalition on the Ground

When we started in 2009, only a few national organizations focused on policy and legislation that addressed the needs of trans people in the United States. TransLatin@ Coalition brought visibility to the voices and experiences of Trans Latin@ immigrants. Based in Los Angeles, the Coalition has expanded to New York, Chicago, Florida, Washington, D.C., Arizona, Georgia, Texas, Minnesota, Maryland, Virginia, California, and more locations. At a time of heightened scrutiny among Latina/o immigrants and criminalization among Latina/os, and as violence against trans women of color became rampant, we—as a coalition—sought to address the intersectional issues facing the lives of Trans Latin@s who are the most vulnerable due to their legal immigration status; gender identity and performance; racial, ethnic, and class background; and who were not represented in the nascent organizing of trans advocacy.

In 2015, as an organization, we decided to expand our network of members to include all trans Latin@s in our scope of work. The Coalition has since continued to focus on immigrants' issues and trans Latin@s but is inclusive of individuals regardless of their migratory status as well as transmasculine members. This expansion has also translated to the type of work the organization conducts. In addition to being an advocacy organization that fights for the rights and dignity of trans Latin@s, we have since incorporated direct services as part of our arsenal in combating structural and societal marginalization. As an organization, we know that providing service is part of empowering or community, and in doing this we take a grassroots, bottom-up approach that focuses on empowerment.

In 2016, our national office, based in Los Angeles, opened the Center for Violence Prevention and Transgender Wellness, which is a direct services program of the Coalition. We are creating the infrastructure and model of the Center and in the following years will roll out similar programs in Washington, D.C., Chicago, and other states where we have representation. The Center is open to all trans- and gender-nonconforming individuals. We offer a drop-in center where individuals can come in to acquire clothing and toiletries; daily food distribution; leadership development; workforce development, ESL classes, peer support; and a computer lab. Additionally, through this programming, we have created a subprogram, Surviving People Unveiling New Knowledge (SPUNK), where we provide trans women who are recently released from immigration detention and incarceration with emergency rental assistance, food vouchers, transportation vouchers, and support in finding temporary housing. Our goal with SPUNK is to reduce and ultimately eliminate the cycle of recidivism and incarceration within the trans community.

As a national organization, we believe that this two-arm operation of policy advocacy and direct services is crucial and necessary to challenge and eventually change the structures that continue to marginalize the trans community. Part of our mission as an organization is to elevate and empower the trans Latin@ community.

Jack: The Report—Community-Based Activism and Scholarship

Bamby and I met in 2015, at UCLA where she was screening "TransVisible: the Bamby Salcedo Story." We were introduced by a mutual friend, and I shared with Bamby my research interests regarding LGBTQ issues with a community focus. At that time, I was engaging in various community actions and events with organizations leading the LGBTQ Latinx movements in Los Angeles, including Familia:

Queer and Trans Liberation Movement, and DeColores's De Orange County, where I was an active member in DeColores's Detainee Visitation Program. After we had developed a friendship, Bamby approached me about collaborating with the Coalition as a researcher and conducting the first needs assessment of trans Latin@s in Southern California.

This would become TransLatin@ Coalition's second report, "The State of Trans Health: Trans Latin@s and their Health Care Needs." Together, we decided to use community-based participatory research (CBPR) as our method of approaching this project and putting together surveys. TransLatin@ Coalition was already familiar with this approach from their previous survey report, "TransVisible: Transgender Latina Immigrants in U.S. Society," put together collaboratively with Dr. Karla Padron. Often used in the field of public health, CBPR is an "orientation to research that focuses on relationships between academic and community partners."[2] In this way, CBPR is based on co-learning and mutual benefit through participation between both the researcher and the community partners. TransLatin@ Coalition decided that Bamby would be the co-principal investigator alongside me, and we would incorporate members of the Coalition in the decision-making processes. Once Bamby and I put together survey questions, we conducted pilot surveys with members of the Coalition and got their feedback on questions and the structure of the overall survey. As a team, we decided on six key areas we needed focus on to understand the holistic health of trans Latin@s in southern California: housing, employment, medical health, mental health, sexual health, and spirituality.

In collaboration with local groups, we eventually collected group surveys in the following locations: El Monte, Long Beach, Los Angeles, San Diego, San Fernando, and Santa Ana. We collected a total of 129 surveys in these six locations from January to August 2016. Bamby and I collectively analyzed the data and wrote the final report.

Because Bamby and Trans Latin@ Coalition members have been doing this work on the ground, I believe as a scholar activist that this type of work is necessary and crucial. I am constantly aware of my own privilege, power, and social justice responsibilities as an academic. As such, it is my responsibility to center the voices and stories of the participants and organizers.

Jack: The State of Trans Latin@s Health | Survey Findings

Of the 129 participants, 91 percent identified transwomen or transfeminine, and 9 percent identified as transmen or transmasculine. Of those participants, 57 percent make less than $10,000 a year and 37 percent were undocumented immigrants. Over one-third of survey participants were homeless, lived in temporary housing, or relied on someone else for housing. Roughly 20 percent of participants had full-time work while 26 percent were unemployed. These harsh realities often push trans people, especially trans Latinas, into sex work, which further criminalizes them.

When it comes to medical health care, we found that close to 50 percent of participants do have health insurance through Medical or Medicaid, yet 28 percent of participants have no health insurance coverage at all. A majority of participants reported that when it came to both medical health care and mental health care, they were not receiving the health care they need because they lacked personal resources and an ability to travel long distances to receive health care.

One surprising finding was the affinity for spirituality services. Seventy-six percent indicated that they believe that their spirituality is important to their overall health and well-being. In addition to peer support groups and the support of trans friends and accepting family members, spirituality is a major source of resilience and empowerment. In particular, spirituality allows individuals to cultivate healing and harmony within oneself[3] and between others and their environment,[4] and a sense of hope for the future.[5]

My (2019) dissertation, "Trans Latinx Lives and Strategies of Self Preservation," builds on these survey findings, with in-depth interviews with survey participants. I expand the focus on employment, family, and spirituality. Quite often, familial ties—both biological and chosen family—and spirituality provide support and allow trans Latin@s to harness the necessary resilience to survive in a hostile world.

Bamby: Scholarship as a Tool for Visibility

In addition to the advocacy, organizing, and direct action, we at TransLatin@ Coalition have, as Jack mentioned, published two reports "TransVisible" and the "State of Trans Health," that demonstrate an urgent need in the trans community. We know that social determinants impact and shape every human-being's livelihood. This is no different for trans people. If you do not have essential things like a job, an education, and safe and stable housing, then you are forced to live in high-risk neighborhoods. In the neighborhoods where trans Latin@s are forced to live, one might get arrested for just walking down the street because this might be labeled as a prostitution zone. There is a stigma attached to trans people—especially trans women of color—that basically everywhere we are and everywhere we go, we get criminalized. We are constantly assumed to be sex workers and drug addicts. The reality is that social constructions push us to be where we are within our society and push us into the streets. This means that as trans people, our bodies are vulnerable to a vicious cycle of incarceration and immigration detention for those who are undocumented. Both prison and immigration detention are places wherein trans Latin@s are assaulted verbally, physically, and sexually simply because of our very being.

That is why we wanted to team up with Jack and conduct the State of Trans Health survey. We were interested in seeing health through a holistic lens. Issues like mental health, medical health, sexual health, housing, employment, and spirituality were critical for us to have a broader sense of what health means to us. The survey supports the Coalition by serving as an educational tool for other organizations, policy makers, and service providers who service trans Latin@s. This report is the first of its kind and has already helped us expand the direct services that we offer through the Center Violence Prevention and Transgender Wellness.

On a personal level, in addition to being an activist, organizer, and president of TransLatin@ Coalition, I am also working to obtain my master's degree in Chican@/Latin@ studies at California State University, Los Angeles. In particular, I am training in social science methods of data collection with an emphasis on trans Latin@ immigrant issues. I am going to do my research and write my thesis on the resilience of trans Latin@ immigrants to figure out what it is that they do to navigate such a marginalizing society. I expect to graduate by the end of 2018. I am not completely sure if a doctoral program is in my future, as I am building an organization and I want for it to be sustainable. I do want to teach Chican@ studies at a community college and bring the trans Latin@ flavor into the conversation to bring awareness to young students who want to pursue higher education.

Bamby and Jack: Imagining a Liberatory Future

My ideal world is a beautiful place. But unfortunately, I also know that I won't live long enough to see the ideal world. I know that as an organization, we at TransLatin@ Coalition are contributing to making other people's ideal world a reality.

We imagine a world where we, as trans- and gender-nonconforming people, can walk freely in the world knowing we can be who we are without being physically, emotionally, or verbally attacked. Liberation means believing in our own livelihood, in our own power, and our own potential. Liberation entails being able to heal our wounds. Once we eliminate our internalized fear of who we are, we can begin to eliminate the fear that exists in our families, our communities, and our larger society.

In order to reach liberation, several things must change, including the multiple systems that do not recognize or value trans- and gender-nonconforming individuals. We as trans- and gender-nonconforming people have been around forever. We have a history of organizing and resisting. We would just tell our community and our people not to give up. If we continue to organize, resist, persist, insist, and understand that our existence is valuable and necessary—then together we can move forward and transform the world.

Notes

1. María C. Lugones and Elizabeth V. Spelman, "Have We Got a Theory for You! Feminist Theory, Cultural Imperialism, and the Demand for Women's Voices," *Women's Studies International Forum* 6, no. 6 (1983): 573–581.

2. Nina B. Wallerstein and Bonnie Duran, "Using Community-Based Participatory Research to Address Health Disparities," *Health Promotion Practice* 7, no. 3 (2006): 312.

3. Elisa Facio and Irene Lara, eds. *Fleshing the Spirit: Spirituality and Activism in Chicana, Latina, and Indigenous Women's Lives* (Tucson: University of Arizona Press, 2014).

4. Ibid.

5. Anneliese A. Singh and Vel S. McKleroy. "'Just Getting out of Bed Is a Revolutionary Act': The Resilience of Transgender People of Color Who Have Survived Traumatic Life Events," *Traumatology* 17, no. 2 (2011): 34–44.

13

Shameless Interruptions

Finding Survival at the Edges of Trans and Queer Migrations

RUBEN ZECENA

In a video produced by the activist organization Trans Queer Pueblo (Pueblo), which is based in Phoenix, Arizona, they ask: "Can we take Phoenix's Pride back to its roots?"[1] The video features one of their key organizers, Karyna Jaramillo, an undocumented transgender woman from Morelos, México, and leader of the group's defense and liberation program. It begins with Jaramillo preparing a Tarot card reading session by lighting a candle, burning sage, organizing her floral decorated Tarot cards, and providing a different genealogy of LGBT history where trans women of color are at the forefront of LGBT liberation. Referencing Sylvia Rivera and Marsha "Pay it no mind" Johnson, cofounders of the Street Transvestite Action Revolutionaries (STAR) and pivotal figures in the 1969 Stonewall uprising, Jaramillo situates the origins of Pride not in corporations or the police, but in the liberatory visions of trans women of color elders. Further, she reminds the Phoenix Pride organizing committee that "Sin justicia, no hay orgullo/without justice, there is no pride."[2] To summarize briefly, this video was produced to promote Pueblo's message and demonstration in the Phoenix Pride parade on April 2, 2017. At this event, Pueblo members interrupted the parade to denounce police brutality and anti-immigrant legislation, but they were publicly shamed with racial slurs and boos from mainly white attendees.[3] Even though this demonstration resulted in the shaming of Pueblo, their decision to challenge a widely celebrated event by LGBT communities signals a refusal to remain silent through their calls for survival. Moreover, Pueblo's interruption of the parade generated an affective response that is suggestive of the racialized shaming that trans and queer migrants face in LGBT public spheres.

In this chapter, I argue that the *shameless interruption* is particularly useful to understand how trans and queer migrants negotiate the complex relationship between alienation in dominant LGBT communities and a commitment to what Karma Chávez (2013) calls a queer migration politics; these politics grapple with coalition building among migrant and LGBT communities.[4] Drawing from queer migration studies and queer theories of affect, this chapter explores shameless interruptions as survival strategies that trans and queer migrants enact when shame alienates them from LGBT public and private spheres.[5] As I suggest, shameless interruptions are affective, performative, and temporal strategies that challenge the constraints of normative belonging within LGBT politics and that ask us to linger with the possibilities of temporal disruption. For example, shameless interruptions can be gleaned in Pueblo's demonstration when they stopped the progression of the parade for five minutes and continued marching even in the face of hostility; more importantly, their decision to interrupt Phoenix Pride draws attention to the connections between trans, queer, and migrant organizing by offering intersectional critiques of institutional power. Furthermore, by gesturing toward the temporal aspects of interruption, I build on scholarship in queer studies that describes interruption as moments where queer temporalities become visible, or as Elizabeth Freeman writes, "points of resistance to the temporal order."[6]

Despite the surge in visibility and acceptance that heteronormative migrant rights organizations have gained, queer migration politics often employ survival strategies, such as shameless interruptions, that are dismissed as uncivil and unnecessary in mainstream media. To counter the dismissal of queer migration politics, this chapter examines online activist documents, including letters and video recordings of protests, and argues that shameless interruptions provide trans and queer migrants with important avenues for critique and survival. These concerns guide my analysis of shamelessness to ask: How do trans and queer migrants perform shamelessness to contest proper modes of LGBT citizenship and belonging? How does shamelessness differ from pride, and what does it enable trans and queer migrants to do? Crucially, then, I address shameless interruptions as more than resistance to normative LGBT politics and citizenship, but rather as poignantly affective survival strategies that resonate with the political orientations of what Lauren Berlant calls lateral agency. Such agency, Berlant writes, is "directed toward making a less-bad experience. It's a relief, a reprieve, not a repair."[7] Under heteronormative and cisnormative racist deportation regimes, survival offers migrants one way to negotiate the violent and precarious conditions of migrant criminalization.

To address these questions, I begin by describing the theoretical framework and materials that the chapter engages. Second, I discuss the contributions and theoretical interventions that shamelessness creates within queer studies and draw from Chicana/Latina Studies to argue that shame has material and lived effects on the lives of minoritarian subjects. Third, I analyze the affective dimensions of Jennicet Gutiérrez's "heckling" of Barack Obama at a White House Pride reception.[8] This section brings to light how Gutiérrez's interruption challenges normative notions of belonging and citizenship and highlights the violence that the president of the United States encouraged. I conclude by analyzing a video of Pueblo's interruption of the Phoenix Pride parade to explore how shameless interruptions illustrate racialized power dynamics in LGBT communities and work as entry points for building further coalitions among trans and queer migrant communities whose futures are precarious. Above all, this chapter conceptualizes shameless interruptions as subversive survival strategies that keep open opportunities for queer migration activism and politics.

Theoretical Framework and Materials

This chapter weaves together affect theory and queer migration studies by making legible the immaterial forces that simultaneously bind trans and queer migrants to inhumane living conditions and those that *move* them into action. Sara Ahmed, whose scholarship is influential to the affective "turn" in the humanities, offers a rich analysis of the circulation of affect in social and public spheres and argues that in "affective economies, emotions *do things*, they align individuals with communities."[9] In this way, Ahmed demonstrates not what affect is, but what it does in the social sphere: sticky alignments among subjects and signs. Her theory of affective economies shows how these alignments, when used to bind and "stick" subjects under the sign of citizenship, helps to form normative structures that govern "democratic norms of behavior and conduct, of what it means to be civil."[10] Her approach to affective economies and citizenship points to the ways in which affect structures social behavior, but it also develops a language to analyze the subversive potential of incivility—what I am calling a shameless interruption. Further, Ahmed's consideration of affect with emotions enables me to engage the affective value of shameless interruptions and make observations in regard to the pain, anger, and hope that trans and queer migrants express.

This attention to affect and citizenship is fortified through queer migration studies, which offers a useful conceptual space to identify the global forces that displace migrants across varying axes of power. It also draws attention to the influence of heteronormativity in early migration scholarship that assumed that all migrants were heterosexual. Further, queer migration scholarship, emerging from the early 1990s, reveals the importance of studying sexuality as a structuring aspect of *all* international migrations and benefits from using "the tools of queer studies as a way to complicate and reexamine assumptions and concepts that unwittingly reify normative notions of gender and sexuality."[11] Eithne Luibhéid argues that this field of study remains an "unruly body of inquiry," with opportunities to investigate the power relations of international migration across many disciplines.[12] She writes that queer migration scholarship reveals how migration regimes participate in the production of binary structures that define some bodies as "deviant," or "queer" and others as normative through racialized, gendered, classed, and sexed discourse.[13] In employing queer theories of affect and queer migration studies, this chapter analyzes how the desire for citizenship and national belonging functions affectively in LGBT communities.

The materials that this chapter examines are produced and circulated by migrant activist organizations such as the Not1More campaign through various media outlets, including online letters, Facebook-live videos, and video recordings uploaded to YouTube. These sources are an important aspect of queer migration politics, particularly when mainstream media continue to label trans and queer migrant activist demonstrations as unnecessary "heckling."[14] In gathering online materials that present a particular angle on Gutiérrez's interruption of Obama and Trans Queer Pueblo's demonstration, this chapter challenges the refusal of dominant LGBT media to address queer migration politics as more than "heckling" and acknowledges the important interventions made in such moments. In making no claims to neutrality, this type of analysis also aims to enact a feminist ethics of self reflexivity. As Richa Nagar reminds us in her important text, *Muddying the Waters*, feminist ethics are fundamental to knowledge production and ask us to reflect on the following questions: "Who are we writing for, how, and why?"[15]

In the next section I engage shamelessness as a critical contribution to queer studies, which has widely focused its attention on embracing shame as a political maneuver.

Shamelessness and the Political Rifts in Queer Studies

Although Gay Shame has been analyzed in useful ways for theorizing nonnormative sexualities and genders, this chapter aims to consider shamelessness as a survival strategy that problematizes theoretical projects in queer studies that omit issues of race and racism. The provocative, innovative, and sexy analyses of shame in queer studies fail to account for the backlash and critiques that queer scholars of color, including Hiram Pérez and Lawrence La Fountain-Stokes, have noted.[16] Their accounts provide sophisticated critiques of the gay male white subject, out of which theories on Gay Shame emerge. In his posthumously published article "Wise Latinas," José Esteban Muñoz addresses this issue when he writes, "When considering the work of affect [through shame], we need to remember that it is always in flux."[17] This observation serves as a reminder about affect's expansive reach. Muñoz elaborates on the need to "cast a fuller picture of affect's volatility," one that does not designate any affect as dominating a specific scene or cultural product.[18] Such understanding of affect offers a strong and vivid description of the affective realities of queers of color in the United States and makes room to theorize affects like shame in relationship to others. Thus, analyzing shamelessness responds to a gap in the study of shame, particularly when little work discusses what happens when migrants refuse to adopt shame as a mobilizing tactic. This emphasis on shamelessness serves as an ethical intervention and contribution that can inform understanding of how migrants survive, relate, and perform when they are scapegoated as criminals by conservative and progressive ideologies.

At its core, my focus on shamelessness builds on Chicana/Latina feminisms. Shamelessness, as discussed by Catrióna Rueda Esquibel, is not a new maneuver for minoritarian subjects but is reflected in the scholarly and literary contributions of Chicana/Latina women. For example, in her genealogical mapping of Chicana lesbian fiction, Rueda Esquibel discusses what she calls "shameless histories" to draw attention to how Chicana writers provide a history of the U.S. Southwest as "always-already queer."[19] The cultural productions that she analyzes, including work by Jo Carrillo, Gloria Anzaldúa, and Rocky Gámez, tell stories that are political, "which marks the writer as *una sinvergüenza*, a woman who knows no shame."[20] Here she invokes the work of tatiana de la tierra, an influential Latina lesbian poet and editor, as Rueda Esquibel's notion of shameless histories is strongly inspired by de la tierra's unpublished anthology on Latina lesbian erotica: *Las Sinvergüenzas*.[21] Sandra Cisneros also adopts shamelessness in a keynote speech she delivered at the National Lesbian and Gay Journalists Association in 1995. While reflecting on her experiences as a graduate student, Cisneros addresses the anger that she felt when she recognized the internalized shame that continuously blocked her from speaking at the Iowa Writers Workshop. She begins her speech by wanting to talk about sex, a topic that she argues is seldom discussed in Latina/o communities due to cultural shaming. Transpiring from her desire to counter sexual shame she writes, "I am a sinvergüenza. I am not ashamed to be shameless."[22] Chicana feminist theorist Edén Torres helps to explain Cisneros's articulation of shame(lessness) when she argues that for people of color in the United States, "Shame is an insidious method of social control."[23] Torres contends that shame is considerably involved in the identity formation of minoritarian subjects. Further, she observes that we acquire shame through multivalent sources and links this negative affect to long legacies of colonization and conquest. Queer and feminist Chicana/Latina scholarship and cultural production thus reveals the importance of shamelessness to minoritarian subjects and makes apparent the reasons why shame cannot be easily embraced in different contexts and by different subjects.

La Fountain-Stokes, who departs from Gay Shame due to its lack of intersectional analysis and the racialized violence that the Gay Shame conference produced, has offered one articulation of shamelessness when he writes that to have no shame, to be shameless is to, "disobey, break the law, disrespect authority (the family, the church, the state), and in a perverse and curious way to be proud of one's transgression or, at the very least, lack a feeling of guilt."[24] While this definition invites us to understand shamelessness as a transgressive performance, my analysis of shamelessness differs in that I am wary of how a claim to nonnormativity may produce a new ideal. In other words, the pride in one's transgression that La Fountain-Stokes provisionally implies, and that Gay Shame articulates, may become the new ideal or norm in LGBT communities. Rather than claim pride in nonnormativity, I argue that shamelessness, when coupled with the strategic use of interruption, enables trans and queer migrants to resist hegemonic orientations and relations with normative structures of power. As Ahmed powerfully observes, the question that drives a queer critique of state power is about "how to be affected by one's relation to, and departures from, the normative in a way that opens up different possibilities for living."[25] This type of critical work is made possible by the queer and feminist antiracist scholarship that I have engaged with and that allow for a rich analysis of queer migration politics in spaces where migrants are criminalized.

TransLatina Survival

Jennicet Gutiérrez is a TransLatina activist and cofounder of Familia: Trans Queer Liberation Movement in Los Angeles, California. This organization works for the collective liberation of Latinx communities through advocacy and education. She received national attention for interrupting Barack Obama on June 24, 2015, at a White House Pride reception celebrating Pride Month and the accomplishments of the LGBT community under the Obama administration.[26] This event was held two days prior to the Supreme Court ruling that legalized marriage equality across the United States. Additionally, executive orders on immigration were issued months prior to this reception. These orders, as Obama adamantly spoke about in a presidential address to the nation, supposedly prioritized the deportation of "felons not families."[27] It is within and against the normative aims of Pride festivities and anti-immigrant rhetoric that Gutiérrez interrupted Obama and was shamed for her actions. In a room full of white gay men taking selfies and applauding Obama for his leadership on "LGBT issues," Gutiérrez's words and actions critiqued the discrepancies between normative LGBT accomplishments and the dire living conditions of undocumented trans women under President Obama, otherwise known as the "deporter in chief."[28] She said, "President Obama, release all LGBTQ [from] detention centers! President Obama, stop the torture and abuse of trans women in detention centers! President Obama, I am a trans woman. I'm tired of the abuse. I'm tired of the violence."[29] As Gutiérrez spoke, a majority of the audience members began to shush her, and Obama immediately responded with, "Listen, you're in my house. As a general rule, I am just fine with a few *hecklers*, but not when I'm up in the house."[30] A telling moment is when Obama, echoing the audience's response and sentiments, told Gutiérrez, "shame on you!"[31]

Perhaps the most chilling or troubling aspect of Obama's and the audience's response to Gutiérrez's interruption is a continued legacy of silencing and violence that trans women of color face in LGBT communities. The dismissal of Gutiérrez as a "heckler" who needs to be silenced is similar to the experience of Sylvia Rivera, who also demonstrated shameless behavior when white attendees tried to shame her into silence. In 1973 at the Christopher Street Liberation Rally in Washington Square park, Rivera was attacked, punched, and almost blocked from speaking.[32] This hostility was encouraged and led by white lesbian feminist Jean O'Leary, who spoke about trans women and drag queens as making a mockery of "womanhood." While Rivera managed to wrestle her way onto the stage and obtain the microphone, this violent moment in history makes explicit the links between trans exclusionary radical feminism, racism, and lesbian separatism. Upon reflecting on the public's participation in keeping her from speaking, Rivera states, "I had to battle my way up on stage, and literally get beaten up and punched around by people I thought were my comrades, to get to that microphone. I got to the microphone and I said my piece."[33]

In his essay, "You can Have my Brown Body and Eat it, Too!" Hiram Pérez alerts us to a historical trend in LGBT communities when he writes, "The shaming of brown bodies is fundamental to dominant U.S. cultures, among them now a dominant queer culture."[34] The dominant queer culture to which Pérez alludes, particularly white gay male sociality, partakes in nation-building projects and global capitalism through alignment with normative citizenship. Given the attempts to silence trans women of color, Gutiérrez's work draws attention to the lack of importance mainstream LGBT politics give to systemic violence against undocumented trans women. Moreover, if normative LGBT politics and communities necessitate the shaming of brown bodies, her interruption demonstrates the affective labor that belonging to dominant LGBT communities requires. It also shows that through interruption and shamelessness behavior, LGBT communities can be (briefly) disrupted. While Gutiérrez could have ended her interruption of Obama early, her refusal to accept public shaming lays bare new possibilities for trans and queer migrants to resist the lure of normative belonging.

Her shameless performance also demonstrates the labor of "shame" in making distinctions between racialized bodies and white bodies in LGBT communities. In a YouTube video uploaded by the Not1More campaign, we can grasp Gutiérrez's shameless interruption when she shouts phrases such as, "I am a trans woman," "I am tired of the abuse," "Stop the abuse, President Obama."[35] Demonstrating no shame in articulating the violence of U.S. immigration control, Gutiérrez draws from her pain and anger to interrupt a scene of nationalism. As the scene unfolds, Gutiérrez begins chanting, "Not one more deportation, ni una mas deportación."[36] It is worth noting that neither the audience nor Obama ever took the time to listen to Gutiérrez's words or treat her with respect. Rather, they filled the room with chants that celebrated masculinist nationalism such as: "OBAMA, OBAMA, OBAMA." They also ruthlessly booed Gutiérrez and the word "shame" was continuously heard throughout the room. Toward the end of the video, a voice appears behind the person who is filming the event saying, "enough . . . this is not for you, this is for all of us." In several ways, this moment contextualizes Gutiérrez's shameless performance within a space that celebrates whiteness and a patriarchal construction of gay sexuality and citizenship. The statement, "this is not for you, this is for all of us," reveals that undocumented trans women like Gutiérrez are outside the realm of the "us." This statement makes explicit the exclusion of trans Latina migrants from LGBT communities. Not surprisingly, Gutiérrez was kicked out of the event but as she was escorted out of the room she continued to chant, "Not one more deportation, ni una mas deportación." Even while being shamed and booed, Gutiérrez behaved shamelessly to mobilize a TransLatina critique against the wishes of liberal white citizens. The use of media to record this event communicates the violence that was performed against Gutiérrez, but it also shows that for almost three minutes, an undocumented TransLatina was able to unsettle the nationalist desires and orientations of dominant LGBT communities.

As her shameless interruption demonstrates, the structural violence against undocumented trans women in and outside of detention centers is sanctioned through the celebration of LGBT "friendly" leaders like Obama. In order to make claims for her own survival and those of other undocumented trans women, Gutiérrez had to be shameless in making her demands. In an interview where she was asked about her reasons for interrupting Obama, Gutiérrez explained that the violence against undocumented trans migrants cannot go without notice. Moreover, she asserts that, "these are stories without humanity . . . these are stories of ridicule, harassment, and physical and verbal abuse in detention centers for undocumented transgender [women]. It is the struggle of my sisters."[37] From this personal account, Gutiérrez grounds pain as an affective structure and reality that *moves her into action*. In addition, her evocation of incivility to counter the normative affective alignment of citizenship raises questions about how her body is read in such occasions. Due to presumed criminality from her undocumented status and corporeal racialization, a shameless interruption was one of the few strategies available to Gutiérrez. As Dean Spade demonstrates, rights-based discourse has historically worked to produce institutionalized violence against LGBT communities of color in hate crime legislation and beyond.[38] Therefore, her shameless interruption does not demand rights but instead asks for liberation from intersecting systems of oppression.

Tracing back to Muñoz's words on the multiple affects and social relations involved in structuring one's experience in the world, Gutiérrez's experience and those of her trans sisters stress anger and pain as affective realities. Muñoz's work on Latina/o affect helps us to understand how these affective experiences come to be registered as excessive to the national body. Writing on what he calls "Feeling Brown," Muñoz notes the difference between "national affect," such as the one that the White House reception displays, and Latina/o affect.[39] He argues, "The failure of Latino affect in relation to the hegemonic protocols of North American affective comportment revolves around an understanding of the Latina or the Latino as affective excess."[40] At the risk of falling into common narratives or clichés that depict Latina/os as "hot 'n' spicy," Muñoz's observation helps to account for the excess that Gutiérrez's body performs through a shameless interruption. In a letter published in *The Washington Blade*, Gutiérrez explains that she spoke at the reception to demand the release of all transgender migrants in detention, some of whom she had spoken with earlier.[41] She explains that these migrants expressed an overwhelming amount of emotional pain when they shared details about their horrific experiences in detention centers. If we follow the logics of hegemonic affective comportment, these experiences are in excess to preestablished narratives of national belonging and unity. As such, any engagement with anger and pain by minoritarian subjects must be dismissed to maintain an affective national community that is grounded in whiteness.

In this case, shameless behavior presented an opportunity to interrupt communities bounded around whiteness. As Muñoz powerfully describes, "the presence of Latina/o affect puts a great deal of pressure on the affective base of whiteness, insofar as it instructs us in a reading of the affect of whiteness as underdeveloped and impoverished."[42] This theoretical move reorients us away from a reading of Latina/o affect as "too much" and shows how Gutiérrez manages to interrupt spaces codified by whiteness. Moreover, queer theorist Eve Kosofsky Sedgwick lucidly describes the violence of shame when she writes of "the double movement shame makes: toward painful individuation, toward uncontrollable relationality."[43] Unlike the affective communities that Obama wants to engage with, which are "uncontrollably" bound toward racialized shaming, Gutiérrez turns a painful scene into one that refuses hegemonic constructions of affective comportment and normative notions of civility. As she continuously reminds dominant LGBT communities and the American public, her existence is indeed *resistance.*

Various forms of violence occurred in Gutiérrez's interaction with Obama and his audience, but upon reflecting on the public's response, she remarks, "For many years, I lived in shame—shame of being a transgender woman of color, shame of being undocumented. Now that I have released my chains of shame, I want my beloved undocumented trans and queer community to find their own power and liberation. This is the vision I see for my community."[44] There is no shame in her response, especially when she expresses disappointment at the Obama administration and the white audience. As she writes, the stories of trans women in detention are stories "of torture and abuse."[45] To be shameful about expressing this violence to an audience that profits from these women's detention follows the goals of normative LGBT citizenship. Certainly, her letter is an extension of her shameless performance at the White House, particularly when she asserts, "In the tradition of how Pride started, I interrupted his speech because it is time for our issues and struggles to be heard."[46] Drawing a link between the liberatory politics of Stonewall and her own interruption, her words clarify that belonging to dominant LGBT communities is not a viable option for TransLatinas who intend to survive.

In what follows, I look toward another moment where the interruption of LGBT public spheres enables trans and queer migrants to critique normative citizenship and belonging and perform alternative modes of politics that center trans and queer feminist coalition.

Violent Public Spheres: Trans Queer Pueblo, Phoenix Pride, and Arizona

Formed in 2016 from a merger between the Arcoiris Liberation Team and the Arizona Queer Undocumented Immigrant Project, Trans Queer Pueblo in Phoenix is a grassroots organization that seeks the liberation of trans and queer migrant communities from all systems of oppression. Pueblo's activist work extends to migrants inside and outside detention centers and cultivates queer and feminist leadership models as integral to their commitment to migrant communities. They garnered national attention in LGBT media outlets for their interruption of the 2017 Phoenix Pride parade. Banners from Pueblo organizers included slogans such as, "Police out of Pride" and "No Justice No Pride." These were strategic messages that critiqued the presence of the police at the parade as well as Pride's relationships with corporations like Bank of America that channel money into the prison industrial complex. The response to this interruption by pride attendees included the use of racial slurs, tackling, and—important to this chapter—the shaming of brown bodies. Similar to the shaming of Gutiérrez and her own corporeal response, Pueblo members faced hostility, but they also refused to fall prey to racialized shaming. Instead, they acted shamelessly and their bodies were in excess to the registers of white LGBT public spheres. What would have happened if either Obama or Pride attendees listened to the experiences of trans and queer migrants? Rather than dismiss the important work of organizations like Pueblo, I want to closely analyze this affective scene as one that offers alternatives to the criminalization of migrant communities. Moreover, I examine the response to their demonstration as one that portrays racialized bodies as excessive, disruptive, and unproductive toward the struggle for gay rights and national belonging. But in so doing, I consider shameless interruptions as subversive survival strategies and an entry point for disrupting LGBT public spheres that cling to normative ideals of citizenship and belonging.

Marching with a banner stating, "Sin Justicia No Hay Orgullo," Trans Queer Pueblo powerfully interrupted the celebration of Pride and the affects that shape LGBT public spheres. And yet, their shameless interruption makes another important intervention that helps to illustrate the affective registers of LGBT public spheres. According to Juana María Rodríguez, there is a viscosity to the corporeal excess of Latina/o bodies. She argues that as queer Latina/os, "We point with our lips, flirt with our eyes, and shimmy our shoulders to mark our delight. Our racialized excess is already read as queer, outside norms of what is useful or productive. (Is that much color, spice, pattern, noise ever truly necessary?)."[47] Her gesture toward Latina/o corporealities and normative notions of affective comportment help to reveal the power relations at work in the shaming of Pueblo. More specifically, the reasons for shaming brown bodies is exposed: affect that is in excess to LGBT public spheres. In essence, shameless behavior subjugates Pueblo members to social and cultural norms that deem their bodies unproductive, noisy, and dangerous. However, when read differently, this excess exposes the color-blind racist politics that underpin LGBT public spheres.

Unlike the Pride parade attendees, I want to address and *listen* to the actual demands that Pueblo members present, as they courageously work to imagine a world beyond prisons, walls, and racialized criminalization. Some of these demands are explicit in their critiques of systems of domination, such as: "make pride safe for LGBTQ people of color by ending Pride collaboration with Police, ending sponsorships that finance the mass incarceration of communities of color and establishing a people-of-color–led review of Pride festivities."[48] Included in their demands was a call for Phoenix Pride to use their influence with the city mayor to put an end to SB 1070, as well as ending the criminalization of sex work, which affects many trans women of color who often have no other means of employment.

Justin Owen, the executive director of Phoenix Pride, received these demands, welcomed new causes for Phoenix Pride to support, and encouraged peaceful protests; interruption of the parade, however, was not to be tolerated "as a matter of safety for the public."[49] His reasoning demonstrates that Owen's imagined public sphere was implicitly white; in other words, his concept of "safety" stems from, reasserts, and normalizes conditions for white citizen safety that are highly racialized. Here, shameless interruptions serve not only to critique normative citizenship as presented in LGBT public spheres, but in this case, they also operate as a means of coalition building among trans and queer communities of color. While Owen makes explicit the racialized logics that alienate migrants from LGBT public spheres, these logics are connected to the criminalization of queer Black Lives Matter protesters with whom Pueblo strategizes. In interrupting Phoenix pride, Pueblo joins activist demonstrations set forth by Black Lives Matter–Toronto. In the summer of 2016, this group shut down Toronto pride with smoke grenades and staged protests to critique the anti-Blackness and anti-Indigeneity that Toronto pride encourages by inviting the police to march at the parade.[50] The impact of this demonstration, as the group gained the attention of Toronto pride leadership who eliminated future police participation in the parade, encouraged Pueblo organizers to define/articulate their own demands and means to challenge Phoenix pride. As Chávez notes, "coalition enables a different understanding of activists' rhetorical invention as they discover and innovate responses—creative and sometimes mundane—to predominant rhetorical imaginaries."[51] These activist responses create possibilities for different organizations to imagine avenues for coalition. Moreover, Pueblo gestures toward the liberatory politics that Black Lives Matter–Toronto initiated and amplifies the means through which trans and queer of color activists organize. This form of coalition "is a present vision and practice that is oriented toward others and a shared commitment to social and political change."[52] Thus, shameless interruptions extend beyond the realm of critique and pursue coalitional practices that generate new knowledges, perspectives, and visions for social change.

Significantly, queer migration politics allow for creative and ethical responses to temporal orders that restrict the possibility of a future for undocumented migrants. We can see the importance of temporality in queer migration scholarship in Chávez's exploration of queer migration politics through her use of "moment" as an analytic. She writes, "Moments expose a queer temporality. Moments taken in this way reveal that time's passage and the meaning assigned to time need not reflect normative assumptions."[53] Similar to "moment," interruptions mobilize alternative configurations of time in complex ways that reflect the temporal realities of undocumented migrants. Building on Nicholas de Genova's concept of migrant deportability, a perpetual state of precarity for undocumented migrants, Rachel Lewis writes, "the condition of deportability leaves migrants unable to make long-term plans, and in some cases unable to imagine any kind of viable future at all."[54] Within temporal orders such as these that designate migrant bodies as having no future due to their presumed deportability, interruption helps to foreground temporal orders that challenge normative structures and provide alternatives. Pueblo's main banner included pictures of Sylvia Rivera and Marsha P. Johnson that can be analyzed as a strategic act of remembrance that threatens the normative temporalities of mainstream LGBT politics by going back to times when other activists also employed shameless tactics. It asks those in LGBT public spheres to remember a time when pride parades were actual protests and sites for communal belonging. Further, by demanding an end to legislation like SB1070, Pueblo insists on making livable futures for undocumented migrants and is shameless in articulating their purposes.

While queer migration politics are vital for Pueblo to articulate their demands, the subversive aspects of such tactics and imaginaries are not welcomed. In a Facebook live video recorded by Pita Samayoa, the director of Media and Communications for the nonprofit organization, One Arizona, Pride attendees are seen harassing Pueblo members, shouting racial slurs, and shaming them for interrupting their festivities.[55] After a white gay man wearing rainbow beads tackles some of the Pueblo organizers carrying the "No Justice No Pride" banner, another white gay man approaches the organizers to repeatedly shout, "SHAME, SHAME, SHAME." Soon after, a Pride attendee yells at the organizers: "This is our day, move it to the park . . . you are ruining our parade." Like the gay man who shouted this angry message against Gutiérrez, Pueblo is shamed for attempting to call attention to structures of domination. As the crowd of angry white attendees tries to shame this activist demonstration, Pueblo members continue to march shamelessly against the direction of the parade chanting: "Pride escucha, estamos en la lucha."[56] Here, Pueblo organizers insist on interrupting the performance of LGBT citizenship, but they also ask for pride attendees to listen to their demands. While I do not intend to romanticize this moment of resistance, it is important to note how affective their tactics are in demanding an end to state-sponsored practices that police racialized bodies. Their model of queer migration politics, which is built upon coalition, responds to violence and racialized shaming with creative and shameless strategies.

Thus, shameless interruptions disrupt societal, temporal, and affective structures as we know them. And it is these moments of interruption that I find useful for revealing the critiques of citizenship and national belonging that migrants mobilize through shamelessness. In this chapter, I have attempted to flesh out how trans and queer migrants negotiate discourses of citizenship, belonging, and normative LGBT politics. We should not disregard Gutiérrez's and Pueblo's interruptions, especially when their shameless behaviors are registered as excessive, unproductive, and noisy. Rather, to be shameless in moments of violence acknowledges the necessary work such interruptions evoke, as they call attention to the racism of LGBT affective communities and signal alternative political orientations: politics born out of coalition that listen to the voices of trans and queer migrants in their struggle for survival.

Coalitional Movements and Otros Futuros

As I have demonstrated through close readings of shameless interruptions, queer migration politics question affective modes of comportment and belonging that construct violent LGBT public and private spheres. These interruptions create useful and meaningful opportunities to acknowledge, respect, and listen to the imaginaries and practices that trans and queer migrants employ. They also call attention to the corporeality of racialized excess and the affective worlds in which migrants are continuously shamed. Shameless interruptions can also lead to coalition work among minoritarian subjects. By focusing on the survival strategies that trans and queer migrants employ, I was able to reframe migrants who question normative notions of belonging and citizenship as much more than "hecklers." Certainly, work on queer migrations continues to develop, and it is my hope that future scholarship further analyzes how affect is involved in shaping migrant experiences. This work is more necessary than ever given how the Trump administration mobilizes fear to criminalize migrants.

In this chapter, I discussed two events where racialized trans and queer migrant bodies were publicly shamed for their shameless interruptions. I close by returning to my original site of inquiry: Pueblo's "Sin Justicia No Hay Orgullo" video. A significant moment in Jaramillo's reading is when she asks if marriage equality "keeps us safe at night?"[57] She maintains a strong critique of normative LGBT politics, in particular its participation in the detention, deportation, and incarceration of trans and queer people of color. But after reflecting on Pride's ties with corporations like Bank of America, Jaramillo reminds us that "the future is not written." She says, "the cards tell of a future when we return to the roots of Pride." Jaramillo deploys a futuristic reading that returns to the past in order to change the present. As such, we can see how queer migration politics is at work in her imagining of futures where lives are more livable. Activists like Gutiérrez and Pueblo organizers will continue to be silenced and excluded from dominant LGBT communities. However, it is their shameless critiques of state power and coalitional strategies that actively illuminate *livable futures in the present*.

Notes

1. Stephanie Figgins, "Sin Justicia No Hay Orgullo/No Justice No Pride," Vimeo, March 31, 2017, https://vimeo.com/210969242.

2. Ibid.

3. Yezmin Villarreal, "LGBT Immigration Activists Interrupt Phoenix Pride," *Advocate*, April 03, 2017, http://www.advocate.com/politics/2017/4/03/lgbt-immigration-activists -interrupt-phoenix-pride.

4. For an excellent rhetorical analysis of queer migration politics, see Karma R. Chávez, *Queer Migration Politics: Activist Rhetoric and Coalitional Possibilities* (Urbana: University of Illinois Press, 2013).

5. My use of *trans and queer migrants* throughout this essay places *trans* before *queer* to acknowledge the important role of trans activists in queer migration politics. When I use *queer migration politics*, I do not mean to erase the political interventions of trans migrants; rather, I follow Chávez in understanding *queerness* as different from the acronym *LGBT* and instead pointing to possibilities for coalition (6).

6. Elizabeth Freeman, *Time Binds: Queer* Temporalities, *Queer Histories* (Durham, N.C.: Duke University Press, 2010), xxii.

7. See Lauren Berlant, *Cruel Optimism* (Durham, N.C.: Duke University Press, 2011), 117. An important difference to note between lateral agency and the survival tactics of shameless interruptions is that the former is not necessarily intentional, whereas shameless interruptions are deployed strategically in moments of racialized shaming.

8. Not One More, "White House Pride Event Interrupted over LGBTQ Detention," *YouTube*, June 24, 2015, https://youtu.be/vv9wRNuptC8.

9. Sara Ahmed, "Affective Economies," *Social Text* 22, no. 2 (2004): 119.

10. Ibid., 134.

11. See Martin F. Manalansan IV, "Queer Intersections: Sexuality and Gender in Migration Studies," *International Migration Review* 40, no. 1 (2006): 226.

12. Eithne Luibhéid, "Queer/Migration: An Unruly Body of Scholarship," *GLQ* 14 nos. 2–3 (2008): 169–190.

13. Ibid., 171–172.

14. Kevin Liptak, "Obama Shuts Down White House Heckler: 'You're in My House,'" *CNN*, June 25, 2015, https://www.cnn.com/2015/06/24/politics/obama-heckler-white-house -lgbt/index.html.

15. Richa Nagar, *Muddying the Waters: Coauthoring Feminisms Across Scholarship and Activism* (Urbana: University of Illinois Press, 2014), 14.

16. See Lawrence La Fountain-Stokes, "Gay Shame, Latina- and Latino-Style: A Critique of Queer White Performativity," in *Gay Latino Studies*, eds. Michael Hames-García and Ernesto Martínez (Durham, N.C.: Duke University Press, 2011), 55–80; and Hiram Pérez, "You Can Have My Brown Body and Eat It Too!" *Social Text* 23, nos. 3–4 (2005): 171–191.

17. José Esteban Muñoz, "Wise Latinas," *Criticism* 56, no. 2 (2014): 257.

18. Ibid.

19. Catrióna Rueda Esquibel, *With Her Machete in Her Hand* (Austin: University of Texas Press, 2006), 7.

20. Ibid., 201.

21. Ibid.

22. Ibid., 78.

23. Eden Torres, *Chicana without Apology: The New Chicana Cultural Studies* (New York: Routledge, 2003), 30.

24. La Fountain-Stokes, "Gay Shame," 72.

25. Sara Ahmed, *The Cultural Politics of Emotion* (New York: Routledge, 2004), 121.

26. Not One More, "White House Pride Event."

27. Zeke Miller, "Obama's Immigration Speech," *Time*, November 20, 2014, http://time.com/3598756/obama-immigration-action/.

28. Caitlin Dickerson, "A Creative Plea from Immigrants, and a Ticking Clock for Obama," *The New York Times*, December 20, 2016, https://www.nytimes.com/2016/12/20/us/a-creative-plea-from-immigrants-and-a-ticking-clock-for-obama.html.

29. Not One More, "White House Pride Event."

30. Ibid.

31. Ibid.

32. Benjamin Shepard, "Sylvia and Sylvia's Children: A Battle for a Queer Public Space," in *That's Revolting! Queer Strategies for Resisting Assimilation*, ed. Mattilda Bernstein Sycamore (Berkeley: Soft Skull Press, 2008), 123–140.

33. Ibid. 127.

34. Pérez, "You Can Have My Brown Body," 175.

35. Not One More, "White House Pride Event."

36. Ibid.

37. Anthony Victoria, "Jennicet Gutiérrez Speaks about Activism and Life Experience," *El Chicano Weekly* 52, no. 30 (2015): A1–A2. https://issuu.com/iecn98/docs/ec-07-16-2015.

38. See Dean Spade, *Normal Life: Administrative Violence, Critical Trans Politics and the Limits of the Law* (Durham, N.C.: Duke University Press, 2011).

39. José Esteban Muñoz, "Feeling Brown: Ethnicity and Affect in Ricardo Bracho's *The Sweetest Hangover (and other STDs),*" in *Gay Latino Studies*, eds. Michael Hames-García and Ernesto Martínez (Durham, N.C.: Duke University Press, 2011), 204–219.

40. Ibid., 206.

41. Jennicet Gutiérrez, "I Interrupted Obama because We Need To be Heard," *The Washington Blade*, June 25, 2015, http://www.washingtonblade.com/2015/06/25/exclusive-i-interrupted-obama-because-we-need-to-be-heard.

42. Muñoz, "Feeling Brown," 207.

43. Eve Kosofsky Sedgwick, *Touching Feeling: Affect, Pedagogy, Performativity* (Durham, N.C.: Duke University Press, 2003), 37.

44. Jennicet Gutiérrez, "Focus on the Issue, Not the Protest," *The Advocate*, July 08, 2015, https://www.advocate.com/commentary/2015/07/08/op-ed-focus-issue-not-protest.

45. Gutiérrez, "I Interrupted Obama."

46. Ibid.

47. Juana María Rodríguez, *Queer Latina Gestures, and Other Latina Longings* (New York: New York University Press, 2014), 2.

48. Antonia Farzan, "Is Phoenix Pride Getting Too Corporate?" *Phoenix New Times*, March 31, 2015, https://www.phoenixnewtimes.com/news/activists-push-phoenix-pride-to-stand-up-for-lgbtq-undocumented-immigrants-9209220.

49. Ibid.

50. Daniel Reynolds, "Toronto Reminds Us that Pride Is a Protest," *Advocate*, July 4, 2016, https://www.advocate.com/pride/2016/7/04/toronto-reminds-us-pride-protest.

51. Chávez, *Queer Migration Politics*, 7.

52. Ibid.

53. Ibid., 9.

54. See Rachel Lewis, "Deportable Subjects: Lesbians and Political Asylum," *Feminist Formations* 25, no. 2 (2013): 185.

55. Pita Samayoa, "Trans Queer Pueblo," *Facebook Live*, April 2, 2017.

56. Ibid.

57. Figgins, "Sin Justicia."

PART IV

Critiquing

14

Monarchs and Queers

YASMIN NAIR

March 6, 2006, saw the most spectacularly successful immigration march in recent history. As television network helicopters hovered, their correspondents reporting on the event in awestruck tones, over 500,000 people poured down the streets of the city's famed downtown to protest the notorious Sensenbrenner bill, which was eventually retracted. It seemed that the immigration rights movement had literally and metaphorically turned a corner. The possibility of change hung thick in the air; butterfly wings, popular if somewhat sentimental symbols of immigration, manifested everywhere, and similar and larger marches across the country over the next few weeks energized activists and immigrants who finally saw hope on the horizon. In the years following the 2006 marches, many thousands of people came out as "undocumented" (refusing the state's categorization of them as "illegal"). Following them, a smaller but far more media-savvy contingent of queer immigrants, nearly all of them millennials, came out and declared that they stood at the intersection of queerness and immigration.

And then: nothing happened. Matters only got worse, with Obama feeling emboldened not only to continue deportations and demonstrate little to no interest in bringing about change, but to exceed the number of deportations carried out by both Bushes combined.

What happened? How did the enormous promise of 2006 fizzle out so fast? And what happened to all that fabulous queer energy, which continues to blaze forth so fiercely in the presence of those who now proudly call themselves the Undocqueers?

The Undocuqueers are a large range of individuals and groups who integrated queerness into immigration by conjoining the act of coming out as queer with the act of coming out as undocumented. On the surface, this made immigration rights vividly, visibly sexy and new. Now, immigration was not simply something that affected adult men and women, often with children in tow, hitherto the main actors in various cases of threatened deportation. Immigration was instead something that affected millennials, who now took center stage.

This was an era when gay, lesbian, and queer identities were fast becoming marketing commodities: *Modern Family*, a television sitcom about an extended family that includes a gay couple with an adopted Chinese child, began in 2009. Now long past the age of *Will and Grace* and *The L Word*, queers no longer need their own shows. The Undocuqueers were led by young, attractive, smart, and photogenic youth who spoke not in the often halting English of their elders but with a fluency in the language of revolution and freedom struggles, of Audre Lorde and Michel Foucault. Rigorously trained in media activism by high-powered organizations like the Illinois Coalition of Immigrant and Refugee Rights (ICIRR), they knew how to deliver sound bites and several, like Tania Unzueta, Jose Antonio Vargas, and Prerna Lal, became acclaimed poster children of the Undocuqueer movement.

Undocuqueers are especially adept at code-switching, rapidly moving between public selves as either sophisticated and deeply articulate spokespersons or sad, untutored immigrants puzzled by The Ways of The White Man. In 2012, Jose Antonio Vargas, by then famous for coming out as undocumented and gay in a *New York Times* essay, crossed a Unite/Here picket line at a Hyatt hotel to make a speech about the need to stop using the word "illegal" in journalism. When *Colorlines*'s Rinku Sen asked him about his act, considered a profound betrayal in union organizing, he responded, "We were an immigrant working class family, but I had no experience with unions at all."[1] While this may be somewhat true—many immigrants work without papers and are often not unionized—Vargas's claim to no *experience* with unions carefully yet casually elided the fact that his career as a journalist from the time he was in high school, in 1998, and which included a jointly won Pulitzer Prize with a *Washington Post* team, made it impossible he could not have understood the significance of what he did.

But by locating his cynical response in a lack of *experience*, Vargas was able to draw upon the leftist guilt that prevented Sen from pressing him any further. By turning his scabbing into something that reflected a lack of *experience*, something defined as personal and thus placed beyond critique, Vargas effectively depoliticized it and made it impossible to criticize him: who would dare call out a queer immigrant of working-class origins who had simply walked unknowingly into a union kerfuffle? No one questioned how a man who had covered national affairs for a national newspaper was somehow unaware of what it meant to cross a picket line. Vargas is, today, one of the most revered figures among the Undocuqueers.

I highlight the Vargas case to raise a critical but hitherto unacknowledged fact: the presence of the Undocuqueers, a hyperextension of the Undocumented movement, has in this and other ways served to erase the fundamental matter of labor, which is, ultimately, what the immigration crisis is really about. Gone today is a sustained conversation on matters like NAFTA or other labor-related matters that have brought about the current immigration crisis. The Undocuqueers have, unwittingly or not, succeeded in queerwashing labor from the landscape of the immigration rights movement.

Undocuqueers allow liberals, progressives, and the left to feel good about themselves and to admire immigrant communities—long demonized as homophobic—as being worthy of admiration after all. Immigrants in turn are able to render themselves as more fully human in the eyes of a majority that ignores the seething presence of homophobia in millions of native-born homes.

This is not your *abuela's* immigration rights movement.

We're Here, We're Queer, We Fucked Things Up

The Undocuqueer movement and its attendant problems have been greatly enabled by the work of academic scholars, journalists, and activists who have turned them into fetish objects of study in their discussions of queerness and immigration. Consider, for instance, Nicholas De Genova's "The Queer Politics of Migration: Reflections on 'Illegality' and Incorrigibility," widely cited as an example of the supposedly necessary celebratory appraisal of the queerness inherent to migration resistance politics.[2]

"What's queer about X?" is the implicit or explicit question asked by queer theorists and scholars upon embarking upon studies of anything queer-related. Here, X stands for an issue like, say, marriage. Asking what is queer about it allows many defenders of the cause of gay marriage to insist that the ability to marry somehow enables a *queering* of the institution, thus transforming its millennia-old misogyny and social inequality into a magically inclusive and somehow feminist institution. Katrina Kimport, in an essay on lesbian wedding photos, insists that the mere presence of such images, because they show same-sex couples, "disrupt normative assumptions about bodies and identity."[3] What Kimport and numerous other apologists for gay marriage miss is the fact that no amount of such "queering" can "disrupt" the ways in which the state sutures vital and life-saving benefits like health care to the *state* of marriage.

This belief in the transformative power of "queering" runs deep through a vast corpus of work on immigration and queerness. For example: Nicholas De Genova reflects upon on the popular slogan of the 2006 marches, *¡Aquí Estamos, y No Nos Vamos!* [Here we are, and we're not leaving!], drawing a clear parallel between that and the queer chant, "We're here, we're queer, get used to it!" and thus, by a familiar form of *queering* declares that the immigrant marchers had queered migration, thus manifesting what he calls the incorrigibility of the migrants. In this, De Genova demonstrates the widespread inability of theorists of matters queer to think about "queer" as more than a cultural production. Academics and commentators who work on queerness place queer politics on the same plane as representation. But the stakes are much lower in representation. Talking about political matters like immigration and rendering them in terms of representational matters results in forms of confabulation, in disappearing the institutional, structural systems that give rise to the queers marching across the plains. In other words, it depoliticizes queers and renders them disruptive figures, with no attention to the fact that queerness actually enables neoliberal configurations of power. "Queering" migration in such ways effectively disappears the entire structure of neoliberal governance that is represented by the Immigration Rights Industrial Complex (IRIC), which controls messaging (including the slogan so celebrated by De Genova) and which has so far failed to come up with a single substantial gain.

From the Closets to the PIC

The parallel between coming out as queer and coming out as undocumented is a strained one. To come out as queer, at least in the United States and much of the Western imaginary, is in general to emerge into situations of less stress, but it is also often to invoke more scrutiny, with damaging results. For a certain kind of gay man, the sort who can pass as cultured and well-off and cute enough to be someone's Best Gay Friend, coming out means an ascension into social mobility. For trans men and women who lack the resources of Caitlyn Jenner, coming out is fraught with danger and humiliation, and even the loss of livelihoods; they run a much greater risk of beatings and even murder as they try to survive in street economies.

Furthermore, what scholarship and reporting has so far failed to take into account is the question of what happens to people who do come out, as either undocumented or undocuqueer. What do they enter into once they "leave the shadows"?

When the undocumented community began to push for DACA (Deferred Action for Childhood Arrivals) and DAPA (Deferred Action for Parents of Americans and Lawful Permanent Residents), several of us in the radical immigrant rights community warned that, as presidential executive orders that could be easily rescinded by even a Democrat president following Obama, both would mostly function as ways to lure undocumented people out into the light of endless governmental surveillance. What we asked was simply, "What are people coming out into?"

Sure enough, with Trump, both orders now face the threat of cancelation but have in the meantime created a massive pool of people who are now literally on federal lists and marked as undocumented. For poster children like Unzueta, with resources and networks to draw upon, ultimate deportation is unlikely, with several administrative roadblocks being thrown up for years by teams of excellent lawyers. For millions of others, the road to deportation is lined with possibly years of imprisonment. For many, deportation is not a return to a beautiful land where monarch butterflies flit around and abuelas gently braid their hair between making vast quantities of fragrant pozole. Among the Undocuqueers, deportation can mean a return to countries where their sexuality, flamboyant and nonconformingly fabulous or not, is punished. For older queers, there may simply be no way to make a livelihood or create new communities of belonging.

Certainly, DACA has brought enormous advantages for many, including health care for those who could now find employment and whose lives may have been saved by access to it. But IRIC, deploying its vast contingent of Undocumented and Undocuqueers, could have easily pressed for much more, for legislation that was actually written into law. While "the shadows" cannot be romanticized, given the stress and precarity they produce, for many that space was safer than the bright light of the state's surveillance.

Where do Undocuqueers end up without the privilege of Change.org campaigns to help keep them out of prison? And who among them has the choice to even come out, when "coming out" has already been effected upon them? Trans people who don't pass by the norms of society, HIV-positive people who need to be on strict medication regimens, gender-nonconforming people whose self-presentation inevitably marks them as wrong, awry—yes, *queer*: all of these groups need never come out to the state, wrapped as they are in the thick fog of surveillance and exclusion. They are always already out.

Rather than ask, "What's queer about X?" we should ask, "How is X enabled or made stronger by 'queer?'" When we ask, "What's queer about immigration?" we can articulate a celebratory discourse that seeks radical potential in the mere presence of queers—as migrants, as disruptors, as figures subverting dominant paradigms. But when we turn the question around, we see that the "queer" does not enable flights of escape but, instead, makes more powerful neoliberal regimes of power and captivity.

Notes

1.-Rinku Sen, "José Antonio Vargas: 'You Know Someone Undocumented,'" *Colorlines*, October 24, 2012, https://www.colorlines.com/articles/jos%C3%A9-antonio-vargas-you-know-someone-undocumented.

2. Nicholas De Genova. "The Queer Politics of Migration: Reflections on 'Illegality' and Incorrigibility," *Studies in Social Justice* 4, no. 2 (2010): 101–126.

3. Katrina Kimport, "Being Seen through Marriage: Lesbian Wedding Photographs and the Troubling of Heteronormativity," in *The Marrying Kind? Debating Same-Sex Marriage within the Lesbian and Gay Movement*, eds. Mary Bernstein and Verta Taylor (Minneapolis: University of Minnesota Press, 2013), 311.

15

The Price of Survival

Family Separation, Coercion, and Help

JOSÉ GUADALUPE HERRERA SOTO

#FamiliesBelongTogether and #KeepFamiliesTogether have become popular hashtags in the moment I write, as Trump and Sessions' "zero tolerance" policy on unauthorized border crossings continues to separate migrant families at the Mexico-U.S. border. Migrant family separation is nothing new; it is and always has been inherent to U.S. immigration policy and practice. Progressives, liberals, and allies are offering themselves as saviors of the moment, leading social movements to fight for immigrant family reunification. I want to offer a story from my personal experience of family separation and reunification to reflect on what liberal efforts at "helping" can look like from another perspective. In this example and in the larger political moment, I show how liberal, "feel-good" desires to help—in the absence of the will to actually lose some of the privileges gained at the expense of people like me, *especially as it pertains to letting go of financial capital accumulated due to race and citizenship privilege*—can create forms of spectacle intended to showcase forms of allyship, free from the burdens of accountability. Distancing themselves from their culpability, especially as it is materialized in disproportionate access to financial wealth, the intervention of liberal allies into our lives can actually further our experiences of disempowerment.

The following pieces are versions of two letters I wrote, one in 2015 and the other in 2017. I wrote these letters because my *abuelita*, who lived in Mexico, was gravely ill, and even though my father lived in Chicago as an undocumented person, it was important that he be able to return to Mexico to see his mother before she passed. It was equally important that he be able to return to the United States to be with his family in Chicago. Like my father, for people who lack the "proper" documentation and who *are made to be undocumented*, the border is an obstacle preventing them to be with their loved ones; it is in their way of moving freely and at will. For the undocumented, the border always separates families.

With my father in Mexico, we made plans for his return. We decided to try the "right way" and to get my father in one of the infamous "lines" that politicians are so fond of talking about. But even to get in the line for a tourist visa requires proof of an immense amount of financial resources. I wrote the first letter in order to obtain those resources, asking my former professors (and their networks) to borrow the $10,000 my family would need. Because they knew me, knew my own struggles with deportation, had expressed their support of my work as a migrant justice organizer, *and* because the money would be returned to them after my father came back, I was certain that these liberal allies would help me. In addition, I asked people who I was certain had personal access to that kind of capital—university professors with full-time, tenured positions.

This plea to turn their verbal solidarity into material support resulted in only a small fraction of the money I needed. I had to figure out how to get the rest from other sources. I was frustrated that my former professors and their friends, people I knew had resources, would not assist me in my time of need. I was more frustrated at *how they went about* responding to my request. Instead of being clear about how much or how little they were willing to loan, the allies put on a big show of reaching out to their networks, putting a tremendous amount of time and effort in pooling resources from their friends and family on my behalf. All of that time and energy on their part produced a financial loan of $3,500. I needed money; instead they offered "efforts," time, social networks, and largely nonmonetary support. It seemed to me that any of the individuals involved in this loan pool easily could have put up more than $3,500 on their own, without the need to go through the whole theatrical-outreach process. Instead of simply stating that they were not willing to risk so much of their personal money, they offered a spectacle of effort, support, and time investment. In witnessing this I felt disempowered to call them out, because they were all "doing *so much.*"

Obviously the "legal route" did not work, my father was denied a visa. Instead, we had to then pay to have him cross without authorization. I had to use all the money I borrowed from my professors, in addition to borrowing ten times that amount on top of it, to pay for my dad's crossing—the more you pay, the less deadly it is.

Following the return of my father, I spoke again with one of my professors who suggested that if I wrote a "thank you" letter to the network assembled for the $3,500 loan, they would most likely feel sorry for me and let me off the hook in terms of repaying the loans, converting the money to a "contribution." By this time, my father was back, but my family was in huge financial debt. I postponed and postponed but eventually felt I had no choice but to write the second letter—in which I thank them for their kindness. I was being sarcastic. The expectation of gratitude and the pressure to write a "thank you" letter from someone so deeply in debt to people with excess resources, was coercive.

I felt that the people I asked for help always claim to be in solidarity with people like me—and yet, when I am coerced to reach out to them, they just threw crumbs. It is not okay to give chump change and expect a "thank you"—that's a problem on its own. But there is more. I felt I had to hold up a mirror to white and middle-class people who claim to be allies, or who see themselves as "helping" people like me and therefore expect gratitude. I wanted them to know, as they engage with people like me, that we are not grateful, that we are not in this together. If you want to be in this with us, it is going to be ugly, and you need to get a taste of our reality—that should be the exchange for people who claim to be allies. I see something different than allies who are willing to throw down—I see academics with vast amounts of financial resources, and I see that the only reason they have these resources is because other people are impoverished, and academics can make careers and salaries off our suffering. Their resources are accumulated at our expense—and I see the ways they are not willing to acknowledge that. Our relationship is not a "nice" one; it is not civil; it is nasty and bad and exploitative and coercive, so maybe would-be allies should think about that if they want to actually be part of our lives. I not only felt coerced to write a thank-you letter, I felt coerced to maintain the bullshit illusion that we are in fact in this together. In exchange for not having to pay back the money, I had to bolster their grotesque desire for redemption.

I didn't know how to express all that at the time; I still do not. Instead, I asked my on-again, off-again, romantic partner (a white woman, an ally, an academic, who also gave me a loan and understands my rage) to help me put it into words at this time. Instead of being able to call them out and to show my rage and claim the validity of my perspective, I reluctantly wrote a thank-you letter in a way that I hoped would sabotage the expectations of the would-be "donors"—their expectations that I would let *them* off the hook. I wrote the letter AND paid them back, because throwing the money in their face was the only direct gesture that reflected the truth from my perspective—knowing full well that they did not need it and knowing full well the extreme measures I had to go through to put together enough money to pay them back. Instead of expressing this in my letter directly, I wrote indirectly. Instead of writing of the violence of so-called allies expecting gratitude and validation in order to forget about money they don't even need to begin with, I wrote of the violence of the border and the coyotes. I detailed the difficulty we had in getting my father back to Chicago. I wanted it to be clear that there is no "line" for people like my dad. I wanted these comfortable, middle-class people in my life to know what people who are very different from them have to go through, like my father, who risked death and injury to return. I was trying to break the cycle of liberal allies contributing little in exchange for being let off the hook in terms of accountability for their own privileges and resources.

* * *

Letter #1

December 8, 2015
Request for financial support

Hello all,

I am a former NEIU [Northeastern Illinois University] student and thanks to the great work and support of NEIU professors, fellow activists, and family, I am currently a PhD student at UIC [University of Illinois, Chicago]. This past summer my *abuelita* passed away after a long battle against liver problems.

Out of all my family who reside in the U.S., I am the only one who was born in México and now has the privilege to cross borders, *muros*, and *fronteras* the "safe" and "correct" way—I have the "proper" documentation needed for international travel. Nonetheless, this privilege involves being pulled aside for questioning during every encounter with U.S. Customs or *la migra*, waiting for hours at the airport inside a U.S. Customs' side room, being selected for in-depth searches by TSA at airports, and so on. As bad as it might sound, it's still a "privilege," since it allows for visiting loved ones in my home country, especially in situations like that of my *abuelita*.

Long story made short, my father (*abuelita's son*) lacks the "proper" documentation or the "privilege" to cross borders, *muros*, and *fronteras*. Nonetheless, this past summer I encouraged him to travel with me to care for *abuelita*, because I knew how much she would want that and I knew, deep inside, that my father needed to go and see his mother. After receiving support from my sister and me, he decided going to care for his mother was the correct thing to do; and so, we left together to care for *abuelita*.

For the last couple of months, following my *abuelita's* death, we have been preparing for my father's return to the United States. We have been figuring out what are some possibilities of getting him back to Chicago without the need to risk his life or put him in any danger. Our plan is the following and here is where I'm requesting your support: My father will be applying for a tourist visa, with the hopes of getting it approved. We are working on having the property (*abuelita's casa*), utility bills, and a bank account under his name, along with meeting other visa requirements.

With the help of your colleague and others, I am trying to raise money to deposit into the bank account we recently opened under my father's name. This will help to show that he has sufficient money to be considered for the visa. The goal is to raise 10,000 U.S. dollars and have it deposited before submitting the visa application. If you are able to contribute financially, please note that your money will be returned to you at the end of April or at an earlier date if possible. We are hoping to raise this money in the next week or so. Your colleague would help collect the funds raised through their networks. Please let us know if you have any questions or need more information. In advance, thank you for your time in reading this and for your support.

* * *

Letter# 2

July 30, 2017

Dear friends and financial supporters,

Thank you for your kind contributions made to my cause in December 2015. Unfortunately, it took me more time than expected to write this letter and to provide follow-up on my initial request for financial support. I have returned your loan to your colleague who will be making the arrangements necessary for your loan amount to be returned to you as soon as possible. Thank you so much for your financial support and my apologies for not dealing with this last year as I initially proposed in my letter.

My father is here with us now, in the United States. Things did not go as originally planned (i.e., getting him across with a visa—even with all the efforts made, the United States denied his visa), but the outcome ended up being the same. It has been a year since he was able to cross the border without the "proper documentation," via the more costly way of crossing borders. Your financial support helped us in many more ways than planned. Thank you.

Border Crossing—First Attempt, Almost Disappeared into the Desert

On March of 2016, following the denial of the visa, my dad first attempted to cross the border via the desert in Arizona, near Agua Prieta, Sonora, which shares a border with Douglas, Arizona. After a 15-hour hike, he and the others were apprehended by Border Patrol—this was a relief on my end, as well as on their end; they were already without water and had completely lost communication. They were on their own with no guidance and were barely holding on—they were apprehended about an hour away from U.S. Route 80. My father endured many injuries both physically and psychologically; this is something quite normal for migrants who are forced to travel in this way. We were relieved to hear from him when he was deported to Mexicali, Baja California, Mexico—500 miles from where he was apprehended.

Border Crossing—Second Attempt, Casa de Seguridad

Following his fast-track deportation to Mexicali, we got my father back to Iguala, his hometown, to recuperate, rest, heal, and get ready for a second crossing attempt. In June 2016, he returned to the U.S.-Mexico border for the second time—same city, Agua Prieta, but with a different coyote. After the first attempt, we could not trust to continue working with the same coyote, thus we forfeited some money by changing coyotes. This second time we agreed that we would not put his life in danger and that out of the different options for crossing borders, we would opt for the less risky in terms of the possibility of losing his life, but riskier in terms of consequences for getting caught and then incarcerated. This form of crossing is the expensive form of crossing that only a very few are able to afford—crossing *en corto* is less lethal, costs more, and comes with higher punishment if caught.

He spent about a week or two in a secure house on the Mexican side while they tried to find U.S. documents for him, documents with age and appearance similar to him. They obtained an Arizona driver's license of a person that looked like my dad; however, we did not fall for it. It was too risky. He would get caught. A driver's license is insufficient to get you across the United States in a border town anymore. He would need a birth certificate and lots of confidence to try to cross with only a driver's license, unless the coyote had a Border Patrol agent working for him. Obviously, the coyote was not going to share the details of how he gets people across, who is involved, or when it does and does not work. Engaging in this type of transaction and contract requires trusting someone you do not know, most of the time it is just luck and going with what your gut tells you. Sometimes you go with what the coyote tells you and it goes perfectly! And most of the other times, it goes horribly wrong. We decided to leave the border town, the coyote, and try our luck somewhere else. Doing so meant risking an actual kidnapping situation. To get him out of the secure house would be risky, but with GPS tracking and a nearby migrant shelter contact we gave it a shot and went for it. We got him out and sent him on a two-day bus ride to Nuevo Laredo.

Border Crossing—Third Attempt,
Everything Is Good Hijo, Ya Pasé

This time we were a bit more prepared, we gained more experience from listening to many coyotes sell their border crossing services and techniques, we became more confident in evaluating pros and cons and deciding who is less trustworthy—differentiating those who actually do the work from those who do not, the professional from the phony. We were not in any rush; we were a bit more autonomous and not fully dependent on the *coyote,* the border crossers. We have a distant relative in Nuevo Laredo who offered their home for my father to stay. He stayed there over a week until things were "right" for the crossing. We prepared my father with cash, cell phones, GPS cell phone tracking, encrypted messaging communication, and so forth. We were able to establish a good system of communication and "surveillance" to know where he was at all times.

My dad would be crossing the Rio Grande to get to Laredo, Texas. That would be part one and the easiest part of the crossing. Even though I thought to myself, what happens if he drowns? What happens if there is fast current? Or high river water levels, and so on? To this, I did my research, using google, looking at terrain and topography maps, and searching for water levels in the area. However, none of this would make any difference; I did this to keep my own sanity. The fact of the matter was that he was going to cross no matter what. At the end, to most people it comes down to hope, no

Photo 15.1. Tracking image screen captured during my father's crossing. Image by José Guadalupe Herrera Soto.

matter how impossible or unrealistic a situation might be. We are just going to give it a try, if it works, great! And if it does not, well, we will try again and again, unless we lose our lives in the attempts. Once in the U.S. side, the second part was riskier and consisted of getting him out of the city and to San Antonio, Texas. He would need to ride a bus and show legal papers when *la migra* boards the bus at the Border Patrol Checkpoint about 30 miles from Laredo on Interstate 35. The second option offered in this second part of the crossing was to walk for several days from Laredo to near San Antonio avoiding roads, basically going around the Interstate 35 checkpoint. I felt more confident about this part of the border since I have driven this before. I also imagined all the things that could go wrong with the *coyote* and fantasized on possible ways that we could try to get him from Mexico into Laredo and to San Antonio. In Chicago, the search for someone with a U.S. passport that looked like my dad began; however, we did not get too far with this and so we left it to the experts, the coyote and their team, rather than me venturing to find ways of getting him safely across the border.

Tracking Image Taken during My Father's Crossing

In the evening of June 30, 2016, my dad crossed the Rio Grande (he has long stories to tell about this). I was there (in spirit) with him. And I was able to see a little red dot on my screen as he crossed the Rio Grande. We lost communication after he crossed the river; however, after an hour or so, he called and stated that he was good but suffered minor injuries in his hands and feet after running, jumping over fences, and hiding behind thorny bushes. My dad was once again in a secured home, this time in the U.S. side.

The next day, the coyote's crossing team got all of my dad's belongings that he had left in Nuevo Laredo and brought them to Laredo, Texas, to the secured home (IDs, clothes, backpack, and so forth). They also provided the documents he would be using to show Border Patrol at the checkpoint (Texas state ID, driver's license, social security card, and green card). Now it was all on him; he would have to purchase his bus ticket to San Antonio at the Greyhound station and ride alone. The coyote reassured us that someone from his team is always on the bus to check on the situation; however more than half of the things the coyote says are not necessarily true but serve to calm and give reassurance to the crossers and their families. Once at the Interstate 35 checkpoint, the bus would stop and a Border Patrol officer would go aboard. My father would show the documentation, answer any question raised by the officer, and hope for the best.

The team took him to the bus stop that evening, the plan was to leave during peak hours, to buy an 11 p.m. or midnight ticket. It was the 4th of July holiday weekend, and the bus had to be full with people to minimize capture since, according to the coyote, Border Patrol is less likely to spend more time reviewing documents in these situations. However, there were no more tickets to San Antonio for the planned departure time. My dad decided to purchase a ticket for the next available bus, Greyhound at 3 a.m. With U.S. legal documents in his pocket and after waiting for so long and going through so much, he just wanted to get it over with. I was hesitant, but in these situations there is no perfect plan and no guarantee—all can go wrong. So we made the decision to go ahead with our new plan, not to postpone, and to give it a shot—he will ride the almost empty 3 a.m. bus.

Thirty minutes on the road and the bus slows down, getting ready to stop at the checkpoint. I'm watching all of this on my screen in Chicago; the cell phone's GPS is working. I can see the red dot not moving on the map while at the checkpoint. A couple of minutes go by. I refresh my page, but the red dot is not found. I refresh again, and the red dot is moving north! I refresh again, and the red dot is back on the road and moving away from the checkpoint. My father replies via messenger and a few minutes later calls me. *Everything is good hijo, ya pasé.* Checkpoint is over and the bus is back on the road heading to San Antonio.

Within the next hour I booked a flight to Austin, Texas—I was going to get my dad. I contacted a fellow activist-scholar in Austin who hosted us there and who let me borrow their transportation to get to San Antonio. That afternoon, I arrived to a trailer home in the outskirts of the city. My father was resting in a small bedroom. I introduced myself to the woman in the home and settled the remaining balance of the crossing cost. We thanked the woman for their service and drove back to Austin. The next morning, we were on our way to Chicago—a road trip from Austin to Chicago, a 20-hour drive.

Today, July 30th, marks the second year my *abuelita* left this world and has reunited with my *abuelito* somewhere in some other universe. I am still recuperating from this entire ordeal. I am glad I was able to provide support to my father in order for him to leave the United States to spend time with *abuelita* and to come back. I did not know how he would get back, but I knew I would have to make it happen somehow—things did not go as planned, but it yielded the same end result: getting my dad back into the United States alive.

Again, thank you all for all your support. Your financial support contributed in many other ways than originally planned. Thank you for all the support and for follow-up on this issue.

Note

The author would like to thank Karma Chávez and Rozalinda Borcilă for help on this piece.

16

The Rhetoric of Family in the U.S. Immigration Movement

A Queer Migration Analysis of the 2014 Central American Child Migrant "Crisis"

KARMA R. CHÁVEZ AND HANA MASRI

In the summer of 2014, reports about an apparent surge in unauthorized crossings of the Mexico-U.S. border by unaccompanied minors from Central America inundated the news. By the end of July, some 60,000 young people had made their way through Mexico and arrived at its northern border. While a similar number of family groups were apprehended during that same time frame, the story was about the children.[1] Mainstream media coupled harrowing stories of the crossings with leaked images of young people being stored in refrigerator-style warehouses along the border. Many stories that accompanied such images framed this as a refugee or humanitarian crisis, noting that the thousands of children crossing the border fled violence in Guatemala, Honduras, and El Salvador, known collectively as the Northern Triangle.[2] Most refugee and immigration organizations shared a similar analysis, though many recognized that this moment had been building for years. Such liberal organizations replicated familiar discourses about refugees, insisting that although the people crossing the border were from the Northern Triangle, a region with extraordinarily low rates of obtaining legal refugee status in the United States, they were refugees, *not* migrants. Thus, these organizations argued, the "crisis" necessitated protective humanitarian responses from the government and good-hearted people nationwide.

With such images circulating and outcry growing, politicians also recognized some kind of crisis, the type of which was hotly debated, ranging from humanitarian, to refugee, to immigration, to border security. The Obama administration looked for places to house busloads of children while they were processed through the immigration system. Conservative locals in places such as Orange County,

California, and parts of Arizona attempted to block the school buses from entering their communities, staging protests with signs reading, "no vacancy, try the White House," and "no new taxes, no new illegals."[3]

Politicians and social groups on all sides of the political spectrum were united—there was a crisis at hand. Yet what exactly made it a crisis? In June 2014, the Chicago-based Moratorium on Deportations Campaign reported that on any given day as many as 4,600 migrant children are detained in 68 child detention centers around the country that have existed since 2002.[4] As early as 2011, the Migration Policy Institute noted that the number of unaccompanied migrant minors to the United States was steadily increasing and had been doing so following political, social, and economic unrest in Latin American countries.[5] In 2001, the Department of Justice Office of the Inspector General issued a report called *Unaccompanied Juveniles in INS Custody*, which indicated that immigration officials encounter "over 100,000 accompanied and unaccompanied illegal juveniles under the age of 18 every year," most of whom are detained for around 72 hours.[6] If thousands of young people are locked in detention centers each day, if the numbers arriving at the Mexico-U.S,. border have been steadily on the rise for years, and if immigration officials have detained more than 100,000 youth annually for more than a decade, what made the summer of 2014 different? What motivated the political and public insistence on naming this migration of youth a crisis? More specifically to our analysis, what agendas does liberal organizing around the figure of the child in the crisis serve?

Employing a queer migration approach—which uses insights from queer theory and activism to draw attention to the operation of racialized gender, sexual, and relational norms within immigration discourses and policy—we analyze the implications of liberal advocate and activist organizing around the child in political and movement discourse about Central American migration. Such an analysis reveals that even when framed as a refugee or humanitarian crisis and therefore supposedly separate from economic migration, images of children, which traffic in rhetorics of vulnerability and innocence, easily pair with the pro-family, pro-child rhetoric of the immigration rights movement to, paradoxically, justify the nation's maintenance and fortification of its borders in ways that harm all migrants.

In this chapter, we first consider the concept of childhood in conjunction with queer and queer migration perspectives, emphasizing the staking of the nation's future on the imagined (white) child. Next, we identify our methods and sources in order to discuss the pro-family, pro-child rhetoric of the immigration movement and specific responses to the 2014 crisis. We also explore the Obama administration's initial response to the 2014 crisis and executive orders issued later that year. Finally, we discuss queer migration activist responses to the crisis and end with some thoughts about the relevance of this analysis to contemporary rhetorics of the immigration movement. Ultimately, we conclude that the fraught nexus between the protectable child and the deportable migrant paradoxically reinforces the exclusionary boundaries of the nation and, in so doing, requires queer critiques and activism that refuse to reproduce logics that include some people at the expense of others. We first turn our attention to queer thought on childhood.

Queer Approaches to the Future/Child

Theorists of childhood note that the concept of childhood as a separate phase of being developed in Europe between the fifteenth and eighteenth centuries.[7] The idea of childhood interweaves with bourgeois conceptions of privacy, family, individualism, and home; childhood prepares children for their future (and hence our future) in the adult world.[8] In modern times, the figure of the child holds an array of cultural meanings that serve myriad cultural and political functions.[9] For this reason, our interest in childhood is not as a state of development but as a description of "'what children mean' in a given society."[10] Critical childhood studies scholars insist that the meanings ascribed to "the child" and an abstract notion of "childhood" are racialized, gendered, and classed, and actual children are therefore treated very differently based on meanings assigned to such factors. For example, in the popular imaginary, children are juxtaposed against non-innocents, particularly gay predators from whom they must be protected.[11] And yet, as Kathryn Bond Stockton claims, "'we' fear the children we would protect."[12] Lawrence Grossberg notes that U.S. depictions of children throughout the 20th century characterized this paradox between what "we" long to protect, and what we find troubling and dangerous.[13] The matter of danger is most acute with regard to nonwhite childhood. Michael J. Dumas and Joseph Derrick Nelson, for instance, note that Black boyhood is "unimagined and unimaginable."[14] Imaginaries of the child and childhood are therefore dense sites at which gender, racial, and national anxieties are constructed and produced.

Significant queer critique, specifically through the lens of "reproductive futurism" interrogates childhood's boundedness to white, middle-class, heteronormative, and nationalistic values. As Sara Ahmed explains, the dominance of reproductive heterosexuality orients us toward conventional lineages: leaving our parents' home to enter a heterosexual union, reproduce, and nurture children.[15] The normativity of reproductive futurism operates in personal and intimate lives, and it has political functions. Lee Edelman describes reproductive futurism as that which sets "an ideological limit on political discourse."[16] In other words, the figure of the child is "the perpetual horizon of every acknowledged politics, the fantasmatic beneficiary of every political intervention."[17] How, Edelman wonders, could anyone take sides against the child? In *No Future*, his much-discussed polemic, Edelman argues,

> queerness names the side of those *not* fighting for the children, the side outside the consensus by which all politics confirms the absolute value of reproductive futurism. The ups and downs of political fortune may measure the social order's pulse, but *queerness*, by contrast, figures, outside and beyond its political symptoms.[18]

In advocating against the future and the child and for an anti-future, Edelman insists queers accept the negativity queerness already represents (as, for example, anti-family and against normative sexuality). In other words, queers should not champion the child or the future or demand to be recognized in the system that celebrates the child. Queers should, instead, embrace negativity and critique the problems with reproductive futurism for queers and others who are excluded, actively expunged, and abjected from its promise. Queer critiques of the child and the future help to explain how heteronormative limits on political discourse function.

José Esteban Muñoz rightly critiques Edelman for the unnamed whiteness of the child figure he critiques. As Muñoz notes, echoing Dumas and Nelson, "all children are not the privileged white babies to whom contemporary society caters."[19] Nevertheless, Edelman's identification of the logics of reproductive futurism remains useful in parsing out the competing impulses that undergird rhetorics about migrant children and the 2014 "crisis."

Edelman's work, alongside important critiques like Muñoz's that emphasize reproductive futurism's racialized dimensions, informs our queer migration approach, which unpacks how racialized gender and sexual norms and values construct, enable, and constrain immigration discourses in, for example, media, policy, and activism. In a smart extension of Edelman's thesis, Eithne Luibhéid examines immigration policy in Ireland to argue that others expunged from reproductive futurism's promise include pregnant migrant women whose reproductive bodies and the children they birth challenge the national future. Through this examination, Luibhéid reveals that the national future is the future of the white, *citizen* child. Luibhéid's critique calls attention to what futures the focus on the white citizen child enable—namely, futures with expanded military, immigrant detention, and prison industrial complexes in the name of the security and protection of that child. Nonwhite, noncitizen children will have very different material futures. That not all children's futures are equal becomes especially clear when children in our midst are, so to speak, "alien" children who violate the nation's laws. Indeed, as Jacqueline Bhabha explains, the presence of child migrants creates for societies an "unresolved ambivalence."[20] Child migrants simultaneously draw "protective attention" because they have no adult care, and "punitive attention" because their presence as "threatening outsiders" disrupts state structures.[21]

Despite the variegated ways different children are actually regarded, liberal politics assume color-blindness in the views and treatment of members of society. Thus, Edelman's theoretical perspective, which insists that queerness intervenes in the terms of the social, helps to make sense of liberal reactions to the child migrant "crisis," which demanded protective attention while simultaneously ignoring the ways that racialized migrant children illuminate anxieties around insecure borders and the national future. Coupling Edelman's insights with Luibhéid and Bhabha reveals the anti-future logic as already attached to the migrant child. Recognizing this logic, in turn, illuminates how liberals' protective attention and pro-family rhetoric in defense of the child colludes with and justifies punitive attention and futures that are decidedly anti-migrant, anti-child, and anti-family.[22]

Immigration and the Rhetoric of Family

Rhetorics of family dominate the campaigns and demands of the immigrant rights and justice movement.[23] Queer migration scholars and activists, meanwhile, draw attention to how the mainstream immigrant rights and justice movement's deployment of familial, relational, and respectability norms harms all migrants, but particularly those most vulnerable.[24] For instance, the 2007 statement "Queers and Immigration: A Vision Statement," issued by the now-defunct organization Queers for Economic Justice, called for the end of immigration reform based on heteronormative family. The authors insisted that advocates broaden or change their definitions of family so as not to be exclusionary to LGBTQ people and all those who cannot or will not conform to narrow and nuclear definitions.[25]

Still, normative family rhetoric has prevailed in the contemporary movement for more than a decade. In the face of unprecedented numbers of deportations and ongoing failures to achieve significant immigration reform, advocates and activists have relied on family rhetoric and imagery to leverage change, and mainstream U.S. media have picked up such narratives. A cursory internet search for "immigrant rights" reveals the prevalence of such slogans as "No More Families Torn Apart," "Keep Our Families Together," and "Families Have No Borders" in pro-immigrant campaigns. Importantly, children are front and center in these appeals, both in images of cute but sad and scared youngsters marching with oversized T-shirts proclaiming "Don't Deport My Mom" and also at the helm of direct actions, as undocumented youth were the main catalysts of immigration-related organizing throughout the Obama era.

Undocumented youth, many who wear or once wore the title "DREAMer"—a reference to the continually ill-fated DREAM Act, which would provide a pathway to citizenship for a select group of undocumented youth—have grown and transformed in their rhetorical appeals.[26] But, especially early on, they pleaded for access to citizenship on the basis of their innocence (it was their parents who broke the law, not them) and on the basis of their desire to assimilate and contribute to the national future. Such appeals sought to expand the conditions of possibility for some, but they did so at the expense of others who would already be considered unworthy immigrants.[27] In liberal discourse around the 2014 summer "crisis," a similar bind between the protectable child and their punishable family, as well as an unwanted national future, is at work.

In the next sections, we analyze the rhetoric of statements produced by the liberal or mainstream immigrant rights movement, primarily United We Dream, alongside statements from the Obama administration during the summer of 2014. We then turn to the Obama administration's rhetoric surrounding its November 2014 executive orders on immigration in conjunction with reactions from radical queer migration activists. We selected these texts in order to define the contours of the debate liberals were having, the way that debate played out in policy, and how queer migration activists responded to those rhetorical and political conditions. The interplay between liberal discourses and federal institutions was of special interest to us here, given the way that rhetorics meant to support the youth in question were adopted into policies that expanded the same border apparatus those youth and their families had to confront.

A queer migration approach informs our analysis in the following sections in two ways: First, we draw on insights from queer and queer migration scholars to help unpack the logics in the rhetoric of liberal advocates and politicians (for example, groups like United We Dream and the Obama Administration). Second, we uplift queer migration activists who offered crucial insight into the work the Obama administration did with the executive order, and we add texture to that theoretical work by making connections to broader liberal frames about family, children, belonging, and normativity.

Protecting the Child Migrant

The youth arriving at the border from Central America would not be eligible for the DREAM Act, but the existing rhetorical landscape regarding family and youth in immigration provided sources of invention for media, politicians, and advocates making sense of what was happening and how various actors should respond. Here, the figure of the child, around which the crisis was organized, links up in political and public discourse with rhetorics about family and family values; the child is valuable, while the rest of the family is disposable or even at fault for the so-called crisis.

Using images of young unaccompanied children in deplorable situations, immigration and humanitarian organizations drew on rhetorics of innocence and vulnerability through their centralizing of the figure of the child to demand protective action. Materially, they insisted upon immediate care of these children, a stop to deportation and detentions, and Obama's refusal to cave to right-wing pressures. Numerous organizations signed on to statements and open letters to Obama demanding such actions. In early July, 190 immigration, civil and human rights, faith, labor, antiviolence, and community organizations signed a letter to Obama expressing their concern that he was placing "far greater emphasis on deterrence of migration than on the importance of protection of children seeking safety."[28] Even the left-of-center National Network for Immigrant and Refugee Rights (NNIRR), which is comprised of over 250 organizations, and individuals implored that, "This is a critical opportunity for the Obama Administration to take clear legal steps and fulfill this country's obligation to provide humanitarian support and protection for these young victims, whose desperate situation is largely a consequence of economic failure in their home countries. These children need essential services and access to justice; they should have due process, liberty and family unity."[29] Both of these statements frame the top priority as protecting children. Although NNIRR mentions U.S. culpability in creating the situation in Central America, both politically and economically, it takes the protection rhetoric one step further, insisting that one of the needs these young people have is family unity, which coheres with existing rhetorical appeals to stop separating families. A queer critique shows that, because of the close connection between rhetorics of the child and the family, it is easy to deploy the child in a way that colludes with discourses that insist only certain people are worthy of inclusion.

United We Dream (UWD), the largest immigrant-youth-led organization in the United States issued several statements on the various political responses to the child migrant crisis and offered its own perspective. Unlike most other statements and organizations, UWD regularly tied the issue of the youth explicitly to other, ongoing immigration issues including Deferred Action for Childhood Arrivals (DACA), separation of families, and comprehensive immigration reform. This rhetoric connects the issue of unaccompanied minors with ongoing struggles for immigration reform, and UWD relies heavily on the same kinds of family appeals familiar to the rest of the movement, despite its early beginnings as a queer-led organization. A June 24th press release cites Cristina Jimenez, the managing director for UWD, who criticized Republican lawmakers:

> Unfortunately, after spending this Congress blocking immigration reform and voting to defund DACA and subject Dreamers to deportation, Republicans are now using the unaccompanied minors crisis to once again demonstrate their opposition

to immigrant youth and families in America. That Republicans' answer to children fleeing violence is to seek to blame DACA sends a loud and clear message—they support and promote inhumane immigration policies that separate families and do not believe Dreamers, like me, living and settled in the United States should be protected from deportation, have the right to be with my family, or able to work and fully contribute to society.[30]

By basing her appeal on the need to keep families together in order to protect innocent youth, Jimenez here draws from the same rhetorical tension that includes those migrants who exist within a normative family structure at the expense of others who do not.

In a July 16th press release, legislative affairs associate Julieta Garibay responded to a Republican-sponsored proposal. Garibay lamented,

We remain committed to reminding America of its moral obligation to truly protect defenseless refugee children, something that is lost between the border and Washington. We will continue fighting so these families are not stripped of their rights by hate-mongering politicians who see them as "invaders" and not as refugees.[31]

This statement also plays into the rhetoric of protecting vulnerable children and families, but it is unique in its description of them as refugees. Describing them as refugees as opposed to migrants plays on an additional set of discourses that hierarchize people who migrate. Humanitarian groups often deploy the child refugee figure to win compassion, but usually that figure is imagined in a faraway place, which is part of the ethical appeal. Moreover, that child is not imagined to have crossed a border without authorization. Although Garibay's argument is steeped in the understanding that refugees are somehow more deserving than migrants, the refugee is often an equally unsympathetic figure, and the distinction between the migrant and the refugee is blurry at best. In direct contrast to Edelman's understanding of the child as the subject upon which the future of the nation is predicated, the refugee, in U.S. and Western discourses, is a mistrusted and threatening subject. As Liisa Malkki explains, states imagine refugees as "an aberration of categories, a zone of pollution," a disruption of the "national order of things" that flood over borders.[32]

Whether using the language of refugees or migrants, UWD responded to Obama's actions in ways that continued to emphasize family and children. On June 30th, UWD put out two press releases, one denouncing the president's intended actions on the Central American migrants and another cautiously supporting his declaration that he would use his executive powers to offer more relief to immigrant families. In the first, Jimenez is quoted as saying, "We are outraged at President Obama's plan to 'fast track' deportations of unaccompanied minors. This humanitarian crisis requires a humanitarian response.

Instead, this Administration has placed children and mothers in cold detention centers and is working fast to disregard the conditions from which they
fled and to potentially deport them to dangerous situations."[33] UWD's Lorella
Praeli is more affirmative in the second press release. Describing Obama's an-
nouncement that he still seeks comprehensive immigration reform and will use
executive orders to achieve some action steps that can't otherwise be achieved
as a "welcome step forward," she cautions, "we are past the point of celebrating mere words. We need to see actual substantive steps forward that protect
immigrant families."[34]

Rhetorically and materially, President Obama paid more punitive than protective attention to the crisis, but, like these groups, he also framed it as a humanitarian problem. In his June 30, 2014, public remarks on "border security
and immigration reform," Obama chastised Republicans for refusing to support
immigration reform and claimed that part of the reason the situation was so
difficult on the border in that moment was because of the broken system.[35] That
same day, he sent a letter to the House and Senate leadership of both parties
asking for support in addressing the "urgent humanitarian situation,"[36] which
included authorization for the Department of Homeland Security to have more
discretion in removing unaccompanied minors and to increase the penalties on
smugglers. He also requested emergency appropriations legislation to apprehend
and process migrants more quickly and effectively, points we expand on later.

Whereas most Republicans showed little protective concern, Obama, like liberal advocates, expressed concern about families and especially children. Though
his concerns about families differed from advocates, he often used similar language of protection and care. In these statements and in interviews with media
outlets, Obama recognized political unrest, violence, and insecurity in Central
American countries. He emphasized the moral and legal obligation to care for
apprehended children. He also stressed the role of parents. In his June 30th remarks, he insisted, "The journey is unbelievably dangerous for these kids. The
children who are fortunate enough to survive it will be taken care of while they
go through the legal process, but in most cases that process will lead to them
being sent back home. I've sent a clear message to parents in these countries not
to put their kids through this."

Despite his recognition of political, social, and economic problems in the
Northern Triangle, and despite U.S. government intervention's role in creating
those problems, Obama reduced the decision for young people to come to the bad
choices of their parents. His admonishments of parents flooded news, making for
headlines on several major outlets. "Our message absolutely is don't send your
children unaccompanied, on trains or through a bunch of smugglers," Obama
told ABC News. "We don't even know how many of these kids don't make it and

may have been waylaid into sex trafficking or killed because they fell off a train. Do not send your children to the borders. . . . If they do make it, they'll get sent back. More importantly, they may not make it."[37] The mainstream media and many organizations repeated this quotation, unquestioning of the administration's motives and accepting it as an appropriate frame and rationale.

A queer migration perspective compels us to consider how the rhetoric of concern for the child on the part of liberal advocates and politicians like Obama naturalizes, obscures, and ultimately justifies a white heteropatriarchal vision of the nation. Such critiques indicate how the tension between imaginings of the migrant child as simultaneous future of—and threat to—the nation is resolved through the shoring up of border enforcement, which does significant harm to those children.

Framing this situation as a humanitarian crisis involving innocent children not only reinforces the savior status of the U.S. nation, but it also plays on existing stereotypes about the poor parenting and family values of racialized migrants. Although equally as many children were apprehended with their families during this time, the disproportionate focus on "unaccompanied" children reinforces the United States as a benevolent protector of those children. This emphasis was present in Obama's language, and it was repeatedly visible in the media imagery accompanying reporting on the matter; most of the images of the crisis, for example, featured children without parents or adults, unless those adults were U.S. immigration officials. Framing this situation foremost as a humanitarian crisis requiring the protection of children also helps to justify the policies of the Obama administration, even though such punitive policies harm those same children.

Deporting Felons, Not Families

At the same time as the crisis covered the news and Obama gave speeches around the country, he crafted shifts in immigration policy to increase penalties for smugglers,[38] as well as to get appropriations for initiatives, including: a border security surge, an aggressive deterrence strategy, and the resources to "to appropriately detain, process, and care for children and adults."[39] Put simply, the political theater of this humanitarian crisis, which embraces the figure of the child, would be used toward punitive ends: more resources for homeland security, including border militarization, detention, and deportation systems. Despite this conservative agenda, Congress refused to assist. Obama did not have to wait for Congress. Via executive action, the Obama administration announced the discontinuance of the controversial Secure Communities or S-Comm program on November 20, 2014.[40]

US Citizenship and Immigration Services summarized the purpose and content of Obama's executive actions in the following way: "On November 20, 2014, the President announced a series of executive actions to crack down on illegal immigration at the border, prioritize deporting felons not families, and require certain undocumented immigrants to pass a criminal background check and pay taxes in order to temporarily stay in the US without fear of deportation."[41] News reports and immigrant rights organizations' press releases primarily centered their attention on this last action, the proposed extension of DACA to the undocumented parents of U.S. citizens or legal permanent residents. Few emphasized the enforcement actions, specifically what DHS Secretary Jeh Johnson introduced as "PEP," the Priority Enforcement Program. Unlike S-Comm, under PEP, immigration officials would target only high "priority" groups such as "those who threaten national security, public safety or border security," those convicted of three nontraffic misdemeanors, and those "with other immigration violations."[42] Arguably, these priority groups could expand to include nearly every deportable person, especially under the ambiguous purview of the third category.

In the face of years of advocate and activist outrage because Obama's deportation practices divided hundreds of thousands of families by deporting nearly 3 million people since 2009, the administration's framing device, deporting "felons, not families" clearly responded directly to established immigrant rights rhetoric. The catchphrase's responsive rhetoric is further obvious because the immigrant rights' movement's pro-family rhetoric has often been paired with contentions that immigrants are not criminals. "Felons, not families" thus mirrors the demands of the mainstream immigrant rights movement. In their framing, both Obama and the mainstream immigration movement ignore families *with* felons, a significant problem since Black and brown immigrants in particular, like their citizen counterparts, are much more likely to have police encounters resulting in arrest and prosecution than white people. In suggesting that he heard the will of the people and changed course to deport "felons not families," in light of the crisis of children on the border, Obama was able to continue to use family rhetoric not as a distraction from the material realities of his policies for families and nonfamilies alike, but to justify those policies and to naturalize a particular kind of law-abiding family that the nation values.[43]

Numerous advocates celebrated Obama's November 2014 deferred action extension,[44] but some queer migration activists lamented the extension's exclusions, focusing on who PEP targeted as deportable priorities. Such activists noted that the following groups were excluded from the deferred action order: parents of undocumented youth who benefited from the 2012 DACA; seasonal workers without connections to U.S. citizen children; LGBT immigrants, especially youth and trans people, who are more likely to have been homeless and therefore to have committed low-level criminal offenses; domestic violence survivors who can't get visas under the Violence Against Women Act; and Black immigrants who are more likely to be racially profiled by police and therefore either have a felony record or have family members who do.[45] The Obama administration either did not acknowledge the family relationships of these groups as real or includable, or the administration failed to acknowledge how even "real" families might harm each other, creating conditions that put someone in a deportable position (for example, a young person flees domestic violence and commits theft in order to survive).

Partners in the Not One More Deportation Campaign, a campaign centrally organized by queer and trans migration activists that claimed a big role in pushing Obama to issue executive orders, also challenged Obama's "felons, not families" framing, elaborating on some of the points mentioned above. Yesenia Valdez, a national organizer for Familia: Trans and Queer Liberation Movement noted:

> As a community, we know that we do not fit the normal definition of families that continue to dominate public discourse. Many LGBTQ undocumented immigrants do not have families that are US citizens or permanent residents that could allow them to qualify for the program. Additionally, we know that our community, especially trans women of color, is unfairly targeted by law enforcement through racial discrimination or for engaging in survival sex work. These daily realities mean that many members of our LGBTQ community will be left out of the president's plan.[46]

Opal Tometi, the executive director for the Black Alliance for Just Immigration and cofounder of Black Lives Matter, a group that centers queer and trans perspectives, emphasized the point that law enforcement measures are always more impactful on Black people, and then added, "we won't stand for a system that criminalizes us, and then pits family against people who may have a criminal record."[47] Tometi's comments also draw attention to the narrow definition of family prescribed in Obama's executive actions as well as the damage done to numerous families by false divisions between alleged "families" and "felons." Thus, the logics underlying Obama's response to the child migrant crisis—logics introduced by liberal immigration organizations—not only traffic in understandings that strengthen the very conditions that create child migrants in the first place, they also function to expand the categories of undesirable immigrants and to marginalize various communities of color.

Conclusion

Employing a queer migration critique to analyze the contrast between Obama's supposedly liberal and pro-family rhetoric during the "child migrant crisis" of

2014 and his seemingly antifamily actions later that year teaches us that queers, immigration activists, and social justice advocates must be wary of arguments that seem to be in line with their values, but that actually work against their interests. A queer migration critique helps us to understand how activists and advocates must find better ways to build coalitions that do not inadvertently issue exclusionary and normalizing mandates.

The concerns that a queer migration critique points to are not merely about gender, sexuality, family, and reproduction. This critique contributes to queer migration studies by drawing our attention to other exclusionary and normalizing mandates, like rhetorics that advocate for the inclusion of refugees at the expense of migrants without considering the complexity of that distinction and the overlap between the two categories. Such rhetorics reinforce divisive discourses that play into draconian policies like Obama's and, at the time we write, Trump's; some are potentially worthy of inclusion, such as children fleeing political and interpersonal violence, while others, such as children fleeing economic violence, are definitively not. As long as advocates engage in these kinds of rhetorics, especially on the backs of children, and let such rhetoric animate politics, advocates and activists will continue not only to exclude, but abjectly treat those they may intend to support. Furthermore, liberal appeals to protect migrant children, within the context of a broader set of appeals to keep families together, are risky given the "unresolved ambivalence" between protective and punitive attention that child migrants conjure[48] and an existing rhetorical landscape that demonizes racialized families. Queer interventions in the operation of discourses like reproductive futurism upon which such pro-family, pro-child appeals rest, are essential to understand the stakes of our politics and to create new horizons that rearrange the conditions of possibility outside of liberal compassion and heteronormative futures.

Obama was not solely to blame, of course, for the record number of removals that occurred during his eight years. He inherited an immense immigration machinery from previous administrations. Apprehensions of unauthorized border crossers were significantly lower during Obama's years than they were under Clinton or Bush, and Obama focused largely on those with criminal convictions and recent arrivals.[49] A queer migration critique of this record reveals that Obama's facile separation between "felons and families," relies upon a narrow definition of family that is inherently racialized and doesn't acknowledge the fact that families of color and immigrant families are more likely to be criminalized than white citizen families. This critique also shows that an unreflexive reliance on family rhetorics by the liberal immigration rights movement is insufficient, and even dangerous, to the task of resolving the migrant child's paradoxical rhetorical status as both a child in need of protection and a migrant against whom the nation-state must protect itself. Such rhetorics, therefore, are easily channeled into logics, like Obama's and Trump's that require a further expansion of the same immigration systems that harm migrant children in the first place.

Notes

1. Muzaffar Chishti and Faye Hipsman, "Unaccompanied Minors Crisis Has Receded from Headlines but Major Issues Remain," Migration Policy Institute, September 25, 2014, http://www.migrationpolicy.org/article/unaccompanied-minors-crisis-has-receded-headlines-major-issues-remain.

2. Although not directly connected to our analysis, a refugee crisis and a humanitarian crisis are not necessarily the same thing. As Didier Fassin explains, often the humanitarian is imagined as something separate from the political. See Didier Fassin, "Compassion and Repression: The Moral Economy of Immigration Policies in France," *Cultural Anthropology* 20, no. 3 (2005): 362–387.

3. Nick O'Malley, "Flight of the Children Finds a US Divided," *Sunday Age*, August 3, 2014, 22.

4. "The Border Is the Problem: Resisting the 'Humanitarian' Solution to Child Migration." *Moratorium on Deportations Campaign*, June 14, 2014, http://moratoriumon deportations.org/2014/06/14/child_migration/.

5. Amanda Levinson, "Unaccompanied Immigrant Children: A Growing Phenomenon with Few Easy Solutions," Migration Policy Institute, January 24, 2011, http://www.migration policy.org/article/unaccompanied-immigrant-children-growing-phenomenon-few-easy-solutions/.

6. *Unaccompanied Juveniles in INS Custody*, Report Number I-2001-009, Department of Justice Office of the Inspector General, September 28, 2001, chapter 1, https://oig.justice.gov/reports/INS/e0109/chapter1.htm.

7. Phillippe Ariès, *Centuries of Childhood: A Social History of Family Life* (New York: Knopf, 1962).

8. Sharon Stephens, ed. *Children and the Politics of Culture* (Princeton, N.J.: Princeton University Press, 1995).

9. Caroline Levander and Carol J. Single, eds., *American Childhood: A Cultural Studies Reader* (New Brunswick, N.J.: Rutgers University Press, 2003).

10. Michael J. Dumas and Joseph Derrick Nelson, "(Re)Imagining Black Boyhood: Toward a Critical Framework for Educational Research," *Harvard Educational Review* 86, no. 1 (2016): 28.

11. Kathryn Bond Stockton, *The Queer Child, or Growing Sideways in the Twentieth Century* (Durham, N.C.: Duke University Press, 2009).

12. "The Queer Child Now and Its Paradoxical Global Effects," *GLQ* 22, no. 4 (2016): 505–506.

13. Lawrence Grossberg, *Caught in the Crossfire: Kids, Politics, and America's Future* (Boulder, Colo.: Paradigm Publishers, 2005).

14. Dumas and Nelson, "(Re)Imagining Black Boyhood."

15. Sara Ahmed, *Queer Phenomenology: Orientations, Objects, Others* (Durham, N.C.: Duke University Press, 2006).

16. Lee Edelman, *No Future: Queer Theory and the Death Drive* (Durham, N.C.: Duke University Press, 2004), 2.

17. Ibid., 3.

18. Ibid.

19. José Esteban Muñoz, "Cruising the Toilet: Leroi Jones/Amiri Baraka, Radical Black Traditions, and Queer Futurity," *GLQ* 13, nos. 2–3 (2007): 363–364.

20. Jacqueline Bhabha, *Child Migration and Human Rights in a Global Age* (Princeton, N.J.: Princeton University Press, 2014), 11.

21. Ibid., 3.

22. Eithne Luibhéid, *Pregnant on Arrival: Making the Illegal Immigrant* (Minneapolis: University of Minnesota Press, 2013).

23. See Karma R. Chávez, *Queer Migration Politics: Activist Rhetoric and Coalitional Possibilities* (Urbana: University of Illinois Press, 2013); Alfonso Gonzales, *Reform without Justice: Latino Migrant Politics and the Homeland Security State* (New York: Oxford University Press, 2013); Bernadette Nadya Jaworsky, *The Boundaries of Belonging: Online Work of Immigration-Related Social Movement Organizations* (New York: Palgrave Macmillan, 2016); Amalia Pallares, *Family Activism: Immigrant Struggles and the Politics of Noncitizenship* (New Brunswick, N.J.: Rutgers University Press, 2015); Amalia Pallares and Nilda Flores-González, eds., *Marcha: Latino Chicago and the Immigrant Rights Movement* (Urbana: University of Illinois Press, 2010); Grace Yukich, *One Family under God: Immigration Politics and Progressive Religion in America* (New York: Oxford University Press, 2013).

24. Ana Milena Ribero, "'Papá, Mamá, I'm Coming Home': Family, Home, and the Neoliberal Immigrant Nation in the National Immigrant Youth Alliance's 'Bring Them Home' Campaign," *Rhetoric Review* 37, no. 3 (2018): 273–285.

25. Queers for Economic Justice, "Queers and Immigration: A Vision Statement," *Scholar and Feminist Online* 6, no. 3 (2008), http://sfonline.barnard.edu/immigration/qej_01.htm.

26. There are numerous examples of the transformation of the appeals of undocumented youth. See: Chávez, *Queer Migration Politics*; Sasha Costanza-Chock, *Out of the Shadows, into the Streets! Transmedia Organizing and the Immigrant Rights Movement* (Cambridge, Mass.: MIT Press, 2014). In the fall of 2017, when young undocumented activists interrupted Nancy Pelosi (D-CA), who was ostensibly speaking on their behalf, they shouted "don't call us DREAMers!" The youth explained that the term "has helped create a narrative of the 'good immigrant vs. the bad immigrant,' pitting younger, better-educated immigrants against other unauthorized immigrants—especially their parents." See Roxana Kopetman and Alejandra Molina, "DACA Debate: Don't Call Them 'Dreamers' or Pawns," *Orange County Register*, September 22, 2017, http://www.ocregister.com/2017/09/22/daca-debate-dont-call-them-dreamers-or-pawns/. This critique has been made by queer migration scholars and radical activists for many years, but its public circulation is newer among undocumented youth at the helm of the movement.

27. Claudia A. Anguiano and Karma R. Chávez, "Dreamers' Discourse: Young Latino/a Immigrants and the Naturalization of the American Dream," in *Latina/o Discourse in Vernacular Spaces: Somos De Una Voz?* eds. Michelle A. Holling and Bernadette Marie Calafell (Lanham, Md.: Lexington Books, 2011).

28. Letter to President Obama Sent by 190 NGOs, July 3, 2014.

29. "NNIRR Urges President Obama to Act for Human Rights and Justice," *National Network for Immigrant and Refugee Rights*, July 1, 2014, http://www.nnirr.org/drupal/ humanitarian-response.

30. "Why Are Republicans Using the Crisis of Children Fleeing Central American Violence to Attack Dreamers?" *United We Dream*, June 24, 2014, http://unitedwedream.org/ press-releases/republicans-using-crisis-children-fleeing-central-american-violence-attack -dreamers/.

31. "HUMANE Bill Embraces Ideology of Hate towards Refugee Children and Families," *United We Dream*, July 16, 2014, http://unitedwedream.org/press-releases/humane-bill -embraces-ideology-hate-towards-refugee-children-families/.

32. Liisa H. Malkki, *Purity and Exile: Violence, Memory, and National Cosmology among Hutu Refugees in Tanzania* (Chicago: University of Chicago Press, 1995), 4.

33. "United We Dream Outraged at President Obama's Plan to Speed Up Deportations of Central American Children," *United We Dream*, June 30, 2014, http://unitedwedream .org/press-releases/united-dream-outraged-president-obamas-plan-speed-deportations -central-american-children/.

34. "UWD Reacts to President's Rose Garden Remarks on Immigration," *United We Dream*, June 30, 2014, http://unitedwedream.org/press-releases/uwd-reacts-presidents -rose-garden-remarks-immigration/.

35. "Remarks by the President on Border Security and Immigration Reform," *White House Press Office*, June 30, 2014, https://www.whitehouse.gov/the-press-office/2014/06/30/ remarks-president-border-security-and-immigration-reform.

36. "Letter from the President—Efforts to Address the Humanitarian Situation in the Rio Grande Valley Areas of Our Nation's Southwest Border," *White House Press Office*, June 30, 2014, https://www.whitehouse.gov/the-press-office/2014/06/30/letter-president -efforts-address-humanitarian-situation-rio-grande-valle.

37. Devin Dwyer, "Obama Warns Central Americans: 'Do Not Send Your Children to the Borders,'" *ABC News*, June 26, 2014, https://abcnews.go.com/Politics/obama-warns -central-americans-send-children-borders/story?id=24320063.

38. A much earlier and slightly different version of the argument in this section was published as a section in: Karma R. Chávez, "Queer Migration Politics as Transnational Activism," *Scholar and Feminist Online* 14, no. 2 (2017), http://sfonline.barnard.edu/thinking -queer-activism-transnationally/queer-migration-politics-as-transnational-activism/.

39. "Letter from the President."

40. S-Comm functioned as an extension of provision 287(g) of the Immigration and Nationality Act, which allows state and local law enforcement agencies to enter an agreement with Immigration and Customs Enforcement (ICE), so they may have delegated authority for immigration enforcement in their jurisdictions.

41. "Executive Actions on Immigration," *US Citizenship and Immigration Services*, November 20, 2014, http://www.uscis.gov/immigrationaction.

42. Jeh Charles Johnson, "Secure Communities," Department of Homeland Security Memorandum, November 20, 2014.

43. This is similar to how Alfonso Gonzales puts it: "Once Latino migrant activists and their allies accept this binary [between good and bad immigrant], they subtly consent to the production of legal violence against migrants" (7).

44. For example, Carlos: "'We should be deporting felons, and not families'—an immigrant student speaks out," *PBS Extras: Student Voices*, December 10, 2014, http://www.pbs .org/newshour/extra/student_voices/we-should-be-deporting-felons-and-not-families -an-immigrant-student-speaks-out/.

45. Julianne Hing, "Who Will Lose under Obama's Executive Action," *Colorlines*, November 21, 2014, http://www.colorlines.com/articles/who-will-lose-under-obamas -executive-action.

46. "#Not1More: Our Victories and Our Fights Will Continue," Not One More Deportation, Press Release, November 20, 2014, http://www.notonemoredeportation.com/ 2014/11/20/not1more-our-victories-and-our-fights-will-continue/.

47. Opal Tometi, "Statement from Opal Tometi, the Executive Director of the Black Alliance for Just Immigration regarding President Obama's executive action on immigration and deportation," *BAJI Blog*, November 22, 2014, http://www.blackalliance.org/ edresponse/.

48. Bhabha, *Child Migration*, 11.

49. Muzaffar Chishti, Sarah Pierce, and Jessica Bolter, "The Obama Record on Deportations: Deporter in Chief or Not?" Migration Policy Institute, January 26, 2017, https:// www.migrationpolicy.org/article/obama-record-deportations-deporter-chief-or-not.

17

Imperialism, Settler Colonialism, and Indigeneity

A Queer Migration Roundtable

LEECE LEE-OLIVER, MONISHA DAS GUPTA,
KATHERINE FOBEAR, AND EDWARD OU JIN LEE

Queer migration analyses and activisms require critically engaging settler colonialisms and Native American and First Nations' sovereignty. We invited four scholar-activists whose work addresses the intersections among queerness, migration, indigeneity, colonialism, settler colonialism, sovereignty, decolonization, and justice struggles to share their knowledge and insights. The scholars—Monisha Das Gupta, Katherine Fobear, Edward Ou Jin Lee, and Leece Lee-Oliver—participated in a rich, online discussion that is reproduced here in edited form.

How do U.S. and/or Canadian state border militarization, interior enforcement, illegalization, detention, and deportation impact Indigenous people? How do these practices draw on and reinforce logics of settler colonialism? What does a queer critique/intervention into these logics/practices do or look like?

MONISHA DAS GUPTA: I want to approach the question about reinforcing the logics of settler colonialism from the angle of discourses and political demands that proliferate in the contemporary immigrant rights movement, with which I am deeply involved. Legalization and a pathway to citizenship are the clarion calls of the movement. That this is what migrants want is rarely questioned outside of radicalized migrant-led spaces. So far, all legislative proposals backed by the mainstream immigrant rights movement have attached legalization to intensified interior enforcement and border militarization, which, in fact, put migrant communities, in particular queer migrants seeking asylum and those subject to criminal legal control, at greater risk. Border militarization compromises the self-determination and territorial integrity of borderland Native American tribal governments.

Consider the pro-immigration characterization of the United States as a "nation of immigrants" or solidarity signs declaring, "We are all migrants," or the portrayal of young undocumented deportable youth as culturally American, estranged from their homelands. Each of these rhetorical moves and political strategies entrench settler colonialism, which operates to erase ongoing Indigenous claims to land and culture, and exercises of self-governance. Each disavows the active presence of Indigenous people as polities, to use Lenape scholar Joanne Barker's words, and the operation of Indigenous self-determination in the domestic space over which the United States asserts its power and sovereignty.[1] Each reinscribes genocidal American exceptionalism that rests on the "New World" immigration story. In the book I am writing, I call these accounts on which much of immigration activism rests "settling stories."

Since 2007, dissident activists—many of them feminist, queer, refugee, and prison abolitionist—have tenaciously pointed out that the string of proposed legislation for comprehensive immigration reform has traded off the intensified militarization of the U.S.-Mexico border, the expansion of for-profit detention centers, and the deepening of interior enforcement for a very limited plan for legalization. My current research and writing focuses on this dissident segment of the movement in Los Angeles and New York. They turn our attention to these "tough on immigration" technologies of violence that have been conjoined with any talk about a plan for legalization. By exposing the transnational impacts of the United States' military, trade, and antidemocratic foreign policies as well as of outright war, all of which spark the migration from Latin America, Asia, and many parts of Africa, the activists reject the story of benevolence that the United States likes to tell about itself. However, their expression of solidarity with Indigenous struggles is based on their identification with them as racialized groups subjected to U.S. imperialism. This is different from the political culture in Hawai'i (and, it seems, from the Canadian context, which Edward describes), where Indigenous struggles over land, culture, and language cannot be skirted by social justice movements. Despite the absence in anti-deportation organizing in Los Angeles and New York of a clear and direct engagement with Indigenous politics, I find potential in this type of organizing to intersect the resistance to U.S. imperialism with a resistance to settler colonialism.

How does a queer critique bear on this dissidence? In my new work, I argue that settler colonialism mediates immigration regulation.[2] Settler colonialism and its convergence with immigration enforcement at the borders and in U.S. domestic space, in my view, are projects that differentially manage normative and nonnormative genders and sexualities. I have been provoked to think across Critical Indigenous Studies and critical migration studies. The modification, *critical*, in both bodies of theory comes with a recognition that questions of gender and sexuality are intrinsic, not incidental, to analyses of imperialism, colonialism, capitalism, nationalism, and modernity, all of which inform our understanding of Indigenous and migration politics.

I am interested in mapping the points of contact between this type of analysis and the centrality of sexuality and gender in practices and imaginings of Indigenous sovereignties. Indigenous queer and feminist frameworks foreground the intimacy between land and Indigenous people. Land and land rights are inseparable from culture and kinship. This is why Indigenous feminist and queer scholars in sovereignty movements argue that any decolonial project will need to undo the violent heteronorms written into colonial-racial policies that congeal around the reproductive politics of blood quantum.[3]

The points of contact among frameworks of settler colonialism, critical migration studies and Indigenous studies, generate an attention to the constitutive work of sexuality in colonial structures as well as decolonial and other struggles of liberation. When we pay attention to these points of contact, questions about Indigenous land and politics come to the fore. They fundamentally challenge us to rethink racial justice and migrant-refugee justice. Such struggles for justice must reject the settler colonial reward of (second-class) citizenship. They need to contend with the importance of land and land rights for Indigenous people. Migrant politics hinges on the right to unrestricted mobility. Consequently, we need to interrogate the tendency to recognize Indigenous people only when they, too, become migrants. This type of false identification opens itself up to settler colonial enticements.

KAT FOBEAR: In *Undoing Border Imperialism*, Harsha Walia writes about how white settler colonialism both controls Indigenous sovereignty and regulates migration and citizenship. She argues that white settler colonialism works to dispossess and make First Nations and nonwhite and nonaffluent migrants a threatening Other.[4] First Nations are a threat to white settler hegemony as they challenge the justification of the Canadian State's forced inhabitation of their unceded territories. Nonwhite, queer, low-income, documented, and undocumented immigrants challenge the very core of Canadian citizenship that is grounded in racial, economic, gendered, and sexual hierarchies. This is where I see a queer intervention taking root. Queer critique can challenge the underlying racial, heterosexist, and classist norms, policies, and historical practices that have worked to strip the sovereignty of First Nations and Native Americans and, at the same time, highly regulate and control migrants' bodies in order to make them disposable and deportable.

Connecting queer critique with postcolonial interventions can also create space to discuss how decolonization is not a singular process with a tidy conclusion. *Decolonization* is a word that is thrown about more than ever by scholars. It has become the new intersectionality. But, what it actually entails or how it is put into practice is often shallowly addressed or doesn't dismantle the very institutions it aims to critique.

Decolonization is messy. It's conflicting. It's very *queer* in that decolonization involves challenging our understanding of society and the institutions that are put into place to maintain power hierarchies. When we talk about decolonization, we need to ask what it means for different groups of people. Decolonization may not mean dismantling national and institutional borders in the same way to all.

For some, the maintaining of borders and the right to control land is core to decolonization. Sovereignty, the right to nationhood, and protecting and ensuring First Nations and Native American peoples' connection to land and culture are pressing issues for many Indigenous persons of Canada and the United States. Both Canada and the United States legally and socially make First Nations and Native Americans wards of the state, which in turn works to highly regulate Indigenous bodies as well as erase their rights for protection and control of their own lands.

At the same time, we know very well that borders kill. The high rates of deaths of migrants crossing the U.S./Mexico and U.S./Canadian borders shows us how highly enforced national borders work to justify economic exploitation, murder, rape, and trafficking of migrants. These borders also cut directly through the traditional territories of Indigenous peoples of North, Central, and South America and place a heavy burden on their communities. Dismantling punitive and militarized border control, white settler citizenship, and the economic apartheid of North America to South America is a crucial step to decolonization.

The challenge for us is to not separate different paths of decolonization as separate issues. Queer postcolonial critique allows us to have both (as well as many other) approaches to decolonization. We do not have to sacrifice one for the other. Far too long, First Nations and Native Americans' voices have been forced out of the national conversation around immigration and border control. It feels like a loss for scholars and activists around immigrant and refugee rights not to listen to and learn from First Nations and Native American scholars, activists, and community leaders who have had a relationship of over five hundred years with settler colonialism and border imperialism. What could come out of a coalition between refugees, undocumented migrants, immigrants, and First Nations/Native Americans? What new dialogues could be birthed? What would queer migration studies look like from a Critically Queer Indigenous perspective? That is how I see queer possibilities coming forward in dismantling white settler colonialism and connecting different paths of decolonization.

EDWARD OU JIN LEE: In order to understand how Canadian state border militarization, illegalization, detention, and deportation practices impact Indigenous peoples, it is crucial to reassemble erased histories of colonial violence. For this reason, I use the term *Canadian immigration/colonization regime*[5] to illuminate a complex set of historical and ongoing relations that organize laws that govern nationality in concert with immigration policy and the Indian Act. The aims of immigration and colonization in Canada have been and continue to be indivisible, as illustrated by the naming, from 1917 to 1936, of the Department of Immigration and Colonization.[6]

A central feature of this regime is the colonial production of the border. The Canada-U.S. border has an extended colonial history, which includes, as Audra Simpson suggests, the creation of the Jay Treaty of 1794, in which the Mohawk, Oneida, Onondaga, Cayuga, Seneca, and Tuscarora Nations had "the right to traverse the boundaries of the U.S.-British divide freely and without levy."[7] The treaty, however, implicitly suggests that Canada and the United States have the power to control who can cross the border.[8] Yet there remain Indigenous communities whose land crosses the Canada and U.S. borders, such as the Mohawk peoples on Akwesasne territories. This colonial border has also been a contested site of immigration/colonization control of Black and Asian people. The most commonly known migration of Black people from the United States to Canada was via the Underground Railroad, organized by Black abolitionist Harriet Tubman.[9] However, there is a more obscured history of slavery in Canada whereby Black slaves became fugitives by fleeing and attempting to cross the border.[10] To stem the tide of Chinese migrants entering the United States, the Canada Agreement (in 1906) was initiated, giving U.S. authorities the power to inspect Chinese migrants through a set of protocols and the imposition of admission certificates.[11] Canadian border inspectors employed health screening techniques to block Asians from colonized India who were determined to be susceptible to chronic disease or disability.[12]

Moreover, same-gender sexuality and gender transgressions were criminalized and used as a state tool to target Asian migrant men for detention and deportation.[13] In contrast, cross-gender practices of white settlers in the 19th and 20th centuries often reproduced heterocisnormative forms of white settler masculinity that further consolidated "anti-immigrant politics, specifically the racializing, feminizing discourses that targeted Chinese residents for exclusion from the nation."[14] The cross-gender practices of white settlers served to reinforce and strengthen white settlement while simultaneously justifying the continued exclusion of Chinese migrants.[15] Although Sears focused on the U.S. context, the geographic proximity and Canada-U.S. border crossings of Chinese migrants during this time period suggest that these racialized and heterocisnormative discourses most likely operated in Canada as well.

The recovery of these erased histories of colonial violence contests the mythology of innocent European settlement and reconstitutes how immigration and colonization are intertwined.[16] The colonial border remains a site of surveillance of racialized bodies, as the threat of Indigenous sovereignty folds "into the seemingly newer threat to settler sovereignty and security— the illegal alien, the always possible terrorist—rendering perhaps all bodies with color as border transgressors with the presumed intent to harm."[17]

A queer and trans of color and diasporic critique suggests that practices of militarization, interior enforcement, illegalization, detention, and deportation informed by colonial and imperial logics cannot be untied from patriarchal cisnormative and heteronormative processes. In order to challenge the colonial border regime, one must also challenge heterocisnormativity and patriarchy. Any anti-normative queer and trans politics that do not interrogate questions of colonization and racialization risk reinforcing a supposedly anti-normative politics imbued by white settler colonial logics. Anti-deportation and anti-border campaigns and actions driven by Indigenous and migrant justice are a queer and trans issue. There are always queer and trans people (whether they are "out" or not) who are part of these campaigns. Processes of racialization often either hyper-visibilize or invisibilize the sexualities and genders of Black, Indigenous, and other bodies of color to further justify their surveillance, detention, and deportation.

LEECE LEE-OLIVER: This question brings to mind something that my mother taught us. Whenever family discussions about mainstream religious piety or politics seemed to suggest to her that we thought of the social phenomenon as fixed or absolute in their truth, she would compel us to see, instead, that "everything is 180 degrees different than what 'they' want you to think." The "they" were known; "they" are the architects and contemporary arbiters of settler colonialism who invested in and erected a system of differential justice that would self-perpetuate in part because people believed in a set

of absolute truths and their natural consequences. Michel Rolph Trouillot's book *Silencing the Past* theorizes the same argument, that part of the
technology of settler colonial oppression relies on the systematic "renewal
of power" via a master narrative.[18] This line of thinking compels me to see
our current notion of citizenship and peoplehood, borders and rights, and
even the concept of deportation as we know it today in the United States
as crafted in relationship to and as part-and-parcel of the business of settler colonialism. I also respond to this question from the perspective of
Indigenous relationship-to-place. It is a concept theorized by Vine Deloria
and Daniel Wildcat, to make visible the frameworks of settler colonialism
and what exactly is disrupted in Indigenous epistemologies and practices
in the era marked by neoliberal coloniality.[19] Settler colonialism and Indigenous co-racialization, I argue, are at the root of imperial militarization,
domestic policing, violence against those viewed as marginalized—aka
dependent—and gender nonconforming peoples. In the United States, Native America is ground zero. The technologies of oppression were tested,
practiced, sophisticated, and refined into a network of interlocking laws
and institutions—ideologies, with assigned arbiters and practitioners,
from vigilantes to homemakers, who operate and mutually produce the
nation-state by performing nativist belonging in a variety of ways. Echoing
your points Monisha, this speaks to Joanne Barker's contention that settler ideology "reinscribes genocidal American exceptionalism." It further
illustrates an underlying white supremacist framework that is at the core
of western exceptionalism.

Commonly trending in Native American analyses, historically and today, is a persistent critique of the ways in which social organization under
settler colonialism is based on an intentional conflation of legal structures
and epistemological frameworks that perpetuate the bifurcation of the civi-
lized/primitive and the segregation of these ostensibly natural enemies. For
settler colonialism to take root, it requires the deracination of Indigenous
peoples first, which enables settlers to descend into the spaces created out of
the genocidal and metaphysical violence that eradicated whole Indigenous
populations. The logics that were employed by colonial architects drew on
certain studied arguments, grounded in ostensibly empirical research, and
then committed to written law, a social contract, that differential human
social groups exist and are naturally unequal in character, morality, capacity,
and sensibility. This point is basic—a sort of Introduction to Critical Race
Studies 101—"Indians" represent the quasi-human/savage realm in the Doc-
trine of Discovery. Useful parallels of negative-positive racialization present
themselves with respect to Immanuel Wallerstein's World Systems theory, to

illustrate how racial stratification, for example, casts "Indians" and Others as subordinates who are natural subjects of white, heteropatriarchal overseers and their *a priori* authority over humankind.[20] The racialization project that most significantly shaped genocidal American exceptionalism, to draw from your point again, Monisha, arises and is fomented in European expansion laws, dime novels, and fantasy fiction together. From the 1550s Valladolid Debate in Spain,[21] to Thomas Jefferson's *Notes on the State of Virginia*,[22] to "captivity narratives" and the Moynihan Report of the 1960s, cast Native American peoples as incomprehensible, incorrigible, and biologically determined to imbibe the cultural knowledge that will always maintain their "Indianness." Member of the Confederated Salish and Kootenai Tribes and Native American scholar Luana Ross critiques the material effects of laws that fomented what Lumbee legal scholar Robert Williams calls "Indianophobia"[23] in her 2004 book *Inventing the Savage*.[24] Ross details legal discourses that predated the criminalizing of Native American ceremony in the Northern Plains during the expansion of the transcontinental railroad system. One example with grave consequences is when federal lawmakers and territorial settler governments argued that Native American ceremonies "ignite the savage"—a throwback to biological determinism.[25]

The most insidious ingredient in this logic is the complex integration of racist heterosexism[26] that engenders beliefs in the immutable nature of being "Indian" or "Other," Indigenous or nonwhite genealogically. The connective tissue between genocidal American exceptionalism is problematically tied to both the sense of white patriarchal heteronormative supremacy and national duty.

Sexuality and gender are often problematically presented as mutually constituted, historically and today. Colonialism and coloniality grow great steam from such a misconception. I see the roots of the technologies of oppression in Native American contexts. I hope the following examples contextualize why an historical analysis of Native American women's racialization illustrates why the point of entry belongs in an analysis of queer–Indigenous intersections. My aim is to contribute a scaffolding, and an intervention, of the way that despite being converted, recapitulated, utilized, iterated, and waged war against "Indian" women and girls speak truths and strategies into conversations about the treatment of women of color, immigrant and citizen, queer, and trans when confronted by U.S. colonialism/coloniality. It is a system perpetrated on Native Americans, women and girls broadly defined, and communities in general. The ways that colonialisms operated involved intersecting Cartesian-like schema/machinery. Colonialism delivered an organized, categorized, and comparative ordering of everyone and everything. The disempowerment of the subaltern required a wall of impenetrable change in order to subject whole peoples across the Americas, and globally, to the colonial overseers and utilization or destruction. The point of arrival of this systematic hierarchy can best be seen in the commodification of everyone and everything as a "resource." It is the truth about the colonization of Indigenous peoples in the Americas, and what was then impacts us all now. The inheritance of colonial ideologies continues to profoundly shape the rights logic that governs all of the laws and institutions we've discussed.

The roles that differential sex and gender constructions and the false promise of assimilation via conformity play in colonial ideology are vast. Most problematic in the logic is the dependence on inferiorized Others that props up the rhetoric of white civility. Most useful to the colonial project, and problematic for the peoples, is the serial subjection to the commodification process. Peoples' sexes, sexualities, and gender identities could be cast as non-normative and studied in comparison to white, patriarchal, capitalist, Christian, heteronormativity and the constructs of white womanhood. If one did not fit the mold, then they could be rearticulated into tools or vermin. For example, the Powhatan child Matoaka, aka the United States' "Pocahontas," and less famous Indigenous girls offer examples of the power of racial-sexual hierarchies. Native American women and girls, who first disappeared into the vanquished status of "Indians," experienced their own entry point into colonial discourses via adult "Indian" masculinity. "Indian" females were at once cast out of their own sovereign status, including those who held esteemed positions within their societies. The racialization of "Indians" further cast "Indian" girls and women out of the scope of white womanhood held by and for cis-white-heteronormative girls and women. Moreover, many white women stewarded colonial and Americanization of Native Americans, as overseers of "Indian" females' entry into domesticity—no matter the age or sociopolitical power in their own communities. In the 1600s, it was commonplace that "Indian squaws" were cast as commodities, like land, who were valueless with the exception of what could be produced from their bodies. Important to note: Simultaneously, their reproductive capacity served as a threat against the growing nation. It is an irony of the right-to-life ethic of white Christian heteronormativity, that not all fetuses are equal. When Indigenous peoples of the Caribbean and Americas became "Indians," Native American girls and women became "squaws." As is evidenced by the current epidemic rate of violence facing Native American women and girls, the racial formation of the "squaw" was and is a death blow that has remained a fixture in the lives [of] Native American girls and women and part-and-parcel of their oppression, negation, and violence ever since. Indigenous women's and girls' hypersexuality, within this context, is assumed. Native American girls and women's bodies, like land and water, are viewed as exploitable for the support of white masculinity and the maintenance of white heteronormative womanhood. Another point of irony, and evidence of the dependence of the colonizer on the logic of human difference, is that the exceptional white woman cannot be "pure" without a comparative "spoil." When we are able to think additionally about transgender identities in Native American communities, we see societies where neither sex nor gender exist in binary antibioses. Rather, Native American epistemologies typically connote anything close to a gender identity as existing in a range of identities and, in many tribes, identification features are malleable and not fixed, not pure or impure in their biological form. Colonial ideology draws on the erasure of information, disinformation, and dehumanization of the Other to organize and assign meaning to those articulated in the social contract.

Two pieces of legislative evidence speak to this postcolonial phenomenological reality. The current epidemic rate of violence against Native American girls and women gave rise to the Tribal Law and Order Act (2010). There was a need for special legislation because the violence against urban and reservation-based Native American women and girls rose to unprecedented levels in the United States, and no one who held jurisdiction (federal or state agencies) was doing anything about it. Rather, a hands-off "murky jurisdiction" has held strong as a logic of inaction. None of the "Violence against Women Acts" before 2013 included Native American girls and women on reservations in any substantial way, nor did legislators accept responsibility for protecting queer/LGBTQ2 peoples or undocumented girls and women— the three groups most vulnerable to abject and constant social and state sponsored violence in the United States. A seemingly semantic by-product of the colonial era, the term *Indian squaw* and the phenomenology of "Indianness" made and continues to make one particularly vulnerable to complex, regular, and systematic state and societal violence exactly because U.S. law uses the term *Indian* in place of tribal communities and citizens. In part, the vulnerability appears to be driven by the usefulness of "Indianophobia,"[27] which calls on the state to keep a vigilant eye and foot on the neck of "Indians," hostile, one and all, including those born and who live as women. Public Law 280 serves to bring this colonial legacy into the present.[28] The U.S. military, likewise, maintains the "Indian" as enemy framework, according to Ross, Williams, Creek-Cherokee scholar Tom Holm, and cultural anthropologist Stephen Silliman.[29] These scholars critically analyze the role of "Indians" in law and how the "Indian" makes up a cornerstone of the U.S.

military lexicon, which illustrates how the "Indian" is inscribed on global Indigenous and non-Indigenous peoples that Western imperialism seeks to uproot. Each scholar, from different perspectives, illustrates how the "Indian," the "squaw," and "Indian country" are used to designate enemies of the West, war zones, and territories as wrongfully occupied by hostile (aka "Indian") forces. The "Indian" and *his* [emphasis mine] "squaw" factor in as ongoing avatars that are used to support the settler colonial project. The ideology of American exceptionalism situates Indigenous, non-Western, non–English-speaking, non-Christian peoples as the primitive "Other," territories and reservations as spaces for vanquishing and vanishing the threat, the Other. Problematically, for Native Americans, reservations and rancherias are still cast in the same light just as "urban Indians" are represented as the visible remnants of America's first burden, its "wards of the state," as the United States' original "domestic dependents." The language of the "dependency" burden is embedded in the legal language used to militarize borders, sanction and carry out interior enforcement, make the legal illegal, and detain or deport those who can be situated and subjected to the abject subjugation of "illegality."

Imperialism generates much contemporary migration across borders, yet when migrants enter the United States or Canada, they are expected to participate in these states' settler colonial logics that dispossess Indigenous communities. How can we engage in political and theoretical migrant rights/justice projects that hold imperialism and settler colonialism in a shared frame? How does the growing presence of Indigenous migrants from Latin America (some of them LGBTQ, genderqueer, and gender nonconforming) present new challenges and new possibilities?

KAT FOBEAR: A couple years ago at a pinkwashing conference in New York I presented a question about what it means to seek asylum in a settler colonial state. What does it mean to seek and be granted protection on stolen Indigenous lands? I talked about how the very same practices that have regulated Indigenous bodies and sovereignty work to categorize, regulate, and determine queer refugees' eligibility for asylum in Canada. An audience member was noticeably upset by my presentation. They asked: if my arguments were correct and the refugee system is a colonial institution, then what's the point of asylum? It would be better to dismantle asylum and not offer it anymore.

As a volunteer for Rainbow Refugee and a researcher whose work focuses on sexual and gender minority refugees, I had given my fair share of talks on heteronormativity, homonormativity, and even homonationalism in the asylum process. But I'd never received a question challenging the very notion of asylum. The person who asked the question did not give an alternative to asylum or what could be changed in the process to avoid reproducing colonial hierarchies. Instead, it was a direct refusal to engage with colonialism and asylum. If that happened, the Canadian government would be responsible for the death of millions of people in need of protection.

I do not share this example to dismiss this person's critique of my presentation or to share one of the many conference presentation horror stories we have all experienced. But, I had never received a reaction like that before. When I had given talks and workshops with scholars, asylum officers, and lawyers about heteronormativity and heterosexism, the reaction was usually about how we need to change the asylum/immigration system in order to better protect and aid sexual and gender minority asylum-seekers and refugees.

Why would pointing out how the asylum system mirrors the very same practices by the Canadian government to regulate Indigenous bodies elicit such a reaction? What is so threatening about colonialism that we avoid it all together?

I have been chewing on that experience for some time. I don't have a clear answer or a solution to the original question I asked. I still think it is very relevant. Yet, I also struggle with this question in my practice. As someone who works with asylum-seekers and helps get them through the process in order for them to be able to stay here and live, I am so overpowered by the immediacy of their situations that it can be hard to confront how I am complicit in reproducing colonial narratives and supporting white settler power structures.

I know that I am not alone in this dilemma. I also know that confronting settler colonialism is difficult since it shapes every part of our reality living in the United States and Canada. I think that many of us recognize that living in a settler state does not mean we have the same relationship or experience to settler colonialism. Sherene Razack writes that while settler colonialism may have allowed certain communities to settle in Canada or the United States, their relationships to settler colonialism may be different.[30] Peoples who were forced to come here either through slavery or other forms of forced migration, who may also have Indigenous heritage from either here or in their countries of origin, have a very different relationship to the white settler colonial politics and practices than others. This is particularly important for settlers such as queer refugees who experience the privileges of settler colonialism that allowed them to settle in Canada or the United States through the state's continued denial of First Nations and Native American sovereignty. However, these settlers also experience violence because of white settler colonialism on account of their race, gender, sexuality, ability, and/or class.

At the same time, we all have a relationship to the land we inhabit and to the original owners of these lands who were forcibly removed from their territories and who are very much alive and present. Recognizing this relationship is the first step to stopping the segmenting or pillarizing of refugees' issues and human rights from First Nations and Native Americans. Seeing how the neoliberal practices of U.S./Canadian governments have worked to destroy Indigenous communities globally is the next step. Confronting what it means to regulate borders and citizenship, whose authority it is based upon, and what can be done to dismantle ongoing power structures is a dialogue that must be fostered between First Nations and Native Americans with undocumented and documented immigrants and refugees. How we actually do this and what needs to be done is the challenge for all of us. Avoidance cannot be the answer.

MONISHA DAS GUPTA: Kat, you raise an essential question here about how to intersect the advocacy for queer refugee appeals to settler states and analyses of colonialism's impact on Indigenous Nations through the medium of reorganizing gender and sexuality. You, Edward and Leece show how colonial regimes of control migrate from laws imposed on Indigenous Nations to regulations that govern immigrants. So, the connections are hardly artificial and your anecdote, Kat, underlines the importance of injecting analyses of colonialism into critical approaches to understanding asylum as a prime site for pinkwashing.

To do so, I feel we need to find a new lexicon. Even as we fight for the right for queer refugees to relocate to the United States or Canada, can we challenge the language of asylum, which as we well know, is steeped in the myths of state benevolence and humanitarianism? We know that both nation-states breed a culture of criminalizing and death-dealing violence toward those who express gender and sexual insubordination, and thus, asylum is elusive at best.

The affective power of "asylum" bolsters the rogue sovereignty of these settler nations, authorizing them to decide who can be admitted and who cannot. Some of the southeast Asian refugee rights organizations with which I work, and which are dedicated to building youth leadership by using anti-imperialist and antioppression curricula, reject the gift of asylum by contextualizing their resettlement process in the violences that stem from war, forced migration, institutionalized racism, xenophobia, heterosexism, and poverty.[31] What you are suggesting, Kat, is that we build politics and language that can simultaneously call out ongoing U.S. and Canadian colonialisms over their domestic space *and* pinkwashing, which invisibilizes colonial violence to project modernity and humanitarianism.

As the conditions that produce global apartheid deepen, accountability on the part of the Global North for the mass displacement from the Global South becomes ever more urgent. So, we cannot abandon speaking to the state to demand justice for queer and transgender refugees. At the same time, we have a responsibility, as you point out so eloquently, to figure out the politics which will enable refugees to inhabit a place and space that continues to be violently settled.

EDWARD OU JIN LEE: What I hear in Kat's reflections is the level of urgency in the ways that queer and trans migrants with precarious status[32] need to navigate the Canadian/U.S. refugee regime that can make it difficult to also center the ways that the refugee/colonization regime also targets Indigenous people. As someone who has been involved with migrant justice for many years, I understand the challenges that come with being part of communities and supporting people who are facing detention and deportation. The term *state of crisis* doesn't begin to describe the range of emotions that are part and parcel of anti-deportation campaigns. The reality is that the most vulnerable among us within queer and trans communities of color, especially those who are poor/working class, disabled, and cis or trans women, have to face state and interpersonal violence on a daily basis. When queer and trans migrants are fighting for their lives, and I am in the thick of an anti-deportation campaign, it is difficult to refocus energy on supporting Indigenous peoples who are also, in their own ways, fighting for their lives.

In this way, I am heartened by Monisha and Leece's response, as they highlight the role of youth leadership development and pushing towards critical models of education that insist on contextualizing refugee processes within the frame of U.S. imperialism, war, and colonial violence. I agree that we "need to find a new lexicon" and both Monisha and Leece remind me that oppressed and colonized people have always, and continue to, fight back and demand justice. Indeed, their reflections gesture to the ways in which the Canadian/U.S. military operates both here and abroad to enforce occupations, borders, and migrations.

One possible strategy is a sustained focus on how the micro processes of anti-deportation campaigns can reveal transformative and life-affirming practices. As Lisa Cacho suggests "in the spaces of social death, empowerment is not contingent on taking power or securing small victories. Empowerment comes from deciding that the outcome of the struggle doesn't matter as much as the decision to struggle."[33] In one instance, the process of supporting a queer migrant who was facing deportation led to an incredible internal transformation—of a shy and gentle-hearted human being who went from being in constant hiding due to his sexual identity and migrant status, to making daily decisions to step outside of the bounds of social death, or perhaps to disidentify[34] with the normative assumptions that queer and trans people are citizens, or migrants serve only as invisible labor. Even though this person was sadly, still deported, I recall the ways in which this person was at the heart of decision-making processes for his campaign, which gave him some degree of control over his own life, at a time when the Canadian state was violently controlling and limiting his life chances. During the campaign, this person and I had many informal discussions about his experience of detention and deportation, alongside the experiences of other communities that were being targeted by the Canadian state, especially Indigenous peoples. As queer and trans migrants learn more about colonial violence in Canada against Indigenous people, they realize the flimsiness of the liberationist discourse and whose interests this discourse preserves. Of course, some queer and trans migrants from the Global South were already aware of colonial violence from their experience in their country of origin.

Anti-deportation campaigns can thus highlight structural violence towards queer and trans migrants and people of color, directly contesting the myth of Canadian benevolence. This further opens discursive space to recognize how the state can also enact violence upon Indigenous peoples. The microprocesses of organizing with queer and trans migrants can also elicit important (but often hidden) conversations and informal learning spaces to discuss the links between state violence towards migrants and Indigenous peoples. However, anti-deportation organizing rarely engages in direct solidarity with Indigenous people and, in particular, struggles for Indigenous sovereignty and land rights. How might those of us who are heavily involved in migrant and racial justice movements reorient organizing practices to emphasize the centrality of white settler colonial and anti-Black logics? How might we ensure that community organizing and educational spaces do not center white and middle-class students with the "best" political rhetoric, but rather support queer trans Black, Indigenous, and other people of color (QTBIPOC) who often have marginal access to university and "activist" spaces? How might intentional long-term relationship building practices along with critical education and leadership development projects across and with QTBIPOC communities eventually hook into urgent anti-deportation and Indigenous sovereignty campaigns? One of the main challenges is mobilizing analytical frameworks that help us to map out the ways in which multiple colonial logics operate simultaneously but also differently, the ways in which white settler colonial logics operate in Canada and the United States to drive migrants out of the Global South while also fostering the genocides of BIPOC communities. The use of the term *white/Western*, as coined by Mahrouse[35] is also useful in the ways that it highlights the interplay between race, nation, and geopolitical center central to understanding the role of the immigrant in ensuring colonial and imperial rule. An analysis of the overlapping processes of cisnormativity, heteronormativity, and patriarchy, as they are embedded within colonial logics, highlights the ways that laws, policies, and practices are organized to promote the making of the white heterocisnormative monogamous couple within a nuclear family structure, in contrast with all those that hierarchically fall outside of this norm, such as QTBIPOC—especially those who are Black, Indigenous, in the western United States.[36] However, these connections are being fostered within academic, activist, and community contexts. Recently, a special issue of the journal *Transgender Studies Quarterly* titled "Decolonizing the Transgender Imaginary" included articles that placed trans Indigenous and Two-Spirit issues alongside decolonizing transness within the South Asian context.[37] Instead of viewing this challenge in a binary manner, we can "zoom out" and "zoom in" in an ongoing iterative manner.

MONISHA DAS GUPTA: In Hawaiʻi, we confront head-on the very uncomfortable question of migrants' relationship to settler colonialism and Indigenous exercise of political, cultural, land, and body sovereignty. The reckoning is uncomfortable because as critical migration scholars we reject push-pull free market theories of migration to expose the imperial labor circuits and processes of colonial and neoliberal displacement that attend mass migration. Thus, the very concept of settlers of color can seem outrageous because migrants and Indigenous people are subject to the same imperial-colonial forces.

Since the publication of Native Hawaiian feminist and nationalist Haunani-Kay Trask's groundbreaking (and controversial) essay on settlers of color and immigrant hegemony in a 2000 *Amerasia Journal* special issue, the debates over who is a settler and who is Native have raged.[38] Building on Trask's insights, Asian American Studies scholars like Candace Fujikane and Dean Saranillio, for example, have challenged us to think carefully about the roles various Asian immigrant groups have played over generations in deepening the U.S. occupation of Hawaiʻi.[39] In the case of Hawaiʻi, settler colonialism depends on encouraging nonwhite immigrants, whose arrival on the islands is thoroughly mediated by labor extractive practices, to invest in statehood and full U.S. citizenship.

Unfortunately, efforts to specify and address the settler colonial invest-ments of migrants of color have too often run into arguments which pit Indigenous rights against migrant rights. A critical look at migrants of color and their complicity with settler colonialism is seen as negating these mi-grants' own histories of colonial-capitalist exploitation. Indigenous self-determination and nation building are misinterpreted to be pro-restriction and anti-immigrant. In the case of Hawaiʻi, Kanaka rights and relationship to land become distorted as a form of dangerous (ethnic) nationalism that ties people to land in essentialist and exclusionary ways.[40]

In my recent publications and current research, I propose a few basic shifts we need to make as migration scholars to understand the United States as an imperial and settler colonial formation. As scholars and activists, we need to recognize that Indigenous people are not racial minorities. This insight comes from Native American and Native Hawaiian scholars and is axiomatic to Indigenous studies. The distinction pivots on Indigenous rela-tions to land and these relations are familial and reciprocal. In the context of Hawaiʻi, for example, as Noenoe Silva and other Native Hawaiian scholars have argued, *aloha ʻāina* expresses not only a ministering and regenerative love for the land, ocean, and skies but also a steady and enduring love for the Hawaiian Nation.[41]

As settlers, we have a responsibility to practice *aloha ʻāina* in all its reg-isters. At our university, we have several community partnerships through which students and faculty practice this ethic. As Kat points out, "[W]e all have a relationship to the land we inhabit and to the original owners of these lands." This sort of intentional engagement invites learning about responsi-bility and mutuality through experience. Our settler *kuleana* (responsibility) is our obligation to Native Hawaiian people, place, land, knowledge, and, above all, self-determination.[42] To be decolonial in this practice of love and care, I strongly feel that we cannot, then, comfort ourselves with the self-interested stories about the nonexclusionary and all-encompassing spirit of *aloha ʻāina* to allay our settler fears about the nature and form of Native self-governance. Such stories exempt migrants of color from contending with their participation in settler colonial projects. To recognize and honor Native Hawaiian genealogical ties to land will require queer formulations of kinship but in ways that are inoculated against cultural appropriation. Here I am thinking of Scott Morgensen's *Spaces between Us*, which tracks the mainstream lesbian, gay, and bisexual movement's appropriation and performance of Indigenous sexual alterity and gender fluidity in ways that bolster and naturalize settler colonialism.[43]

This orientation, in turn, can allow us to break out of the binary formulation of mobility and rootedness. As I mentioned before, Indigenous people become legible to us as migration scholars only when we consider their mobility. We need to grapple with Indigeneity as a place-based and highly diverse political formation. We need to parse the distinction between conditions of *displacement* that create migrants, who may or may not be Indigenous, and *dispossession*, which raises very specific questions about land rights and access to land.

Relatedly, the exercise of Indigenous sovereignty has to be treated in the present tense and as operating alongside or intersecting with other social justice movements. As Kanaka Maoli feminist scholar J. Kēhaulani Kauanui has shown, guaranteeing access to land for non-gender binary and sexually variant Kanaka in blueprints of self-determination proposed by various sectors of the Hawaiian sovereignty movement is crucial and cannot be managed by the multicultural settler state's legalization of same-sex marriage.[44] One lesson I have learned from my situatedness in Hawai'i, as a person who teaches and writes about social justice–oriented movements, is that no vision of justice is complete without a serious discussion of and commitment to the return of lands to Kanaka Maoli from government and military control.

If queer is a settler formation (Morgensen), can queer be a decolonial resource? Does "queer" offer resources for making connections or building useful relationships among Indigenous, anti-imperialist, and migration studies research or activisms?

EDWARD OU JIN LEE: I am particularly interested in exploring the theoretical and political possibilities when we dive into the heart of empire, which, in Canada, includes places like major urban areas like Tkaronto/Toronto and Tiohtià:ke/Montreal or major development and resource extraction sites in Northern Alberta and Quebec. What are the kinds of messy tensions, violences AND solidarities being formed in the factories, the hotels, and on the streets? In what ways do university spaces serve as both the engine for empire and a site of resistance against it? How might these politically and economically driven spaces also serve as sites of intimacy, abuse, and pleasure? How might decolonizing practices serve as a response to the coloniality of power?

These questions bring me to small, untraceable interactions, relationships, and stories of what happens when Black, Indigenous, and other people of color meet each other in the heart of empire. I recall a few years ago when my parents went through financial devastation to, yet again, find themselves with nothing. My mother, in her '60s, was compelled to work in the Alberta oilsands as a cook for a South Korean company that hired mostly temporary workers. She told me stories of being the oldest woman worker that she knew, but that the second oldest worker was an Indigenous woman and how they would talk about their families and my mother would bring her 한국 (Hanguk/Corean) food. I wondered how Indigenous people and migrants met each other within the oilsands, and how, often nearby, Indigenous people and allies were protesting the oilsands and their contribution to colonialism and the devastation of nearby Indigenous communities.

The theoretical and political practice of decolonizing genders and sexualities explores how sexuality, race, class, gender, and religion intersect to produce colonial violence on a transnational scale with particular impacts on queer and trans people in the Global South and QTBIPOC who live in Western nation-states.[45] However, the intentional creation of a queer and trans decolonial politics can also reimagine vibrant and sustainable futures. Paola Bacchetta encourages us to imagine a politics that includes strategies that resist all forms of oppression simultaneously while also creating space or "holding space" for altogether new ways of being.[46] What might generative possibilities and space-making that occurs in the heart of empire look like, especially by QTBIPOC, whose lives are organized for elimination and erasure?

I have realized, over time, that my life (our lives) will always be in struggle, and the question becomes, how do we find ways to hold onto moments of collective belonging, mutual understanding, self, and collective dignity in the face of ongoing struggle and crisis due to state and interpersonal violence? All of these complexities remind me that at the heart of empire, the violences and solidarities can come from anywhere and from anyone, so it is important to be vigilant and intentional when fostering coalitions and solidarities.

MONISHA DAS GUPTA: Edward, I am moved by the way in which you ended your response to this question by pointing to the everyday, small, even "untraceable interactions, relationships, and stories of what happens when Black, Indigenous and other people of color meet each other in the heart of empire." You note that "violences and solidarities can come from anywhere and from anyone." I have learned the power of storytelling as a way to build coalitions through my involvement with the anti-deportation movement.

I have realized that these stories bind together people with very different experiences with migration and state apparatuses. For example, the process invites direct and difficult engagements about the ways in which queer and transgender people experience police violence and criminalization as compared to those who are cisgender. Difference rather than identification is shaped into coalitional politics. So many youth leaders in the anti-deportation movement have been deeply influenced by women and queer of color feminism (whether they have been able to afford college). They have tutored me in the profound and consequential differences that exist within the U.S. immigrant rights movement. And, as we move to bridge migrant justice and Indigenous justice—a political project you outline in introducing yourself—how can we operationalize irreducibility and incommensurability?

This brings me to your reflections on feeling out of place and never at home anywhere until you experienced fleeting moments of belonging in the company of queer and trans people of color. I have come to value the feeling of uprootedness as a person who comes from a family impacted by the partition of India (as your family must have been by the partition of Corea) and, then, my life in the United States as a migrant-turned-citizen of color. I navigate the worlds in which I live from that generative sense of never belonging. I want to hold on to that feeling of discomfort and use it as the source of my activism and scholarship.

Queer youth in anti-deportation struggles often refuse to participate in the assimilative tropes of DREAMer narratives. In this refusal, they produce a queer time and place. Here, I am influenced analytically by Jack Halberstam and Lisa Cacho.[47] Unlike DREAMers who represent themselves as instantiations of the American Dream to demand a pathway to U.S. citizenship, the queer activists, with whom I have trained and whom I have interviewed, testify to the states of eviction. They are evicted from places, spaces, and people for which or whom they feel an affinity. They feel evicted from their bodies. They speak and act from the epistemological-political space of non-belonging as QTBIPOC—migrants and refugees sin papeles. Displacement structures their condition. Their suspension in time, their uncertainty about status and, therefore, uncertainty about residence, generate important analytics for a queer migrant framework.

Even as this type of queer migrant politics can sow the seeds of a healthy skepticism about belonging, I struggle with how they line up with another set of political sensibilities to which I am also exposed every day—the profound emphasis on a sense of place in all Kanaka Maoli struggles for sovereignty. This disjuncture confronts the movement for migrant justice with incommensurability. This uncomfortable reckoning, as we have learned from queer and feminist women of color, is the starting point of meaningful solidarity.

LEECE LEE-OLIVER: I am so grateful to sit in and be a part of this discussion. I want to speak to the threads you've all shared about learning to cultivate richer and sustainable liberatory praxes. I draw on everyone's thinking about the relationship between lexicons of oppression and our liberation. I hope to add to the conversation something that I struggle with, which is the dual, but not mutual, use of terms and sites of liberation that become the traps of coloniality. I vacillate here between terms and problematics that I see manifest from their appropriation. My aim stems from my hope that we may collectively see possibilities for moving the discourse forward and advance the real possibility of liberatory justice.

There are critical fissures that are created when people, maybe subconsciously, grapple with belonging in colonized spaces. Feminist discourses and DREAMers alike rely on legal and conceptual freedoms promised by the colonial/Western government. Juridical equality stems from a lack thereof since the social contract's legal structures were constructed differential pathways to economic, spiritual, and political freedom. Freedom, in the house of the master, is limited at best.[48] Liberation cannot occur in that house. Angela Davis, bell hooks, and Janet McCloud teach that liberation is the goal. This current in our conversation brings to mind decoloniality as praxis, what it looks like, manifests as, stems from, and how to keep it real, honest, and liberatory. Theoretically, decolonial activists and scholars consider what rubrics are necessary to create viable, sustainable, and positive change. Many of us recognize the need for coalitional and intersectional efforts and yet we often commit to decolonial praxes at the individual level. We ask that allies learn about our struggles and do real work. In 2018, we are literally over half a century into decolonialism and we find ourselves in a world that is devolving into white supremacy. How do we move forward without truly reconstructing normativities in our own hypotheses and projections for change? What does decoloniality look like in hegemonic systems that foster, foment, and reward individualism? When one is in community and, yet, not of the community—the act of solidarity—how does one find his/her "place" and resist the temptation to talk, take the lead, or school others on what "real" decolonial struggles look like? I am speaking to the act of solidarity as an act of decoloniality. As you suggest, Edward, it seems that learning to zoom in and out is critical. How does one hold on to the broader knowledge of the oppressed communities, remain in conversation with, and work to avoid "fronting solidarity," which in actuality is an appropriation of a struggle? That is part of the multifold task of decolonialists. When immigrants struggle with their own settler identity, often times Indigenous peoples become a scapegoat—questions arise about phenotype [You don't look like Tonto? Well, the actor was Italian, so . . .], locational identities [Have you ever lived on a reservation?], and clothing and culture. Finding a sense of belonging and place in a colonized state creates states of being that must be defended. How that defense is mounted matters. The defense that does not acknowledge Native Americans and Indigenous peoples, no matter the ethical stance on behalf of the oppressed, is still a stance of oppression. As an urban Blackfeet and Choctaw person, I am aware that wherever I live is another Indigenous person's homeland. For many non-Indigenous Americans and immigrants, this reconciliation and self-acceptance seems far more challenging.

How can decoloniality perpetuate liberation? I draw on the work of Chela Sandoval in *Methodologies of the Oppressed*,[49] a critical thinker who has nearly vanished from the very decolonial discourses rooted in part in her instrumentation of critical strategies for decolonial workers. One of the strategies Sandoval lays out in *Methodologies* is that the revolutionary, the civil rights worker, even those called protectors today, are called on by the author to avoid rearticulating hierarchical power structures within their work to undo other hierarchical systems. Sandoval's implicit critique speaks to a tendency among some activists who so vigorously defend one's "people" and simultaneously erase other oppressed peoples' struggles and rights. I speak here from a methodological standpoint.

We must begin to disempower the structures of imperial power by changing the language of the colonizer. I believe that is a critical part of the larger project of decolonization and liberation. For example, earlier this year I participated in a consultation project, working with the Native American staff in the Department of Justice who are rewriting the Violence Against Women Act, which has expired—again. My colleagues, Native American leaders throughout the country, call on the agencies' understanding that: 1) Native American societies are highly vulnerable to unique forms of societal and state violence; 2) restricting tribal jurisdictional power and granting federal agencies jurisdiction leaves Native Americans wide open to violation; and 3) the common use of the terms "Indian" and "Indian country" in laws problematically renders Native Americans a monolithic racial/sexed body and falsely reifies the racist primitivity that perpetuates the stereotypes that make Native Americans vulnerable to the very violence the act is supposed to halt.

Another example comes from a current Indigenous social movement and the intentional effort to shift language usage in order to elevate and advance the efforts of Native American sovereignty movements. This example comes from the protectors at Standing Rock who used social media to make visible their effort to end the development of yet another crude oil pipeline through a Treaty-protected land and water system. They assert that the term *activist* is not an accurate portrayal of the work that Indigenous protectors do. The protectors reached audiences on a global scale and, within their posts, several women began posting live video feeds with an unequivocal message on terminology. They stated, "We are protectors, not activists" and then they would explain the connections between Native American treaties, sovereignty, epistemology, and praxis. The term *protector* asserts a new intersectional social-political-cultural positionality that assumes the Treaty right to exercise political-cultural-sovereign authority to enact changes that protect that which Native American epistemologies assert as a human right and responsibility—to live on the earth with respect to the sacred and the generations to come. The term *protector* in the context of Standing Rock, applies directly to the power granted to the Lakota Sioux peoples under the Treaty of Fort Laramie (1851). The Treaty expresses the rules of engagement whenever U.S. interests, or non-Sioux interests, encroach on these, the lands and water systems beholding to the Sioux. It protects the rights of the Lakota Sioux peoples and their multifold responsibilities to their peoples, the land, and water systems—to themselves and to all in existence.

In sharing, the protectors at Standing Rock gave the world new tools of liberation. It is not the first time that Native Americans or Indigenous peoples asserted complex Indigenous political positionalities and the urgent redress. Joy Harjo and Gloria Bird's *Reinventing the Enemy's Language*[50] adroitly showcases Native American women's testimonials critiquing white, heteronormative, Christian supremacy, their negative impacts on Native American women and communities, and the language that supports the structures of oppression of Native Americans. The protector standpoint offers an opportunity not only to learn about the relationships between Indigenous peoples and non-people entities (land, water, air, mountains, and more), it also gives us an opportunity to enrich the ways that we promote and think about social justice as a form of protection, and protection as humble stewardship.

While some news syndicates and audiences adopted the terminology, there seems to be a missed opportunity to change the lexicon of imperialism and subordination technologies on the larger scale. In short, the term *protector* was repeated, but less understood. Instead, news feeds appropriated the term *protector* and equivocated rather than explored it as part-and-parcel of the Treaty rights of Native American tribes. In this example, we might consider how language is appropriated, in the capitalist sense, as a way for news to appear current. Similar in the case of the Hawaiian sovereignty movement, protests occasionally make mainstream news, but little is made clear about the history and relevance of the movement to today's Indigenous Hawaiian rights, suffering, and protection of sacred sites, like Mauna Kea. The term *protector*, then, becomes a commodity that bolsters the viewership of the program, newspaper, blog, etc. To identify "feel-good" solidarity, including the appropriation of the term *protector*, we might ask ourselves what is gained and what is lost. What might we do to move beyond the commoditization of liberatory lexiconography?

On the flip side, the matrix of power and individualism leaves us open to what Sandoval cautions against. In the mix of social media posts, verité footage also captures the lived experiences of allies who helped to occupy Standing Rock. Among them, likely well-intentioned allies speak of their reasoning for shoring up tents and committing their time and energy to the protection of Lakota rights vis-à-vis water. In most cases, they talk about the importance of protecting Indigenous lands and waters, acknowledging the connectedness of all living entities. The language of relationality abounds in these stories, just as the ethic of "seven generations," and being on the right side of history seem prevalent. The lessons of communal existence were well honed. Often, at the end of the interviews, allies were asked to identify their heritage. Some appeared, phenotypically, to be Native American, but were not. Brown hair and skin served as mediums of positive identification and therefore garnered interviews. Their long testimonials also bore witness to the use of state-sanctioned police and military violence. At the end, however, camera crews were often surprised to learn that their interviewee was not Native American, nor did they see themselves as Indigenous. Respectfully, I understand, rather, that everyone is Indigenous in some part of their family history. Here, the focus is on those who are Native American and live within Indigenous cultural-intellectual systems. In some cases, a sort of quietness ensued when the interviewee's phenotypes seemed to betray the interviewer who learned that their "subject" was an immigrant, or even a settler of sorts. What this easily calls to mind is the power of colorism and the seductive nature of positive racism (exoticization and passing). Some allies appeared to feel a sense of responsibility to speak about the issues when they accepted the interviewer's request. I wonder the difference between their sense of responsibility and the egocentric sense that their voice in the struggle mattered. In this sense, one is holding power and authority to speak on an issue in the first person, rather than as a clear and unequivocal ally, which can altogether collapse into appropriation. This is the stuff of which Sandoval warns. It is an appropriated power that is relevant when considering using colonial terms in a new way—the term and the lexicon of queer liberation.

To the question about using the term *queer*, I would argue that using the term *queer* is complex and can be problematic because, like phenotypical irrelevance, when power is seen within the marginalized, third world, dark skin/hair, nonnormativity, and "queerness" one may be induced to adopt the term in order to find comfort in one's not-quite-normative lived experience. The appropriation of the term *queer* and simultaneous oppression of queer identities has been widespread in the West. As a term arising in the context of colonialism, *queer* was used to designate and induce a necessary, for the state, powerlessness. State-sanctioned violence against "queered" persons and communities is rooted in the notion that queer peoples can and should be equated with difference-as-bad, and extant threats, and even illness—the linkages in language are notable because the term *queer*—like *Indian, Black, woman, immigrant, trans* (a seemingly endless list)—stands in for myriad negative transgressions against colonial/Western supremacy. Like so many linguistic resurrections, in the context of decoloniality *queer* has been occupied as a term of power, agency, insight, brilliance, and strength, where different-as-bad-ass exemplifies power, agency, and survival in the face of abjection and struggle. In the middle of the two, coloniality/decoloniality, the appropriation of *queer* has been used to qualify any practice that is resistant or adjacent to the confines of modernity, including everything from family formations, to dress codes, to sexual deviance. The latter, problematically invigorates the term *queer* as a justification for the very types of intimacy that continue to be used to mark queer and trans peoples, collapsed through a fear of non-missionary-heteronormative sexualities, as deviant and illegal.[51] In the current climate, a white, cis, heteronormative, able-bodied, capitalist can appropriate the term *queer* in defense of their desire for everything from nonnormative dress codes to non-hetero-binary intimacy. Every day, people who appropriate the term *queer* are not seeking liberation in the public sphere or facing state and societal violence like actual queer peoples. The subalternity of queer identity leaves one open to vast and multifold forms of violence, vulnerability to state and societal violence, unemployment, housing and food insecurity, and medical negligence.

Another facet of the complexities of this discussion has to do with those who necessarily seek solitude and safety from hostile environments. Some forge ahead without critical decolonial strategies and end up fostering and giving power to oppressive regimes. One clue can be seen when one's sense of rights overshadows his/her own settler positionality. As an example, Alyssa Howe's "Queer Pilgrimage"[52] explores an important part of the history of queer subjectivity and freedom in the United States and details how San Francisco became a "homeland" and "mecca" to queer people escaping hostility, confinement, and other forms of vulnerability to violence across the United States. In the essay, San Francisco is identified as a "tourist mecca" and "homeland" for queer tourists who embark on "pilgrimages" to the bay area's Castro district. Drawing on Indigenous and Muslim ideologies, the "homeland" narrative is coupled with the Muslim sacred practice of pilgrimage. Donning religiosity, San Francisco—and the Castro—is made to be the rightful lands of non-Indigenous settlers who seek refuge from the violent oppressions used to maintain heteronormativity that envelops the nation.

It is completely understandable that any person wishes to secure and reach safe spaces. It is often empathy that silences criticism of oppressed strategies for survival. For example, overtly expressed racism is often countered with empathy and pity; anti-queer sentimentalities are often countered with distanced notions of tolerance in diversity and legal discourses. It is the language that is questioned here, because language is the manner through which we are led to imagine our world, ourselves, and the laws that bind us to sociogenic systems. The language of "safe spaces," or the "homeland" in this case, is the very same language that has been adopted on college and university campuses throughout the United States wherever spaces—rooms—are condoned as "safe." Diversity mandates, which yield campuses millions of dollars annually, meagerly offer spaces where students can come together, ally, and feel a sense of inclusion temporarily. Ironically, what is actually a form of induced self-isolation is presented as a provision in the form of safe spaces. Rather, if safe spaces were adopted campus-wide, attention would go toward the broader nature of hostility, abuse, and violence on campuses, in classrooms, and administrative spaces. So too, San Francisco's Castro District was for a long time a site of state-sanctioned violence, where the use of the term *gay bashing* came to fruition as police and vigilantes entered into queer spaces in attempts to beat the queerness out of the United States.

Given the brutality waged against and the vulnerability of queer peoples, it could become difficult and disheartening to engage in a critique that challenges oppressed peoples for appropriating the concept of Indigenous homelands or *mecca*. However, such critiques address the ways in which the appropriation ignores the genocide, deracination, and displacement of California's Indigenous peoples, in order for the very same lands and waters to become havens for other peoples fleeing oppression elsewhere. The term *mecca* may have religious or sacred undertones, but appropriation requires no commitment to that decree.

My critique here aims to identify the dangers of appropriation, within civil rights efforts that move from healthy separatism—where we can acknowledge that it is good to share time together and time with people who most closely share our experiences—to unhealthy division—where we can lose sight of our own sense of onus, make excuses that we have less work to do on ourselves than others, and where we have simplistically taken "a side," where in reality, we created a side, boundary, and negation of Others.

When I participated in an immigrants' rights protest several years ago, because white supremacy and anti-immigrant of color violence has never stopped in the United States, I listened as people of color took to the microphone to assert their solidarity with "Mexicans." I wondered why they (non-Mexican immigrants of color) thought the issue was about "Mexicans" when the legislation was opaquely broad and pointed at immigrants. Why did they think of themselves as safe from the threat of deportation and police violence? It brings the issue full circle for me. Decoloniality holds a basic tenet that the world/cosmos exists in great and necessary complexity. The work of the decolonial workers is to avert binary, Western, colonial, hierarchical power structures and assert life affirming alternatives. The projects, diverse in their global formations, seem to start with understanding the self as a complex natural phenomenon within complex, overlapping, intersecting, and coexisting systems. From here humility, responsibility, diversity, and solidarity can become familiar co-equals, comfortable positionalities, and engender positive, humane, ways of being and engaging with other life forms.

Notes

1. Joanne Barker, "Indigenous Feminisms," in *Handbook on Indigenous People's Politics*, eds. José Antonio Lucero, Dale Turner, and Donna Lee Van Cott (New York: Oxford University Press, 2015); Joanne Barker, "Introduction: Critically Sovereign," in *Critically Sovereign: Indigenous Gender, Sexuality and Feminist Studies* ed. Joanne Barker (Durham, N.C.: Duke University Press, 2017), 5.

2. Monisha Das Gupta and Sue Haglund, "Mexican Migration to Hawai'i and US Settler Colonialism," *Latino Studies* 13, no. 4 (2015): 455–480.

3. In the context of Hawai'i, see J. Kēhaulani Kauanui, "Indigenous Hawaiian Sexuality and the Politics of Nationalist Decolonization," in Barker, *Critically Sovereign*.

4. Harsha Walia, *Undoing Border Imperialism* (Oakland, Calif.: AK Press, 2013).

5. Edward Ou Jin Lee, "Tracing the Coloniality of Queer and Trans Migrations: Resituating Heterocisnormative Violence in the Global South and Encounters with Migrant Visa Ineligibility to Canada," *Refuge: Canada's Journal on Refugees* 34, no. 1 (2018).

6. Ibid.

7. Audra Simpson, *Mohawk Interruptus: Political Life across the Borders of Settler States* (Durham, N.C.: Duke University Press, 2014), 133.

8. Ibid.

9. Henrietta Buckmaster, *Let My People Go: The Story of the Underground Railroad and the Growth of the Abolition Movement* (London: Reaktion Books, 1992).

10. Charmaine A. Nelson, "'Ran Away from Her Master . . . a Negroe Girl Named Thursday': Examining Evidence of Punishment, Isolation, and Trauma in Nova Scotia and Quebec Fugitive Slave Advertisements," in *Legal Violence and the Limits of the Law*, ed. Amy Swiffen and Joshua Nichols (New York: Routledge, 2017), 177–78.

11. Kornel Chang, "Enforcing Transnational White Solidarity: Asian Migration and the Formation of the US-Canadian Boundary," *American Quarterly* 60, no. 3 (2008): 671–696.

12. Nayan Shah, *Stranger Intimacy: Contesting Race, Sexuality and the Law in the North American West* (Berkeley: University of California Press, 2011).

13. Ibid.; Gordon Brent Ingram. "Returning to the Scene of the Crime: Uses of Trial Dossiers on Consensual Male Homosexuality for Urban Research, with Examples from Twentieth-Century British Columbia," *GLQ* 10, no. 1 (2003): 77–110.

14. Clare Sears, "All that Glitters: Trans-ing California's Gold Rush Migrations," *GLQ* 14, no. 2–3 (2008): 383–402.

15. Ibid.

16. Sherene Razack, ed. *Race, Space, and the Law: Unmapping a White Settler Society* (Toronto: Between the Lines, 2002); Harsha Walia, "Transient Servitude: Migrant Labour in Canada and the Apartheid of Citizenship," *Race & Class* 52, no. 1 (2010): 71–84.

17. Simpson, *Mohawk Interruptus*, 12.

18. Michel Rolph Trouillot, *Silencing the Past: Power and the Production of History* (Boston, Mass.: Beacon Press, 1995).

19. Vine Deloria and Daniel Wildcat, *Power and Place: Indian Education in America* (Golden, Colo.: Fulcrum Publishing, 2001).

20. Immanuel Wallerstein, *World-Systems Analysis* (Durham, N.C.: Duke University Press, 2004).

21. Lewis Hanke, *All Mankind Is One: A Study of the Disputation between Bartolome De Las Casas and Juan Gines De Sepulveda in 1550 on the Religious and Intellectual Capacity of the American Indians* (DeKalb: Northern Illinois University Press, 1994).

22. Thomas Jefferson, *Notes on the State of Virginia* (New York: Penguin Books, 1998).

23. Robert Williams, *Like a Loaded Weapon: The Rehnquist Court, Indian Rights and the Legal History of Racism in America* (Minneapolis: University of Minnesota Press, 2005).

24. Luana Ross, *Inventing the Savage: The Social Construction of Native American Criminality* (Austin: University of Texas Press, 2004).

25. Jeff Ostler, *The Plains Sioux and U.S. Colonialism from Lewis and Clark to Wounded Knee* (New York: Cambridge University Press, 2004).

26. María Lugones, "Heterosexualism and the Colonial/Modern Gender System," *Hypatia* 22, no. 1 (Winter 2007): 186–209.

27. Williams, *Like a Loaded Weapon*.

28. Ross, *Inventing the Savage*; U.S. Public Law 280 gave some states jurisdiction over tribal nations. See: https://www.govinfo.gov/content/pkg/STATUTE-67/pdf/STATUTE -67-Pg588.pdf.

29. Stephen W. Silliman, "The 'Old West' in the Middle East: U.S. Military Metaphors in Real and Imagined Indian Country," *American Anthropologist* 110, no. 2 (2008): 237–247. Thomas Holm, "The National Survey of Vietnam Era American Indian Veterans: A Preliminary Reconnaissance," *Wicazo Sa Review* 1, no. 1 (Spring 1985): 36-37.

30. Razack, *Race, Space and the Law.*

31. Monisha Das Gupta, "KNOw History, KNOw Self: Khmer Youth Organizing for Justice in Long Beach," *Amerasia Journal* 45, no.2 (2019): 137–156.

32. Lee, "Tracing the Coloniality."

33. Lisa Marie Cacho, *Social Death: Racialized Rightlessness and the Criminalization of the Unprotected* (New York: New York University Press, 2012), 32.

34. José Esteban Muñoz, *Disidentifications: Queers of Color and the Performance of Politics* (Minneapolis: University of Minnesota Press, 1999).

35. Gada Mahrouse, *Conflicted Commitments: Race, Privilege, and Power in Transnational Solidarity Activism* (Montreal: McGill-Queen's University Press, 2014).

36. Shah, *Stranger Intimacy.*

37. Aniruddha Dutta and Raina Roy, "Decolonizing Transgender in India: Some Reflections," *Transgender Studies Quarterly* 1, no. 3 (2014): 320–337; Saylesh Wesley, "Twin-Spirited Woman: Sts' iyóye smestíyexw slhá: li." *Transgender Studies Quarterly* 1, no. 3 (2014): 338–351.

38. Haunani-Kay Trask, "Settlers of Color and 'Immigrant' Hegemony: 'Locals' in Hawai'i," *Amerasia Journal* 26, no. 2 (2000): 1–24.

39. Candace Fujikane, "Foregrounding Native Nationalisms: A Critique of Antinationalist Sentiment in Asian American Studies," in *Asian American Studies after Critical Mass*, ed. Kent A. Ono (Malden, Mass.: Blackwell, 2005): 73–97; Candace Fujikane, "Introduction: Asian Settler Colonialism in the U.S. Colony of Hawai'i," in *Asian Settler Colonialism: From Local Governance to the Habits of Everyday Life in Hawai'i*, eds. Candace Fujikane and Jonathan Okamura (Honolulu: University of Hawai'i Press, 2008): 1–42; Dean I. Saranillio, "Why Asian Settler Colonialism Matters: A Thought Piece on Critiques, Debates, and Indigenous Difference," *Settler Colonial Studies* 3, no. 3–4 (2013): 280–294.

40. See Nandita Sharma and Cynthia Wright, "Decolonizing Resistance: Challenging Colonial States," *Social Justice* 35, no. 3 (2009): 120–138, for exemplifying this type of argument. For critiques of their position, see Jodi Byrd, *The Transit of Empire: Indigenous Critiques of Colonialism* (Minneapolis: University of Minnesota Press, 2011), 204; Scott Lauria Morgensen, *Spaces between Us: Queer Settler Colonialism and Indigenous Decolonization* (Minneapolis: University of Minnesota Press, 2011), 19; Saranillio, "Why Asian Settler Colonialism Matters."

41. Noenoe Silva, *Aloha Betrayed: Native Hawaiian Resistance to American Colonialism* (Durham, N.C.: Duke University Press, 2004). Silva's work has laid the foundation for the rich body of work being produced by Native Hawaiian scholars. For a collection of exemplary essays, see Noelani Goodyear-Ka'ōpua, Ikaika Hussey, and Erin Kahunawaika'ala

Wright, eds. *A Nation Rising: Hawaiian Movements for Life, Land, and Sovereignty* (Durham, N.C.: Duke University Press, 2014).

42. Hōkūlani Aikau, Noelani Goodyear-Kaʻōpua, and Noenoe Silva, "The Practice of Kuleana: Reflections on Critical Indigenous Studies through Transindigenous Exchange," in *Critical Indigenous Studies: Engagements in First World Locations*, ed. Aileen Moreton-Robinson (Tucson: University of Arizona Press, 2016), 157–175.

43. Morgensen, *Spaces between Us.*

44. Kauanui, "Indigenous Hawaiian Sexuality."

45. Sandeep Bakshi, Suhraiya Jivraj, and Silvia Posocco, eds., *Decolonizing Sexualities: Transnational Perspectives, Critical Interventions* (Oxford: Counterpress, 2016).

46. Paola Bacchetta, "QTPOC Critiques of 'Post-Raciality,' Segregationality, Coloniality and Capitalism in France," in Bakshi et al., *Decolonizing Sexualities*, 264–281.

47. J. Jack Halberstam, *In a Queer Time and Place: Transgender Bodies, Subcultural Lives* (New York: New York University Press, 2005); Cacho, *Social Death.*

48. Audre Lorde, "The Master's Tools Will Never Dismantle the Master's House," *Sister Outsider: Essays and Speeches* (Berkeley, Calif.: Crossing Press, 2007), 110–114.

49. Chela Sandoval, *Methodology of the Oppressed* (Minneapolis: University of Minnesota Press, 2000).

50. Joy Harjo and Gloria Bird, *Reinventing the Enemy's Language* (New York: W. W. Norton and Co, 1997).

51. Nayan Shah, "Between 'Oriental Depravity' and 'Natural Degenerates': Spatial Borderlands and the Making of Ordinary Americans," *American Quarterly* 57, no. 3 (2005): 703–725.

52. Alyssa Howe, "Queer Pilgrimage: The San Francisco Homeland and Identity Tourism," *Cultural Anthropology* 16, no. 1 (2001): 35–61.

Contributors

MYISHA ARELLANUS is a painter from Mexico City raised in the San Fernando Valley. At the age of 16, she led and completed her first mural project in Van Nuys, California. As a result, Arellanus became an immigrant youth organizer and educator in the SFV community. Since then, she has led several public art projects and collaborated with various muralists throughout Los Angeles County.

FELIPE BAEZA utilizes art as a tool to create political spaces, and his most recent practice investigates how memory, migration, and displacement work to create a state of hybridity and "fugitivity." He primarily works on paper and incorporates different techniques via collage and de-collage. He also utilizes his own biography to reflect and explore the persistent effects of social institutions and cultural practices on the individual. He uses this strategy to imagine structures and possibilities for the self-emancipation of the hybrid-fugitive body that lives in/is persistently susceptible to hostile conditions. The possibility of self-emancipation is forged by the necessity to survive and thrive, wherein one is forced to create new forms and structures that produce liminal spaces of belonging. Additionally, his practice aims to challenge those notions that keep people on the margins by using collage and its ability to be reconfigured to insert excluded people into conversations and provide the missing pages of histories. He completed a BFA at Cooper Union in 2009 and an MFA at Yale University in 2018.

GREG BAL's approach to photography is primarily informed by his experiences growing up as a minority immigrant in the United States. These experiences cultivated in him deep respect and appreciation for different cultures and peoples and a passion for working on social justice issues. They are also what led him to work as a public defender for most of his career and gave him the lens through which he takes/creates his photographs. Much of his recent work has been in response to the increasing intolerance against "the other," addressing issues such as immigration rights, religion, race, and the LGBTQ community. Many of his conceptual works merge images from the present with archival images as a means of connecting to and honoring those who have paved the way. His work has been published in the *New York Times*, *Vogue India*, and *Tehelka* magazine and has been exhibited at the Center for Fine Art Photography in Fort Collins, Colorado.

AB BROWN received their PhD in Performance Studies from Northwestern University and is assistant professor of Contemporary Performance at Colby College. Their scholarly research draws on over 7 years of performance ethnography with LGBTIQ asylum seekers in South Africa and argues for quotidian and aesthetic performances of statelessness as strategic practices of unbelonging that propose alternative configurations of citizenship, subjectivity, and community. Their work has been published in *Women and Performance*, *Theatre Survey*, *Performing Arts Resources*, and *Theatre Research International*. As Sister James, they create historically situated and place-based performances that range from ethnographic, socially engaged ensemble work to conceptual solo performance. www.sister-james.com.

JULIO CAPÓ JR. is associate professor of History and deputy director of the Wolfsonian Public Humanities Lab at Florida International University. Capó researches inter-American histories, with a focus on queer, Latinx, race, (im)migration, and empire studies. His book, *Welcome to Fairyland: Queer Miami before 1940* (University of North Carolina Press, 2017), has received six honors, including the Charles S. Sydnor award from the Southern Historical Association for the best book written on the U.S. South. His work has appeared in the *Journal of American History*, *Radical History Review*, *Diplomatic History*, *Journal of American Ethnic History*, and *Modern American History*. A former journalist, he has also written for *Time*, the *Washington Post*, *The Miami Herald*, and other outlets. He is cochair of the Committee on Lesbian, Gay, Bisexual & Transgender History and has held fellowships at Yale University and the United States Studies Centre at the University of Sydney.

ANNA CARASTATHIS (PhD Philosophy, McGill University) is a codirector of the Feminist Autonomous Centre for Research in Athens. She is the author of *Intersectionality: Origins, Contestations, Horizons* (University of Nebraska Press, 2016) and coauthor of *Reproducing Refugees: Photographia of a Crisis* (Rowman and Littlefield, 2020). Anna is a founding member of the network, Feminist Researchers against Borders, and coeditor of a special issue of *Refuge* journal on "Intersectional Feminist Interventions in the 'Refugee Crisis'" (2018).

JACK CÁRAVES is an activist scholar and assistant professor of Women, Gender, and Sexuality Studies at San José State University. Their research and activism takes an intersectional lens to understand how gender works as a structure of power to discipline and police queer and trans people of color. Their research uses community-based mixed methods approaches, in-depth interviews, and participant observation, and focuses on the experiences of Trans Latinxs in Southern California and the role of family and spirituality in serving as spaces of empowerment and resistance.

KARMA R. CHÁVEZ is chair and associate professor in the Department of Mexican American and Latina/o Studies at the University of Texas-Austin. She is coeditor of *Text + Field: Innovations in Rhetorical Method* (Penn State Press, 2016) and *Standing in the Intersection: Feminist Voices, Feminist Practices in Communication Studies* (SUNY Press, 2012). She is author of *Queer Migration Politics: Activist Rhetoric and Coalitional Possibilities* (2013) and *Palestine on the Air* (2019), both from the University of Illinois Press. She is also a member of the radical queer collective Against Equality.

RYAN CONRAD is an SSHRC postdoctoral fellow in the cinema and media studies program at York University where he is working on a manuscript entitled *Radical VIHsion: Canadian AIDS Film & Video*. Previously he was a postdoctoral fellow at Carleton University with the AIDS Activist History Project. He holds a PhD from the Centre for Interdisciplinary Studies in Society and Culture at Concordia University and an MFA in Interdisciplinary Studio Arts from the Maine College of Art. Conrad is the cofounder of Against Equality (againstequality.org), a digital archive and publishing collective based in the United States and Canada. He is the editor of the collective's anthology series that are compiled together in *Against Equality: Queer Revolution, Not Mere Inclusion* (2014). His record of visual, written, and activist work is archived online at faggotz.org.

MONISHA DAS GUPTA holds a joint appointment as professor in the Department of Ethnic Studies and Department of Women's Studies at the University of Hawai'i at Mānoa. She specializes in cross-border migration and migrant-led social justice movements to which she brings a critical and feminist transnational perspective. Her research is closely tied to community-based organizing. Her book, *Unruly Immigrants: Rights, Activism, and Transnational South Asian Politics in the United States*, (Duke University Press, 2006), looks at feminist, queer, and labor organizing. Her journal articles and book chapters cover post-9/11 struggles for migrant rights in the face of surveillance and deportation, transnational feminist analyses of U.S. imperialism, and transpacific migration. Currently, she is working on a book tentatively titled, "Settling Migration: Migrant Organizing in an Era of

Deportation and Dispossession." It considers migrancy and Indigeneity together to understand U.S. immigration policies.

MOLLY FAIR is a multidisciplinary artist and archivist, whose practice explores the possibilities of radical cultural transformation. As a member of Justseeds Artists' Cooperative, she has worked on numerous campaigns with grassroots organizations to produce graphics addressing issues such as environmental justice, prison abolition, survivor support, and migration. She is a founding member of Interference Archive and is interested in documenting and celebrating the histories of social justice movements.

KATHERINE FOBEAR's research and activism focuses on the intersections of race, sexuality, and gender in migration and transitional justice. Her most recent work is with LGBTQ refugees and undocumented persons in Canada. Her new work focuses on the issues that transgender asylum seekers and undocumented persons face in the United States and Canada. She is also a queer oral historian and is currently working on a queer community public history initiative in California's Central Valley, an area until recently ignored by most LGBTQ+ historical records. Katherine serves on the board of Trans-E-Motion, a Central Valley transgender advocacy and support organization.

JAMILA HAMMAMI, MSW, is a queer nonbinary first-generation Tunisian Arab American person of color community organizer and social worker from the South, now based in NYC. They come to this work with personal and familial experiences with the incarceration system, a background in reproductive justice, and experience witnessing the impacts of migration, mass incarceration/industrialized punishment, and racism in their formative years in Texas. They were the founder and executive director of the Queer Detainee Empowerment Project until 2018. Founded in 2014, Jamila has worked with LGBTQI/ HIV+ immigrants in detention and post-detention. Now, they are a PhD student in Social Welfare at the City University of New York, focusing on community organizing. They are an adjunct professor of community organizing at Hunter College, an MSW-level Social Work Field Instruction at Silberman School of Social Work and Columbia School of Social Work in New York City, an organizer at the Adjunct Project, as well as a consultant.

JOSÉ GUADALUPE HERRERA SOTO became a migrant justice organizer during his four-year struggle to resist the U.S. government's attempt to deport him. José has existed without white-papers/legal status for most of the 28 years he has lived in the United States. José has worked closely with the No Name Collective, Moratorium on Deportations Campaign, and other autonomous groups in Chicago. Today he labors for pay at a large not-for-profit (something he is not proud of) and collaborates on developing critical analysis and popular education of current immigration issues from a border abolition perspective (something he is very proud of). José lives in Chicago with his son, Josue, and his always-struggling undocumented family. www.MoratoriumOnDeportations.org.

EDWARD OU JIN LEE is an assistant professor at the School of Social Work at the Université de Montréal. Edward's research and practice interests are within the realms of critical, decolonizing, and anti-oppressive social work as well as critical, participatory, and digital media research methodologies. Edward also engages in social policy advocacy and community organizing with Queer, Trans, Black, Indigenous, and other People of Color (QTBIPOC) communities and, in particular, queer and trans migrants with precarious status.

LEECE LEE-OLIVER (Blackfeet/Choctaw/Cherokee/Wyandot) is assistant professor of Women's Studies and director of American Indian Studies at California State University, Fresno. Dr. Lee-Oliver's research and activism centralize American Indian, Indigenous, and Third World decolonialism. Her work engages oral tradition, law, critical auto-ethnography, and cultural-artistic expression to explore how American Indian, transnational Indigenous, and subaltern peoples respond to colonial, hetero-patriarchal, white supremacist oppression locally and globally. Her current project interrogates the contemporary epidemic rate of violence against American Indian women and girls as a by-product of coloniality and pays homage to American Indian women leaders. Dr. Lee-Oliver serves on the board of the Fresno American Indian Health Project, which provides cultural and wellness services to American Indians in the Central Valley.

ADELA C. LICONA is a photographer, associate professor emerita of English, University of Arizona, and the founder and director of The Art of Change Agency. Her photography has appeared in *Community Literacy Journal, Collective Terrain: Edible Baja, Kairos, Proximities, Terrain, TRIVIA, Versal,* and *Zócalo.* Adela is author of *Zines in Third Space: Radical Cooperation and Borderlands Rhetoric* (SUNY, 2012) and coeditor of *Feminist Pedagogy: Looking Back to Move Forward* (JHUP, 2009) and *Precarious Rhetorics* (OSU Press, 2018). She was the past director of the UA's Institute for LGBT Studies and is cofounder of Feminist Action Research in Rhetoric, FARR, a group of progressive feminist scholars. She is editor emerita of *Feminist Formations* and serves on the boards for *QED: A Journal of GLBTQ Worldmaking, Feminist Formations,* the Primavera Foundation, and the Tucson Youth Poetry Slam.

EITHNE LUIBHÉID is a professor of Gender and Women's Studies at the University of Arizona. She holds a PhD in Ethnic Studies from UC-Berkeley, and her research focuses on the connections among queer lives, state immigration controls, and justice struggles. Luibhéid is the author of *Pregnant on Arrival: Making the 'Illegal' Immigrant* (University of Minnesota Press, 2013) and *Entry Denied: Controlling Sexuality at the Border* (University of Minnesota Press, 2002). She is the editor of "'Lives That Resist Telling': Migrant and Refugee Lesbians," a special issue of the *Journal of Lesbian Studies* (2020) and "Queer Migrations," a special issue of *GLQ* (2008); and the coeditor of *A Global History of Sexuality* (Wiley Blackwell, 2014); *Queer Migrations: Sexuality, Citizenship, and Border Crossings* (University of Minnesota Press, 2005); and "Representing Migrant Women in Ireland and the E.U.," a special issue of *Women's Studies International Forum* (2004).

HANA MASRI received her PhD in Rhetoric and Language from the Department of Communication at the University of Texas, Austin. Her work examines how materiality animates rhetorical constructions and contestations of migration, citizenship, and sovereignty in contexts from the U.S.-Mexican borderlands to the Levant. She is particularly interested in how what gets designated *trash* can function both to render groups of people as waste or surplus and, at times, challenge such designations.

MATICE MOORE is a Black, nonbinary artist originally from Arizona. They sell liberation-themed art and apparel through their etsy shop. https://www.etsy.com/shop/LoveLttrs4Liberation.

YASMIN NAIR is a writer, academic, and activist whose work can be found at www.yasminnair.com. She is the cofounder of the queer radical editorial collective, Against Equality, and policy director of Gender JUST in Chicago. Nair is currently working on her book *Strange Love: The Invention of Social Justice*.

BAMBY SALCEDO is a transgender Latina woman who received her master's degree in Latin@ Studies from California State University–Los Angeles. She is the president and CEO of the TransLatin@ Coalition, a national organization that focuses on addressing the issues of transgender Latin@s in the United States. Bamby also developed the Center for Violence Prevention & Transgender Wellness, a multipurpose, multiservice space for transgender people in Los Angeles. Bamby has been invited to participate on several panels at the White House including in 2016, "The United State of Women," where she shared the stage with Vice President Joe Biden at the opening plenary session, and in 2015, the Transgender Women of Color and Violence and LGBTQ People of Color Summit. Bamby has also participated as the opening plenary speaker at several conferences, including The 2015 National HIV Prevention Conference and the United States Conference on AIDS in 2009 and 2012. Bamby has been featured and recognized in multiple media outlets such as *People en Español, Latina Magazine, Cosmopolitan*, the *Los Angeles Times, Los Angeles Magazine*, and *OUT 100*, and featured in the HBO documentary, *The Trans List*.

FADI SALEH is a PhD candidate at the Institute for Cultural Anthropology and European Ethnology at the University of Göttingen, Germany. In his PhD project, he traces the recent emergence of Syrian LGBTIQ refugees as a constituency in discourses around humanitarianism, asylum, and queerness. In addition to his academic research, Fadi continues to work with many LGBTIQ organizations in Europe and across the Middle East and North Africa region in a variety of consultancy, research, training, and advocacy capacities.

ELIF SARI is a PhD candidate in Socio-Cultural Anthropology and Feminist, Gender, and Sexuality Studies at Cornell University. Her research and teaching interests include transnational sexualities, queer (im)mobility, asylum, borders, queer diasporic critique, and humanitarianism, with an interdisciplinary focus on the Middle East and Global South. Her current research explores the practices, processes, and geopolitics of LGBTI asylum from the Middle East to the United States and Canada via Turkey, as well as the everyday lives and experiences of Iranian LGBTI refugees awaiting resettlement to North America in small Turkish towns. Her work has been published in *Journal of Lesbian Studies* and *Movements*. She is coeditor of the Turkey Page at *Jadaliyya* e-zine.

RAFAEL RAMIREZ SOLÓRZANO has been an educational and migrant rights advocate for over 20 years. He participates in campaigns designed to counter racial violence, achieve educational justice, and end the school-to-prison-to-deportation pipeline. He is currently an assistant professor of Social Justice in the Department of Chicana(o) and Latina(o) Studies at Cal State L.A. In his current book project, he documents the political ingenuity led by undocuqueer activists along the Trail of Dreams, a four-month, 1,500-mile walk to Washington D.C. His interdisciplinary research includes Chicanx and Latinx freedom movements, racial geographies, and queer-of-color critique.

MARÍA INÉS TARACENA is a multi–award-winning print and radio journalist from Guatemala, who lived in the Arizona-Sonora borderlands for more than half her life. She's currently the News Production Fellow at Democracy Now!, an independent global news outlet based in New York City. María Inés tells stories of immigration, the U.S.-Mexico border, LGBTIQ+ resistance, and gender violence in Central America.

ROMMY TORRICO is a queer, trans, formerly undocumented artist born in Iquique, Chile, raised in Naples, Florida, and currently based out of New York. Along with infusing their art with powerful stories from their own life, Torrico's work consistently uplifts the experiences and identities of their communities. Their work has been exhibited in galleries throughout the Americas and has been featured in a number of books and publications worldwide.

MYRTO TSILIMPOUNIDI is a social researcher and photographer. Her research focuses on the interface between urbanism, culture, and innovative methodologies. She is the author of *Sociology of Crisis: Visualising Urban Austerity* (Routledge, 2017); coauthor of *Reproducing Refugees: Photographia of a Crisis* (Rowman & Littlefield, 2020); and coeditor of *Remapping Crisis: A Guide to Athens* (Zero Books, 2014) and *Street Art & Graffiti: Reading, Writing & Representing the City* (Routledge, 2017). Myrto is the codirector of the Feminist Autonomous Centre for Research (FAC Research) in Athens.

SUYAPA G. PORTILLO VILLEDA is associate professor of Chicano/a-Latino/a transnational studies at Pitzer College and a member of the Intercollegiate Department of Chicanx Latinx Studies at the Claremont Colleges. As a Fulbright Scholar Fellow to Honduras in 2018, she studied root causes for migration and displacement. She has served as an expert witness for numerous LGBTI Central American asylum cases and is a historian of Honduras and Central America.

SASHA WIJEYERATNE is the former organizing director at the National Queer Asian Pacific Islander Alliance, working to build the power of LGBTQ API communities toward a world where all queer and trans people of color can thrive. Sasha is currently the executive director of CAAAV: Organizing Asian Communities, organizing working-class Asian immigrants in Chinatown and Queens in New York City. Sasha has been part of a number of grassroots and national organizing campaigns and deeply believes in the power of organizing to win impossible battles. They are confident that we have what we need to transform ourselves and our world and that working-class immigrant and people of color organizing will get us free. Sasha has also been part of a variety of organizing and political education projects, including: South Asian Youth Movement, No Dane County Jail Coalition, VigilantLove, Asians for Black Lives, DC Desi Summer, Queer South Asian National Network, and more.

RUBEN ZECENA is a PhD candidate in the Department of Gender & Women's Studies at the University of Arizona. Born in El Salvador, he is on a constant search for "home" and specializes in queer migration studies. His work appears in *WSQ: Women's Studies Quarterly, Constellations: A Cultural Rhetorics Publishing Space* and *Border-Lines*. His dissertation explores the relational politics of queer and trans migrants as imaginative acts of transgression that enable their survival.

Index

DISSIDENT FEMINISMS

The University of Illinois Press
is a founding member of the
Association of University Presses.

———————————————————

University of Illinois Press
1325 South Oak Street
Champaign, IL 61820-6903
www.press.uillinois.edu

Printed by Printforce, United Kingdom